MARIO ASEF, GOLO F
GEORG KLEIN, BRANDON L

ERRANT SOUND READER

THOUGHTS
AND PRACTICES
FROM THE
BERLIN ARTIST–RUN
SPACE

ERRANT BODIES PRESS

TABLE OF CONTENTS

ERRANT SOUND: A CHRONOLOGY 5

Kirsten Reese : VOICES OF INSECTS AND VOICES OF ALGORITHMS 20
Antje Vowinckel : AUTOMATIC SPEAKING AND DIALECT KARAOKE 28
Gerriet Krishna Sharma : TRACING THE NON–EUCLIDEAN DRIFT IN EVERYDAY LIFE –
    CONSTRUCTING LIQUID ARCHITECTURES I. – X. 40
Georg Klein : BASED ON RE–SEARCH 47
Alessandra Eramo : ROARS BANGS BOOMS: 7 VARIATIONS FOR VOICE AND ONOMATOPOEIA
    PERFORMANCE, 2013 – 2015 59
Holger Schulze : WHAT DO SOUNDS NEED, WHAT DO WE GRANT THEM OR NOT?
    A FEW CONSIDERATIONS ON THE AFFORDANCES OF THE SONIC 69
Jeremy Woodruff : COMMUNITY WORLDING AS SOCIAL COMPOSITION:
    URBAN GARDENING SOUND ART PROJECTS 2012 – 2022 79
Janine Eisenächer : READY MAKING: ON THE ACTION–BASED SONIC KNOW–HOW AND
    AUDITORY KNOWLEDGE IN SOUND PERFORMANCES WITH THINGS 95
Nico Daleman & Jutta Ravenna : KINETIC SOUND ART 112
Laura Mello & Vanessa De Michelis : BEYOND THE BINARIES: FROM DYSTOPIA TO *TOPIA ... 125
Brandon LaBelle : LISTENING BETWEEN THE LINES:
    IN CONVERSATION WITH LILIAN CAMPESATO 130
Mario Asef : S < L > E : THE LANGUAGE OF/IN THINGS 137
Roberta Busechian : WE ARE WHAT WE HEAR AND HOW WE REMEMBER IT 153
Golo Föllmer : HINGES. CONVERSING ABOUT DO–WORDS 161

BIOGRAPHIES 195
COLOPHON 200

GEORG KLEIN, MARIO ASEF, BRANDON LABELLE ET. AL.

Errant Sound

A CHRONOLOGY / EINE CHRONOLOGIE

Berlin, a city marked by war-induced voids and desolate landscapes, served as a divided metropolis on the Cold War's front lines, offering a distinctive ambience and unique liberties to the art and music scenes in both East and West. Within the dilapidated neighborhoods of Prenzlauer Berg, Kreuzberg, and Schöneberg, self-organized spaces began sprouting as early as the 1970s. Following the collapse of the Wall in 1989, these spaces proliferated to such an extent that they evolved into a distinctive cultural hallmark of Berlin. Amidst an atmosphere characterized by fragmentation, rupture, and the incomplete, realms of possibility emerged – found in squats, abandoned shops, basements, bunkers, and even the former state bank of the GDR. Alongside clubs and galleries, an artistic project space scene flourished, drawing in artists from every corner of the globe and profoundly influencing the city's diversity and international character.

Berlin als Stadt der kriegsbedingten Lücken und Brachen, als geteilte Stadt an der Frontlinie des kalten Kriegs bot der Kunst- und Musikszene sowohl im Osten wie im Westen nicht nur eine besondere Atmosphäre sondern auch besondere Freiheiten. In den heruntergekommenen Altbaukiezen in Prenzlauer Berg, Kreuzberg und Schöneberg entstanden schon in den 1970ern selbstorganisierte Räume, die sich nach dem Mauerfall 1989 so stark verbreiteten, dass sie zu einem einzigartigen, kulturellen Charakteristikum Berlins werden sollten. In dieser Atmosphäre des Zerbrochenen, Aufbrechenden und Unfertigen entstanden Möglichkeitsräume – in besetzten Häusern, verlassenen Läden, Kellern und Bunkern bis hin zur ehem. Staatsbank der DDR – und es entwickelte sich neben Clubs und Gallerien eine künst-

Following the onset of the new millennium, the vitality of this artistic scene began to wane, facing mounting challenges posed by the expanding repurposing of spaces for interim use and the swift surge in rents following the financial crisis of 2007/8. Compounded by successive rounds of budget cuts by the Berlin Senate, artists found themselves navigating increasingly precarious financial conditions. In response, a resistance emerged in 2009 through the Berliner Netzwerk freier Projekträume und -initiativen (Berlin Network of Independent Project Spaces and Initiatives), advocating for political intervention.[1] This advocacy bore fruit with the inception of the "project space award" in 2012, marking an initial stride toward structural support.

During this period, Berlin boasted the presence of more than 150 self-organized project spaces, each implementing diverse organizational structures. In 2010, Brandon LaBelle established his studio in Prenzlauer Berg, transforming it into a hub for performances and lectures centered around sound. Named Errant Bodies, in reference to Errant Bodies Press, this space swiftly evolved into a focal point for artists and researchers dedicated to the sonic arts.

Alongside organizing public events, as a studio environment Errant Bodies was loosely comprised of a group of local artists, including Riccardo Benassi, Valeria Merlini, Michael Fresca and Anna Bromley, as well as providing residencies for visiting artists. As a project space, it felt important to support not only the presentation of work, but to also give room for artists to stay in Berlin, and to pursue their research and creative process in a free manner.

lerische Projektraumszene, die unzählige Künstler*innen aus aller Welt anzog und so die Vielfalt und Internationalität der Stadt entscheidend prägte.

Nach der Jahrtausendwende geriet diese Szene durch die zunehmende Bebauung der zwischengenutzten Flächen wie auch die seit der Finanzkrise 2007/8 rasant steigende Mietentwicklung nach und nach in Bedrängnis, abgesehen von den zahlreichen Kürzungsrunden des Berliner Senats und den damit immer prekärer werdenden finanziellen Verhältnissen für Künstler*innen. Ab 2009 formierte sich mit dem *netzwerk projekträume* ein Widerstand, um gegenüber der Politik Forderungen durchzusetzen[1], was ab 2012 zur Einführung des "Projektraumpreises" als eine erste Form der Strukturförderung führte.

In dieser Zeit gab es in Berlin mehr als 150 selbstorganisierte Projekträume, die jeweils unterschiedliche Organisationsstrukturen aufwiesen. Bereits im Jahr 2010 richtete Brandon LaBelle sein Studio in Prenzlauer Berg ein und verwandelte es in einen Verlags- und Projektraum, in dem kleine Ausstellungen, Performances und Vorträge rund um das Thema Klang stattfanden. Unter dem Namen *Errant Bodies* – parallel zu *Errant Bodies Press* – entwickelte sich dieser Raum schnell zu einem Anlaufpunkt für Künstler*innen und Forscher*innen, die sich der Klangkunst widmeten. Neben der Organisation von öffentlichen Veranstaltungen fungierte Errant Bodies als Atelierumgebung für eine Gruppe lokaler Künstler*innen, darunter Riccardo Benassi, Valeria Merlini, Michael Fresca und Anna Bromley, und bot Gastkünstler*innen die Möglichkeit zu einem Aufenthalt.

Um das Jahr 2013 wurde die Situation jedoch auch für die Klangkunst in Berlin immer schwieriger: während die 90er noch von einer Aufbruchstimmung und der Herausbildung des Genrebegriffs Klangkunst geprägt waren, standen die 00er-Jahre zunächst für eine Etablierung und Konsolidierung der Klangkunst – mit der *sonambien-*

Around 2013, the landscape for sound art in Berlin faced escalating challenges. While the 1990s witnessed the conceptualization of the genre of "sound art" with the first *sonambiente* exhibition in 1996, the 2000s were initially marked by its establishment and consolidation, culminating in the second *sonambiente* exhibition in 2006. However, the subsequent years saw a gradual erosion of crucial platforms for presenting sound art. As early as the end of 2007, venues like TESLA (then not associated with the automotive giant but a medien>kunst<labor) and the *singuhr-hoergalerie*, which has been nomadic since 2013, began to fade from the city's sonic landscape.

In this context Brandon LaBelle approached several Berlin sound artists to jointly run the project space at Kollwitzstraße 97. Their collective goal was to uphold and cultivate it as a space for discourse within the sound art community. In January 2014, they inaugurated the space with the exhibition *Unsound*, featuring works by Serge Baghdassarians & Boris Baltschun, Anke Eckardt, Georg Klein, Brandon LaBelle, and Jeremy Woodruff as part of the *transmediale* event.

Silence can be appreciated as the pre-condition for a sounded event – an empty room, a blank page, an open horizon allowing for the sudden movements of sonic energy. Silence never goes away, instead it is a shadow that follows, a double that supports as well as haunts the body of sound. Following such themes, the exhibition brings together works that take us closer to silence, materializing its underheard presence and appropriating it through states of observation. Silence is captured, as the unconscious of sound – the unsound that surrounds and ghosts listening. (Programmtext zur Ausstellung 'Unsound' 2014, transmediale Vorspiel)

Im Nachhinein besehen scheint die Programmatik der kleinen Ausstellung bezeichnend für die Stimmung in dieser Zeit, wie auch für die Ausrichtung des Projektraums:

... dedicated to experimental work in sound, performance, voice and spatial practices. Through residencies, workshops, events and exhibitions, Errant Bodies emphasizes an engagement with process and

---

1 https://www.projektraeume-berlin.net/netzwerk/mission/

captured, as the unconscious of sound – the unsound that surrounds and ghosts listening. (exhibition flyer "Unsound," *transmediale Vorspiel* 2014)

Looking back, the focused nature of the compact exhibition appears to mirror both the prevailing mood of that era and the overarching direction of the project space:

[...] *dedicated to experimental work in sound, performance, voice and spatial practices. Through residencies, workshops, events and exhibitions, Errant Bodies emphasizes an engagement with process and dialogue, encouraging a dynamic and diverse approach to the sound arts. As a project space, it also intends to foster social and public activities, contributing to the creative scene in Berlin. It is organized and developed through its working group comprised of Berlin-based sound artists and researchers.* (Website Errant Bodies, 2014)

Comprising individual artists, the group operated without a hierarchical structure. From the outset, members organized themselves into small groups, coordinating projects based on ideas arising from collective dialogue. The challenge was to establish an open organizational system accessible to all members,[2] allowing anyone interested in organizing an event to freely access the calendar and check the space without complications. Events were executed without external funding; each member, aside from paying a monthly venue rental fee, bore the costs of the events they wished to organize. This system provided significant flexibility for decision-making, en-

dialogue, encouraging a dynamic and diverse approach to the sound arts. As a project space, it also intends to foster social and public activities, contributing to the creative scene in Berlin. It is organized and developed through its working group comprised of Berlin-based sound artists and researchers. (Errant Bodies Website, 2016)

Als Gruppe, wie sie sich im Laufe des Jahres 2014 allmählich formierte[2], weist sie keinen künstlerischen Leiter und keine ausgewiesene Hierarchie aus, sondern es sind die Mitglieder der Gruppe, die sich projektweise zusammenfinden, um ein Vorhaben zu realisieren. Die Herausforderung bestand darin, ein offenes, für alle Mitglieder zugängliches Organisationssystem zu schaffen, das es jedem*, der* an der Organisation einer Veranstaltung interessiert ist, ermöglicht, den Raum nutzen zu können. Die Veranstaltungen wurden ohne externe Finanzierung durchgeführt; jedes Mitglied trug, abgesehen von der Zahlung eines Anteils an der monatlichen Raummiete, die Kosten für die Veranstaltungen, die es organisieren wollte selbst. Dieses System bot erhebliche Flexibilität bei der Entscheidungsfindung und ermöglichte die spontane Einbeziehung von Gastkünstlern für *lectures, performances, listening sessions* usw. Das Fehlen finanzieller Mittel stellte jedoch eine erhebliche Herausforderung für die Entwicklung umfangreicherer Ausstellungen und Projekte dar.

Mit der moderierten Veranstaltungsreihe *Stadt Klang Text*, konzipiert von Georg Klein, Mario Asef und Antje Vowinckel, wurde 2014 ein erstes Vorhaben öffentlich gefördert, das programmatisch auch für den Bezug zur Stadt und zum öffentlichen Raum steht. Die Reihe befasste sich mit der Frage, wie klangliche Erfahrungen zu sozialem Engagement und der Erfahrung eines gemeinsamen Raums beitragen, insbesondere durch interventionistische Formen im urbanen Raum. In jeder Ausstellung präsentierten zwei Künstler ihre Arbeiten, die in einer abendlichen Diskussion mit externen Gästen zusätzlich

abling the spontaneous inclusion of visiting artists for talks, performances, listening sessions, and more within a short timeframe. However, the absence of funding posed considerable challenges in developing more elaborate exhibitions and projects.

Under the direction of a three-person team (Georg Klein, Mario Asef, Antje Vowinckel) overseeing the concept and applications, the moderated event series *Stadt Klang Text* (*City Sound Text*) marked the inaugural publicly funded project. The exhibition and discussion series from August to December 2014 showcased ten artistic perspectives from sound artists exploring urban spaces. The series delved into the inquiry of how auditory experiences and sonic endeavors could contribute to fostering civic engagement, mutual spaces, and disruptive forms within the urban sphere. Each exhibition featured two artists presenting their work in an evening discussion led by a scholar, providing an open forum for public participation.

Beyond individual lectures, sound performances, book launches, guest presentations, and solo exhibitions, specific series emerged as central components defining the programming at Errant Bodies. Notable among these are the *Acousmatic Lecture Series* (2014 – 2021), *The Voice Observatory* (2015), *In The Sound Field* (2017), and *Social Acoustics* (since 2017), among others.

The *Acousmatic Lecture Series*,[3] initiated by Mario Asef, draws inspiration from a Pythagorean tradition, wherein only Pythagoras's most dedicated disciples were granted the privilege of seeing him during his lectures. In the contrary, newcomers would sit in front

---

ein offenes Forum für die Öffentlichkeit bot.

Neben Vorträgen, Sound Performances, Buchvorstellungen, Gastpräsentationen und Einzelausstellungen sind es insbesondere die Serien, die das Programm des Projektraums prägen: Acousmatic Lecture Series" (2014–2021), *The Voice Observatory* (2015), *Social Acoustics* (seit 2017), *Field Recording* (2017) und weitere.

Die von Mario Asef ins Leben gerufene *Acousmatic Lecture Series*[3] geht auf eine Tradition der Pythagoräer zurück, nach der nur die treuesten Schüler des Pythagoras das Privileg hatten, ihn bei seinen Vorträgen zu sehen. Im Gegensatz dazu saßen Neulinge vor einem Vorhang und waren gezwungen, die Erklärungen des Meisters allein durch das Zuhören aufzunehmen. In dieser Reihe wurden Wissenschaftler und Forscher eingeladen, Vorträge hinter einem Vorhang zu halten, um die Anwendung von Pierre Schaefers Konzept des "reduzierten Zuhörens" in der akusmatischen Musik auf die Methoden des Zuhörens im Zusammenhang mit der Vermittlung und Schaffung von Wissen zu untersuchen. Diese Vortragsreihe war bis 2021 fester Bestandteil des Programms, mit dem Auftritt von Mladen Dolar als Abschluss der Reihe. Aus dieser Serie ging auch die Publikation mit dem Titel "Akusmatik als Labor: Kunst-Kultur-Medien" hervor, herausgegeben von Mario Asef und Sven Spieker.

Die einjährige Initiative *The Voice Observatory*[4], die von Ernesto Estrella, Brandon LaBelle und Mario Asef organisiert wurde, entwickelte sich 2015 zu einem Labor, das sich der Erforschung von Phänomenen widmete, die mit der Stimme in ihren akustischen, performativen und soziopolitischen Dimensionen verbunden sind. Die-

---

[2] Members end of 2014: Mario Asef, Gilles Aubry, Serge Baghdassarians, Ylva Bentancor, Elena Biserna, Anke Eckardt, Ernesto Estrella, Hanna Hartman, Jacob Kirkegaard, Georg Klein, Brandon LaBelle, Ines Lechleitner, Kirsten Reese, Åsa Stjerna, Antje Vowinckel, Jeremy Woodruff.

[3] www.acousmaticlectures.com

of a curtain, compelled to absorb the masters' explanations solely through the sense of listening. In this series, scholars and researchers were invited to deliver lectures from behind a curtain, exploring the application of Pierre Schaeffer's concept of "reduced listening" in musique acousmatique to methods of listening associated with knowledge transfer and creation. This distinctive series remained an integral part of the program until 2021, featuring Mladen Dolar, serving as the culmination of the series. This event was also featured in a publication titled *Akusmatik als Labor: Kunst–Kultur–Medien*, edited by Mario Asef and Sven Spieker.

In 2015, a year-long initiative named *The Voice Observatory*,[4] organized by Mario Asef, Ernesto Estrella, and Brandon LaBelle, unfolded as a laboratory dedicated to the exploration of phenomena associated with the voice across its acoustic, informative, performative, and socio-political dimensions. This comprehensive program united sound installations, theoretical presentations, panel discussions, and performances on a shared platform. The overarching objective of this series was to establish a space conducive to a productive dialogue wherein both established and innovative hypotheses, artistic processes, and theoretical concepts pertaining to the voice could converge and interact.

The initiatives of the Berlin Network of Independent Project Spaces and Initiatives played a central role in establishing a broader funding program for the art scene in Berlin. During these years, they developed funding and funding instruments together with the administration and successfully implemented them through political channels. In 2016, Errant Bodies received the Proj-

ses umfassende Programm vereinte Klanginstallationen, theoretische Präsentationen, Podiumsdiskussionen und Performances auf einer gemeinsamen Plattform. Das übergreifende Ziel dieser Reihe war es, einen Raum zu schaffen, der einen produktiven Dialog ermöglicht, in dem sowohl etablierte als auch innovative Hypothesen, künstlerische Prozesse und theoretische Konzepte mit der Stimme zusammenkommen und interagieren können.

Die Initiativen des Berliner *netzwerks unabhängiger projekträume und initiativen* spielten eine zentrale Rolle bei der Etablierung eines breiteren Förderprogramms für die Kunstszene in Berlin. In diesen Jahren haben sie gemeinsam mit der Verwaltung Förder- und Finanzierungsinstrumente entwickelt und erfolgreich auf politischem Wege durchgesetzt. Im Jahr 2016 erhielt auch Errant Bodies den *Projektraumpreis*, den die Senatsverwaltung vergibt und den das Netzwerk seit 2012 mit einer großen Party feierte.

Diese Auszeichnung markierte einen wichtigen Wendepunkt für Errant Bodies, da mit diesem Budget die Schaffung einer ersten Infrastruktur zur Verbesserung der Funktionalität der Gruppe möglich wurde. Um dies zu organisieren, wurde ein gemeinnütziger Verein gegründet, um Finanzen besser verwalten zu können und eine rechtliche Grundlage für die Beantragung weiterer Mittel zu schaffen. Gleichzeitig tauchte in der Gruppe die Frage nach einem neuen Namen auf, um die Vereinsaktivitäten von den Belangen des Verlags *Errant Bodies* zu trennen und unabhängig zu agieren. So wurde der Verein *Errant Sound e.V.* benannt.

Mit der Vereinsgründung haben sich die Aktivitäten von Errant Sound im Bereich der Klangkunst kontinuierlich ausgeweitet – mit Installationen, Performances, radiophonen Arbeiten sowie räumlichen und diskursiven Praktiken. Mit seinen Ausstellungen, Präsentationen, konzertanten Events, Residencies und Workshops unterstreicht Errant Sound sein Engagement, Prozess und Dialog zu fördern für ei-

ect Space Award, the fifth prize of its kind awarded by the Senate Administration and organized by the network since 2012.

This accolade marked a significant turning point for Errant Bodies as it received its first modest budget, enabling the creation of a small infrastructure to enhance group functionality. To facilitate this, a non-profit association was established, providing a structured financial administration system for the project and a legal foundation for applying for additional funding. Simultaneously, after extensive deliberations, the group initiated discussions about adopting a new name. This decision was driven by the desire to differentiate the activities of Errant Bodies Press and to attain financial and spatial independence. Thus, the group was rebranded as Errant Sound e.V.

Since that time, Errant Sound has remained devoted to experimental endeavors in sound-related arts, encompassing installation, performance, fieldwork, voice, radio, as well as spatial and discursive practices. Employing exhibitions, presentations, events, residencies and workshops, Errant Sound is dedicated to process and dialogue, promoting a dynamic and diverse approach to the field of sound arts. Functioning as a project space, it also strives to nurture public activities, thereby contributing to the vibrancy of Berlin's creative scene and fostering connections within its artistic communities.

During this period, two new series were conceived. Within the *In The Sound Field* series in 2017, Errant Sound artists delved into their field recording practices, elucidating how their personal methodologies are intertwined with and influenced by the recording of environ-

nen dynamischen und vielfältigen Ansatz im Bereich der Klangkunst. Als Projektraum ist er auch bestrebt, soziale und öffentliche Aktivitäten zu vernetzen und so zur Vielfältigkeit der Berliner Kunstszene beizutragen.

In diesem Zeitraum wurden zwei neue Serien konzipiert. Im Rahmen der Reihe "*In The Sound Field*" (2017) befassten sich die Künstler*innen von Errant Sound mit ihrer Praxis der field recordings (Feldaufnahmen) und erläuterten, wie ihre persönlichen Methoden mit der Aufnahme von Umwelt- und anderen Geräuschen verwoben sind und von ihnen beeinflusst werden. Verschiedene ästhetische und künstlerische Ansätze sowie Strategien für Aufnahmen "im Feld" wurden durch Diskussionen mit weiteren Gästen, darunter der Mitbegründer von Gruenrekorder Lasse-Marc Riek, erkundet.

Social Acoustics von Brandon LaBelle konzentrierte sich auf die Erkundung der Erfahrungen und Möglichkeiten, die den relationalen und soziologischen Qualitäten von Klang innewohnen. Die teilnehmenden Künstlerinnen María Andueza und Barbara Lázara beleuchteten insbesondere die mit Arbeit und Sprache verbundenen Bedingungen. Sie beschäftigten sich mit den Feinheiten von Stress und körperlichen Reaktionen und legten Prozesse offen, durch die sich Ideen und Wünsche im sozialen Bereich manifestieren.

Nach wie vor waren die räumlichen Möglichkeiten in der Kollwitzstraße – trotz Erschließung zweier Kellerräume – bescheiden. Erst mit dem *Dystopie Sound Art Festival* im Jahr 2018 gelang schließlich eine räumliche Ausweitung, sowohl in der Stadt wie auch international, durch die Kooperation mit Institutionen in Istanbul (MIAM – Center for Advanced Studies in Music). Initiiert von Georg Klein, Jeremy Woodruff und Golo

4 www.thevoiceobservatory.wordpress.com

mental and other sounds. Various aesthetic and artistic approaches, as well as strategies for recording "in the field," were explored through discussions featuring special guests, including the cofounder of Gruenrekorder Lasse-Marc Riek.

Social Acoustics by Brandon LaBelle centered on exploring the experiences and potentialities inherent in the relational and sociological qualities of sound. Notably, participating artists María Andueza and Barbara Lázara spotlighted the conditions and experiences associated with work and speech. They delved into the intricacies of stress and saliva, uncovering the processes through which ideas and desires manifest within the social realm.

The *DYSTOPIE Sound Art Festival* in 2018, initiated by Georg Klein, Jeremy Woodruff and Golo Föllmer, marked a significant turning point for Errant Sound, both within the city and on the international stage. This festival, funded by the Senate of Berlin, unfolded over a 10-day exhibition at various locations, including Wasserspeicher, Errant Sound, Meinblau project space, and public spaces like Kollwitzplatz, Tempelhofer Feld, and Teufelsberg.[5] The title of the festival alluded to the dystopian global developments foreseen by factors such as climate change, the growing influence of tech corporations, and authoritarian governments. These themes were also reflected in the more recent sound-artistic productions featured in the festival.

With the creation of "atmospheres" (Gernot Böhme) and the performance of 'non-places' (Marc Augé), sound art has a special potential to make this ambivalence of dys-

Föllmer markierte das Festival auf Basis einer Ausstellung einen bedeutenden Wendepunkt für Errant Sound. Vom Berliner Senat gefördert, verband es mehrere Klangkunst-Locations: die Wasserspeicher im Prenzlauer Berg, der Errant Sound Projektraum, der Projektraum Meinblau sowie öffentliche Räume wie den Kollwitzplatz, das Tempelhofer Feld und den Teufelsberg[5].

Der Titel des Festivals spielte auf die dystopischen globalen Entwicklungen an, die sich durch Faktoren wie den Klimawandel, den wachsenden Einfluss von Technologiekonzernen und autoritäre Regierungen abzeichneten. Diese Themen spiegelten sich auch in den jüngeren klangkünstlerischen Produktionen des Festivals wider.

Klangkunst besitzt mit der Gestaltung von ›Atmosphären‹ (Gernot Böhme) und der Bespielung von ›Nicht-Orten‹ (Marc Augé) ein besonderes Potential, diese Ambivalenz von Dystopie und Utopie in einer sinnlichen, nicht-narrativen Form erscheinen zu lassen. Für das Dystopie Festival haben 26 internationale Künstler*innen in Klang gefasste Szenarien entwickelt, in denen sie sich mit technologischen, biologischen und politischen Dystopien auseinandersetzen. Eine aktuelle politische Zuspitzung bekommt das Festival durch den Länderschwerpunkt Türkei mit vielen Gästen aus Istanbul.[6]

Ein Ziel des Festivals war die nachhaltige Kooperation mit einem Land, in dem durch die politische Entwicklung die Freiheit der Kunstproduktion gefährdet ist. Mit Hilfe des Goethe-Instituts konnte eine weitere Festivalauflage 2019 in Istanbul realisiert werden, die sich 2021 selbständig als *Distopya* fortsetzte.

Ende 2018 musste Errant Sound den Raum in der Kollwitzstraße 97 aufgrund der Beendigung des Mietvertrags verlassen, was eine Phase der Unsicherheit einleitete. Ein Drittel der Mitglieder verließ den Verein. Glücklicherweise konnte Errant Sound dank eines jurierten Verfahrens des Berliner Senats einen geförderten Projektraum in der

topia and utopia appear in a sensual, non-narrative form. For the Dystopia Festival, 26 international artists* have developed sound scenarios in which they deal with technological, biological and political dystopias. The festival's focus on Turkey, with many guests from Istanbul, gives the festival a topical, political edge (Dystopie Festival webpage).[6]

One of the objectives of the festival was to forge lasting collaborations with a country where the freedom of art production faced threats from political developments. In collaboration with Turkish curators we developed the festival in Berlin and in cooperation with the MIAM Institute Istanbul a following festival edition took place in Istanbul in 2019 and went on independently in 2021, with support by Goethe-Institute.

At the end of 2018 Errant Sound had to leave the space at Kollwitzstraße 97 due to the termination of the rental contract, ushering in a period of uncertainty. One third of the members departed during this challenging time, and as a nomadic project space, Errant Sound had to navigate new obstacles. Fortunately, thanks to a juried procedure of the Berlin Senate, Errant Sound secured a funded project space at Rungestraße 20 in 2019. The Netzwerk Projekträume consistent political efforts expanded financial funding instruments, leading to partial improvements in studios and project spaces, helping against the overall rental development situation in the city. With the financial support of a basic funding (*Basisförderung*), our project space successfully solidified its position as a significant hub for the local, national, and international sound art scene within a span of four years (2020/21–2022/23).

Rungestraße 20 für 2019 erhalten. Durch die konsequente politische Arbeit des *netzwerks projekträume* wurden die finanziellen Förderinstrumente erweitert, was zu partiellen Verbesserungen in den Ateliers und der Projektraumszene führte und der allgemeinen Mietentwicklung in der Stadt entgegenwirkte. Mit der finanziellen Unterstützung einer Basisförderung ist es unserem Projektraum gelungen, innerhalb von vier Jahren (2020/21-2022/23) seine Position als bedeutender Knotenpunkt für die lokale, nationale und internationale Klangkunstszene auszubauen und zu festigen.

Die Wiedereröffnung Ende März 2019 markierte auch den Beginn eines fortlaufenden künstlerischen Forschungsprojekts, der Ausstellung und der Veranstaltungsreihe mit dem Titel *Ready Making*. Konzeptioniert von Janine Eisenächer und Steffi Weismann ist *Ready Making*[7] ein Forschungsprojekt, das Künstlerinnen und Künstler dazu einlädt, gemeinsam über die Bedeutung von Klängen und Geräuschen nachzudenken, die durch "klangpraktische Handlungen" erzeugt werden (nach einem von Elena Ungeheuer geprägten Begriff). Dabei geht es um die Interaktion von Objekten und Materialien innerhalb von Performances, die die Bereiche Performance Art, Sound Art, experimentelle Musik, Theater und Tanz abdecken. Darüber hinaus befasst sich das Projekt mit dem stillschweigenden Wissen und dem auditiven Verständnis, das in Klangperformances eingebettet ist. Es zielt darauf ab, herauszufinden, was wir lernen und erfahren, wenn wir das akustische Potenzial von Alltagsgegenständen spielerisch erkunden und ihnen zuhören. Das Projekt wirft Fragen über die diesen Dingen innewohnende Macht und die von den Materia-

---

5 Kirsten Reese offers an insight into her work for Dystopie 2018 in this book.

6 www.dystopie-festival.net/2018.

7 See Janine Eisenächer's contribution in this book.

8 www.readymaking.com

The reopening in late March 2019 also marked the beginning of the ongoing artistic research project, exhibition, and event series titled *Ready Making*. This initiative by Janine Eisenächer and Steffi Weismann delves into the nuanced sounds within sound performances and the performative aspects of sound art, contextualizing them within discursive frameworks.[7]

Ready Making[8] is an artistic research project that invites artists to collectively contemplate the significance of sounds and noises generated through sound-practical actions (translated by Eisenächer from the term "klangpraktisches Handeln" coined by Elena Ungeheuer). This exploration involves the interaction of objects and materials within performances spanning the realms of performance art, sound art, experimental music, theatre, and dance. Additionally, the project delves into the tacit knowledge and auditory understanding embedded in sound performances. It aims to uncover what we learn and experience when we playfully explore the acoustic potential of everyday objects and listen to them. The project raises questions about the agency inherent in these things and the sounds produced by materials. It prompts an exploration of how we can perceive them as non-human actors or entities, and how they become a part of our coexistent reality.

Conversely, the *Visual Approach to Sound* exhibition series seeks to examine sound through the lens of visual art.[9] In this series, visual artists were extended invitations to showcase works that draw on the forms and methodologies of visual art, yet are inherently shaped by a central acoustic dimension. During the fall of 2019, the *sonomemo* exhibition, funded by

lien erzeugten Klänge auf. Es regt dazu an, zu erforschen, wie wir sie als nicht-menschliche Akteure oder Entitäten wahrnehmen können und wie sie zu einem Teil unserer koexistenten Realität werden.

Die Ausstellungsreihe *Visual Approach to Sound* hingegen versuchte, Klang durch die Linse der bildenden Kunst zu betrachten[8]. In dieser Reihe wurden bildende Künstlerinnen und Künstler eingeladen, Werke zu präsentieren, die auf Formen und Methoden der bildenden Kunst zurückgreifen, aber von einer zentralen akustischen Dimension geprägt sind. Im Herbst 2019 präsentierte die vom Musikfonds geförderte Ausstellung sonomemo Werke der neu zusammengesetzten Gruppe in einer Kollektivausstellung zum Thema "Klang und Erinnerung"[9]. Der neue Veranstaltungsort zog inzwischen nicht nur mehr Besucher an, sondern auch interessierte Künstlerinnen und Künstler, so dass die Gruppe aufgrund der großen Nachfrage ihre Mitgliederzahl zunächst auf 20 beschränkte.

Die von den Errant Sound Mitgliedern Andrei Cucu, Daniela Fromberg und Stefan Roigk initiierte Ausstellung *as we entwine* zum Auftakt der transmediale im Januar 2020 war eine der letzten Veranstaltungen, die wir vor der COVID anbieten konnten. Wie viele andere Kulturräume befand sich auch Errant Sound aufgrund der Pandemie in einer enormen Unsicherheit. Als Reaktion darauf begann die Gruppe alternative Formen der Kunstausstellung zu erkunden. Es war zwar von entscheidender Bedeutung, die künstlerische Produktion aufrechtzuerhalten, aber der Kontakt mit dem Publikum wurde nun schwieriger. Während des Lockdowns entwickelte Errant Sound verschiedene Strategien, um mit der Öffentlichkeit in Kontakt zu bleiben. *Audiovisual Screening* z.B. war eine Reihe von Online-Klangperformances, die Künstler und Publikum an verschiedenen Orten miteinander verbanden. Diese Reihe wurde zur Errant *Shutdown Sound Night*, die das Konzept auf einen gemeinsamen Raum ausweitete.

Musikfonds, showcased works from the newly formed group in a collective exhibition centered around sound and memory.[10] The new venue not only drew more visitors but also attracted interested artists, prompting the group to cap its membership at 20 due to the high demand for participation.

The exhibition *as we entwine*, initiated by Andrei Cucu, Daniela Fromberg and Stefan Roigk for the *transmediale* prelude in January 2020, was one of the last events we could offer before the COVID-19 pandemic. Similar to many other cultural spaces, Errant Sound faced significant challenges due to the pandemic. The group, in response, began exploring alternative forms of exhibition making. While it was crucial to maintain artistic production, preserving contact with the public became even more paramount. This led to the adoption of digital presentations such as live screenings and podcasts as essential means to showcase, perform, and discuss art.

During the lockdown, Errant Sound developed various strategies to stay in touch with the public. *Audiovisual Screening* was a series of online sound performances that connected artists and audiences in different locations. This series became *Errant Shutdown Sound Night*, which expanded the concept to a shared space.

Sine 2020, there has been a growing imperative to collectively address political issues and foster collaboration with other project spaces in Berlin. Following the racist murders in Hanau, the collaborative initiative by Steffi Weismann and Georg Klein called AARC (Artists Against Racism Collaborative) emerged in partnership

---

Nach den rassistischen Morden in Hanau 2020 gab es ein wachsendes Bedürfnis, politische Themen anzugehen und die Zusammenarbeit mit anderen Projekträumen in Berlin zu suchen. Auf Initiative von Steffi Weismann und Georg Klein enstand die *Artists Against Racism Collaborative* (AARC) in Zusammenarbeit mit *Apartment Project* – einem Projektraum mit türkischem Background, die sich der kollaborativen künstlerischen Praxis widmet. Ziel war es, trotz Corona einen gemeinsamen künstlerischen Diskurs zu pflegen, gemeinschaftliche Prozesse zu ermöglichen und innovative Formen der Solidarität zu erforschen. Dies führte zu zwei Gruppenausstellungen mit Performances, partizipatorischen Formaten und Diskussionsveranstaltungen im selben Jahr sowie in 2021 zur Ausstellung Haters[10].

Trotz strenger Coronabedingungen für Ausstellungen, Performances und Konzerte konnte das Festival "DYSTOPIE 2020" im Herbst stattfinden. Diese Ausgabe, mit einem Fokus auf Brasilien, fand in der Alten Münze am Spreeufer und bei Errant Sound statt und umfasste 24 Projekte mit Installationen und Performances unter Beteiligung von 40 Künstler*innen, sowie ein Symposium unter dem Titel "Listening as a tool to blow out the bubble". Künstlerische Leiter*in waren Georg Klein und Laura Mello, zusammen mit Mario Asef für die Projektleitung. Gefördert wurde das Festival erstmalig durch die Kulturstiftung des Bundes[11], mit DeutschlandFunk Kultur als Medienpartner. Das Untergeschoss der Alten Münze mit seinen verlassenen Tresorräumen, der von der Feuchtigkeit der Spree angegriffenen Betons-

---

9 See Mario Asef's contribution in this book.

10 Participating artists: Mario Asef / Roberta Busechian / Janine Eisenächer / Alexandre Fenerich / Golo Föllmer / Georg Klein / Laura Mello / Jutta Ravenna / Kirsten Reese / Antje Vowinckel / Steffi Weismann. Roberta Busechian offers an insight to her work for sonomemo in this book.

11 See Georg Klein's contribution to this book.

with Apartment Project – an organization with Turkish background devoted to collaborative artistic practice. The aim was to cultivate a shared artistic discourse, facilitate collaborative processes, and explore innovative forms of solidarity. This led to the creation of two group exhibitions, performances, participatory formats, and discussion events in the same year, then in 2021 to the exhibition *Haters*.[11]

Despite stringent attendance regulations for exhibitions, performances, and concerts, the DYSTOPIE 2020 festival managed to proceed with extreme caution. This edition, focused on Brazil as a partner, unfolded from October 16th to November 1st at Alte Münze, Spreeufer, and Errant Sound, featuring installations, performances, and a symposium showcasing 24 projects by 40 artists (Artistic directors: Georg Klein, Laura Mello. Project management: Mario Asef, Georg Klein. Funding by Kulturstiftung des Bundes).[12]

The basement of Alte Münze, the old Berlin mint with its abandoned treasure chambers, concrete structure affected by the humidity of the river Spree, and large boiler room, provided a highly evocative stage for the current times, in particular global right-wing populism and the COVID-19 pandemic. As an extension of the exchange initiated in 2020 in DYSTOPIE Berlin-Brasilien festival among artists residing in Brazil and expatriate artists residing abroad the festival *Topia took place in Brazil in 2021. Their common interest was the listening experience as a (de-)construction and (re)signification tool.[13]

The commitment to exchange and collaboration extended beyond Berlin in 2022. ANIMA MUNDI, initiated by Janine Eisenächer and Bartosz Nowak, leverages

---

truktur und dem großen Maschinenraum bot eine höchst suggestive Bühne für die aktuelle Zeit, insbesondere den globalen Rechtspopulismus und die Corona-Pandemie. Die Abschlussperformance "*El Intruso*" von Mario de Vega einen Tag vor dem nächsten Lockdown griff die düstere gesellschaftliche Stimmung auf und verwandelte sie in ein kathartisches audiovisuelles Erlebnis. Durch den initiierten Austausch mit brasilianischen Künstler*innen konnte dann in 2021 eine Fortsetzung des Festivals als *TOPIA in Brasilien stattfinden. Ihr gemeinsames Interesse galt der Hörerfahrung als (De-)Konstruktions- und (Re-)Signifikationsinstrument, wie in Laura Mellos und Vanessa De Michelis Beitrag beschrieben.[12]

In 2022 wurde eine neue Ausstellungsreihe von Janine Eisenächer und Bartosz Nowak initiiert: ANIMA MUNDI nutzt die Klangkunst, um neue Verbindungen zu Umwelterfahrungen, Nachhaltigkeitsfragen und künstlerische Antworten auf die Klimakrise herzustellen. Die ersten Ausgaben von ANIMA MUNDI fanden bei Errant Sound und 2023 im MOS-Kunstzentrum in Gorzów Wielkopolski, Polen, statt und werden 2024 als deutsch-polnisch-irische Kooperation weitergeführt.

Nach der restriktiven Coronazeit waren dann auch wieder gemeinsame Hörerfahrungen möglich. Im Jahr 2023 führte MaxJoy die Sonic Art Bar ein, ein monatliches Treffen im Errant Sound in der Rungestraße 20. Diese Initiative bot ein Forum für die gemeinsame Hörerfahrung von Audiostücken in einer einladenden Atmosphäre, verbunden mit persönlichen Gesprächen.

Für Herbst 2022 war bereits eine neue Ausgabe von DYSTOPIE in Vorbereitung, in Zusammenarbeit mit dem Klangkunst-Projektraum SA))-Gallery in Moskau, so dass Russland zu unserem Fokus werden sollte. Der verheerende russische Angriffskrieg gegen die Ukraine führte jedoch zur Absage des Festivals. Für 2024 wurde das Festival dann als Klangkunst-Biennale DYSTOPIA neu aufgelegt, wo-

sound art to establish novel connections to environmental experiences, sustainability concerns, and responses to the climate crisis. The inaugural editions of ANIMA MUNDI were hosted at Errant Sound and the MOS art center in Gorzów Wielkopolski, Poland, with subsequent expansion in 2023 as a German-Polish-Irish cooperative effort.

Another avenue for exchange revolves around shared listening experiences. In 2023, MaxJoy introduced the *Sonic Art Bar*, a monthly gathering held at Errant Sound on Rungestraße 20. This initiative provided a forum for collectively appreciating works of sound art in an inviting atmosphere, coupled with personal discussions.

At this juncture, our sound art festival DYSTOPIE, scheduled for fall 2022, was already in progress with Russia as the new focus country in cooperation with a sound art project space in Moscow. Unfortunately, the devastating Russian war in Ukraine was leading to the cancellation of the festival. But in 2024, DYSTOPIA will relaunches as a Sound Art Biennial,[15] directing its focus toward sound-related practices emerging from the Indian subcontinent (artistic directors Georg Klein and Nida Ghouse). Additionally, another edition of the biennial is already in the works for 2026, both funded by the Berlin Senate and represents an important step towards establishing this art form between music, visual art and media art and making it visible in an international context.

In 2024, our project space once again faces the challenge of being without a physical location. As our funding is not renewed without justification, we are forced to vacate our space at Rungestrasse 20 in Berlin-Mitte.

bei in diesem Jahr der Schwerpunkt auf klangkünstlerischen Praktiken aus dem indischen Subkontinent liegt (künstlerische Leitung Georg Klein und Nida Ghouse). Darüber hinaus ist bereits eine weitere Ausgabe der Biennale für 2026 in Arbeit, beide durch den Festivalfond des Berliner Senats finanziert. Die Entwicklung einer "Biennale der Klangkunst" stellt einen wichtigen Schritt dar, diese Kunstform zwischen Musik, Bildender Kunst und Medienkunst zu etablieren und im internationalen Kontext sichtbar zu machen.

Im Jahr 2024 steht unser Projektraum erneut vor der Herausforderung, ohne Raum zu sein. Unser Mietvertrag wurde von der Genossenschaft Rungestraße 20 nicht verlängert und zusätzlich fiel die finanzielle Basisförderung durch den Berliner Senat weg. Die Zukunft von Errant Sound wie auch die Produktion und Präsentation von Klangkunst in Berlin generell bleibt ungewiss – ähnlich ist die Lage vieler anderer Projekträume in der Stadt. Es scheint, dass wir uns in der gleichen Situation befinden wie vor 10 Jahren, als wir als Errant Bodies Gruppe begannen einen Projektraum zu entwickeln. Trotzdem liegt unser aktueller Fokus darauf, Klangkunst und ihre Möglichkeiten zu erweitern, indem wir mit neuen Positionen und Formaten arbeiten – und hoffentlich auch bald wieder mit eigenen Räumen.

Dieses Buch ist ein Versuch, die verschiedenen Ansätze zu Klangpraktiken und -diskursen des Errant Sound-Projektraums aufzuzeigen, wobei wir nicht alle Positionen der letzten 10 Jahre berücksichtigen können. Die heterogenen Beiträge sollen zum Verständnis von

---

12 www.dystopie-festival.net/2020.

13 See Laura Mello and Vanessa De Michelis' contribution in this book. The artist, Lilian Campesato, featured in this book, was also a participating artist.

14 www.listeningbiennial.net

15 www.dystopia.berlin

The future of Errant Sound, as well as the landscape for producing and presenting sound art in Berlin, remains uncertain – similar to the predicament faced by many other project spaces in the city. It seems that we are facing the same situation as from 10 years ago when we started as the Errant Bodies group. Despite this, our current focus is on expanding sound art and its knowledge by introducing new positions and formats – and with new spaces.

This book is an attempt to expose the diverse approaches to sound practices and discourses within the Errant Sound project space. Herein lies our earnest endeavor to contribute to the understanding of sound, exploring its social, political, and cultural dimensions.

Comprising a collection of insightful essays crafted by members and allies of Errant Sound, this text compilation delves into diverse facets of sonic practice and contemplation.[16] These essays, born from ongoing research projects and experiences within Errant Sound, intertwine thematically, weaving a tapestry of shared terms and discourses. Listen, explore, and resonate with discussions on themes such as listening, voice and speech,[17] installation sound art,[18] performance and "social composition,"[19] sound object, new technologies,[20] and artistic research.[21] We ask "What do sounds need, what do we grant them—or not?"[22] This book is a testament to the interconnectedness of these sonic realms, inviting readers to ponder the intricate threads that bind them together.

Klang in unserer Gesellschaft beitragen und seine sozialen, politischen und kulturellen Dimensionen erforschen. Die von Mitgliedern und Assoziierten von Errant Sound verfassten Essays befassen sich mit verschiedenen Facetten der klangkünstlerischen Praxis und Reflexion[14]. Sie sind aus laufenden Forschungsprojekten und Erfahrungen innerhalb von Errant Sound entstanden, greifen thematisch ineinander und weben einen Teppich aus gemeinsamen Begriffen und Diskursen. Mit dem Reader sollen Resonanzräume diskursiver Art entstehen zu Themen wie Zuhören, Stimme und Sprache[15], zu Klanginstallation[16], *performance art* und *social composition*[17], Klangobjekten und neue Technologien[18], sowie zu *artistic research*[19]. Wir fragen: "Was braucht der Klang, was gewähren wir ihm – oder nicht?"[20] Dieses Buch ist ein Zeugnis für die Verflechtung dieser Klangwelten und lädt die Leser*innen ein, über die verschlungenen Fäden nachzudenken, die sie miteinander verbinden.

---

16 See Golo Föllmer and Brandon LaBelle's contribution to this book.

17 See Antje Vowinckel and Alessandra Eramo's contribution to this book.

18 See Jutta Ravenna and Nico Daleman's contribution to this book.

19 See Jeremy Woodruff's contribution to this book.

20 See Gerriet K. Sharma's contribution to this book.

21 See Georg Klein's contribution to this book.

22 See Holger Schultze's contribution to this book.

23 January 2025.

CURRENT MEMBERS:[23]

Mario Asef
Roberta Busechian
Andrei Cucu
Nico Daleman
Janine Eisenächer
Alessandra Eramo
Özcan Ertek
Golo Föllmer
Alifiyah Imani
Georg Klein
Thom Kubli
Brandon LaBelle
Verena Lercher

MaxJoy
Laura Mello
Oliver Möst
Jutta Ravenna
Kirsten Reese
Stefan Roigk
Gerriet K. Sharma
Bea Targosz
Steffi Weismann
Georg Werner
Zorka Wollny
Jeremy Woodruff

FORMER MEMBERS:

Alex Arteaga
Gilles Aubry
Serge Baghdassarians
Ylva Bentancor
Julia Cremers
Peter Cusack
Ernesto Estrella
Alexandre Fenerich
Berit Fischer
Daniela Fromberg
Hanna Hartman
Klaas Huebner
Jacob Kirkegaard

Ines Lechleitner
Åsa Stjerna
Antje Vowinckel

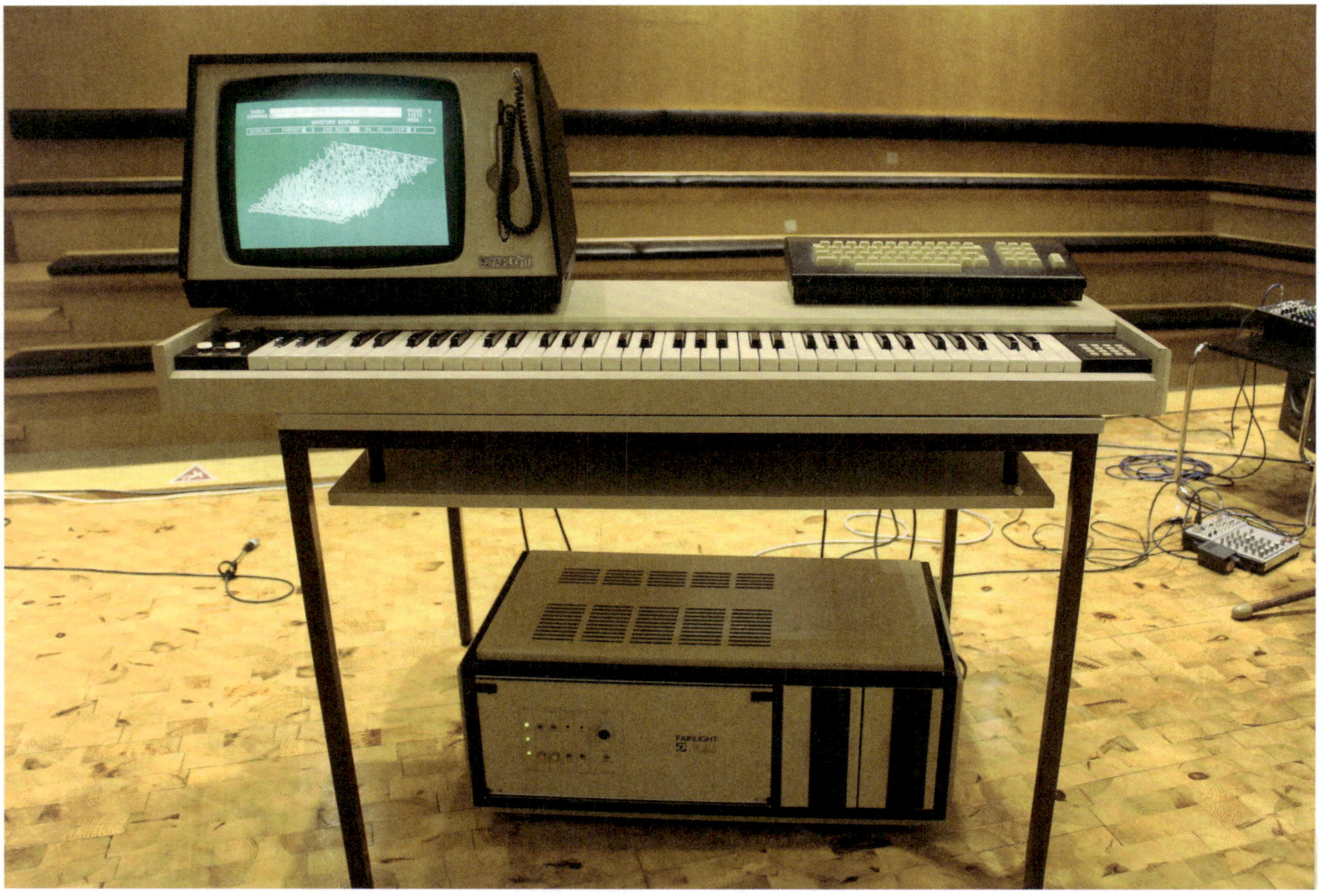

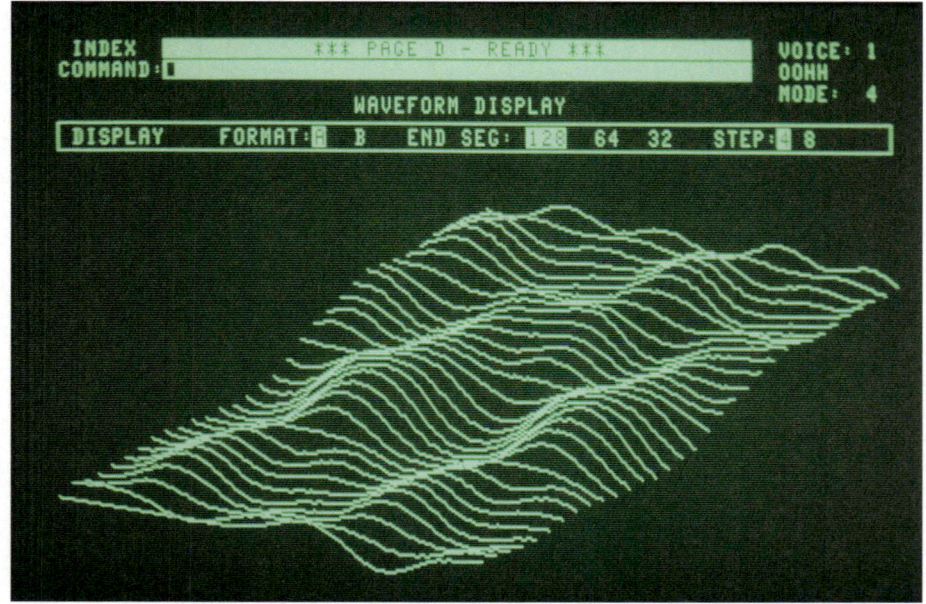

↑: Fairlight CMI
(Computer Musical Instrument)

↘: Fairlight screen
Photos: Kirsten Reese

KIRSTEN REESE

Voices of Insects and Voices of Algorithms

Creatures and Signals for archival insect recordings and Fairlight CMI was composed for the Dystopia Festival 2018[1] and was first performed at the unique environment of the historic Teufelsberg listening station in Berlin. The work brings together insect recordings from the *Tierstimmenarchiv* (Animal Sound Archive) of the Museum of Natural History Berlin with "speculative" insect voices generated by the Fairlight CMI, one of the first digital synthesizers and samplers.

The work related to the festival theme "dystopia" by featuring actual archival recordings of insect voices and imagined creatures represented by the "voices" of an electronic, digital instrument. *Creatures and Signals* posed speculative questions around this juxtaposition ... Which animals will survive (us) on earth? What kind of beings will they evolve into? Will they develop new languages? Will they change the way they communicate with other beings and life forms? Quite a few of the recordings from the *Tierstimmenarchiv* date back to the 1960s; the Fairlight is an instrument that stands equally for historicism and futurism; and the performance of *Creatures and Signals* took place in the ambience of *Teufelsberg*, a historic site from the Cold War-era that today is characterized by decay and overgrowth – all of which contributed to the work's overall atmosphere of dystopic retro-futurism. Moreover, it raised broader questions concerning the musical interaction between voices of non-human living beings and machine voices (questions I have continued to explore in other works since 2018[2]).

INSECT VOICES

Insects represent the majority of living creatures in the so-called "animal kingdom," yet most species have often been regarded (by humans) as mundane and seemingly insignificant. In times of growing awareness of ecological crises and the mass extinction of insects ("Insektensterben") this view might be shifting. But still, while the visual appearance of certain insects, especially when magnified, is spectacular, often insects are associated with filth and met with aversion, they are combatted as pests or disease carriers, and many thrive under the most unwelcoming of conditions ... – all of which links to the dystopian theme of the composition. Most importantly, of the millions of insect species presumably inhabiting the earth most are "undiscovered," unknown. Their insignificance – being too small or unimportant to be worth consideration – and the aspect of the *unknown* sparked the speculative sound investigation of *Creatures and Signals* into unknown future sounds of undiscovered or newly evolving creatures.

What is remarkable about insects, on the other hand, is how the countless different species have followed a highly differentiated path in their evolutionary development in terms of their specialized adaptation to habitats, food sources, symbiotic relationships with other animals or plants, etc. This specialization and differentiation is also true for insect calls.

What characterizes the voices of insects? Insect vocalizations can be grouped into five categories in relation to the sound production mechanisms involved: vibration/tremulation, percussion, stridulation, click mechanisms and air expulsion.[3] Stridulation in particular, a frictional mechanism in which two specialized body parts move against each other in systematic patterns, is common: most often one body part with ridges is scraped across another, which causes vibrations in different patterns depending on how close the ridges are and how fast the movement is. Although the sound-producing tools (body parts) are highly specialized and diversified, their utilization is based on simple mechanisms and mostly results in simple sound structures that are repeated in small time units. Often the repetition of minute sounds is so fast that this results in distinct frequencies and high pitched oscillations. And when hundreds or thousands of animals sound together in the open, dense sound choruses in complex spatial formations emerge.

FAIRLIGHT VOICES

What characterizes the voice of the Fairlight? The Fairlight CMI (Computer Musical Instrument) was introduced in 1979 and was one of the first digital instruments. (The model I used for my compositions belongs to the UNI.K Studio of the University of the Arts Berlin and is from 1983). It is a synthesizer and a sampler: waveform synthesis is done by shaping envelopes for up to 32 harmonics, and samples can be retrieved from a sound library and also recorded and edited. Both stored synthesized sounds and samples are called "voices" (and several voices can be grouped to form an "instrument"). The Fairlight carries the aura of the early days of the digital: when the system disk, an 8-inch floppy disk, is installed or when the "voices" and "instruments" are retrieved from the floppy disk the two disk drives emit archaic noises. The instrument is operated by choosing commands on a monitor screen using a light pen or alternatively through commands on an alphanumeric keyboard. The Fairlight's digital capacities are extremely limited in comparison to today's sound synthesis and sampling possibilities: it operates in 8-bit, the maximum sampling rate is 32000 Hz, the maximum size of a sample is 16kb. But the sound design is well thought-out and endows the instrument with a characteristic sonority, unique and beautiful (and also very different from analogue synthesizer sounds).

Not only regarding its sound, but also concerning its operational workflow (and its touch and feel in general) the Fairlight has proven to be an extremely versatile instrument: differentiated sonic designs and manipulations can be controlled through the computer keyboard or the light pen (even drawing wave form envelopes on the monitor screen). The touch-sensitive piano keyboard can be scaled to different tunings. Algorithmic processes can be triggered via the piano keyboard, for example the *Portamento* function: if you press a note on the keyboard followed by another one, a glissando towards this last note begins, continuously (by holding the new note) or in the time intervals that you press the key – until this note is finally reached; if you trigger several of these glissandi, you end up with overlaying changing rhythmic, harmonic and timbral processes of great complexity. Overall, the real-time possibilities of sound manipulation and transformation of the Fairlight are impressive because they allow the interaction of many processes resulting in complex, stimulating sonic and structural responses from the instrument.

LIKENESS OF MODULATED SAMPLES AND INSECT CALLS

This real-time modulation was what I concentrated on when developing *Creatures and Signals*. Experimenting with the Fairlight samples/voices, I aimed for electronic voices that could be heard in relation to the insect voices from the archive. Where in other pieces I worked with the sound synthesis possibilities of the Fairlight,[4] for *Creatures and Signals* the starting point was the sample library that came with the instrument at its time. 33 discs hold around 25 samples each, around 800 samples altogether, instrumental sounds, human voice and other human sounds, one disc features animal sounds, other discs are labeled "weather," "effects," etc. (The sample library of the Fairlight can be regarded as an archive of emblematic sound representations.) Many of the non-instrumental samples in particular show a certain "roughness" due to their limited resolution and noise artefacts, so that often a single sample or a short loop seems to be alluding to insect sounds already.

When performing the piece, or listening back into recordings of the performance, sometimes I could not distinguish between certain digital and real insect sounds myself. The resemblance lies mainly in the way samples of the Fairlight and insect vocalizations build on simple patterns on micro levels. Also, playing chords or clusters of adjacent notes on the Fairlight creates a temporal density similar to when many small insects sound together. There is an interesting correlation to granular synthesis, one of the most important digital sound synthesis/processing techniques, where samples are split into small grains of sounds of around 1 to 50ms. Multiple grains may be layered and played back at different speeds, phases, volume and frequency; waveform, envelope, duration, spatial position, density of grains may be varied. Low speeds of playback result in clouds of sound, higher speeds in pitches with novel timbres. As mentioned before, on the Fairlight various parameter values can be controlled in realtime, three sliders, two pushbuttons/ control knobs and optionally three more pedals and pushbuttons can be mapped to the control parameters. I used the following parameters to shape the "maxi-grains" (minimum size 50ms) and transform the samples: *Loop Start – Loop Length – Start Segment – Vibrato Depth – Slur – Damping – Portamento*. Loop start and Loop length define a starting point and length of the sample extract to be looped, the loop can become as short as 50ms. *Start segment* determines were the sample starts to play (not necessarily where the loop begins). *Vibrato* depth modulates the pitch of the sample, which has different effects depending on the loop length. *Slur* means notes don't end with key release, but add up when a new note is played (the setting of polyphony in the general settings of the voice determines how many notes can be piled up). *Damping* is the fade out time, it can usually be up to 16 seconds (up to 65 seconds in the sampling Mode 4). *Portamento* I already explained earlier.

FORM / COMPOSITION

When researching insect sounds in archives, in collections or other online resources one finds different categories of recordings. Insect voices are often captured in a field recording as a soundscape of different animals sounding together rather than as a "pure" high quality recording of isolated calls. In laboratories – where sometimes animals were dissected and isolated body parts activated through electrodes to produce their sound – recordings often feature a background hum as ambience. In general, the recording quality regarding overall fidelity and noise ratios varies immensely.

The *Tierstimmenarchiv* belongs to the Natural History Museum of Berlin, which before reunification was a GDR (German Democratic Republic) institution, and because travel opportunities for researchers especially to Western countries were very limited, many recordings were made in areas in former East Germany and even from around Berlin – and not, for example, in exotic rain forest locations in faraway countries. I embraced the characteristics of this not-so-spectacular and heterogeneous material, and, browsing through the comprehensive database of digitized insect recordings to which I had been given full access, followed an intuitive strategy for choosing sounds. (The database also included bat vocalizations, and given that transpositions of ultrasonic frequencies sound especially electronic I integrated these – bats chase and eat insects: this provided the connection to insect sounds.) I also included some of the recordist's/researcher's comments on the sound files, their voices, accents and manner of speech emphasize the local specificity and history of the archive.[5]

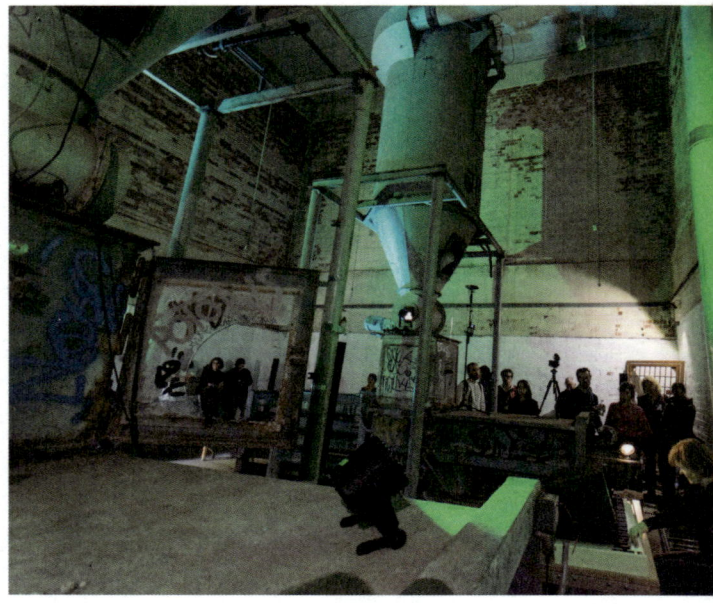

Regarding the form of the work, it was important to me to follow a "not-so-clean," non-hierarchical approach and to have a looseness in the musical dramaturgy. This reflects the multitude of voices that exist in the insect sound world, and the gaps that exist in our (human) knowledge about this world. From a selection of around 50 recordings, I condensed the material by extracting and overlaying the extracts in different tracks in the DAW. This way, there are always several different insect voices present, with new ones emerging or fading away, at other times beginning to call or ending quite abruptly.

Similarly, on the Fairlight, I chose samples (around 12) from the library of discs, then experimented with modulation possibilities and improvised with the insect tracks. I regarded the Fairlight sounds as individual voices of other creatures joining the soundscape, at the same time anticipating musical relationships in terms of matching or contrapuntal timbre, rhythmic patterns, envelope and development of the voice, etc. Some of the insect vocalizations have a more unique coloring than others, are more expressive or evocative, with a kind of build-up, an urgency – for example the queen bee "piping, quacking and tooting" (this is beekeepers jargon for the call the queen causes by vibrating the air around

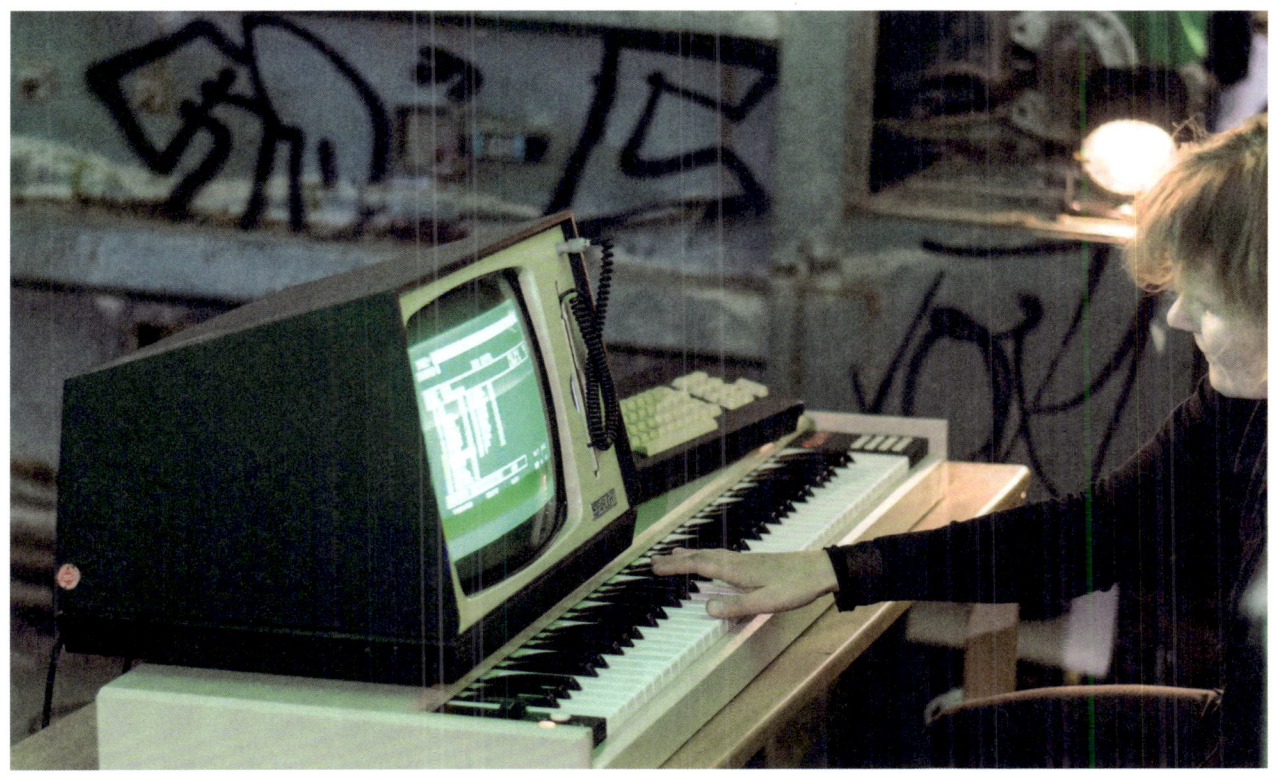

↖/↑: Performance of Creatures and Signals at Teufelsberg, Dystopie Festival 2018
Photos: Golo Föllmer

her body with wing beats – in German: "quacken und tüten"). The Fairlight samples, being played on a keyboard as notes, tend to have a harmonic feel to them, even when the harmonies are dissonant – and as with the insects some show a more intense, evocative expression. The atmosphere that emerged in some parts I would describe as melancholic. The listening attitude is one of observation: observing "nature" ... observing something that happens, without interference.

I performed several versions of *Creatures and Signals* with different durations in different contexts, for example in the Lange Nacht der Wissenschaften at the Museum für Naturkunde in 2022, sitting opposite a large spider model. The version *Creatures Sound Tracking* was developed for the Lange/Berweck/Lorenz synthesizer trio and premiered in 2023, here three electronic synthesizer voices accompany the insect and (reduced) Fairlight voices.

INSECT VOICES – VOICES OF ALGORITHMS

The confrontation of insect vocalizations with electronic signals raises questions about the relationship between the voices of humans, non-human beings and machines. It questions human listening: do we hear the electronic sonorities as if they resemble insect voices, or do algorithms actually have a voice of their own? Voices originate from *living* beings – what can this *aliveness* mean in regard to electronics? We call an electronic process *live-electronic* when it is running on its own (at least for a while) and it evolves and can be listened to in realtime. But equally important is the aspect of sound as a phenomenological, physical event. Even in the days when composers programming computers had to wait for the sounding result for hours, or even days and nights, they were surprised by what the machine spat out as a result, and inspired.[6] An electronic/digital sound process is the translation from numbers to sensuous sound. We perceive this sound with our aural sense, a form of perception which we ascribe meaning to in an expressive connotation (voice as an expression). An algorithm is defined as an exact sequence of instructions, which under the same preconditions always returns the same result, where a specific input yields a defined output – but in electronic/digital music, the output is a transformation into a different medium, an interaction with the physical world (hardware, loudspeakers, our ears). Moreover, the combination of algorithms quickly has the potential to produce a complexity of sound waves in a physical space which is not foreseeable – *forhearable*. This is true for sound synthesis, and even more when working with samples – recordings from the real world, not synthesized in the black box but saturated with complexity. When algorithmic sound is not designed with a predetermined output in mind, but when it is created in a reciprocal process between human and machine, we hear algorithms converted to complex physically sounding entities with an aura of aliveness, and possibly as voices.

What signifies a voice? – To hear a voice means to acknowledge the expression of a subject (and maybe to react, to enter a communication process). Philosophical questions concerning subjectivity and consciousness are currently very present in the debate about artificial intelligence – but corresponding questions have been raised regarding animals, especially concerning the smallest and "least worthy" of animals, insects. In the 1970s, the American composer David Dunn developed a series of experimental setups with speakers and microphones entitled *Music, language and the environment* intended to establish communication with animals or vast landscapes.[7] In 1990, Dunn composed a work with recordings of the sounds of microorganisms in a lake, titled *Chaos or the Emergent Mind of the Pond*.[8] (Dunn also recorded signals from tree bark beetles, noxious beetles that threaten vast expanses of California tree cover, whose growing numbers are believed to be a marker of climate change.) What does Dunn hear in the sounds of water insects and organisms of the pond? He can't "accept the assumption that the creatures themselves are meaningless specks of protoplasm, forever doomed to repeat a few automatic mating calls or territorial assertions." As a musician, he hears urgency, vitality, a joy of self-expression in these calls/signals, and even a mysterious "autonomous knowing" as patterns emerge in a complex system. According to Dunn, all creatures would then be "distributed sensors" of this system that could even be called mind.[9]

Such speculations may help us in dealing with the challenges of our global ecological situation today. By listening, we realize that the other living beings out there have a voice, which we hear not necessarily as a singular subjectivity (or "intelligence," or "consciousness"), but as collectives of voices/soundings representing different species. We hear them, sometimes connecting to the expressiveness that reaches us, feeling that we might be able to understand – and sometimes only recognizing the voice of the "other." In any case, we know that in the current situation on the planet we share we have to listen more.

With electronic voices, I believe our insights might lie at the other end of the spectrum of listening as a communicative, interactive and embodied process. Electronic voices come into being and exist as an extension and a counterpart of our mind and our senses – listening to them and interacting with them enhances our self-reflexivity, expands our imagination and, ideally, transcends our self,[10] especially when we regard these voices as equally embedded in their (physical) environment as all of nature. To connect the natures of these voices of insects and voices of algorithms is what it is all about.

NOTES:

1. Produced by Errant Sound e.V., https://www.dystopie-festival.net/2018

2. s. kirstenreese.de/werkee.html

3. Edith Julieta Sarmiento Ponce in *Acoustic communication in insects*, Quehacer Científico en Chiapas 9 (2) 2014 compiles five categories of sound-producing mechanisms in insects: vibration/tremulation (generally oscillations of the abdomen or other unspecialised body parts), percussion (striking one part of the body against another), stridulation (frictional mechanisms, involving the movements of two specialized body parts against each other in a systematic patterned manner), click mechanisms (contraction and relaxation of specialized musculature results in a succession of clicks which may be repeated quickly in distinctive patterns) and air expulsion (exhalatory sound, unusual in insects). The hearing organs of insects are also highly diversified.

4. Other works with Fairlight: *the lightest words had the weight of oracles* for Fairlight CMI Synthesizer and electric guitar (2014) focuses the specific sonority of the Fairlight in relation to its "digitalness". The synthesis function is (mis)used to create small melodies and tone clusters from sine tones. Digital artefacts or grissling noises in the lower register are included as well as glitches in the sound when polyphonic possibilities are exceeded. *Light Green Rituals* for Fairlight CMI Synthesizer and ensemble (2018) revolves around ritualistic acts and sound archetypes, using "iconic" samples from the Fairlight disc library as sound symbols.

5. To include different categories of recordings of animal voices is also important in regard to realizing that there is no "true" way to document these sounds, no true way of hearing them. Firstly, the recording technology influences the recording, and secondly our hearing sense functions differently from those of animals for whom these voices as form of communication are intended: insects have varied listening organs which pick up sound in a multitude of ways. I explored this theme more in a recent work with underwater recordings of creatures living in the ocean: *Homeostasis*, an audiovisual installation for the Ozeaneum museum in Stralsund and the Zoological museum in Kiel. Marine animal vocalizations are emitted in a medium – water – where sound waves travel differently than in the air – the medium for sound transmission for human ears, so of course humans will hear these documentations of marine sound in fundamentally different ways than the animals in their habitat. For an interesting elaboration on water as medium in the context of media studies see John Durham Peters, *The Marvelous Clouds, Toward a Philosophy of Elemental Media*, The University of Chicago Press, 2015 (Chapter 2).

6. John Chowning talks about the relationship of imagination and intellect, technology and perception in an interview with Johannes Goebel in 1987: "Technology is also leading our ear. Let's assume that some composer would say there is nothing that I'll ever hear that I couldn't have imagined – I would disagree. There is a lot that we will hear that we ourselves could not have imagined but for the fact that we were in contact with technology and one another. Our intellect leads our perceptions and our perceptions lead our intellect, and given any point in time it's one or the other." In CD Liner Notes *John Chowning* Wergo 2012-50 1983, p.14.

7. *Music, language and environment, environmental sound works 1973-1985*, CD released 1996, also available on bandcamp.

8. *Angels and Insects* CD, released 1990, also available on bandcamp.

9. Accordingly, John Durham Peters in *The Marvelous Clouds* points out that marine biologists like to say that dolphins possess "distributed cognition", "networked beehive- or cyborg-like knowledge and perception", p.76.

10. Inspiring and well worth a read and re-read in this regard is Donna Haraway's *Cyborg Manifesto*.

ANTJE VOWINCKEL

Automatic Speaking and Dialect Karaoke

AT THE BOUNDARIES OF LITERATURE AND MUSIC; DIEGESIS AND MIMESIS, ANALOG AND DIGITAL

One focus of my work is composition with O-Ton (sound bites). Many of my pieces have been broadcast on radio in radio play and sound art programs, and recently I have increasingly been producing pieces without speech that take place performatively and in public spaces. Digitality determines my routines and sometimes leads to a new workflow. My essay begins with reflections on the fundamental differences between music and language and then shows examples of my own methods in which I reflect on these differences and try to use them creatively.

WAV.WAV.WAV.

Digital practice obscures the differences between speech and music. Aliens watching a terrestrial radio station might think that to make a program, you simply play one or more .wav files and everyone listens. So they land on Earth and take over the DAW.[1] They select various files from the audio pool and click on "send," but gradually the audience switches off. An earthling comes along and notices: five voice files, plus different languages and a music file. "That's not possible!" "Why?" – Well… This conversation is a nice two-person role-playing game for workshops or long train journeys. The premise: aliens know file formats, but have no idea about semiotics. They have never heard of De Saussure or other sign models. So far, they have shared information via screenshots of their thoughts.

Speech and music can be saved as .wav (mp3, flac), etc. and both can be made to sound via loudspeakers. There seems to be only one common digital code: the file format. "They're all sound waves, you're just moving air," say the aliens. But it doesn't help them to choose the right .wav files to make a program for earthlings. They first have to understand that some of the sound waves we hear are double-coded, that there is a whole world behind them, which only opens up if the listeners can perceive and decode them linearly. And people can only do this if they hear the alphabetically and phonetically coded signal in a linear sequence. Because we humans learn the speech code as children (initially through mimesis), we are often unaware of it. It is therefore worth occasionally being as naive as a few aliens when trying to combine speech and music, and to realize once again how differently the seemingly identically coded file information affects our perception.

DIGGIN' IN MIMESIS

Language is diegesis, with it I can show. "This is …" Once my brain has deciphered the code of the sound waves, I can abstract, I can point out from my immediate surroundings. "Yesterday I was in …," "Aliens are …," I can ask, comment and even lie "Yesterday I wasn't in …"

Music is mimesis – that is imitation, imitation in a broader, more abstract sense – sometimes encoded in written notes, but what you hear is not a code. It imitates, suggests or reshapes, without coding.[2] Digital formats disguise this fundamental difference: either I use the phonetic-alphabetic code to open a diegesis barrel that allows me to talk about an infinite number of places and times and inform listeners about them; in a news program, I invite them to follow my index finger and jump back and forth between many countries, people and topics. In a radio play or song lyrics, I create a broader, more visual track that inspires imaginary scenes. Or I can opt for the mimesis barrel, which does not offer these possibilities, but only contains analog waveforms. But I can reach into it again and again and superimpose, shift, interweave and condense many things into complex textures that we experience in real time, or rather: experience in "pure duration."[3] The difference between diegesis and mimesis is closely linked to Henri Bergson's distinction between time and duration.[4]

In order to follow the finger of a speaker or writer who points to the world he or she is describing linguistically, with its various settings and logical sequences, I have to arrange them side by side in my head. I place myself in other real or fictional realities, and to do this I have to abstract from my immediate surroundings. What is happening around me right now, and in what order, is irrelevant to the enjoyment of a story and its sequence. I imagine a different time and can jump back and forth in it without changing the work.

Mimesis, especially music, requires an engagement with the present, a holistic perception. A melody only works if I hear the notes in exactly this order, in this duration.[5] Ontologically speaking, diegesis and mimesis are mutually exclusive. Either the whole world or the immediate present. Is that a boundary? The human brain is not so particular about it. Of course, texts have always been sung, pointing to the kingdom of heaven (liturgy) or to the emotional world (song, opera). People want both, and often at the same time: nowadays, for example, news accompanied by music or images, music and speech simultaneously in a TikTok video. A clear hierarchy helps here. In most cases, either the music dominates (song, aria, rap) and the text is more or less dispensable, or vice versa (movie, radio play, game). In addition, the music almost always relates to the world told in the text. I accept the music as the atmosphere of these distant places or I beam myself to my own fantasized places and don't care that I don't understand the text at all.

In opera, the spheres were initially still clearly differentiated. Important plot information was conveyed in the recitative, while the experience of the present, the duration, was intensified in the arias with emotional expression. Later, the spheres became intermingled. We can switch easily, but we don't want to feel the switching too clearly. Perhaps this is why speaking in music has experienced a discovery and revaluation of prosody over the centuries. Composers such as Arnold Schönberg, Harry Partch, Leos Janáček and Robert Ashley were inspired by speech melodies. With the beginning of sound recording, recordings were also integrated, for example in musique concrète, later by Steve Reich or René Lussier.

Even in the theater, in a dramatic text, passages in which life is imitated (often somewhat exaggerated) usually work better than wall shows or political discourse, in which I as a spectator not only have to abstract from my own situation in the theater, but also from the situation on stage. The mimetic situation is then shown far beyond, so that one could also read. The stage set becomes secondary and when I am supposed to perceive it again, I feel the switching, the changeover from seeing the just linguistically evoked images that may be playing at some point and somewhere to the real present image of the stage space.

So there are tried and tested strategies that indicate that people have a sense for the differences between diegesis and mimesis and their combinations, even if they are not very conscious of them. The newsroom that puts music under its news may say that it simply wants to sound modern.

But perhaps it also fears that its listeners cannot cope with the change between so many places and people and want them to stay "on," "on" with the present good mood, "on" with the present feeling of being informed. Others, like me, don't like music under news. The mood of the music doesn't match the content, it's supposed to put me in a good mood. The attempt is too transparent for me and may not fit my mood at all. If I really want to follow the news, the music distracts me as I jump between different places and people. – Although I have to admit that there are people who don't even notice whether there's music on or not. In other words, they manage to be infected by the music, to imitate it emotionally and still follow the news. Then you can also experience catastrophe reports in a good mood. You could also discuss the pros and cons with aliens.

There has long been a model in which the hierarchy (which results from the fact that we always subordinate the music to the text) is almost abolished: "Ping-Pong," "Tick-Tock," "hum," "buzz" and "squeak" are onomatopoeic expressions that both show and imitate. A kind of "mimdieg." However, the brief moments of mimesis in these expressions pass so quickly that they are hardly noticeable; at least it is enough for a little pleasure, a joy in taking shortcuts when bypassing the code. The desire to break down hierarchies is known to be a constant driver for the arts.

Currently, many approaches aim to break down the hierarchy of musicians and audience, which is usually also architecturally cemented. The audience can walk through the performers or join in. The mimesis is shifted from content to representation, the breaking down of hierarchies is not depicted but performed by both sides, at least for a moment. This also applies to casts that depict a non-hierarchical diversity. In this way, the duration of the event can also refer to something else (if one knows or senses the background). The Chinese demonstrators probably also understood this when they held up white leaves in November 2022.[6] Instead of pointing out grievances with written posters, they imitated other demonstrators and at the same time depicted the silence that was imposed on them.

Abstract mimetic forms and representations are important because they challenge freedom and a change of perspective without excluding those who think differently, as discursive formats often do.

The desire to break up hierarchies also drives me when I am constantly looking for new relationships between text and music. I try out very different combinations and genres: a musical silent film performance with text projections,[7] a sound aquarium with waterproof text plants, a crossover of science and sound art. The relationship between mimesis and diegesis is perhaps most vividly illustrated in a passage from my piece "Call me yesterday," which I composed in 2005, before I even knew the terms diegesis and mimesis. In a passage of this composition with language courses, the phrase "This is a door" is imitated, repeated, and varied so that pointing eventually becomes music. But when? I have created a kind of slide; the speed at which you slide down it and when you feel the ground under your feet remains open. In any case, everyone changed their perspective at some point during the passage.

AUTOMATIC SPEAKING

After "Call me yesterday," I looked more specifically for suitable material that would allow a similar work. Digital processes crept in, which for me were more practical solutions on the way to a certain performative result. I don't see the pieces explicitly as digital art.

The speech melodies led me to the dialects that I describe in the next section. What interested me most about the vocabulary lists and grammar exercises in the language courses was their semi-literate state. They say something about the world, but do not have the character of a work. They can be assembled and utilized without offending anyone.

These thoughts, as well as other inspirations, led me to the method of automatic speaking. This resulted in the audio pieces "rochenununterbrochen,"[8] "Ginsterdings,"[9] "Folgen Sie mir pausenlos,"[10] "Goethe to go,"[11] and "mp-droste high mud beat."[12] Automatic Speaking is reminiscent of the Écriture automatique of the French surrealists, but is based more on the principle of repetition and a series of rules. There are also references to nature writing, deep listening, sound poetry, the stream of consciousness, the writing landscapes of Carlfriedrich Claus and Berlin real-time music (echtzeitmusik).

The artistic role models were joined by repulsive energy.[13] So often I would have liked to give the sounds more space in the radio play, but the text always wants to move forward, the sounds can't last, can't unfold, you always relate them to the text because we are used to this hierarchy. I've also noticed that I like poetry, but I don't tend to like volumes of poetry, and certainly not read aloud. And also, like many people and poets, I like walking through the much-sung-about forest – but how to talk or sing about it today? There are no contemporary hiking songs.

I would like to see a real-time oral poetics and imagine combining and balancing the practical skills that improvising musicians have with those of lyricists, similar to onomatopoeia.[14]

Automatic Speaking begins with choosing a route in nature and a workshop in which the speakers learn a few rules. Some are quite banal, e.g. they have to walk very slowly because otherwise the sounds of breathing will dominate the recording, others are aimed at unleashing creativity and achieving a unity of time and place. Equipped with a recording device, everyone then walks along this route one after the other. Everyone records themselves and then makes the recording available. The participants are paid and named when the recording is published. They can also create their own pieces from the material.

Automatic Speaking is oral,[15] multicultural, multi-perspective and multilingual. It overcomes the succession of text and music. Sound and language are created simultaneously. It is poetic and at the same time performative and musical. *Automatic Speaking* creates transitions between non-art and art, it promotes creative processes. It is inspired by nature and at the same time overwrites it.

Improvising musicians have the ability of permanent acoustic monitoring. This allows them to create short circuits, create structures and integrate mistakes. The very fact that they create in real-time in front of the audience and do not have the opportunity to weigh anything on the gold scale and decide whether it is good or bad forces them to take everything that comes along as it is and continue with it. Nothing is sorted out, but everything is integrated, transformed and structured. This is only possible if you listen carefully to yourself and others and always listen back while moving forward. Good improvisation is therefore based at least as much on memory as on spontaneity. This is why improvising musicians often understand *Automatic Speaking* quite intuitively. And it leads, for example, to such beautiful reinterpretations as "high mud" to "Heimat" – Korhan Erel, who spoke German, English and Turkish as he trudged through the mud of Münsterland, pointed to what he saw. Not only did he know that he was talking about mud, he also heard it and was able to reinterpret his own output in this way. Diegesi's "This is deep mud" becomes mimesis: "high mud" sounds like "home." Yes, admittedly, you can also find that in books of poetry. But to hear someone change their perspective through pure repetition and listening is something else. You can almost physically feel the shift in perception and see how the speaker surprises themselves. You gain access to the functioning of creative processes instead of the repeatedly weighed, evaluated, proofread and bound end product.

Poets bring other qualities to the table, but it's difficult for them to incorporate them so quickly. That's why I don't think I've exhausted my method yet. Instead of a short workshop, it would take more time to teach this monitoring to lyricists, while at the same time it would be interesting if lyricists could teach musicians how to create metaphors.[16] When a person combines both abilities, I think that's when it really gets going! Then completely different poetic fantasy spaces and more complex musical structures open up, where some things still sound too epic to me.

Experiencing creative processes such as letting go, monitoring and repetition shows that the hurdle between life and art, which is so often experienced as a boundary, is a flexible transition. Just as evolutionary research has long since shown that the formation of species takes place in a constant back and forth,[17] *Automatic Speaking* allows us to understand that art can also emerge and disappear anywhere.

This comes in handy for the further artistic working process, because I combine the speech streams with sound recordings of the same route and use the break-off points as docking points. While the performers wear headset microphones so that they are not even tempted to adopt a reporter's stance, I then walk along the route again with a stereo microphone and record sounds – not realistic atmospheres, but the materials are now brought into play acoustically, musically. I bend branches, throw stones at metal objects along the way, move stones etc. and compose with the sounds of the objects that the performers encounter along the way. (So that it doesn't become illustrative. Sentences in which the speakers talk about sounds are dropped.)

As I said, the streams of speech do not always flow easily, they falter and also dry up. I accept that. The condensation then takes place digitally. While the performers only act orally, preferably in the pure duration, and are not supposed to sort anything out, I then make a selection.[18] I put all the performers' audio tracks together in the digital editing program. Ten times the same course, about an hour each time. The path that everyone has taken is thus depicted on the timeline, and I can create "trail markers" that show me approximately where the tower, the stone, the fallen tree are located on the timeline. (With Bergson, you could say: I project the pure duration I experienced beforehand onto the space afterwards.) For example, if I click on minute 7'30", everyone will be talking about the fallen tree at approximately this point.[19] When I then zap vertically through the tracks, I hear ten different perceptions, linguistic–musical forms of expression, overwritings of this one place in nature in a very short time. This is only made possible by the digital way of working.[20] I can also set short keywords in the track, which then appear in alphabetical order in the clip list. This makes it easy for me to search for semantic parallels. From this I make a selection by listening, but this still resembles a written process, as I move back and forth in the speech stream and compare.

The original ideas are only captivating when listening to the streams of speech for the first time. The longer I immerse myself in the montage, the more the emphasis shifts to the coincidence of sometimes downright boring repetitions, which, however, open up a space, a musical structure in the encounter. I am also comfortable with the drying up and breaking off, because sounds and music can dock on here without being just background music. Music can take on linguistic rhythms and colors. In this way, diegesis and mimesis are constantly changing and are permeable to each other. The poetry and music created in this way are open to slips of the tongue, multilingualism, spontaneous translations by multilingual performers; it is physical, musical and diverse. The streams of speech literally remain on the (natural) surface. That is exactly what they are supposed to do, because instead of semantic internal references on paper, this opens up the possibility of encounters with others and musical structures. A different kind of complexity emerges.

For example, at one point a performer repeats the word "Fichten." He dissects it, divides it into syllables: "Ficht-ten. Fich-ten." Then it suddenly continues "ten-eleven." You can tell that the speaker has been listening to himself and starts counting in English, creating a rhythm that matches – in my ears –the flow of speech of another speaker. The rules for *Automatic Speaking* are about generating as much imagery and music as possible in contrast to normal speech. Nobody can do this for over an hour. It is therefore part of the process that a lot falls out again at the end and only a few minutes can be heard from each person.

After my experience with the language course material in "Call me yesterday," I deliberately set out in search of new, oral and semi-poetic material. I don't want print-ready poems or compositions with the character of a work, but something unfinished, raw. That way I can allow myself to continue working with it and it also takes pressure off the performers. In contrast to Écriture Automatique, the performers here have a microphone in front of their mouths the whole time and they know that a piece is to emerge from it. Repetition helps to eliminate the resulting inhibition. If you get involved and listen to yourself, you will eventually forget the microphone.

The finally composed piece is an invitation to creative perception. It works with means that everyone has at their disposal. In no way do I want it to be understood as a sound walk. So don't take it along the same path and compare, that was that and that was that. Rather do it yourself. But I could imagine filming all the participants from above using a drone and projecting this recording of the performers moving in the forest onto a floor, where visitors could then dance on the performers' heads while listening to the piece.

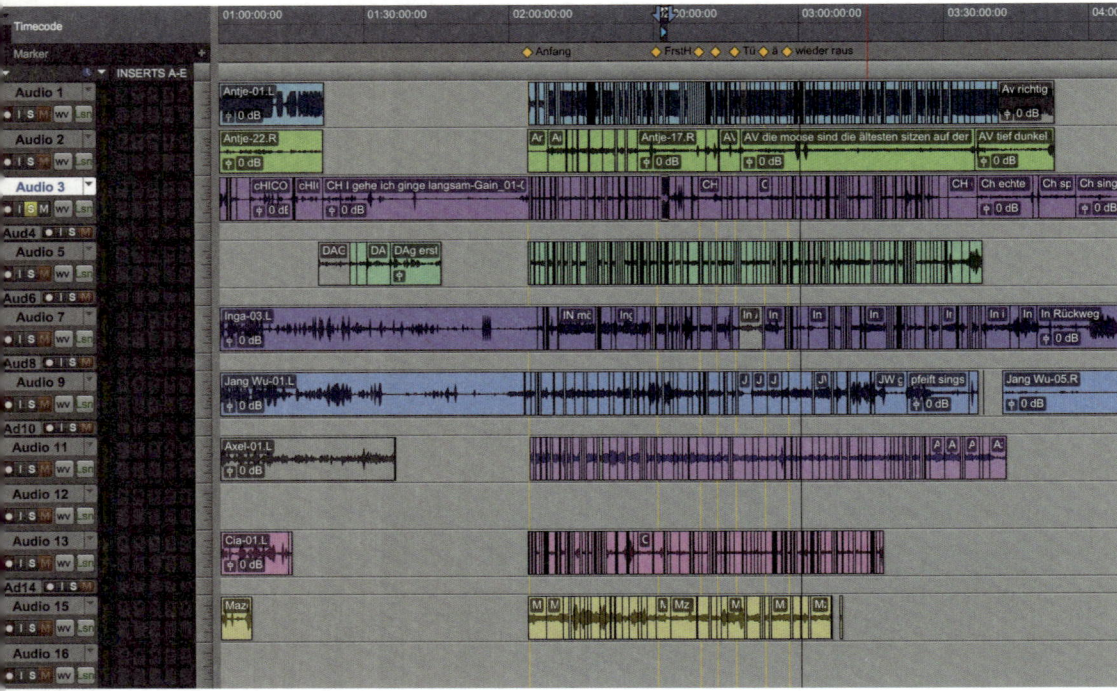
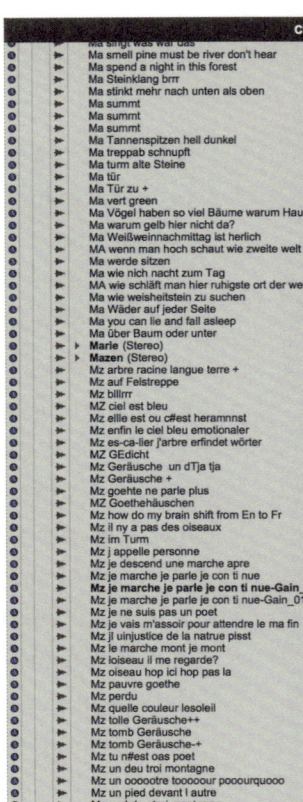

↑: Goethe to go. Anfangsphase: Zehn Sprachaufnahmen mit Wegmarken
↗: Goethe to go. Clipliste mit Notizen

DIALECT KARAOKE

For dialect karaoke, I use dialect recordings that are as melodic as possible. I either make the recording myself or I use archives. They are always short, coherent everyday stories that have arisen in conversation. The content of these stories is irrelevant. Sometimes you understand something, often you don't. Whether dialect or vernacular – these definitions are of little interest to me, the main thing is a lot of singsong, or rather: a modulated prosody, so always nice and high and low.

Previous pieces are "Terra Prosodia,"[21] "Melody minus one"[22] and "Gipfeltreffen."[23] In this way, I am following a tradition of upgrading mimesis in the perception of language (as mentioned above). In the first two series "Terra Prosodia" and "Melody minus one" I still worked with acoustic and virtual instruments. Software programs make it possible to convert audio recordings into midi files and convert them into notes. This makes it easy to extract spoken melodies and transfer them to other instruments. The melodies, which contain many glissandi (continuous slurring), are mapped to a chromatic scale – this is where digitality comes into play. At least in the usual setting. You can then use pitch bending to help things along. However, the results sounded terrible. Although the mapping was realistic, it seemed far too complex both rhythmically and melodically. It didn't sound like the beautiful melodies I had in my head, but more like a technical beeping in an intensive care unit. I therefore simplified it arbitrarily. At lectures, people occasionally criticized the fact that I had used a chromatic scale at all when transferring it to the Midi protocol.

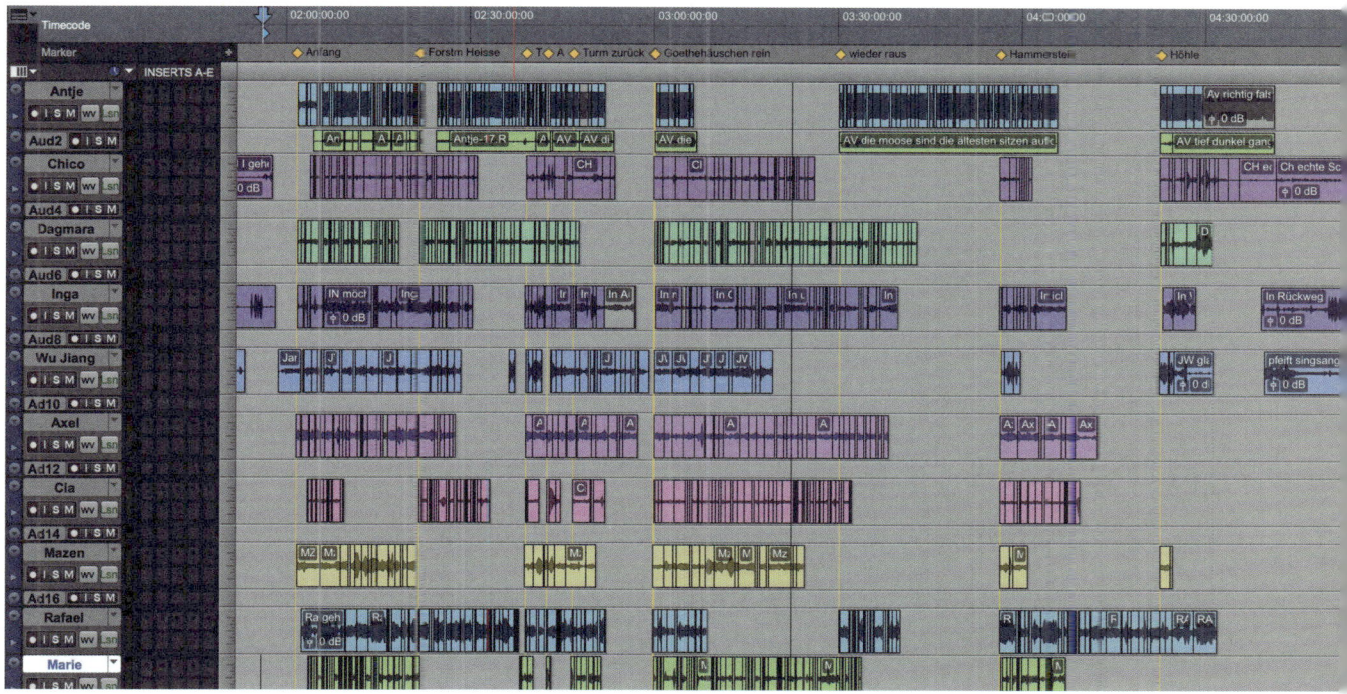

↑ / ↘ : Goethe to go, spätere Stadien

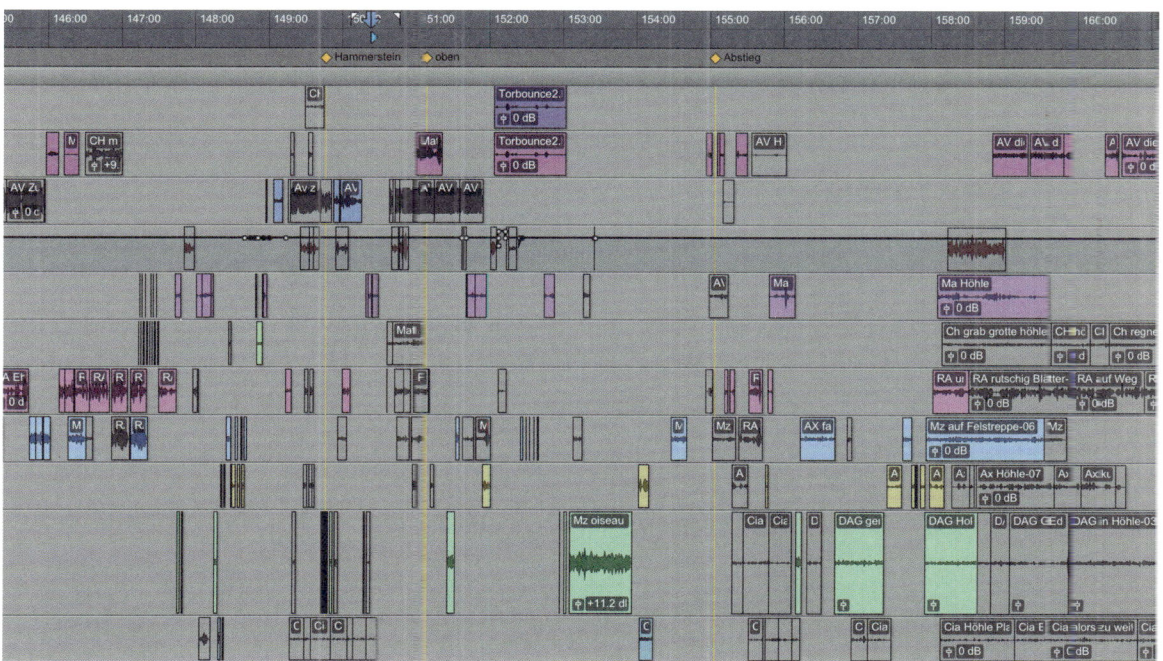

34 / 35

"I have nothing to say
and I say it."
John Cage

Instructions for Automatic-Speaking-Tour by Antje Vowinckel

Go. Speak.

Speak continuously without any pause. Two seconds is a pause!

Repeating is very important.

Speak slowly or quickly, loudly or softly, but keep your walking pace.

Speak only of the present. Not of the future, not of the past.

The present is your surroundings.

You are alone. You lead neither blind nor kids nor tourists.

Remain yourself. Say "I" – not "you" or "we".

Use your tongue as a camera.

Use it to scan the environment.

Film it, don't explain it.

Break down the environment into individual images.

Break down your language into single words, syllables, letters.

Repeat them.

Zoom into the landscape and out again … in and out …

Connect your observations to parts of your body.

Repeat. Change only one letter or syllable. Keep repeating.

Repeat until a new observation creeps in.

Or: stretch words until something new comes in or you run out of breath.

Babble, shout, grumble, whistle, rhyme, use foreign languages.

Keep repeating.

Avoid judgmental comments.

Avoid well-known songs.

Accept "mistakes". That means: never interrupt or correct yourself.

If you think you made one, repeat it, vary it. Take it as a detour.

Even finer scale subdivisions have long been technically possible, i.e. even more realistic acoustic representations. Later, I felt confirmed by the studies of the American psychologist Diana Deutsch on the perception of speech melodies.[24] Repetition alone causes us to perceive speech melodies more melodically after a while, apparently mapping them onto a chromatic scale. Of course, this exact repetition is rarely experienced in reality, it is mainly a side effect of my constant digital cutting of original sounds, but it has changed my perception in such a way that I focus on the melody the first time I hear it.

Working with the virtual instruments was interesting for a while, but then I decided to simulate the digital process with analog means. I invited a group of musicians individually into the studio. There they listen to small snippets of a dialect recording in a loop with short pauses via headphones. They were asked to hum along to these short snippets of speech. No consonants, just "mm" and at the very front of the lips (otherwise it sounds comic-like). They have to completely abstract from the person, the content and the phonetics and concentrate entirely on the melody. This works completely differently than when actors imitate dialects. They rely on holistic perception and imagine a specific person with their attitude and mannerisms and imitate them by putting themselves in their place.[25]

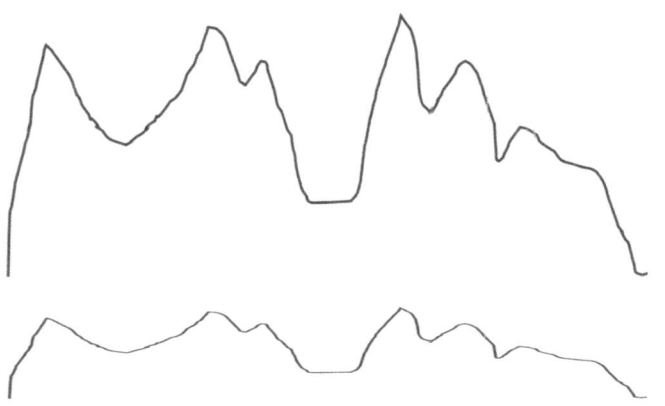

↑: Gipfeltreffen, 2020

Immediately beguiled by this, I immediately passed this approach on to the next performers as a guide and – because not everyone found it so easy – slowed the headphone fragments down to four or eight times as much in the next step. This sounds terrible on the headphones because the plug-ins digitally distort the recording in an unpleasant way. But nobody hears it in the end. In this way, the small, squiggly glissandi expand into wide landscapes with valleys and highs on which the hummers can glide smoothly. The digitally slowed down original material only serves as a foil, it cannot be heard in the composition, but the slowing down of the imitative humming reinforces the impression of approaching and feeling one's way along. The ups and downs of the dialect, which often originated in the landscape, out of the landscape, now become a musical landscape themselves.

In this way – I hope – a paradox of the dialect becomes tangible: although dialects have existed for thousands of years and are passed on from generation to generation, they only arise spontaneously, only in the moment. You cannot pass on a dialect as a technique. Dialect is the subtext of trust. Outside of familiar spaces, it is quickly discarded. When I make my own recordings of dialects, I often feel like a butterfly catcher. Because the dialect usually flies away immediately in the face of the microphone net.[26]

I'm not a savior of dying languages and dialects – it's often about regional and political identities – but it's a shame that a universe of melodies is also being lost, and possibly unbiased speech in general. Dialect melodies have no meaning, they arise unconsciously and want nothing. In contrast, the seductive speech melodies of some presenters, readers and actors are based on rhetoric. They serve the power of persuasion.[27]

I use the dialect melodies to compose electro-acoustic pieces. They consist of the unadulterated dialect recording (structured only by pauses and repetitions) and the humming melodies of the performers, which approximate the recording. It remains recognizable that these are linear stories in the original, I have not – at least so far – fragmented the material any further, but the content is not important. I just wanted to make sure that you can feel the natural character and not get the idea that the original has already been played. Although everything is analog in the end, the parts are only created by slowing down and sequencing the digital film in between.

The fact that the impression of spontaneous approximation was retained despite all the effort was demonstrated at a concert performance in the semi-darkness, when an audience member said afterwards that he believed he had heard the piece live.

Initially, I thought it would be better to use as many foreign dialects as possible so that no hierarchy would impose itself on the listener. There should be no guesswork about the content. In the meantime, I have started using German, English and Italian recordings again because it is important to me that the prosodies are perceived as dialect melodies. They are never completely pure anyway. They mix with rhetorically (diegetically) based sentence melodies and in a familiar language the audience can perceive these differences more clearly. It becomes clearer that the sentence melodies arise arbitrarily and are not controlled.

(I was also offered recordings of dialects that were obviously spoken by heart, where the overlay of rhetorical-narrative melodies is so dominant that I can't use them. In toning languages such as Chinese, where prosody has a much stronger semantic meaning, this distinction is almost impossible for our ears to make.)

The laborious appropriation of the melodies can, if you like, also be seen as a futile cultural appropriation. Of course, the meticulous copying never leads to the imitators using the typical dialect prosodies afterwards; the copy-and-paste results in something completely different. But the process possibly points to the role that dialects (still) play today. Sometimes they come across as positively authentic or even funny, sometimes negatively provincial, sometimes treacherous (when it comes to verifying origin in asylum procedures) and sometimes even disruptive when conveying information on the telephone. The constant presence of standardized language in the media means that dialects and accents are disappearing more and more. But for some, this is not happening fast enough: Stanford has now developed the first software that makes it possible to eliminate prosodically deviating accents, such as Indian, from call center employees.[28]

The program may reduce discrimination and ensure equal opportunities, but what a musical loss! And what a world it would be if instead, before setting up a conversation with the call center employee, you first practiced a few minutes of dialect karaoke with a corresponding voice recording.

... mm   mm   mm   mm   mm   mm   mm ...

SUMMARY

Almost all of my works are created using digital recording technology, sequencer programs and plug-ins in combination with human voices, acoustic instruments and sound recordings. The results do not usually count as digital art, as the digital technology primarily simulates the old analogue technology and the results do not exhibit or analyze anything digital. Similar means have already been used for montage and filtering. However, some digital processes allow intermediate steps, which I would call mapping or interlayers, that were not possible before. They allow the material to be sorted and arranged in new ways or performative techniques to be invented that would previously have been unthinkable or extremely cumbersome.

NOTES:

1. Abbreviation for: "Digital Audio Workstation."
2. Seen from the outside, it can stand for certain eras and milieus, but only if you already know something about them.
3. Bergson, Henri (1920): "Zeit und Freiheit", Frankfurt am Main, Athenäum Bd. 135, S. 68.
4. According to Bergson, "time" is always to be equated with "space", as this idea enables a comparative arrangement.
5. Bergson, Henri (1920): "Zeit und Freiheit", Frankfurt am Main, Athenäum Bd. 135, S. 78.
6. https://www.zeit.de/kultur/2022-11/china-proteste-corona-lockdown-xinjiang-brand, called up 15. 12. 2022
7. In Places of Logic. (Stadt Logik). Sound performance with Text projections for organ, objects, PowerPoint.
8. rochenununterbrochen, WDR Studio Akustische Kunst 2007
9. Ginsterdings, Autorenproduktion 2014
10. Folgen Sie mir pausenlos, Deutschlandfunk Kultur, 2012
11. Goethe to go, DLR Kultur, 2018
12. Mpdroste high mud beat, Lyrikweg-App, Stiftung Burg-Hülshoff, 2020.
13. A term by Oswald Egger.
14. Rap and poetry slam are stylistically too limited for me, but the impetus for the scene may be similar.
15. What is meant is a secondary orality, as Walter Ong describes it. Ong, Walter (1982): Oralität und Literalität, Opladen: Westdeutscher Verlag 1987, S. 18.
16. Anyone interested is welcome to contact me ...
17. Grant, Peter, Grant, B. Rosemary (2014): "40 years of evolution." New Jersey: Princeton University Press
18. I myself am always there as a performer and change roles after the tour.
19. Hollow paths are more suitable than panoramic paths.
20. This would be very laborious to be done analog: you would have to transcribe all the speech streams, then arrange the sentences of one speaker linearly one after the other and those of all the others one below the other. It would be a paper chore that would require a large display area.
21. Terra Prosodia, WDR Studio Akustische Kunst, 11. 11. 2011, CD: gruenrekorder 2013
22. Melody minus one, WDR Studio Akustische Kunst, 2. 7. 2016
23. Gipfeltreffen, Autorenproduktion, 2020, auf CD: im hier und jetzt oder nie, DEGEM (Deutsche Gesellschaft für Elektroakustische Musik, CD20, 2020.
24. Deutsch, Diana (2019) Musical Illusions and Phantom Words: How Music and Speech Unlock Mysteries of the Brain, Oxford University Press; https://deutsch.ucsd.edu/psychology/pages.php?i=212
25. Best examples: Amy Walker, 21 accents. https://www.youtube.com/watch?v=3UgpfSp2t6k
26. The difficulties of dialect recording are the subject of Tuning Butterflies (2018,Englisch), Errant Bodies Records #12.
27. Linguistics also distinguishes between conscious A and unconscious B prosody. vgl. Tillmann, Wolfgang: https://www.phonetik.uni-muenchen.de/studium/skripten/AP/APKap3.html.
28. https://edition.cnn.com/2021/12/19/us/sanas-accent-translation-cec/index.html.

With the kind permission of the Academy of Sciences and Literature Mainz. The following essay is based on a lecture by Vowinckel at the symposium "Grenzen der Künste" (Borders of the Arts) conceived by Dr. Marlene Meuer for the Young Academy of the ADW Mainz. The contributions to the symposium can be found in the anthology of the same name, published by the ADW Mainz, 2024.

BIBLIOGRAPHY:

Bergson, Henri (1920): "Zeit und Freiheit", Frankfurt am Main, Athenäum Bd. 135.

Deutsch, Diana (2019) Musical Illusions and Phantom Words: How Music and Speech Unlock Mysteries of the Brain, Oxford University Press.

Grant, Peter, Grant, B. Rosemary (2014): "40 years of evolution." New Jersey: Princeton University Press.

Maye, Harun, Reiber, Cornelius, Wegmann, Nikolaus (Hg (2007)): Original/Ton. Zur Mediengeschichte des O–Tons. UVK Verlagsgesellschaft 2007.

Ong, Walter J.: Oralität und Literalität. Die Technologisierung des Wortes (1982), 2. Auflage, Springer 2016.

Vowinckel, Antje: Tuning Butterflies, errant bodies records, 2019.

GERRIET KRISHNA SHARMA

Tracing the Non–Euclidean Drift in Everyday Life

CONSTRUCTING LIQUID ARCHITECTURES I. – X.

TRACKED HEADS AND CAPTURED EARS

Today, more and more media devices provide control and customization of individuals' sonic environments. These fast-spreading technologies include not just headphones with noise-cancelling, but, smartphone apps designed to make a noisy office sound like a rural countryside, the cacophony of public transport like a seashore and the fragmented events of the home office a well-tempered and idealized, vivid-yet-mellow office ambient. We find wearable sound generators to suppress the sound of tinnitus and new in-ear smart devices called "hearables"[1] that filter, alter, and augment the sounds of everyday lives. As the newest development with the advent of on-board head-tracking in consumer headphones since 2021, it is now possible to adjust virtual sound source positions to the rotation of the head to the effect that we can compose and produce even more *realistic* or plausible soundscapes. Scenes like the water stream, the reading voice, the fireplace, the coffee machine, or the piano now stay in their position, in relation to our individual head. Whereas in common stereo-displays, these sounds will turn with the head, in so-called binaural and head-tracked 3D-audio scenes, sources stay fixed in the virtual coordinate, producing the mental image of a lived space. Although these tools are still too expensive for most people, they will soon be common and standardized and therefore built into most of the existing devices, presumably then retailed by all the competing providers of the audio technology market.

At the moment, this newer development heralded by the biggest consumer tech company in 2023 trades under the term "spatial audio" and is marketed as "3D audio" by others. It is a metaphor for a department store with various new ephemeral digital toys bound to some easy-to-use and accessible hardware. However, it is remarkable that a single company that wants to overrun the existing VR market in the coming years[2] is claiming the next steps to "spatial computing" by first working on a head-tracked spatial audio environment. By this, a single commercial institution is affecting the worldwide production of music, changing the format, turning the switch from stereo to spatial and offering containers of fashionable headphones and Goggles as gates to this new world. This operation is unprecedented in the history of music, sound art and architecture. In other words: The spatiality of sound has climbed another level of impact and importance in our mediatized societies.

SEAMLESS SPATIAL DRIFT

Considering predictions that average homes in cities will become smaller and smaller, hyper-realistic spatial audio solutions for "enlarging" the aural architecture of your own walls and blocking out unwanted sounds from the neighbors, streets and skies will become an important aspect of a healthy and peaceful life. Therefore, we can, and likely will, more and more live in our individualized 3D audio bubbles. We know that technologies and labor practices reshaped perception, absorbing and immobilizing subjects through attentive practices aimed at production or consumption.[3] From this perspective, isolating our ears looks less like a dubious act of rebellion or a fashionable act of entertainment and more like a radical requirement of modern living.

My prognosis for the coming years is that NOT wearing headphones will sound strange to our ears. We are about to enter a completely mediatized sound world technically produced not in front or around – but inside our ears. In other words: The future world is likely to sound unrealistic without headphones. Thus, there will be more and more moments where it is hard to tell whether this is "Metaverse" – or not. Until only a couple of months ago, loudspeaker environments could still be considered as equipment with the certain potential to develop (augmented) immersive sound architectures within a given and noticeable technical setup and built architecture. The potentiality of mediatized immersion unfolds the moment one forgets about the technical setup and blends into the virtual scenery. Creating this moment was dependent on a plethora of variables interlinked and weighted differently from piece to piece, scene to scene, e.g. compositional skills, audience's pre-conditioning, socialization, lighting, and flawless technical performance. The most successful devices capable of exploiting this potential were mostly part of academic labs and prestigious concert halls or hidden inside a few venues worldwide. Now, we can purchase consumer devices that we deliberately place into or onto our ears and forget about the act and the fact only moments after this. We do not see them, and there is no loudspeaker, no cable, there are no stands, no plinths, no acoustic or visual artefacts. The certainty of the sonic presence is detached from the assertion or inkling of the physical source. Only moments after switching on Apps like "Odio"[4] or "Endel"[5] the mind is building an environment that is augmented, constantly shifting between haptic and visual everyday objects and sound sources that define the place like a radiator, a half-open window, the subtle noise pattern of a door, the static appearance of a wall, the vertical orientation of a floor, the openness of a high ceiling, birds in a tree … all this becomes like a magic cape that we put on and disappear into *a* world morphed into *the* world.

During the development of this text, another surprising phenomenon appeared in everyday observations: The Bluetooth headphone-earplug became a fashionable accessory. More and more, you see people "wearing" headphones as part of, and integrated into, their personal visual expression combined with earrings and glasses as well-composed ensembles on the head. And maybe, similar to what happened to glasses in the past 50 years, being upgraded from ugly, almost discriminating medical aids to fashionable, characteristic, must-have accessories, hearing aids might just become not distinguishable from headphones or mobile phones, technoid, futuristic yet common body jewelry.

THE LIQUEFACTION OF THE INTERFACE

Since 2021, spæs Lab Berlin[6] and I have been collaborating with Volst, a Dutch software company that has developed Odio-App, a surprising 3D-Audio App utilizing head-tracking built into the Apple Airpods and Airpods Max and virtual interactive sound sources with a visual interface. Binaural soundscapes are treated and distributed like formerly tracks or songs, with individually adjustable sound sources in your headphone world. By touching the circular source representation on the screen and smoothly finger-swipe the symbol to a new

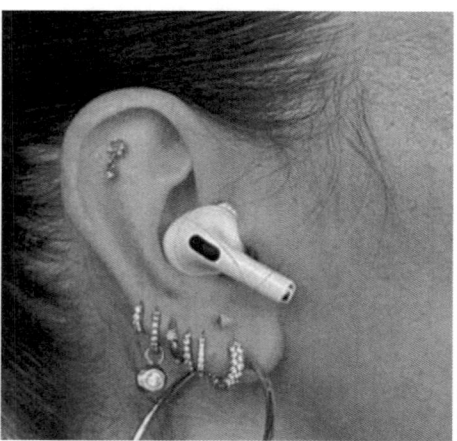

position, in feedback with the auditive perception, one is remixing the aural architecture[7] seamlessly. To artistically challenge this technology and to interpret this tool as an instrument in the context of world-making, together with spæs lab I developed *liquid architectures I. – X.*, a series of soundscapes exploring and modelling the overlaps of technically induced realities in our everyday lives. For a year, we used this App daily, trying to understand how virtual soundscapes in headphones alter and change our perception of trains, houses, places, and communicative situations between human beings. We worked on different interactive spatial arrangements with simple and more and more complex sound textures composed by use of various digital and analogue tools and references.[8]

By this, we were investigating how personal binaural headphone space is modulated by atmospheres, moods, spatial cognition and constraints of the medium. It came as a surprise that some of us would not take off our headphones when not working on the App, using the transparency mode (one click on a button at the device) for communication, e.g. ordering a coffee, but even more the noise-cancelling function (press the button again) for blocking out the rest of the noisy world, e.g. the coffee place, to find concentration and quiet during the day. And for incoming calls, you just tap the second button to blend from one space into the next and back again. This "tap" becomes a smooth unconscious gesture, like swiping functions on the mobile phone, browsing the web with endless cascades of mouse clicks or just brushing your teeth. Everyone who tried out this simple-looking setup, with many different pre-conditions (examples: "I do not like the brand, I do not like head-phones, I do not like synthetic sounds, I have experienced bad head-tracking before, I have never experienced binaural sound propagation before, I have no idea what 3D audio is about, I think stereo is great and cannot be replaced, I do not like soundscapes"), was acting similarly: These people were not talking about being convinced, at all. Before words, their body was already reacting according to the effect of the medium. They blended in moments before the intellect started analyzing the altered situation, understanding the severeness of the shift. We frequently observed the moment of awareness of the fact that perception signalled: "it is there and therefore it is real" – "… although I know it is not. Or: what do I know?".

THE PHENOMENOLOGICAL SHIFT

According to Goodman,[9] worlds are made through processes of eversion that include composition and decomposition; weighting; ordering; deletion and supplementation; and deformation. All these processes could be considered a confrontation with the world and a means whereby to produce alternatives to it. The domain of worldmaking is that of possibility. "When we make worlds, we conject the Other. In doing so, we also help shape the world and its trajectory."[10]

Within recent years, the use of spatial audio (e.g. Ambisonics, Wave Field Synthesis, Dolby Atmos, Spatial) has come into the focus of game design, online platforms, such as YouTube, and companies like Apple, Google, Sony, and Facebook, consumer electronics, event locations, and architecture. Quite likely, in the near future artificial auditory environments will be part of everyday life and, for a great number of people, a part of their reality. We have arrived at a 90% plausible production of aural architectures directly inside our heads, without the affordance of the advanced handling of a tool, fragile mediation of air and constraints and properties of built architecture. No knowledge of a manual nor intellectual or physical training is necessary. I call this a historical paradigm shift. We have entered the stage of post-Euclidian worldmaking within everyday experience.

"A paradigm shift is underway; as technological constraints are rolled back, so must conceptual constraints be re-evaluated. Some of these are concerned with what spatiality actually is. Although we think of three-dimensional Euclidean space, it is by no means clear that this is anything other than a conceptual latecomer (however useful)."[11]

That does not mean we will not feel our feet on the ground anymore or that software is not based on three-dimensional mathematical models nor that there are no unwanted sound artefacts while wearing the headphones, but the commercial power by which these tools will be getting cheaper and spread will have its effect on phenomenology, thus affecting bodies and mindsets.

The emerging question is, who creates these environments and with which intentions, and how can music, sound art and architecture contribute with their own strategies to such a reality?[12]

"However, to make a (different) world is to know (differently). Shifting perception then is the means by which to critique and question the world. We change the frame, change the perspective, and thereby change our understanding of it."

These new possibilities open pathways to a *terra incognita* in a time when every pixel of the world seemed to be charted, scanned and categorized. Nevertheless, the substances of these spaces are multi-layered and need a different knowledge compared to former ideas of navigation, composition and research.

As Kendall and Ardila implied already in 2008, "[…] we do not want to simply copy the real world; we want to build on it. But, we do want to use everything we can of what we know about human spatial perception, how it works in different contexts, why it works, and so on."[13]

We have arrived at a point that gives us access to a mobile, interactive, and personal world-making that takes references from the past ideas of Euclidian and built spaces and drifts seamlessly into a procedural and imaginary, at the same time, plausible and lived conception of spaces. As playful as this might appear for some, as grave and unpredictable the consequences will be. Aural perception, sonic worldmaking, hearing and listening modes, the perceiving body, all the debates around these will have to face a new, very different, technically induced hybrid space. And this is NOT a game, as we are talking about the future of social engagement and exchange, the production and sharing of cultural goods, and the growing atmosphere of loneliness among individuals.

SENSING LIQUID ARCHITECTURES

Using *liquid architectures I. – X.* we can constantly engage with and observe alternative and altered spatial models. They are composed as a self-test scenarios for mediatized sonic environments. Each soundscape has a title that references a spatial concept, including historical, literary, philosophical, architectural and hybrid forms.

The title of this series is a reference to architect and theorist Marcus Novak. Novak is probably best known for his essay, "Liquid Architectures in Cyberspace,"[14] a fundamental and radical text about the poetics of cyberspace. The text describes a fluidity between the virtual and the real, made possible by the domain of the digital, as extending to all aspects of data, information, and form. According to Novak, the extreme changes brought forth by technology create unprecedented new opportunities to conceive of new kinds of spaces (or worlds).

"Architecture becomes liquid, music becomes navigable, cinema becomes habitable, dance becomes disembodied. As distant as these new options seem from their origins and from each other, they are related to one another by what can only be called 'worldmaking.' Worldmaking is, in my estimation, the key metaphor of the new arts."[15]

For *liquid architectures I. – X.*, each soundscape is composed of 5 – 8 individual sound sources that together form the aural architecture of the virtual environment. Each of these sound sources has an indication (e.g. guardian (grd), core (cor), poem (poe), belfry (bel), void (voi), dome (dom), intra (int)) referring to the title (e.g. shelter) of the soundscape. Each indication, linked to a certain sound as part of the scene, can take on a concrete Cartesian function and/or figurative connection with other sounds and their indications. By this, every soundscape is a helix of terms that form a spatial entity as a result of a multi-layered production of space through sound. At any moment, it can become an integral part of the built architecture as well as cocooning the listener into another shell, another world of plausible yet utopian spatial descriptions. The mode of morphing between these shells is not technically induced but triggered by the shifting attention and the focus of the listener. Each sound is individually developed for its soundscape and composed as part of the spatial ensemble. Each sound has a different length and is seamlessly looped. Therefore, the soundscapes are not generative, and they have individual characteristics, atmospheres, recognizable, yet always changing the textural consistency over time. The positions of the virtual sound sources are represented by visual objects (circles with abbreviations of the sources' indication) on the screen. They are meticulously arranged and part of the overall spatial composition. Once the listener opens a soundscape, the positioning of the objects appears as a pre-composed arrangement, an aural architecture concentrically placed around the idealized head position (i.e. the center of the screen) and in distinct directions and distances from this vantage point. However, the listener is free to swipe and reposition these sources, multiply or erase them due to personal situations, preferences and needs. The farther they are placed from the head, the fainter their volume becomes. Overlapping objects produce new spatial textures amalgamating the original sources of the respective soundscape. These soundscapes have the

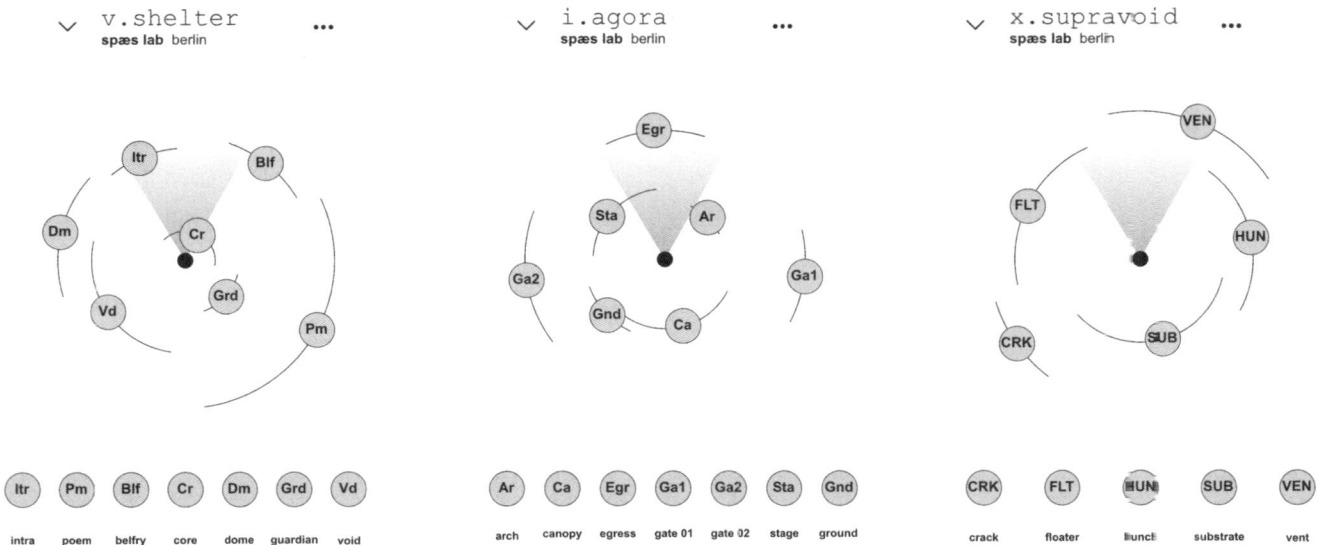

following spatial structures simplified in a two-dimensional scheme.

QUESTIONING AN ART OF IMMERSION — RENDERING THE REAL DIFFERENTLY

I sincerely hope that artists understand the seriousness of the situation, as others own the mainframe already. I trust that artists will take this as an opportunity to rethink their processes and find adequate ways for creation, distribution, and communication. This process will change the concepts of our musicianship, craftsmanship, performance, writing, production, technical setups, audience, and education. Everyday listening will become mediated by *immersive* technologies inside our ears and alter our conception of the world. The fact that hearables are in the process of replacing hearing aids becoming objects of fashion and "individual taste" designed by so-called *immersive marketing*[16] will even speed this process up in the coming months and years. However, an "art of immersion" should describe and stage the moment of transition from one world description into the other. The object of investigation is the brink, the borderline between "in" and "out."

Admittedly, immersion can be an intellectually stimulating process; however, in the present, as in the past, in most cases, immersion is mentally absorbing and a process, a change, a passage from one mental state to another. It is characterized by diminishing critical distance[17] to what is shown and increasing emotional involvement in what is happening. Similar to how film has made time manipulable, virtual acoustics as part of virtual reality makes this possible for space when experiencing spaces, meeting places and n-dimensional worlds – in the near future, more than ever, we will be able to decide what we surround ourselves with. But by that, we will not alter a virtual reality; we will change the everyday and how we perceive and understand it. As artists, we will have to overcome the current situation in which we are using the same tools as every marketing specialist with a team of very well-payed and fully equipped engineers and designers to instantly fulfil every strategic wish to manipulate bodies and minds constantly and with entrance to the private everyday life of so many. We have to find a way of sharing experiences in immersive environments. What do we know about the perception and perceptibility of spatial phenomena in n-D environments? With *liquid architectures I. – X.*, I developed and composed ten utopian environments, reactive, not even interactive, synthetic, artificial, recognizable but every time different. They mark a crucial moment in time – the now. They comment on the irresistible drift from traditional spatial concepts, emphasized and augmented by audio-visual mediations over centuries, from simulations towards a hybrid conceptualized spatiality closely linked to our hearing organs, producing an experience of immediate presence and individual "Wirklichkeit." The thoughts and questions raised in this text are only tiny spots on the field hidden underneath the terminology of marketing and multi-media venues, trying to make people believe that this is the next "great thing." In short: 3D sound is the ingredient to render the Metaverse "alive," creating presence and personality. We need artists, designers and architects who can form this *terra incognita*, a place of surprises and demanding (not just smooth, entertaining, and pleasant) new concepts for alternative social engagement and future cultural pathways. Maybe some will find a way to professionalize strategies of amateurism, minimalism, Dada and Glitch in VR, higher order loudspeaker environments and headphone spaces to contrast the spotless appearances of common media products and foster a fundamental aesthetic debate on immersive effects and phenomena. Maybe then we can formulate an alternative and open invitation to the listener to share an extended ontology of sonic spatial arts by composing sound as space.

NOTES:

1 Hagood, Mack, Hush : media and sonic self-control, Durham : Duke University Press, 2019.

2 This text was drafted in February 2023. Apple announced their VR Goggles Vision Pro in June 2023, when this text was finished.

3 Hagood, Mack, Hush : media and sonic self-control, 2019.

4 https://odio.app/

5 https://endel.io/

6 Lab for Spatial Aesthetics in Sound Berlin: www.spaes.org // For 20 years, the members of spaes work through cross-disciplinary collaboration and experimentation with practitioners, artists, scholars, engineers, and researchers from all disciplines including arts, architecture, XR, games, music, and design, to explore the relationships between sound, space, and human experience from the perspective of aesthetics. This exchange of ideas, skills, and knowledge on the interface of science, practice, and academia allows us to cultivate a critical interdisciplinary reflection and to push the development and dissemination of practices within the field of aesthetics, space, and sound further. spæs thinks of spatial aesthetics as a day-to-day practice of world-making inherent to every compositional act with sound as one of its raw materials, and with loudspeakers in particular.

7 For the concept of aural architecture I refer to Blesser, B., Salter, L., "Spaces Speak, Are You Listening?" Experiencing Aural Architecture Cambridge, Massachusetts: MIT Press, 2006.

8 A more detailed description of the compositional process is going to be published in the upcoming Routledge Companion on "Sound of Space" in 2024.

9 Goodman, Nelson. "Ways of Worldmaking." Vol. 51. Hackett Publishing, 1978.

10 Worldmaking as Techné, Participartory Art, Music, And Architecture, editors: Mark-David Hosale, Sana Murrani, and Alberto de Campo. Library and Archives Canada Cataloguing in Publication, 2018 Riverside Architectural Press.

11 Lennox, P., (2009) The Oxford Handbook of Computer Music, edited by R. Dean, New York 2009, p. 259.

12 Worldmaking as Techné, Participartory Art, Music, And Architecture, Editors: Mark-David Hosale, Sana Murrani, and Alberto de Campo. Library and Archives Canada Cataloguing in Publication, 2018 Riverside Architectural Press.

13 Kendall, G. S., and Ardila, M., (2008). The artistic play of spatial organization: Spatial attributes, scene analysis and auditory spatial schemata. In CMMR 2007, Lecture Notes in Computer Science 4969, ed. R. Kronland-Martinet, S. Ystad, and K. Jensen. Berlin: Springer, pp. 125–138.

14 Marcos, Novak, Liquid Architectures in Cyberspace, first appearing in "Cyberspace: First Steps." Michael Benedikt. ed. 1991. pp. 225–254.

15 Ibid.

16 Rose, F., From "The Power of Immersive Media", ISSUE Spring (2015), strategy + business magazine, published by PwC Strategy & Inc.

17 Grau, O. (2003). Virtual Art: From Illusion to Immersion (Rev. ed.). Cambridge, Mass., London: MIT Press., p. 49.

GEORG KLEIN

Based on Re – Search

research (n.)
1570s, "act of searching closely" for a specific person or thing, from French recerche (1530s, Modern French recherche), back-formation from Old French recercher "seek out, search closely", from re-, here perhaps an intensive prefix (see re-), + cercher "to seek for," from Latin circare "go about, wander, traverse," in Late Latin "to wander hither and thither," from circus "circle"[1]

"Art is and always has been a research practice"[2] emphasizes Dieter Mersch in his Epistemology of the Aesthetic, and Henk Borgdorff also has to ask himself whether "not all artistic practice is also research to a certain extent" in order to address the problem: When does artistic practice count as research?

Can criteria possibly be formulated that facilitate a distinction between artistic practice as such and artistic practice as research? This is accompanied by the question: How does artistic research differ from academic or established scientific research?[3]

Finding criteria for this – and defining the term research at all – has become the subject of countless essays, including normative approaches that aim for a system-compliant canon to make artistic practice suitable for PhDs and generate research funding under the label "artistic research."[4] Public opinion fluctuates between swansong ("Praxis Dr. Kunst geschlossen" / "Practice Dr. Art closed")[5] and overload ("Uncharted waters: How research vibes flood the art world"),[6] but in the meantime artistic research seems to have developed a pull that the art world – or at least the art academies – can no longer escape.

The fact that this pull ends in bureaucratic disciplining was already opposed in 2010 by Hito Steyerl in her essay "Aesthetics of resistance? Artistic Research as Discipline and Conflict." She points out that the practices of artistic research have a long and far-reaching history in the 20th century, in order to then address the question of which sources of conflict and tension underlie this new academic discipline.[7]

I see the concept of conflict as central not only as a crucial element of an academic discipline, but also as crucial for the content or motives of artistic research. This is not only evident in current trends in which colonialism, racism and gender issues play an increasing role in the art world.[8] Steyerl states this already for earlier forms of artistic research – as resistance: "A power/knowledge/art, which reduced whole populations to objects of knowledge, domination and representation had to be countered not only by social struggle and revolt, but also by epistemological and aesthetic innovation."[9]

First, however, I would like to trace the term *research* back to its linguistic roots in order to gain methodological terms and discuss them in the field of sound art. The subjective artist's perspective seems to me not unimportant in this self-defining process of "artistic research," so I would like to describe a little of my own way into it and to present at the end one example in more detail: the genesis of the installation Dark Matter on the subject of hate speech in radical right-wing music and propaganda, whose research began more than 20 years ago.

SEARCHING

The search has always been a central component of artistic activity. Be it material or form or subject, finding always presupposes a search movement, sometimes described as a struggle, sometimes as an intensive rehearsal process or experimentation phase or as a preliminary study, sometimes as a brilliant idea that has been long awaited, and even coincidences usually require attention that is characterized by an open, searching attitude. Since often you don't even know what you're looking for, intuition plays no insignificant role.

It is hard to point out when this searching becomes researching, especially in art, but the French origin – Old French *recercher* "to look for, to examine closely," not only points to an intensification of the search process. The Latin derivation – *circare* "to go around, wander, traverse," in late Latin "to wander here and there," from *circus* – specifies the kind of search movement, wandering back and forth, circling. With the prefix *re-*, it becomes repeated circling, which indicates a certain exploratory persistence.

For me, this repeated circling began with a concrete place: the forecourt of the *Philharmonie* concert hall in Berlin, where Richard Serra's sculpture *Berlin Junction* is set up: two curved, rusty steel plates inclined towards each other, forming a passageway. Initially fascinated by the acoustic space and the claustrophobic atmosphere in the space in between, shaped by form and material, the "repeated circling" led me deeper and deeper into the context of the sculpture as well as the installation site.

Created in 1987 for the 750th anniversary of the city, it reflected the solidified front of the two halves of Berlin. The site of the installation itself led into even deeper, historical layers: at Tiergartenstraße 4 there was a villa before the Second World War in which the Nazis organized the systematic killing of mentally handicapped people even before the Holocaust began, with a cover name named after this address: *Aktion T4*. At the time, the Geschichtswerkstatt protested in vain[10] against the fact that Serra's sculpture, which had no relation to this historical site, was set up exactly here. What I came across in the course of my research changed my concept decisively: instead of working only with pure sound transformations, voices with spoken texts coming from the ground were now also to play a role.[11]

With each further encirclement of this place, more and more *extra-musical* aspects entered into the conception and realization of my work, which finally ran as an interactive installation in this sculptural interspace in 2001/02 (title: transition). The years before, my way of working as a composer had been more *inner-musical* and within the framework of what can be understood as an artistic search, e.g. in experimental forms of sound generation or in medial sound reflections. With *transition*, on the other hand, the repeated circling of the site led for me to a completely new kind of contact with reality, with a conflict-ridden reality that entered directly into the work with the installation on site, also with regard to the reception side.

Mersch emphasizes this point when he refers to the fact that "a distinction must then be drawn between art and artistic research" and that we are dealing with a "changed genre" that "redefines artistic work and enriches it with a current, socially relevant dimension,"[12] or, to put it even more forcefully, "catapults it into a sphere of the social and of political and public significance." The concept of art is thus "removed from the traditional framework of autonomy and work aesthetics," "freed from the noble attributes of transcendence and sublimity" and "the permanent abandonment of its self-criticism, of reflexive navel-gazing," whereby, however, the potential of a critique that emerged in the horizon of modernity is preserved and continued.

ARTISTIC SEARCH – ARTISTIC RE-SEARCH

Since *transition*, I have been using the term "artistic research"[13] in my artistic practice, which, compared to "artistic search," takes place to a significant extent in a non-artistic terrain. In this way, the context from which something is extracted and in which something takes place gains a much greater significance and is incorporated into the work with a completely different intensity. I also consider this to be one of the great strengths of sound art, that unlike music, it can create an almost "intrinsic" connection to external reality, with the inclusion of space, architecture, objects, visual material as well as the social situation. Sound artists generally work not only on the sound part of a work but also on the visual part, the spatial reference and the perception situation, the reception side.[14] A personal or institutional division into sections does not usually take place here. Sound Art is transdisciplinary in itself.

Following Kenneth Clark, Nelson Goodman and Arthur Danto, Mersch characterizes artistic practice as:

> always a form of "research" involving the investigation of perception and of media, etc. (…). It is the singularity of involvement in the world, its violence or subjectivation that is put to the test, so that the meticulous labor of art is to reveal each of these aspects as well as the unseen and the hidden, and to give them voice and visibility.[15]

Making a place speak was the focus of my work *Ortsklang Marl Mitte* (2002). Here, hidden scribbled graffiti slogans at the railway station in Marl were given a completely new – acoustic – presence on site via a hanging raw horn loudspeaker, uncensored between left-wing and right-wing radical, between obscene and amorous, accompanied by two iron grid sounds recorded on the spot.[16]

In contrast to *transition* the year before, there was no clear starting point in Marl. The city in the Ruhr area had been unknown to me and I first had to make contact with the reality there, in a kind of aimless wandering for several days, similar to the *dérive* of the situationists, which Guy Debord developed in Paris in the 1950s: a wandering or strolling around, with subjective perceptions and experiences through which one perceives the different moods of an urban space.

> People who engage themselves in the dérive renounce, for a longer or shorter period of time, the reasons for moving and acting that they normally

know, the relationships, work and leisure activities that are theirs, in order to surrender to the influences of the terrain and the encounters that come with it.[17]

Alongside "repeated encircling," this is the second aspect in the word origin of research: from *circare* "to go around, wander, traverse," "to wander here and there," which in its initial aimlessness and subjectivity also characterizes my artistic research of a place.

RESEARCH – INVESTIGATION

In contrast to scientific research, which is defined by an initial question, a definition of methods, by verifiability and repeatability, by generalization and objectification (which must be permanently questioned, but is nevertheless predominant as a goal), artistic research is characterized by an individual artistic sensibility, "a kind of questioning observation," as the artist Itamar Gov once put it: "He enjoys tracking down hidden micro-histories or forgotten people, events and objects. Especially those that do not seem to be connected at first glance, but make sense in constellation."[18] This research is based on a perception that has not been trimmed by scientific methodological constraints and controlled framework conditions.

> This goes hand in hand with art's obsession, its permanent creation of scandal by uncovering the repressed, the monstrous or the uncanny, as well as with art's unique ability to explore possibilities or worlds that lie outside scientific explicability and yet form facts that cannot be revealed otherwise. Art always begins anew. There is no finality in the arts, no satisfying closure, state of peace, or generalizable results. At most there is the singular, the disturbing exception.[19]

Art or artistic research appears here, as Steyerl has put it, as an "act of translation":

> It takes place in at least two languages and can sometimes even produce new languages. It speaks the language of quality as well as that of quantity, the language of the singular as well as that of the specific. It uses values as well as exchange values or the values of the spectacle, discipline as well as conflict. And it translates between all of these. This does not mean that it translates correctly – but it translates nonetheless.[20]

The fact that art starts anew each time, as Mersch has described, points to a further contrast to scientific research, which is located in a research community, i.e. historically as well as globally in a research continuum, in which researchers confirm or refute each other, in the sense of a "progress," however conceived. Themes and research questions are carried forward in this community, while artists tend to deal with a theme or aspect singularly, even if thematic series of works can emerge or collectives are increasingly at work.

Carrying on this kind of wandering, the year after *Ortsklang Marl Mitte*, I came across an abandoned construction trailer in the countryside of Saxony / Germany in the February fog, which turned out to be a former neo-Nazi disco. Inside, the van was painted completely black with white runes and "Doitschland" lettering next to large speaker cut-outs. However, it took almost 20 years – until after the radical right-wing attack in Halle in 2019 – until I was able to realize an artistic work from the initial find. This also changed my investigation activities: while in 2003 I was still mainly concerned with radical right-wing music as a recruitment phenomenon in a subcultural milieu, by 2020 the field of right-wing populism had expanded so much and had become so modernized and multiplied via the internet that a correspondingly expanded research was necessary. This brought my *artistic research* close to *journalistic research* – or better said: my artistic investigation close to journalistic investigation.

On contrast to (humanities') academic research, which is primarily based on taking note of what has already been published in so-called literature studies, journalistic investigation is described as:

> the independent acquisition of information as opposed to merely processing press releases, agency material or press conferences. It gathers the widest possible range of information that illuminates a particular topic from different and conflicting perspectives, in order to enable balanced reporting. Journalistic research uses many sources: among others, archives, databases, personal conversations (interviews) with affected persons, experts and eyewitnesses, official press material, enquiries at press offices, requests based on freedom of information laws, specialised literature or the internet.[21]

In fact, this describes my approach in this case quite well, except that the end result became something quite different from a press article.

SAYING – SHOWING

If we now ask what the difference is between artistic research and scientific research, it is not only at the beginning – in the artistic methods of acquiring material, of subjective contact with reality with an individual, artistic sensibility – but also at the end, in the form of publication: not as a written article but as a condensed form in which both an emotional and an intellectual address takes place, operating primarily in the sensual. As Mersch puts it, it is not a matter of "saying" but of "showing."[22]

In the installation *Dark Matter*, which developed out of the neo-Nazi construction trailer and ran for the first time in 2021 at the Errant Sound Gallery, this condensation already begins with the space designed for the showing: a non-rectangular, small room of about 16sqm for 1 person, surrounded by a jet-black but light-reflecting curtain. One enters this room via an airlock with a radio headset equipped with a directional sensor. The room has three projection sides and, depending on which side the visitor looks at, what is heard changes, sometimes also what is seen.

The reception situation is immersive: you are alone in an isolation, but without completely losing your orientation as with VR glasses. Movements – not only with the head – are possible in a small range, i.e. one can actively turn to one side. The three-part piece begins in a visual reconstruction of the interior of this neo-Nazi construction van from 2003: one is virtually standing in this van and listening to German, right-wing extremist *Oi!* music by the band "Noie Werte" from the decade after the fall of the Wall. What makes this beginning particularly delicate is that the NSU TRIO, who perpetrated the racist murders of 9 people in Germany undetected, also lived and hid in such a construction trailer in East Germany at the time (which was only uncovered years later).

My research work began here with the music, which is now indexed and can only be found on hidden websites. What concerned me most at first was that it celebrates hate as a positive emotion. Together with a contempt for the ruling "system of state and capital," which is not far from left-wing circles (also in the musical punk aesthetic), there is the feeling of being an underdog neo-Nazi, despised and marginalized by society, in a national freedom struggle, as exemplified by the song "Kraft für Deutschland" ("Strength for Germany"). In the installation, excerpts of three pieces of music are repeatedly played back extremely slowed down. The sound mix is influenced by the interactive movements of the listener between the three sides and fluctuates between self-pitying lament and brute self-empowerment.

At this point, I would like to go a little deeper into the work in order to be able to better present the research levels and connections.

The first research phase, however, had to include extra-musical material, the visual signs in the wagon: the white runes and inscriptions that could later be followed as an iconic trace into our own time and that are used ever further transformed as identity markers in the right-wing scene. In the course of the first part, more and more current signs from the international White Supremacy movement replace the hand-painted characters from the construction trailer. Here, visually, the bridge is laid to the present, because the themes run through: the white race as the "nowadays oppressed minority," which is becoming aware of itself again (the "Red Pill" from the film *Matrix* as a revival symbol) and must finally fight back, which should lead to a national revolution (as seen on January 6, 2021, during the storming of the Capitol in Washington).

The second part then also leads right into the modern forms of radical right-wing propaganda, which tries to influence the media and recruit followers by means of hate speech and troll armies. The research work here led deeper and deeper into a brown swamp, with many branches to *Q-Anons* and *Incels*, which has taken on frightening proportions under the radar of the general media public.

A live leak of a recruitment by the right-wing online organization *Reconquista Germanica*, which manipulated the 2017 German Bundestag election through shitposting and trolling, was suitable as central material here. It is flanked by excerpts from the right-wing "Handbook for Media Guerrillas" and concrete memes and hate speech posts including counter-reactions by those affected. What is crucial here is not only how formerly left-wing strategies (as in the "Handbook of Communicative Guerrilla"[23]) are used by the right, but also the use of sarcastic wit, the production of funny memes that have a nasty content, in order to be able to distance oneself in this way at any time ("not meant that way") in case of legal disputes.

This text-dominated passage, which leads into a deliberate overload due to the three-sided condensation, then moves on to the next musical stage: the parallel development to German-language hip-hop with right-wing lyrics about self-defense and resistance against left-

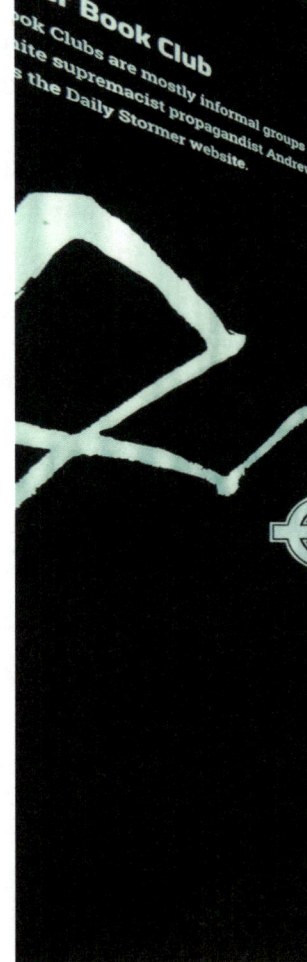

→: Dark Matter Part 1: Old hate symbols out of the wagon, new hate symbols, 3-side projection, visitor with wireless headphones

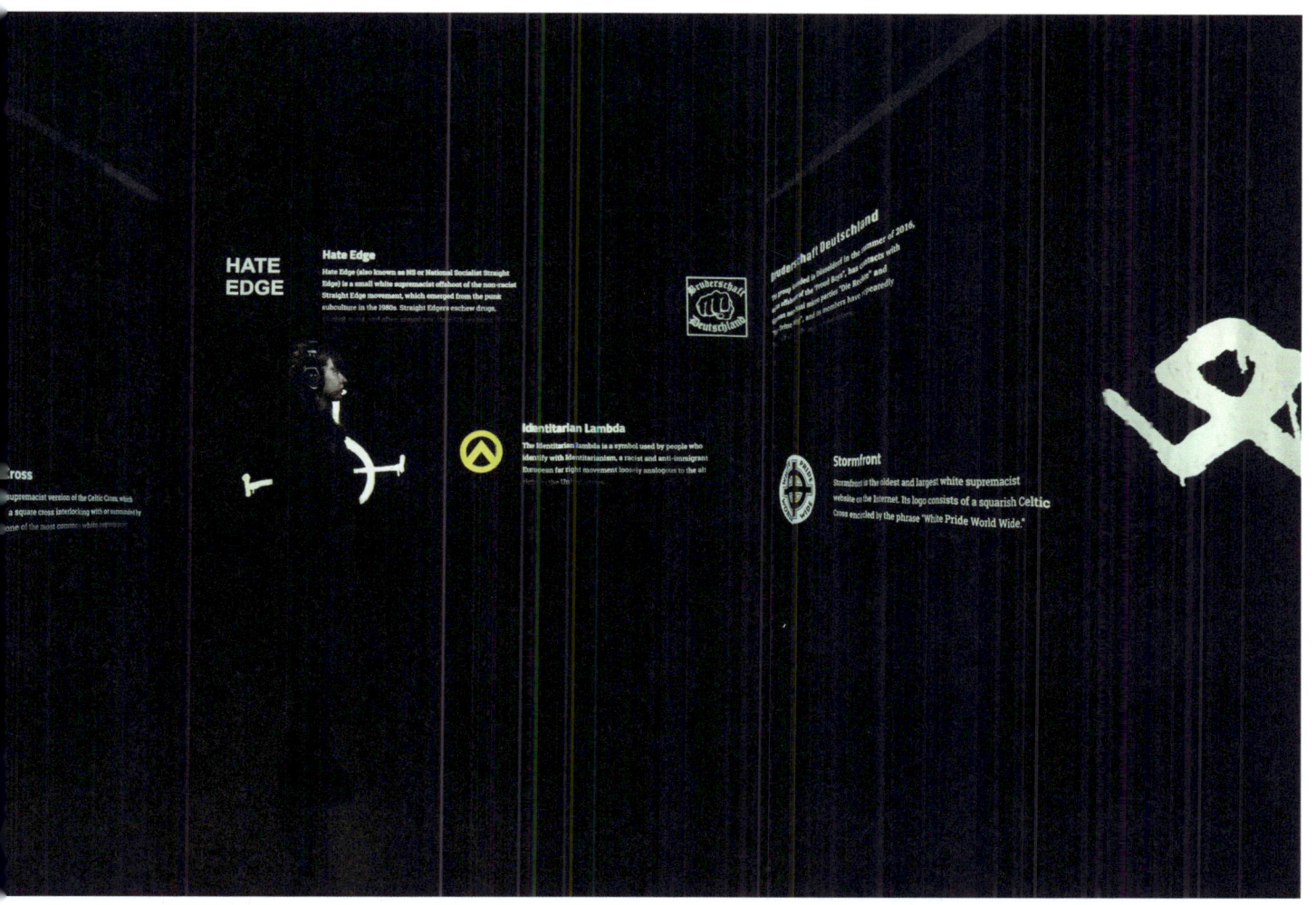

wing mainstream politics and media. In contrast to the schoolyard CDs of the old right-wing rock scene, not only a modernized musical style comes into play here (which was controversial in the right-wing scene – until success became apparent) but also music videos whose imagery conveys right-wing subtexts with professional skill.

It then also ends on the level of the film, the internationally successful blockbuster "300" from 2007: the fight of the (white) Spartans against an overpowering opponent, the Persians. The symbol on the shield of the Spartans later became the symbol of the right-wing "Identitären Bewegung" / "Identitarian Movement" in Germany and Austria (which was not only involved in the shitposting campaigns of *Reconquista Germanica*, but also wanted to create a counter-public sphere in protest actions, including a house project in Halle, Saxony-Anhalt).

Here also appears in pure form the masculinist cult that accompanies the right-wing scene and, in addition to fighting and defensiveness, also stages the traditional cliché of the protective role of the man vis-à-vis the woman, who in turn gives her consent to the then so justified and unavoidable exercise of violence.

This exercise of violence is then the subject of the third part, but no longer in a musical, linguistic or cinematic form but as real violence – which is, however, also staged. The right-wing assassin from Halle not only targeted the visitors of the synagogue he wanted to kill in 2019 on Yom Kippur, the highest Jewish holiday, but also staged his act in the form of a live stream on twitch, so to speak in front of a worldwide audience. The aim was not only to gain fame in the right-wing community on 8chan and other forums, but also to motivate imitators to do the same. Accordingly, the live stream[24] is flanked by his "manifesto" in English, which not only reflects his ideology but also presents his self-made weapons along with a list of "achievements" like in a video game.

The playback of the live stream stops in the installation with the first murder, and two different analysis comments begin that immediately reacted to the attack: on

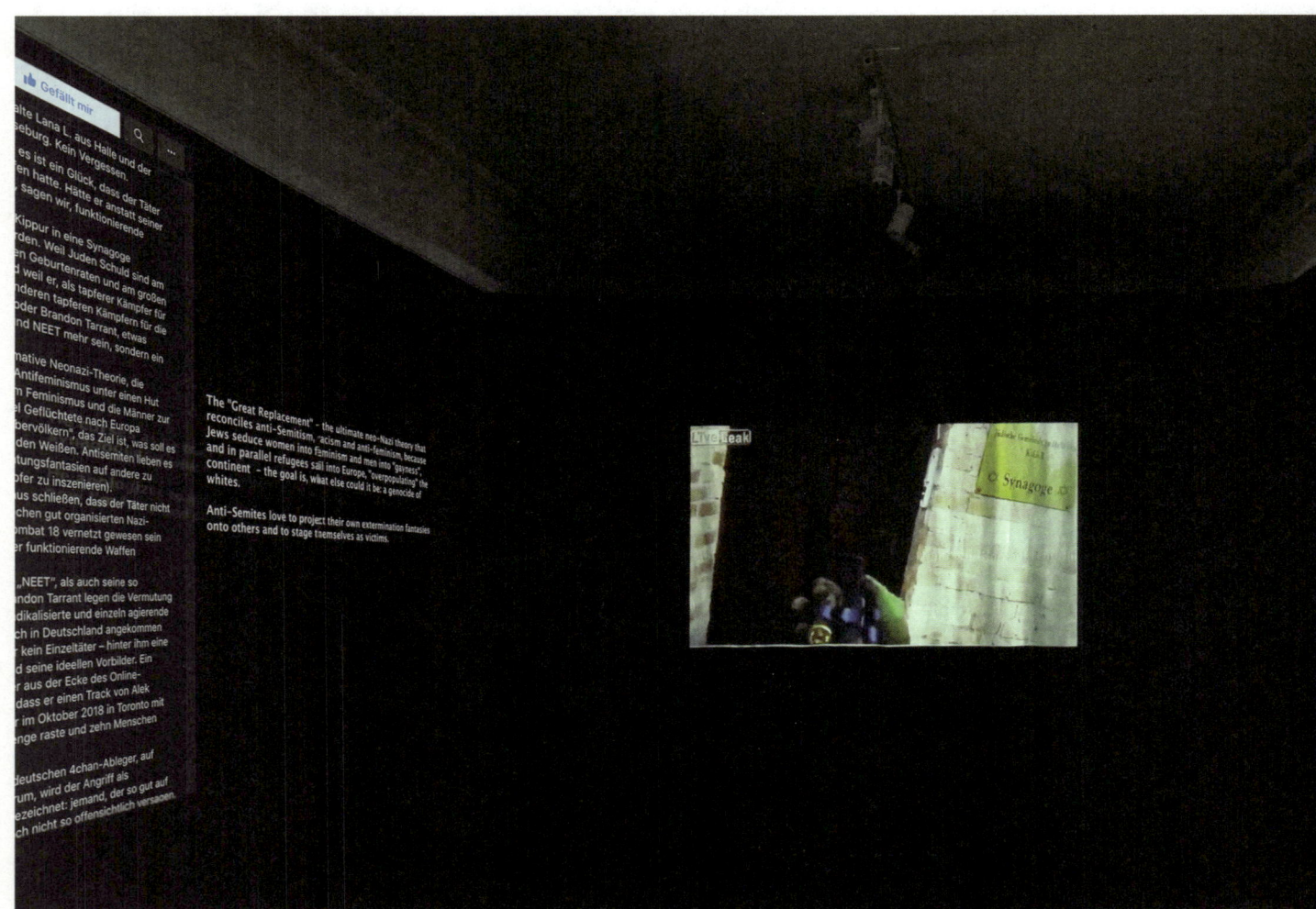

the right side by an anonymous US-American, who wants to expose the assassination as a fake. On the left a Facebook comment by the German journalist Veronika Kracher – surprisingly with a similar conclusion: it is a staging – but as a video game in real, that ends in a "gamification of terror."[25]

For me as a researcher, it was enormously important to be clear about this whole context of the development of right-wing extremist propaganda, in order not to miss an important detail in the live stream of the assassin: after his somewhat laboriously delivered, racist, anti-Semitic and misogynist address to the international audience, the assassin says almost in passing and as if to himself:

"Ah, Musik"

and you see the assassin's hand pushing aside weapons and ammunition boxes in the footwell of the car, turning on a small loudspeaker and then playing a song.

Barely heard properly in the stream, the song he uses to get in the mood sounds like "Mask off" by the African-American rapper Future, however in a strange version: in fact, this song was given right-wing lyrics by a "Mr. Bond" in a professional manner, so it was appropriated from a black man and turned into a song for "Aryans,"[26] and brings the whole range of neo-Nazi symbolism into play in this Nazi rap, from the *red pill* to the *black sun*[27]:

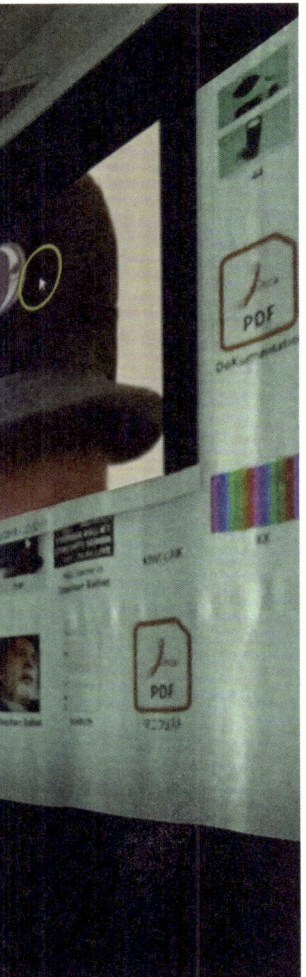

←: Dark Matter Part 3: analysis page (V. Kracher), centre: assassin live stream, right: analysis page (US Anon.)

Mr Bond: "Powerlevel"
power level, reveal my power level
dropping red-pills, on the normal-gs
[verse 1]
aryan, toast up with the gang
from atlantis to a whole 'nother domain
hyperborea, i'm the livin' proof (super)
master race, ant-thesis to the jew
pyramids, from china to peru
in plain sight, a return is overdue
free energy, implosive how we move
highjump n-gg-, byrdie knew the truth
vril force, from the black sun
open doors, to aldebaran
maria, sigrun, are the medium
ultima thule, seeking our elysium
percocets, molly, percocets
chase a check, never chase a b-tch
don't chase no b-tches

Future: "Mask off"
[verse 1]
two cups, toast up with the gang
from food stamps to a whole 'nother domain
out the bottom, i'm the livin' proof (super)
ain't compromising, half a million on a coupe
drug houses, lookin' like peru
graduated, i was overdue
pink molly, i can barely move
ask about me, i'm gon' bust a move
rick james, thirty-three chains
ocean air, cruisin' biscayne
top off, that's a liability
hit the gas, boostin' my adrenaline

Similar to the icons and propaganda, radical right-wing music has evolved from a subculture niche into a widespread alt-right cosmos that is trying to become mainstream in the sense of a right-wing cultural revolution. What was still simple right-wing rock and Oi!-music around 2000 became quite respectably produced hip-hop with German lyrics and visuals 10 years later and landed 20 years later as rap musically on the cutting edge and with English lyrics aimed at an international audience.

And this music is more than just background music: it is incredibly powerful in creating the right feeling, a cool attitude – and the racist and anti-Semitic lyrics embedded in catchy grooves burn themselves into the brain all by themselves. In the installation, the music with lyrics of "Powerlevel" appears twice briefly with full sound before the assassin arrives at the scene.

REFLECTION – EXPERIENCE

Exposure to this music, to this propaganda and also to this live stream is an imposition.

It is difficult for the individual viewers to cope with, which is why the work needs a strong framing, an individual visitor guidance. Everyone is guided in and out. The supervisory staff is instructed to pay attention to the psychological state of the visitors coming out and, if necessary, to offer to talk to them. Any voyeurism or chance encounter with the material is avoided. It is not an installation that you can go in and out of, as is usually the case in the art world.

The three parts form a dramaturgy that runs towards the assassination in Halle, and it is important that the individual visitor must first pass through the phases of musical-visual and propagandistic preparation before encountering this reality. Therefore, the 22-minute piece is restarted with each visitor.

This imposition – as it confronts one in the case of *Dark Matter* (one visitor called it a "confrontation therapy") – is possible in the field of art, in contrast to science, and points to an important difference: artistic research serves a different outcome, a very different form of presentation than scientific research: in the "showing," in the mediation of a sensory-reflexive experience, it is about a different kind of knowledge, "a felt knowledge,"[28] a production of knowledge whose "centre is the constitution of forms of non-subjective reflexivity that operate in the sensory."[29]

The result – the artwork that offers a reflexive space of experience – in turn affects the methodology, the beginning of the artistic process: artistic research is characterized by the fact that at the end there is no text but a sensually perceptible artwork, an experience.

The nature of this experience is as diverse as there are artists and also multiplies in the diversity of reception. So it is not about unambiguity and general validity. But despite this double subjectivity, it is about a "non-subjective reflexivity" that is conveyed in works of art and has its own epistemic quality.[30]

Whether this is successful depends – especially in view of the accumulations of material offered in the course of artistic research – on how this experience is shaped:

"For it is not enough to just put something together or associate it with something else. Rather it is the 'event of situating', the individual 'face' or the unmistakable hue which it takes on that is important. The way in which each respective compositio is able to come back to itself, remark itself and create a self-reference is crucial."[31]

Mersch calls the capacity for re-marking a "simultaneity of exposition and de-setting," an interplay of "exposition and transposition":

> These can work in many ways: by stretching the interstices, the distances between, the dislocation or incommensurability of the relata, by exhibiting a conflict or "rift," or through a contradiction or discord in the "togetherness" of its elements.[32]

Generating a *compositio* of this kind already has its beginning in artistic research with a search that traces tensions, follows traces, explores terrain and thereby pursues conflicts.[33]

What is the conflict – this question accompanies my research work, and where I end up and how the result shows up has become more and more open over time, both in terms of the topics tracked down and the materials used. Both the methodology and the result are primarily aimed at an experience that can lie somewhere between the enjoyment of art and the experience of shock.

For me, these aesthetic possibilities of mediation – their translation – are the central difference to the scientific research result, which should not be lost in efforts to institutionalize *artistic research*. Seen both from the beginning – in artistic investigation – and from the end – in the artistic work – it differs from scientific research, which at the same time results in the best conditions for cross-fertilization.

NOTES:

1. etymonline.com

2. Mersch, Dieter. Epistemologien des Ästhetischen, Diaphanes. English: Epistemologies of Aesthetics, Translated by Laura Radosh, Diaphanes, Zürich 2015, p. 24.

3. Borgdorff, Henk. Die Debatte über Forschung in der Kunst, in Rey and Schöbi, eds., Ku!nstlerische Forschung, p. 25.

4. s. Vienna Declaration on Artistic Research, 2020, and the response to it: What Is Wrong with the Vienna Declaration on Artistic Research? by Florian Cramer, Nienke Terpsma, 2021, open Academy, file:///Users/gk/Downloads/What%20Is%20Wrong%20with%20the%20Vienna%20Declaration%20on%20Artistic%20Research%20.pdf

5. Hornuff, Daniel. Praxis Dr. Kunst geschlossen, FAZ, 17.5.2015.

6. Hauenstein, Hanno. Unerforschte Gefilde: Wie Research-Vibes die Kunstwelt fluten, Berliner Zeitung, 6.5. 2023.

7. Steyerl, Hito. Aesthetics of resistance? Artistic Research as Discipline and Conflict, maHKUzine. Journal of Artistic Research, Utrecht School of Arts, 8, 31–37, Winter 2010. German: Ästhetik des Widerstands? Ku!nstlerische Forschung als Disziplin und Konflikt, pp. 2–4, translated by Birgit Mennel, transversal texts 01/2010.

8. At documenta 15 (2022), for example, a wide variety of collectives used scientific-artistic methods to bring hitherto unnoticed perspectives of global communities into the field of vision of the Eurocentric art canon.

9. Steyerl, op.cit. p. 35.

10. Independent History Work Association. Incidentally, it was not until 30 years later that a memorial was erected next door.

11. See more in Text Book transition, Saarbrücken, 2002, and the documentation at https://www.georgklein.de/installations/001_transition_e.html

12. Mersch op.cit. p. 28/29.

13. The German term "Künstlerische Recherche", in contrast to the English "artistic research", offers a distinction to the term "Künstlerische Forschung", in English also "artistic research". "Forschung" is strongly connected to science, while "Recherche" is more various and methodologically open and might better be translated as "investigation".

14. The visitor situation in public space and thus the perceptual situation is completely different from that in a concert or gallery context, which sometimes leads to surprising experiences.

15. Mersch, op.cit. p. 25/26

16. Recorded with young people from Marl, see Deutscher Klangkunstpreis 2002, ed. Uwe Rüth, Skulpturenmuseum Marl, and documentation at: https://www.georgklein.de/installations/002_MarlMitte_e.html

17. Guy Debord: Théorie de la dérive, Les Lèvres nues n° 9, décembre 1956 et Internationale Situationniste n° 2, décembre 1958. Translated by Ken Knabb.

18. Hauenstein, Hanno, op.cit. p. 8.

19. Mersch, op.cit. p. 26.

20. Steyerl, op.cit. p. 5. "At this point it must be emphasised that this also applies to so-called autonomous artworks, which do not claim to carry out any kind of research."

21. Wikipedia, https://de.wikipedia.org/wiki/Recherche#Journalistische_Recherche

22. Mersch, op.cit. p. 170.

23. autonome a.f.r.i.k.a.-gruppe, Luther Blissett, Sonja Brünzels: Handbuch der Kommunikationsguerilla, Hamburg, Berlin, Göttingen, 1997.

24. Published on twitch, who deleted the video relatively quickly, but it can still be found on the darknet.

25. Kracher, Veronika: CN: Mord, Antisemitismus, Facebook comment on Oct. 9, 2019, reprinted in: Klein, Georg: HATERS, exhibition brochure, Errant Sound, 2021.

26. See Khamis, Sammy. Der Soundtrack rechten Terrors – NS-Propaganda reinsten Wassers, Deutschlandfunk Corso, 25.10.2019.

27. "Mask off": https://azlyrics.biz/f/future-lyrics/future-mask-off-remix-lyrics/ "Power Level": https://azlyrics.biz/m/mr-bond-lyrics/mr-bond-power-level-lyrics/

28. Klein, Julian. "Was ist ku!nstlerische Forschung?" (What is artstic research?), Gegenworte 23, Wissenschaft trifft Kunst, Berlin-Brandenburgische Akademie der Wissenschaften: Akademie Verlag 2010, S. 25–28.

29. Mersch, op.cit. p. 169.

30. In his concluding chapter, "Epistemic Practices of the Arts", Mersch offers a lucid description of further features of "aesthetic thinking", which I can neither adequately summarise nor comment on here.

31. Mersch, op.cit. p. 160.

32. Mersch, op.cit. p. 162.

33. See Klein, Georg. Site-Sounds. On Strategies of Sound Art in Public Space, Cambridge University Press, 2009.

ALESSANDRA ERAMO

ROARS
BANGS
BOOMS

SEVEN VARIATIONS FOR VOICE AND ONOMATOPOEIA PERFORMANCE, 2013 – 2015

The variety of noises is infinite. If today, when we have perhaps a thousand different machines, we can distinguish a thousand different noises – tomorrow, as new machines multiply, we will be able to distinguish ten, twenty, or thirty thousand different noises, not merely in a simply imitative way, but to combine them according to our imagination.

Luigi Russolo, "The Art of Noises: Futurist Manifesto," 1913

In his manifesto, the futurist artist Luigi Russolo classifies six noise families in order to be performed on *Intonarumori*: For producing a broad spectrum of modulated, rhythmic sounds similar to those made by machines, the *Intonarumori* are audio devices, considered the first mechanical sound synthesizer. Thunder, Whistles, Booms, Grumbles, Snorts, … These onomatopoeic words recall the different sounds of the modern industrial landscape. As part of the Manifesto of Futurist Music "The Art of Noises' by Luigi Russolo, this onomatopoeia is the starting point of my performance work: from his intuition projected into the future about the importance of noise in music, 100 years later I have written seven variations for human voice in which noise not only becomes a leitmotiv in music, but it also turns into musical material itself.

Onomatopoeia became one of my main interests, and, from a contemporary perspective, I focus on the interpretation of onomatopoeia and its extension with my voice and other media such as drawing, movement, gesture, field recordings and text. Onomatopoeia has become so enchanting for me, probably because I am immersed in multilingualism in my daily life in Berlin, it is a kind of Babylonian sound poem that resonates in me – I don't think I could live without this great linguistic chaos anymore, I love it! – that makes me perceive some words as pure sound, in a mental exercise in which the onomatopoeic word forms an idea of sound, an image of sound. Interestingly in German, the word Onomatopoeia is called "Lautmalerei," which is the composition of the two words "Laut = Sound" and "Malerei = Painting."

My mouth tries to express a noise through a word that at the same time is already sound in itself. It is an image of sound, turning into a vocal gesture in which the signifier and the signified are playing in unison. And how many images emerge in the listener's mind when they hear, for example, the Italian word "Scricchiolio" – in English, "Creaking"?

Since onomatopoeia differs from one languages to another, I adapted my performance variations "Roars Bangs Booms" to different European languages and performed it in different versions in Germany, Czech Republic, Austria and Italy. I embody these noises, I hear them, I perceive them as urban soundscapes of the present, I transcribe these sounds in drawings and interpret them with my voice and with my body, revealing the beauty of these noises, while playing with the audience's expectation, fancy, and imagination. Onomatopoeia is an exploration of phonic figures consisting of a kind of imitation of a noise through the creation of a new word. Onomatopoeia can be primary ("tic-tac," "boom-boom") or secondary (word of onomatopoeic origin: "ticking," "booming"). The sounds have the archetypical quality of a pre-linguistic state, as when a child repeats sounds it has heard, the babbling of a child who is learning to speak, while it is trying to name and give a voice to events, things, sounds, people, the world around by imitating the noises.

The number seven of the work's variations of course was chosen on purpose: seven is a sacred number, and I wanted the sense of the sacred to accompany me on this journey while exploring the world of noise and onomatopoeia. An important recurrent element in the performance variations are small paper sheets with onomatopoeic words from the Manifesto of Futurist Music and the reading instructions on it for the audience.

The first live-performance took place on 24th May 2013 in the Haus am Lützowplatz Gallery in Berlin. There was an almost sacral atmosphere, in the middle of the exhibition "Streitobjekt Arbeit" with early 20th century art works, including paintings and prints by George Grosz and Käthe Kollwitz, treating the themes of industrial landscapes, exploitation of workers in the dawn of industrialization and first labour unions that gave voice to workers in early capitalism. The people depicted in these paintings probably heard the same, new industrial noises that Luigi Russolo heard and that inspired him to write his manifesto.

Paper sheets with onomatopoeic words in Italian (*thunder, whistles, booms, grumbles, snorts, ...*) are handed to the audience, which is asked to read them aloud. While doing so, most of the people don't know the meaning of the word they are reading, as many do not know the Italian language. So I perform every onomatopoeic word as a distinctive but also very subjective vocal expression. Through my voice and gesture, the audience is imagining the meaning of each word and is associating it with their own noisy incidents or experiences with noises. An idea, a memory becomes voice.

I was always particularly interested in the more mysterious aspect of noise, the one related to both individual and collective memory, so I wanted to investigate this "mistery" in my artistic work. Reading Luigi Russolo's Manifesto of Futurist Music, that was written 100 years before "Roars, Bangs, Booms" I was amused and immediately felt at ease. Russolo, in his artistic research, dealt with themes of the occult and mystery, and as he wrote in his manifesto, ancient cultures always attributed sound to the gods, so sound itself was considered sacred and therefore reserved for priests or shamans for their healing rituals in which contact with the non-human was sought. God, Divinity or Saints were often contacted through the use of dance and music, such as altered voices, singing, speaking in tongues, noises and repetitive rhythms, all those sound elements served primarily to lead the participants into a trance-like state. In this sense, sound can be understood as a separate entity, distinct and isolated from everyday life of human beings. Luigi Russolo in his manifesto states that ancient life probably was silence most of the time, or rather the noises were primarily from nature, animals, humans and some rudimentary machinery. The life of us modern humans instead is full of noise. He probably refers to the rural Italian soundscape before industrialization, especially the Padanian plain between Venice and Milan where he spent most of his life – which today is one of the most densely populated and industrialized regions in Europe. Furthermore, Russolo, exploring the origins of human-made sounds, states that noise essentially first came into being as a result of the invention and use of machines in the 19th century, hence the evolution of music must be synchronized with the evolution of machines that interact with humans with all positive and negative side effects.

There is not always a clear reason why we artists develop a particular interest rather than another for our projects. In artistic research sometimes reason can be happily surpassed by intuition. Artists certainly follow their own sensibility and worldview. Yet in the creative process of "Roars Bangs Booms" I wondered where this deep interest in exploring aspects of noise and onomatopoeia came from. I think it probably stems from the "noisy" places in southern Italy I listened to as a child, and which I listened to again as an adult.

For the live-performance variation on 1st February 2014 at Echo Bücher in Berlin, I've chosen a more profane setting with a great number of pecorino-cheese cubes on a stainless steel plate, decorated with handmade Italian toothpick flags. Many small paper sheets with the onomatopoeic words were handed to the audience, who is asked to freely interpret the words when indicated. While the audience interprets the onomatopoeic words aloud, we're all immersed in a soundscape, based on field recordings I collected between 2008 and 2013 in the industrial city of Taranto, the city where I was born. At the end of the performance, I offered to the audience the delicious sheep milk cheese to eat together. Savouring this first quality cheese is the happy and cathartic conclusion of the performance, as a way to remind and transform a traumatic event which Tarantinians and myself have experienced in 2008: a mass slaughtering of thousands of sheep in the polluted Taranto area because of the high dioxin level found in their milk.

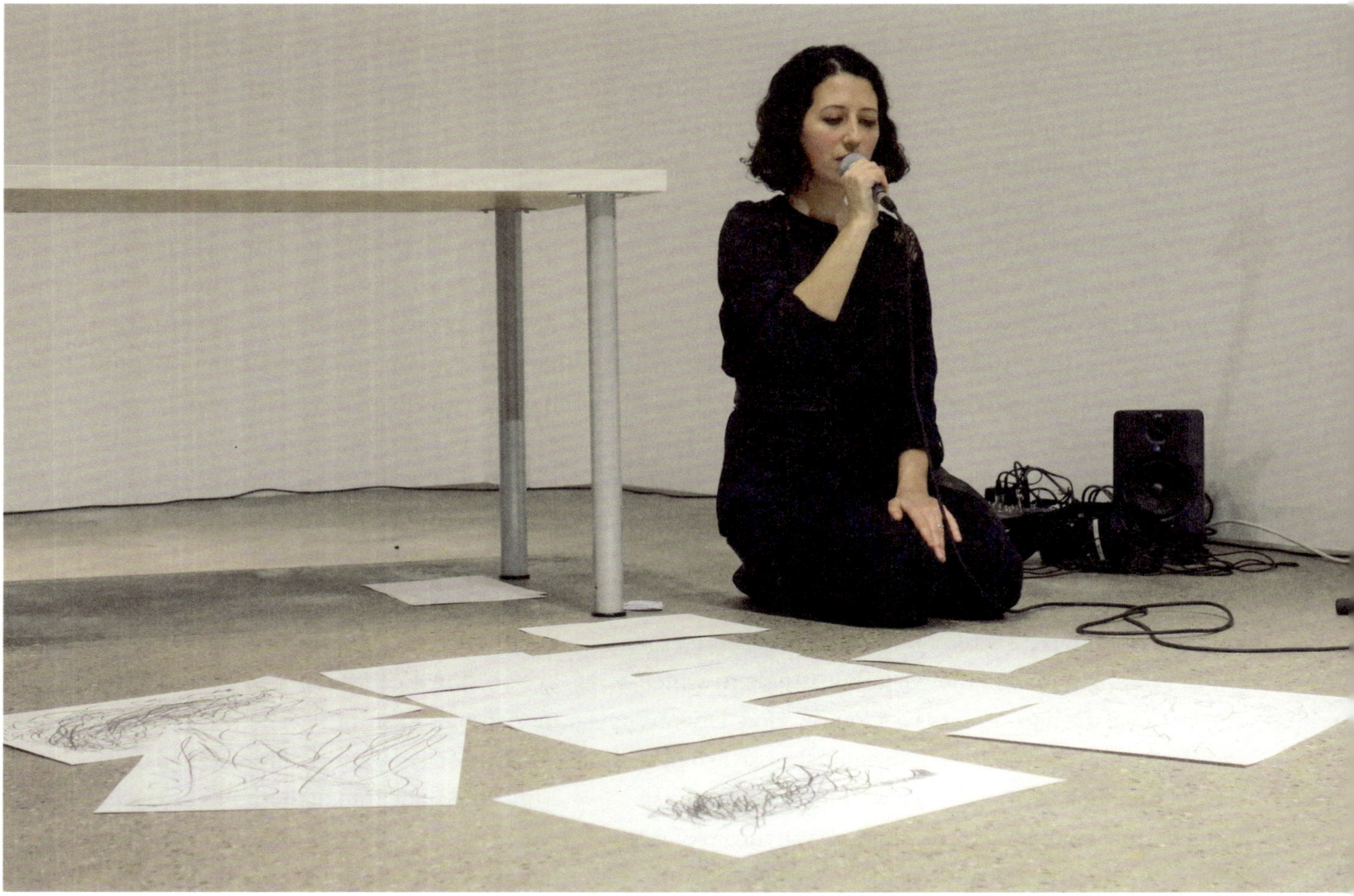

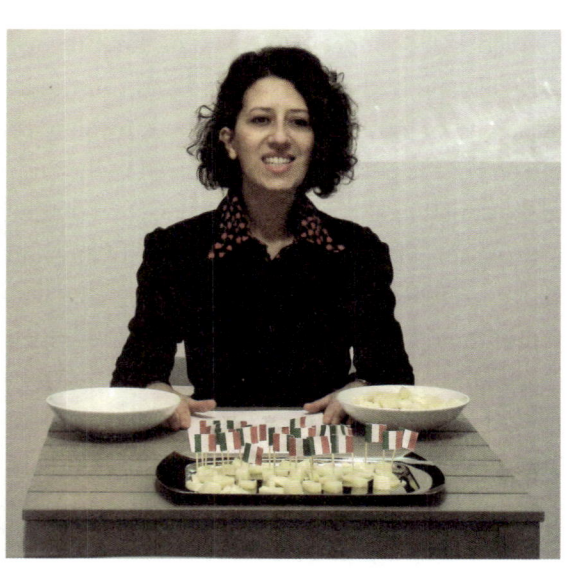
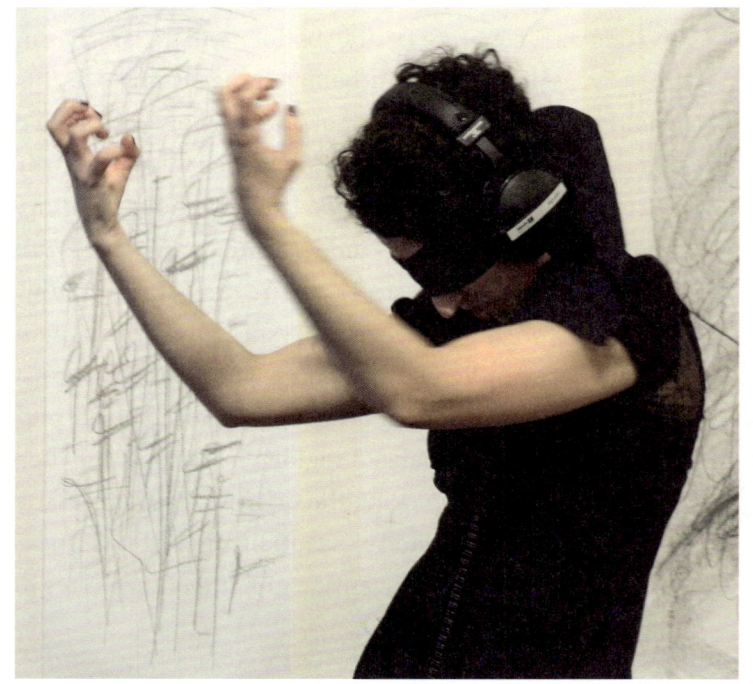

SOME FACTS ABOUT THE INDUSTRIAL CITY OF TARANTO TAKEN AT RANDOM AND IN NO PARTICULAR ORDER

In 2013, I curated "Correnti Seduttive" (*Seductive Currents*), a sound art, interactive performance and audio-visual art project in Taranto, dealing with the city's biggest issue: the pollution caused by the industry and the military base. I invited a group of internationally renowned artists living in Berlin: composer, visual and sound artist Georg Klein; performer and video artist Steffi Weismann; field recordist and sonic journalism pioneer Peter Cusack, all members of Errant Sound and artistic director of Corvo Records Wendelin Büchler, to participate with me in a three-week residency at the Aragonese Castle in the Old Town in Taranto to build an anthropology of the sounds of Taranto and present the developed works in an exhibition in March 2014. The main questions were: "How do the human, visual and sonic landscape of Taranto present themselves today?" and "Which aspects and features of the Beauty/Danger dichotomy can be illuminated through observation and research in the field?"

Taranto, the city of two seas, once known as the pearl of the Ionian Sea and Magna Grecia owns a vast maritime culture heritage like the production and trade of sea silk, an extremely fine fabric that is made from the long silky filaments or byssus that grows in certain types of pen shells like Pinna nobilis, a large (120cm) species of Mediterranean clam. The cultivation of the rare, and valuable fabric was one of the main economic factors and reason the Taranto area became very wealthy since the 1st century B.C.

In 1965 one of Europe's biggest iron and steel complex ILVA (now ArcelorMittal group) became operational in Taranto, employing 5,000 workers at peak time and later occupying an area more than twice the size of the city. Apart from being a major center of the European steel industry, Taranto is also an important NATO base. It's a place of social tension, high emigration and disastrous environmental problems. Toxic dioxine and red oxidized iron powder, released by the steel industry and covering parts of the city, are the main health threats.

In 2012 local prosecutors ordered the partial seizure of ILVA because of abnormally high cancer incidence, linked to the pollution. The closure dramatically and suddenly brought the underlying conflict of interests between health and employment in the city out into the open. Taranto's circumstances clearly demonstrate the limits of European capitalism but, so far, little has changed on the ground. The steel plant is still working and the pollution continues. Today, in 2023 tourism is increasing. And there are cultural associations like the multidisciplinary performance/architect group "Post Disaster Rooftops" operating on marginal territories and aiming to decentralize the production and sharing of knowledge: The association organizes experimental music shows, performances and actions on the roofs of the inhabited or abandoned and precarious buildings of the Old Town, a place of great beauty but extremely fragile and symbolic of the "disaster" of Taranto, just between the sea and the immense steel plant. Also, the famous traditional easter procession in Taranto, showing statues of the Holy Virgin full of grief, has become a tourist attraction, broadcast live on prime-time television – just like the weekly demonstrations of Tarantinian mothers, who lost their children to leukemia, covered even by the New York Times. Taranto is certainly a very interesting place whose noises evoke contrasts and confusion.

Russolo realizes the importance of noise in music; he states that noise, coming to us irregularly from the unpredictable confusion of life, never reveals itself entirely to us: Noise is mysterious, it provides us with many surprises. Indeed, every manifestation of our life is accompanied by noise, like the sound of a mother's breathing when the baby is still in her womb, or the sound of birds chirping that marks the beginning of spring. Noise, although mysterious, has something familiar to our ears and has the power to immediately call us back to life, to our memories and emotions. Music that includes noise from the real world enchants me, as it can be mysterious and superimposed on the real, therefore this music can be sacred.

For the live performance on 3rd May 2014 at the old project space of Errant Bodies in Berlin Prenzlauer Berg, I am standing blindfolded in the room in front of the audience. Wearing headphones, I'm listening to my own vocal interpretation of the onomatopoetic words from the Manifesto of Futurist Music. With my body and through gestures, I interpret the recording of my voice. The audience cannot hear what I'm listening to, but can imagine or guess each noise/onomatopoetic word just by observing my body in movement: sometimes as if electrified, sometimes fluid, sometimes crawling, sometimes heavy as lead, sometimes light as feather, the movements are genuine, in a kind of a silent, bizarre dance with a focus on voice moving between inside and outside. Exploring oral and written phenomena in sound, I exhibited also my large-format drawings as graphic transcriptions of the onomatopoeic words: each drawing is a gestural interpretation of one noise. In this work I explore a new space between sound, voice, gesture, writing and drawing. A drawing that becomes onomatopoeic word, a dance that is noise. Finally, after my performance, the audience is invited to hear the original recordings at a listening station in the gallery space.

"From Luigi Russolo's Manifesto to industrial soundscapes of today" is the title of a lecture/ performance, precisely another variation of "Roars Bangs Booms" I presented on 3rd March 2014 in Taranto at the Ex-Caserma Rossarol, University of Taranto. As part of my live performance, I read aloud a letter addressed to the ghost of Luigi Russolo. While listening to my lecture, the audience is immersed in the noise of the city's industrial soundscape that mingles with the onomatopoeic words read aloud and the sounds of daily life in the Old Town of Taranto.

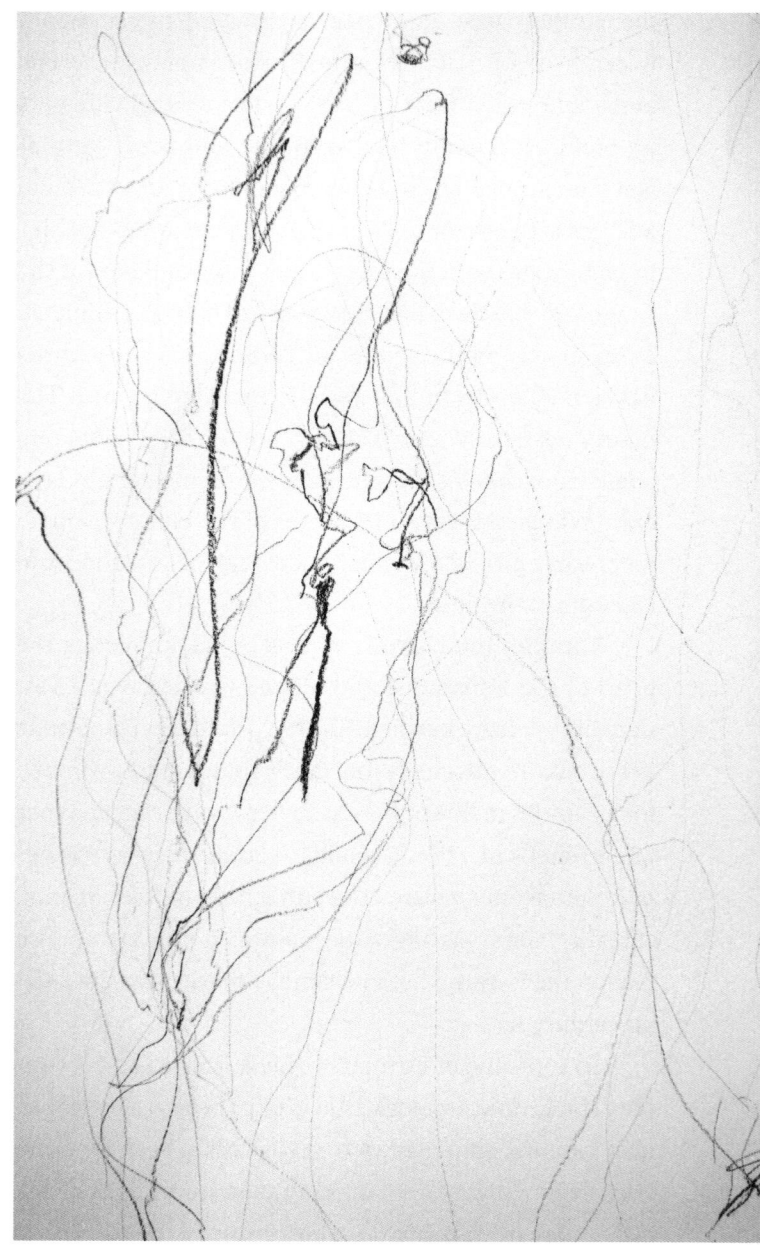

"Dear Luigi Russolo,

I am at the University of Bari – Campus of Taranto, in a former church now used for meetings, symposiums and conferences. I know that you and your colleague Francesco Pratella provoked the masses with your call for emptying the conservatories, colleges, universities and academies to determine the closure and celebrate their funeral in order to give absolute freedom to musical studies. I'm sorry to tell you that after 101 years here in Italy, music continues to be taught the same way as before – if it is taught at all – because I heard that recently music education, as well as visual art education, was definitely eliminated from programs in public school. But I'm glad to tell you that your intuitions, your ideas and your work have been very, very useful for the renewal of Italian music. You brought some fresh air and your ideas have also built the base for the international avant-garde music from the 1950s to today. Your spirit is here with us today and I know you can hear us, as you have been able to listen to the new sounds of your time, the sounds of the new Italy from the early 1900 just in the beginning of the new industrial era.

I welcomed your enthusiasm and that of your Futurist colleagues – female and male artists, poets, dancers and composers – for your rejection of passivism and love for the new. You, a painter, a multifaceted artist, a composer, revolutionzed Italian classical music. I had to smile at first when I read some of your statements that were as ingenious as they were necessary, rightly so, for example when you said that "We must break this narrow circle of pure sounds – referring to orchestral timbres – and we must conquer the infinite variety of sounds-noises." And I fully concurred when you stated that "In the age of technology we need to turn to 'the throbbing of valves, the comings and goings of pistons, the screeching of metal saws, the rattling of railways, spinning mills, printing presses, power stations and railways'." Or when you said that "the already heard sounds are boring, and classics like Beethoven and Wagner have 'shaken the nerves and the heart'." "Now we are fed up with them," you then stated radically, "and we enjoy much more ideally combining noises […] than hearing again, for example, the Eroica or the Pastorale."

I have read in history books that especially the first performances of your Futurist Music punctually triggered brawls between audience and performers, which were eventually quelled by police intervention. I hope the same does not happen today, as I, unlike you, reject all forms of violence. However, I would like to tell you today that I particularly liked the manifesto you wrote on 11 March 1913, "The Art of Noises," where you state that music must be made predominantly of noises, not only based on tonality. In particular, I liked your idea of using the noises of everyday life in composition, because they are living, real sounds.

By creating the Intonarumori, these incredible musical instruments which are noise generators, you have enriched listening with sounds unheard before. Convinced of the new aural sensitivity of contemporary man and convinced that in the 19th century, with the invention of machines, noise would triumph and dominate human's sensitivity, you wrote your Manifesto classifying all the possible noises of the modern era: howls, rumbles, crinkles, gurgles, hisses and buzzes. You ranked them one by one. An all-Italian genius. You launched the seeds of the European musical avant-garde.

I can confirm that your intuition, namely that noise can be considered a component of artistic expression, has deeply penetrated into the poetics of musical exploration of sound in the 20th century. The beautiful audience here with me in this room and also myself know very well the sounds and noises you have been talking about 101 years ago. In this sense we are already experienced with the Futurist Music. We find these sounds every time we open the window, pointing our ear to the outside, when we walk on the streets, listening to the noises, to nice noises, to ugly noises and to unsupportable noises that surround us. In this city of industry. Or the industry of the city ... depending on the point of view, the perspective, the experience or the geographic location. We have learned to listen also thanks to your Manifesto.

While I am writing you this letter, I am immersed in a multi-faceted soundscape: my fingers typing computer keys, a navy helicopter is flying over the buildings, a man* shouts "SIGNORAAAAA!" (Laaaadyyy!) and he answers himself "Whaaaat?". A car was just parked, an illegal parking assistant comes closer and shakes the change coins in his hand, a scooter has just passed an elderly lady walking, the red and white chimneys of the steel plant are blowing smoke in the air, the neighbor's tv is playing the latest songs of Sanremo Festival**, a group of seagulls are screaming while flying over the sea, a small truck loaded with vegetables is stuck in traffic, a man sings neomelodic songs from Naples, and then he sneezes. It all sounds pretty interesting, all worthy of a possible composition of Futurist music. But I wanted to ask you if all these sounds can be considered "futurist sounds" or "sounds from the industrial city." Would you say that these sounds belong to any given place? Or are they perhaps special sounds, unique, specific sounds from an industrial city? Maybe one of those beautiful industrial cities that you and your Futurists colleagues were deeply fascinated by?

So I take this wonderful opportunity to let you hear an 11-minute composition I made, which is based on the sounds of Taranto that I recorded between 2010 and 2014. The sounds you will hear are all original and not manipulated.

Dear Luigi Russolo, if you will allow me, I would like to pay homage to you by kindly asking the beautiful audience present here to participate in the musical performance, interpreting with their voices the onomatopoeia from your manifesto "The Art of Noises." You conceived these onomatopoeic words as a list of noises that the musical instrument you invented, Intonarumori, could reproduce. Considering the voice as an exceptional and eternal instrument, I would therefore like our audience here and now to interpret the list of noises with their own voice, freely and as they see fit. We are about to distribute to the audience the paper sheets with the words, so we'll create a chorus of noisy onomatopoeias together.

I hope you will appreciate.

A noisy greeting, Alessandra Eramo

*The man is called Aldo. All Tarantinians know him as the most famous homeless and heroin addict begging for money and screaming around weird insults against the Holy Virgin in the city center.

**Most popular music Festival contest in Italy, dedicated to "Canzone Italiana" (Sanremo Italian Song festival)

Let us begin from the body.
We are body listening in a landscape. A body that is born in that landscape. It knows it and is familiar with it.
A landscape that is an environment made of air, earth, sun, sky, colors, architecture, nearby shapes, distant shapes, smells, and voices and noises. Human noises and non-human noises. Industrial noises.
It is now 2023, ten years after the realization of my project "Roars Bangs Booms," and the sky of Taranto is still red with the smoke from the chimneys of the huge steel plant, towering in the landscape of the industrial city, a seagull's cry mingles with the symphony of the industry that hardly stops, while nato planes and helicopters are training for war over our heads. Their deafening noise shakes everything, the windows of our homes are vibrating, the sea churns in small waves as the helicopter passes, we would like to faint for a moment, absent ourselves, stop breathing, or shout at the top of our lungs that we do not like the logic of war and the war industry. Then we remember that this big factory needs laborers, and the laborers work in it while being poisoned, while getting sick, and killed. For 70 years. 70 years ago peasants enthusiastically left the countryside and much of their economic misery to live in the industrial city, many became laborers in the biggest factory of the South.

In the pink-red landscape of this South, the noises remind us that we are not alone. We even start to become attached to these sounds.
We are not alone; animated and unanimated creatures and things are all around us.
Let us imagine that we are bodies immersed in the landscape, listening is like breathing in the landscape, with moments of apnea, and moments when we resume breathing strongly and decisively, and let's imagine that we are breathing heavily, a sweeping movement of arms open, chest out, the body expanding and becoming part of the landscape a hiss of larynx - it is the sound of air passing through our throat - we taste the landscape, it passes through the cavity of the mouth.
But the landscape poisons us. Because the air is poisoned here. We are left with a strange taste of rust and iron on our palate.
We blow the air through our nose - strongly, vehemently.
Here's the sound, it's a kind of puffing, a clanking roar, screeching of train tracks, squeaking of machines and pulleys, harsh, shrieky noises, a gentle rumble, beating heart, pressing rhythm of venous flow. Mouth of metal, taste of steel. I become poison.
The sunset over the Taranto sea is a shattered mirror of dazzling light. Let us try to listen to this fiery red sunset,
red in the evening
red is the light
red is the dust of iron red is the tar We breathe red - the smoke of smokestacks
contemporary industry - past and present and future wrecks of warehouses, buildings and crumbling tracks among the red-pink eucalyptus trees and the sea shaped like a wide-open smile.
Engines and mopeds whine in the night - in those deserted streets,
while mothers in their beds continue to hope for a sleep,
they get disturbed by the perennial nightly rumble of the plant which was built next to the apartment buildings, the mothers close their windows, fall asleep, in their beds of sheets embroidered with byssus silk, the sea silk, the memory of a glorious Magna Graecia past, of an ancient economy and wealth of

this part of the Mediterranean. The mothers have sour dreams of a better future for their children, other than the one spent in the bed of an oncology ward.

Hoping mothers, in tristezza siderurgica (steel sadness), dreaming mothers in this poisoned South, today still die hoping.

Pink-red dust settles everywhere, on the balconies, on fallen leaves, on the sidewalks, on the graves in the cemetery.

In the city the fragments of light dazzle the eye, it is infinite beauty, changing, iridescent, the marching band passes by playing the symphony of scrap metal in the Easter procession of pathetic music where Mother Mary searches for her holy son.

Post-Disaster. The cameras are on, the world is watching us, the world is listening to us.

Pietas.

Perhaps it is like a thud that deafens us for a few seconds, tinnitus that whistles in our bodies, and does not leave us, lingers in our ears, tinnitus colored red, purple, pink, iridescent, we are deaf as if overwhelmed by too much life, a hyper-oxygenation from too much baroque poison.

While the sea is a caress. The sea-cemetery of new emigrants. The joyous sea of dolphins and inflamed sunsets. We shall return one day to this sea – we who have emigrated – to rediscover all this light.

In the delirium of the future, in the catastrophe, our bodies absorb every vibration, reproduce it through a timid voice, the voice soon learns to rise to the clear sky full of stars and smoke, an intonarumori voice rises, it incorporates spirituality in an ecstatic dance, it appropriates the industrial, familiar noises, futurist architecture that marks the difficult coexistence of humans and nature. The voice accommodates in its larynx the crackling of lava, interpreting words that are sounds, dancing, leaping, the body cannot sit still, the body registers every belly movement, every lips smacking, spitting out saliva that expands, like a snake's tongue, spits out venom that becomes sound, and is transformed into beneficial elixir, a new music for our ears.

These noises are screeching of steel, they are rumbling of engines expanding and vanishing, roars, – bangs – booms – they are tumult of sea waves, sound of a mother's cradle at the passing of the last fisherman's boat returning home, smiling, hunting seagull's cry, endless echo tracing the horizon of smokestacks reaching for the sky, the great mystery of the industrial sky.

– what sound does this sky make?

LIVE PERFORMANCES OF ROARS – BANGS – BOOMS:

Haus am Lützowplatz Gallery, Berlin, 24 May 2013

Echo Bücher Berlin, 1 February 2014

Chiesetta San Francesco c/o Ex-Caserma Rossarol, Taranto, 3 – March 2014

Errant Bodies Berlin, 3 – 11 May 2014

Museum FLUXUS+ Potsdam (Germany), 29 November 2014

MuseRuole Festival, Innsbruck (Austria), 24 May 2014

Geh8 Dresden (Germany), 23 April 2015

Školská28 Prague (Czech Republic), 24 April 2015

"Neue Musik St. Ruprecht" St. Ruprecht Church Vienna, 3 May 2015

www.correnti-seduttive.com

HOLGER SCHULZE

What do Sounds need, what do we grant them or not?

A FEW CONSIDERATIONS ON THE AFFORDANCES OF THE SONIC

Sounds don't want anything. Sounds are there; or they are not.
To assume that sounds have intentions, desires, needs, suspicions or dislikes would be a serious categorical error.
Sounds are not actors.
Or ... are they?

In the year 2015, on September 9, one could attend a performance by sound artists Mendi + Keith Obadike, at the Ryan Lee Gallery in New York. In this performance, both artists sit across each other, at a rather small table. On the table one can detect an assortment of rather historical tape machines, a mixing desk, older, heavier headphones, and – most importantly – brochures with long lists of numbers as it seems. "009, 383, 010, 277." They read these numbers in a very focused, neutral, but at times also grave manner. "013, 167, 014, 409." Alongside with reading those numbers in alternation – one sequence read by Mendi Obadike, another sequence read by Keith Obadike – peculiar feedback sounds emerged from their readings. They resonated, now and then pretty painfully, within this particular gallery space. People gathered, listened, stood, left. The performance lasted for 25 minutes. Its name: *Numbers Station (furtive movements)*.[1]

It would – most certainly – be a complete anthropomorphization of all the sounds, vibrations, reflections and timbres involved in this case to attribute any direct and explicit agency to them. Is it at all conceivable that these individual sounds, which are essentially physical effects, could really have an intrinsic and intentional power to act – without any humanoid agents assigning this agency to them in the first place? It is indeed very difficult to imagine such an interpretation; at least outside an animistic or pantheistic framework and worldview. And, to put it mildly, an animistic approach to life, existence and the interpenetration of life forms, activities, seemingly inanimate objects and their processes is not at all ridiculous and out of the question when we are investigating artistic practices.

Yet these particular sounds have power. While the mere numbers, as read by Mendi + Keith Obadike, can seem purely neutral and abstract as such, they immediately take on a different impact and power when contextualized by the artists. "017, 92, 018, 167." The numbers arouse doubt and irritation in us; we continue to listen. We want to understand. "019, 105, 020, 157." The two interlocking series of numbers are taken from the New York Police Department's self-reported stop-and-frisk data from over 123 precincts. The underscoring composition of overlapping sine tones of different frequencies fading in and out is generated from the same NYPD database, taking stop numbers and translating them into frequencies. This practice of stop and frisk is neutral and bureaucratic in its official description. "023, 379, 024, 175." But deeply racist and oppressive in its actual implementation: mainly black and brown people have been subjected to this oppressive practice of control, surveillance and threat. "025, 255, 026, 212." The numbers document a racist threat of state repression.

In their performance, Mendi + Keith Obadike read out first the number of the quarter and then the number of stops. "028, 190, 030, 186." In doing so, they make audible the structural racism and oppression that these stop-and-frisk actions by the New York Police Department actually represent. They manifest this violence, not in argument or visual documentation, but with a sonic argument,[2] with sonic evidence. "032, 048, 033, 452." I can actually hear this sonification of the *Banalität des Bösen, the banality of evil* (Hannah Arendt) inherent in these acts of repression.

In what follows, I would like to explore the needs, affordances and agency of sound comparable to those present in this work by Mendi + Keith Obadike. A number of works from the last 15 years of sound art will therefore serve as starting points for various aspects of sonic affordances. These include several examples from the performance series *Ready Making*, curated by artists and performers Janine Eisenächer and Steffi Weismann at Errant Sound. These examples might actually help to make sense of what needs and possibilities sound has to offer: these are the affordances of sound events, sound effects and sound practices. To this end, I will focus primarily on four aspects that shape the affordances of sound in a particular intervention or artwork:

(a) the situation

(b) the instrument, tool or apparatus

(c) the actor – whether human or non-human, a single actor or a collective group of actors;

and

(d) the particular activity in its temporal and relational structure.

SONIC AFFORDANCES OF A MATERIAL SITUATION

This situation is limited. At the moment, the situation is that of a written, edited, typeset, and printed text. You are reading it under whatever circumstances you happen to encounter it, be it in the form of a digital file or even a printed book. However, its constraints are very different from those of a spatial situation of sound art. In such a situation there will be walls and light sources, windows and power sockets, chairs, tables. There are people present, of course. We are present. We wear certain clothes, according to cultural customs and seasonal requirements, personal styles. Our hairstyles and accessories bring in another range of materials and their effects. There is a certain protocol of how to speak or not to speak in this situation, how calm or agitated we are, before, during a conversation, a performance, a lecture, and afterwards. These constituents of a situation are, if you like, the material framework within which any given sound artwork, any given sound practice, might take place today.

The possibilities within are not limitless. They are fixed. Often there are not really many ways to extend, change, transform or add to these options. But they can be played with. They can be subverted and reversed, ignored or underlined, undermined or simply exhausted. But only rarely is it possible to expand the given options beyond these existing limits. These strong constituents, these implicit assignments to anyone approaching this situation, are: *the affordances of this situation.*

In 1979, psychologist James Jerome Gibson defined affordances in the context of visual perception and their relation to an ecological interpretation of environmental stimuli. For Gibson, affordances included "what [the environment] offers [to the actors], what it provides or furnishes, either for good or ill."[3] Affordances are thus, to a large extent, unintentional. They simply exist – whether or not a human agent can make good use of them. They exist regardless of one's use of them, one's respect for them, or one's ignorance of their effects. The affordances of a situation are a factual reality.

A few years later, in 1988, cognitive researcher Donald Norman expanded the notion of affordance to include a relational dimension. He emphasized that each affordance may be factual, but it exists only in relation to particular agents outside of it. According to Norman, an affordance is, more precisely, "a relationship between the properties of an object and the capabilities of the agent that determine just how the object could possibly be used."[4] Affordances continue to be regarded as objective reality, but this reality does not consist of isolated atoms or things. This reality is populated by interrelated and often interpenetrating entities. The total isolation of entities is actually a very rare and rather exotic case. It rarely occurs in this reality.

In a more recent step, sound scholar Carla Jana Maier has been working with me to apply these concepts of affordance to sound art and its material aspects. We recognize affordances within the artistic practices that use instruments, or any object that can be used as an instrument:

> Every instrument incorporates its own discursive and material attributes which become sonic affordances for instrumentalists or sound artists who play, interpret or manipulate the instrument.[5]

The attributes of each performance situation, the material sound sources, and the material sound agents provide the framework for what can be done with sound. These affordances exist whatever a sound artist, sound engineer, or sound art curator might wish. Any given situation is therefore quite different in its possibilities and limitations: a dance floor offers a set of material affordances that are radically different from those of a lecture hall; a raw industrial loft again offers significantly different possibilities for what can be done with sound in it than a newly built opera house or a contemporary radio recording studio. The materials of each of these situations are fundamental.

These materials and their precise constellation affect what you and I tend to do: what you and I have learned as customs and habitual ways of using and reacting to these materials. No doubt: it is still possible to act and perform willfully against all these given affordances or constraints, but one could easily get stuck at some point. Stopped by a lack of electricity, by house rules, perhaps by fire regulations, by the time-frame of an evening performance, by cultural conventions, or even by the laws of physics and social propriety: a performance announced to last twenty minutes could, of course, be extended to twenty hours without interruption; without allowing an audience to leave the venue. It would be possible, no doubt. But it would also provoke certain reactions, activities, noises from the members of that very audience. Protest, anger, aggression, leaving the venue, abandoned chairs and rows, even lawsuits: these could be the consequences of acting so radically against the conventions, expectations, and given framework of a performance. They are also part of the affordances of a performance or artwork.

Let us listen to an example: "Between the winter of 2001 and the summer of 2004" the composer and artist Annea Lockwood "made five field-recording trips, moving slowly down the Danube from the sources in the Black Forest through Germany, Austria, Slovakia, Hungary, Croatia, Serbia, Bulgaria and Romania to the great delta on the Black Sea, recording the river's sounds (at the surface and underwater), aquatic insects, and the various inhabitants of its banks."[6] In this piece, Lockwood worked with the boundaries of this one particular environment: the material situation of a river, its affordances, its physical properties, and the various people who live with or near it – in this case: the Danube, the *Donau*. Listening to *A Sound Map of the Danube* (2008), we might notice the surprisingly deep and sonorous gurgling of this river at its source in the Black Forest. Are we surprised by the great and wide chorus of sheep, all over some meadows? Then the gurgling sounds lighter, more agile and dynamic; in the background we hear the distant sound of the same river. And then even heavier sounds of falling water, downstream, with higher velocity and more impact, become audible. The bells of a larger church are heard.

For Lockwood, this river has agency. She writes:

It created its sounds through the way it shapes its banks in collaboration with rocks, soil, silt, etc., but I was also recording aquatic and terrestrial insects, frogs and tadpoles, fish, geese and other birds, humans, and the wind in reed beds and in trees, listening to how they all interweave, how all are dependent on the river, and thus how the river shapes its whole environment far beyond its banks.[7]

In this case, then, it is the material situation of the river, its impact on beings and plants, animals and all sorts of potential life forms and activities, that provides the sonic affordance. Annea Lockwood studied these affordances – and provided an arrangement in her sound recording that represents a perspective on these affordances of this particular stretch of water.

Sonic affordances, in this case, operate in the macro-structure and resonant effects of sound, its possible repertoire. They are the first amplifier. They are the affordances of a *material situation*.

SONIC AFFORDANCES OF A MATERIAL APPARATUS

A tool is an object with inherent limitations. An instrument is such a tool, as well as virtually any apparatus one might work with, also in the arts and in sound art. An instrument or such a tool is an apparatus that requires trained and refined handling. A performer must therefore explore, understand, and embody the possibilities, the factual resistance, and the instabilities of such a tool with which one works. It is then this instrument that tends to dictate most of the dynamics, resonance, volume, and even a certain placement of the audience within a performance situation, potentially altered only by contemporary technologies of sound amplification. It is rather difficult, if not impossible, to play a flute under water and enjoy such a performance. It might also not make much sense to invite a large choir to sing on top of Mount Everest. If you expect a large and diverse audience to enjoy such a performance, it might only be possible at certain times of the day and if you can provide certain means of transportation. In general, I would not advise expecting a huge crowd in such a case. Also, it might not make sense to perform with a set of turntables if you intend to perform while walking or hiking across the Rocky Mountains; and a set of MAX/MSP patches might not be the most ideal choice if you primarily want to draw the listener's attention to a particular experience of corporeal materiality, plasticity, the fluids and mucus of a body.

These inherent limitations of an instrument, software or hardware tool are, of course, never absolute. On the contrary, they often serve as provocative inspirations or challenges to achieve the very goal they seem to oppose! In the end, they may all make a lot of sense artistically – just because they seem almost impossible or useless to do. This is what artistic challenges are about, at least in part.

The performer and composer Marianthi Papalexandri-Alexandri chose a rather extreme artistic challenge. She decided to disassemble, abstract, and reassemble various specimens of flutes. She decided to explore what possibilities they offer and how they can be used, reversed, and developed in new ways? In a performance from February 9, 2014, at the Theaterhaus Stuttgart by the Neue Vocalsolisten, one can witness the staging and instrumental practice of Papalexandri-Alexandri's piece *Untitled VI für drei Männerstimmen und Klangobjekte* (2013/14).[8]

This piece is performed by male singers who sing not into the audience, but into the openings of a series of transparent plastic tubes containing membranes and other resonating and amplifying materials and mechanisms. One hears, so to speak, not the voices of the singers, but how they are transformed by these new instruments, which resemble flutes or organ pipes, perhaps even a kind of futuristic and grotesquely inflated panflute. Moreover, the sound is not really inflated and more audible than one would expect in such a case. It is even less audible, quieter and enriched with more hiss and noise, friction and overtones that are not thoroughly controlled by the singers. It is indeed an alien experience – alien in terms of sound, in terms of performance and in terms of listening. Papalexandri-Alexandri outlines her artistic approach as follows:

> The works in the *Untitled* series center on a unique frictional mechanism that allows me to acoustically activate musical instruments, everyday objects, and architectural spaces into resonant bodies. Some adaptations of these new technologies are presented as mechanical sound sculpture and motor-driven sound installations. Some of them have been presented in the context of a solo live performance.[9]

Friction and activation are central to her work. The adaptations to which they give way then create new and surprising, also uncomfortable or even disturbing, sometimes confusing affordances. The microstructure of sounds is affected and altered, as are the accompanying noises and the supposedly central activities of sound production and propagation. All of these aspects are transformed to the extent that the overall sonic affordances are fundamentally altered. Papalexandri-Alexandri has studied these affordances – and her work presents the wide range of potential sounds that can be provided by the limitations of a flute – but also of a vocal ensemble and its vocal characteristics.

In this case, sonic affordances operate not in the macro- but in the minuscule micro-structure of sound events: the selection and shaping of sounds that this apparatus can produce, this aggregation of materials and activities, is transformed. Frequencies, overtones, and timbres are not the same as they were before this transformation, nor is the performance practice, the stage setting, or our listening experience. The affordances affected in this case, however, are primarily the affordances of a *material apparatus*.

SONIC AFFORDANCES OF A MATERIAL ACTOR

What an actor can do on any stage for the performance of sound art may seem endless. At least that is how many in the audience tend to imagine the possibilities an artist can work with. But even these possibilities are limited. The potential inclinations, desires, fears, avoidances, or inhibitions are certainly a force that enacts and perpetuates many limitations. Any group of actors, be they humans or animals, insects, groups of people, or other types of agents, never perform thoroughly identical actions. Their detailed actions vary widely and are often largely unstable, sometimes uncertain, highly volatile in their precise realization. Even if some actors perform identical tasks, and even if they rehearse performing those tasks over and over again, they never do so in exactly the same way. Differences in detail cannot be avoided or eliminated, not in a space-time continuum characterized by minute particles, detours, and serendipity at any given moment. As actors, you and I, as well as any artist, we are random and aleatoric agents in spatial arrangements that contain social assemblages and constitute linkages between apparatuses and practices.

This becomes particularly relevant when those present or passersby are to be considered as the main contributors to the work. A perfect example of this is the work of sculptor and performer Benoît Maubrey. In the summer and early fall of 2019, he worked in Berlin and built a so-called *Speakers' Arena* at Pallasstraße 5. This arena was indeed a material curve of benches in three rows, inviting to sit, but also to stand, to linger, to perform on them. These benches, their backs, and a kind of reflective backdrop actually consisted of more than 300 loudspeakers that could be used for amplification. Maubrey writes that his work is a:

"participative public sculpture made out of 320 connected loudspeakers that people can use to express themselves. The public, local artists and musicians can participate via a number of ways:

– by calling either one of two telephone numbers to express themselves for 3 minutes.

– via Bluetooth they can relay songs and messages to the sculpture.

– via direct "line in" they can connect their devices and instruments or speak directly through a microphone.

– via an "audio twitter" (to #speakersarena) their messages are automatically read out loud.

Additionally the sculpture can be used as a PA system for events, DJs, and small concerts."[10]

Sound art scholar Vadim Keylin from Aarhus, Denmark, discusses this particular work extensively – primarily in its characteristic affordances.[11] And I agree with Keylin when he states that Maubrey's works of this kind can be read as "intermedia artworks, where the creative agencies of the artist and the participants are split between the different media – sculptural and sonic."[12]

In the artist's documentation of this work, one can witness how the stage was built; how the residents were surprised, perhaps irritated at first, when it was erected on the square in front of their huge apartment buildings. But over time, a process of appropriation and domestication of this stage, with all its rather peculiar possibilities, took place. People spoke and rapped, small children sang their favorite lullabies, chart hits, or silly rhymes; groups performed, and performances with strong emotional baggage could be witnessed. Some people added color and graffiti to the speaker stage. All of these individual performances by passersby could certainly be placed outside the realm of any rigidly defined sound art aesthetic or repertoire. However, in their recombination and situated appropriateness, they alone and exclusively made this sound artwork a truly intriguing work: they actually activated the stage and explored its potential. Without their de facto contribution, this stage might have turned into one of those very ambitious, often grandiose, but mostly abandoned and empty promises of participation. Participatory art movements have seen an abundance of these abandoned open works. They are the reason why scholars have had to write mainly about the conceptual ambitions and manifestos of the artists rather than about the actual occurrences of participation. Because actual participation did not happen.

In the case of Maubrey's *Speakers' Arena*, however, the protagonists actually participated and performed. They may not always have been fully aware of their resulting function within the artwork. But this is actually not an uncommon effect of participatory artworks as such. It might even be worthwhile to consider a somewhat clear, but in other respects opaque, idea of what a participatory artwork actually results in as a general marker of these artworks: it points to the openness and generativity that these artworks allow. They are indeed *opera aperta* in the sense of Umberto Eco.

In this case, all the performers or protagonists who take the stage serve as connectors and activators, so to speak. They activate the sonic potential of this object by actively connecting the sounding parts of the object. They are the ones who make the various possibilities inherent in this sound artwork audible and tangible. They bring it to life.

The sonic affordances in this example operate in the medium range, focusing on the combination of sound contributions, the organization and timing of sound performances that actors can contribute. They are the affordances of a *material actor*.

SONIC AFFORDANCES OF A MATERIAL ACTIVITY

Anything that moves can emit sound. This is neither an aesthetic nor a theoretical statement. It is the result of the laws of physics as applied to a planet with the gravity and atmosphere that the species to which I, and presumably you, belong, has inhabited for the past 10,000 years or so. Any activity that sets things in motion on our home planet causes a sonic reaction of materials: pressure waves are created – and they reach our ears as more or less distinct sound events. This is the very material definition of sound, as documented in this famous encyclopedia entry: "sound, a mechanical disturbance from a state of equilibrium that propagates through an elastic material medium."[13]

A mechanical disturbance of this kind can be induced by a wide variety of activities. I can clap my hands,

I can whistle, I can snap or knock on wood. I can touch things, bang on them, run my fingers over them gently or hard, breathe over them or blow into them. I can jump on them, kick them, or even throw them violently away. And these are not even close to all the activities I can do to make a sound. In fact, any conceivable activity that a person, living being, or even inorganic object can perform with its material body will result in some sort of sound event.

However, the potential activities that human aliens like you and me can perform are actually limited. Our extremities can only apply a certain amount of pressure or impact to things. The speed at which one can do this is also limited. However, with a lot of training, some performers on our home planet can actually achieve incredible speed and accuracy combined with impressive dynamics and highly differentiated phrasing when they hit drums, press keys, or compress some air directly from their respiratory tract into an instrument. It seems that some of our physical limitations can be transcended into unimaginable dimensions through training, refinement, and understanding more and more about how our bodies and our instruments actually interact.

For the most part, these activities take place in rather specific places and enclosed spaces. These spaces must also provide certain acoustic qualities. So some of the most outstanding performances on this planet do not primarily take place in extremely noisy industrial sites, in inaccessible closets or caves, or in some of the coldest polar regions or hottest deserts on this planet. They do not usually take place far from other life forms, and they are not usually carried out by natural disasters or solely by swarms or herds of animals, or by automated structures after the extinction of all life on this planet. It is true, however, that all this may be quite normal in a few years, decades, or centuries – but right now it is not a common thing to observe, to do, or to participate in. Musical and sound performances on our home planet do not usually involve objects that are too gigantic or too microscopic for our fellow anthropoid life forms to handle – and our musical instruments must have at least some basic, sound-producing, moving and oscillating mechanical or electronic components.

Needless to say, by excluding all of these spatial, environmental, and chronotopic qualities, they become a rare but potential and perhaps exciting and provocative choice to perform music under precisely these circumstances. In other words, all of these extreme environmental qualities can indeed be chosen for performance. They can be explored. Perhaps they will be mastered at some future point in the cultural history of music. For now, however, they represent more of a target for some Guinness World Record attempt or some compositional and performative extremism. To be honest, I would be very happy to attend such a performance.

An example of an extreme sound performance was presented on May 24, 2021 by the artist Gwendolin Robin. In her performance *Sous les lunes de Jupiter* (2018/21),[14] Robin works with specific materials, her physical movements, a given space and floor, and surprising skills. She arranges a set of discs, rings and a set of spheres and balls in two sequences, rectangularly lined up against each other. The materials of which these moving objects are made are stone and glass, steel or lead, wood or any other amalgamation of substances. In her actual performance, she rolls and pushes, catches and energizes this set of spheres and discs, one after the other. The performance can seem like a kind of children's game, but with rather unclear rules and a completely open set of activities. Robin moves and steps quickly across the room, starting a sphere here, slowing down another ring, accelerating another sphere, catching another before it bounces off the wall, setting another ring in motion, walking quickly across the room to catch yet another sphere, and so on.

Her movements are precise: a dance and a catch within a new, still undiscovered ballgame of mainly aesthetic and sonic character. This ballgame emphasizes the peculiar material qualities of the place, the climate and the audience present, the alertness and the mood of the performer. The performer becomes a medium for analyzing this situation, materially through her truly unique ballgame – and as an audience member, I can partake in and learn from her performative investigation.

Robin performs an improvisation that responds to the affordances of a floor's materials, the humidity, heat or pressure present, the attention of an audience focused on her, and the unstable and fleeting motions, detours, stops or speeds of her balls and discs. It is a universe that she sets in motion: the rings of Saturn, glass discs or oxidizing rings flying in space; massive, metallic globes rolling sluggishly, while smaller marbles or balls quickly cross the entire performance space. She dances with walls and floors, discs and spheres, focused attention and excitement. Only rarely does a ball crash against a glass ring and even break it: a myriad of particles suddenly traverse the entire floor.

In the case of these activities, what we see and hear are primarily their relational effects. We experience how the artist connects certain sounds and sonic affordances.

Sonic affordances in this case therefore operate in the relation between particular affordances. They refer to potential transformations and formants inherent in the given situation, the objects or apparatuses used, and the performers. They are the affordances of *material activity*.

WHAT ARE THE AFFORDANCES OF SOUND?

Sound is an intervention. It intervenes as such in the given material environment. It does this by setting existing materials in motion. Their activation produces audible pressure waves. The triggering activities are therefore not abstract. They do not take place independently of the material substances, designed forms or other situated aspects that are present: sound practices and their resulting sound events are strictly relational to the situation in which they take place and to the affordances that make them possible. Four main areas of affordances can be observed in sound performances. Following the artistic examples discussed here, I propose to describe them as follows:

(a) the situation: sonic affordances operate here within a macro-structure of affordances. A situation and its material, spatial circumstances serve as the very first amplifier of any sounds that occur, as well as the provider of a basic repertoire of sounds that a performance might wish to employ.

(b) the apparatus: sonic affordances here affect the micro-structure of affordances. Material tools, machines, and objects serve as intrinsic generators and selectors of sounds that might be articulated within a given material situation.

(c) the actor: sonic affordances operate here in the medium range of affordances. They affect the combinations of sounds and the way they are organized when certain actors, themselves characterized by a range of possibilities and limitations, intervene as a disturbance to their current mechanical equilibrium.

(d) the activity: here a sonic affordance is linked to the particular relation between affordances and the mutual transformations and formants of sounds. These activities usually represent the main and decisive force in a sound performance, since they actually cause some material movement and thereby activate the relations between these constituents.

These four categories of situation, apparatus, actor, and activity, as well as their particular affordances, make it possible to reflect on the potential and artistic challenges, achievements, and particular practices involved in a sound performance or sound artwork. Any given artwork or performance alters one or more of these categories within a framework of materials, actors, their tools and actions. Taken as a basic overview, they are obviously not complete. To sound artists and sound art scholars, however, they offer a matrix for reflection, critique, and further work in exploring, expanding, and excavating what sounds might need, what we might give them – or what we might not be able to give them at all. Or could we?

BIBLIOGRAPHY:

Richard E. Berg, "sound", in: Encyclopedia Britannica, May 11, 2023. Online: https://www.britannica.com/science/sound-physics.

James Jerome Gibson, The Ecological Approach to Visual Perception, London: Routledge 1979.

Sanne Krogh Groth and Stefan Östersjö, "Sonic Argumentation I – Editorial", in: Seismograf (2019). Online: https://seismograf.org/fokus/sonic-argumentation-i

Vadim Keylin, Materialities and Socialities of Participation in Sound Art, PhD Dissertation Aarhus University 2020.

Annea Lockwood, A Sound Map of the Danube, New York: Lovely Music, Ltd. 2008. Online: https://www.youtube.com/watch?v=PuLzv53gM_0

Annea Lockwood, "Working in the Sounding Field", in: Sanne Krogh Groth and Holger Schulze (eds.), The Bloomsbury Handbook of Sound Art, New York: Bloomsbury Academic 2020, 260-266.

Jessica Lynne, "Reading the Numbers of Stop-and-Frisk", in: Hyperallergic, Brooklyn: Hyperallergic Media Inc., September 15, 2015. Online: https://hyperallergic.com/237694/reading-the-numbers-of-stop-and-frisk/.

Carla J. Maier and Marianthi Papalexandri-Alexandri, "Membrane: Materialities and Intensities of Sound", in: Sanne Krogh Groth and Holger Schulze (eds.), The Bloomsbury Handbook of Sound Art, New York: Bloomsbury Academic 2020, 447-457.

Carla J. Maier and Holger Schulze, "The Tacit Grooves of Sound Art. Aesthetic Artefacts as Analogue Archives", in: SoundEffects – An Interdisciplinary Journal of Sound and Sound Experience, Vol. 7 (2017), No. 3, 20-35.

Benoît Maubrey, Speakers' Arena (2019), Berlin: Pallasseum July 1 to November 2019. Online: https://benoitmaubrey.com/arena-berlin/

Donald Norman, The Design of Everyday Things: Revised and Expanded Edition, New York: Basic Books 2013.

Mendi + Keith Obadike, Numbers Station (furtive movements) (2015). New York: Ryan Lee Gallery September 9, 2015. Online: https://www.youtube.com/watch?v=PuLzv53gM_0

Marianthi Papalexandri-Alexandri and Neue Vocalsolisten, Untitled VI für drei Männerstimmen und Klangobjekte (2013/14) Stuttgart: Theaterhaus Stuttgart February 9, 2014. Online: https://www.youtube.com/watch?v=H9vuEFftqyg

Gwendolyn Robin, Sous les lunes de Jupiter (2018/21) in: READY MAKING #03 – on the object-based know-how and auditory knowledge in sound performances, (concept: Janine Eisenächer & Steffi Weismann), Berlin: Flutgraben e.V. May 24, 2021. Online: https://www.facebook.com/errantsound/videos/402986127365380

Holger Schulze, Sound Works. A Cultural Theory of Sound Design, New York: Bloomsbury Academic 2019.

Naomi Waltham-Smith, Shattering Biopolitics: Militant Listening and the Sound of Life, New York: Fordham University Press 2021.

Soyoung Yoon, "Do a Number: The Facticity of the Voice, or Reading Stop-and-Frisk Data", in: Discourse Vol. 39, No. 3, Documentary Audibilities (Fall 2017), 397–424.

NOTES:

1 Obadike 2015, Lynne 2015, Yoon 2017, Schulze 2019, 185f., Waltham-Smith 2021, 38-48.

2 Groth and Östersjö 2019.

3 Gibson 1979, 127.

4 Norman 2013, 9.

5 Maier & Schulze 2017, 23.

6 Lockwood 2008, booklet.

7 Lockwood 2020, 262.

8 Papalexandri-Alexandri 2014. https://www.youtube.com/watch?v=H9vuEftqyg

9 Maier & Papalexandri-Alexandri 2020, 448.

10 Maubrey 2019.

11 Keylin 2020.

12 Keylin 2020, 162.

13 Berg 2023.

14 Robin 2021.

JEREMY WOODRUFF

Community Worlding as Social Composition

URBAN GARDENING SOUND ART PROJECTS 2012 – 2022

INTRODUCTION: SPECULATIVE FORMS OF LISTENING IN GARDEN SOUNDSCAPES

In a series of sound art works, I investigated sonic and musical perceptions in a group of gardeners' and musicians' lives, in relation to the garden soundscape and how food is grown there in Pittsburgh, Copenhagen, Berlin, and Bangalore. My sound art works were more focused on process, while I thought of the installations themselves as rather secondary, or as remnants perhaps, of that research, rather than results. The work has consisted of talking to gardeners and getting them in touch with musicians, thereby opening possibilities of collaboration for a combined practice of listening, recording, music making and gardening. The idea of financing the gardening efforts through music was suggested via the value of the artwork, whether this was offered in return for donations on the internet, or through the work's value in an exhibition, as commercial objects, or as good publicity for the garden. More importantly, however, the works provided the opportunity for me to consider how aesthetic processes of listening might both compliment, and feed off, local ecologically minded garden projects; I speculated thereby how sound and listening might best be adapted to, and embedded within, global food systems to possibly transform reception and tastes. I have conceived of these collaborative projects as proofs of concept in this regard. Below I describe the questions raised by the artworks which were only partly answered, but which suggested how one could best follow up this research with future projects of this kind. This way of working artistically is one example of a process I have come to call *composing sociality* (Woodruff 2020).

Sound art scholarship demonstrates the indispensable value of writing subjectively to understand complicated social processes in relation to the environment. Voegelin (2014: 21) states, "the artist listens to and produces the possibility of the landscape from the possibility of time and the possibility of space, hinting at the plurality of reality and challenging the singular actuality it is presented as. The invisible mobility of sound informs and incites this exploration and invites the listener to … participate in its reconstruction." Similarly, Schulze (2020), advocating the theories of Goodman (2009) and Eshun (1998), utilizes the approach of what he calls "sonic fiction." To zoom in on symbioses between garden and sound, I appropriate LaBelle's (2010) strategy of "micro-epistemologies" in my artwork's rhetorical stance: I use experiential metaphor via episodic variations relating other experiences to the theme of gardens to demonstrate effects of sound's radical political polyvalence. Altogether these writers led me to consider the textual element to the sound art (such as this piece of writing itself) as a crucial part of the artworks. Finally, I've been inspired by the concept of solving "wicked problems," from the field of co-creational design, to understand the connection between sound, sociality, and the environment (Buchanan 1992: 5).

In both public and private life, music clearly plays a role in generating the momentum that directs and helps accumulate agricultural forms of energy. One reason for this is that music has always been regarded as a means of caring for the human soul. And music has also always played a role in mitigating the distribution of wealth through political influence. Tia DeNora (2015) has recently explored the theme of "asylum" as overarching metaphor for music. She points out that music can be a marker in various degrees between public and private space and maps these zones onto various concepts of wellness and illness. She shows how music itself becomes a way to creating and preserving wellness by being a form of shelter and a buffer against psychological pain and social alienation. All the foregoing authors show how music is a form of nourishment, a parallel food for the inner self. Finally, however, music has of course also been literally manifested in multiple ways as a motivating force during planting work, in folk song, musically coordinated forms of movement during work, etc. Allen S. Weiss writes, "Gardens constitute a primal *Gesamtkunstwerk*, the site of all sites, the ground of all the arts, the unstated nexus of heterogeneity in the system of fine arts, the source of synaesthesia, the analogue of all correspondences" (Weiss 2008: 12). With such thoughts continually in the background as an underpinning to the research, I sought to tap into the energy of these connections in my artwork.

SOCIAL TONALITY

Using in-situ sonic documentation, interviews, and music, I considered how what I call *social tonality* (2014) in garden-sound relates to garden participation; and I considered how the introduction of aesthetic listening practices to food production organization might provide more resilient counter-capitalistic frameworks by functioning as a kind of workshare. Is it possible to convert urban gardens into spaces of sonic performance? Is it possible to embed sonic art in ecological gardening and local food structures? Does engaging in this way raise awareness on the part of both musicians and gardeners and create the possibility of relationships that could be of help to foster autonomous communities including them both? Having formulated the concept of social composition, I speculate that by activating the foregoing questions in social scenarios involving group listening, speculating new places for music to exist in the everyday life of gardeners and by following up on community activities that focus on these propositions, a group artwork arises that may address the needs of a larger collectivity.

A profusion of literature on ecological art such as Lucy Lippard's *Undermining: A Wild Ride Through Land Use, Politics, and Art in the Changing West* (2014) or Sue Spaid's *Green Acres: Artists Farming Fields, Greenhouses and Abandoned Lots* (2012) for example, have described how movements such as earth art and urban gardening art focus important issues in the context of ongoing environmental struggles of various communities. More research has emerged focusing purely on ecological sound art (see Bianchi 2016, Gilmurray 2017 and Solomos 2023). But no scholars or artists I know have of yet directly, systematically, and exclusively analyzed aesthetic qualities and strategies which are inherent to the working communities concerned with bettering the natural ecology in and of themselves, rather than turning only to what artists external to these communities have (symbolically) added or accomplished for environmental change by temporarily creating a self-contained work. The social cohesion of a group of workers in urban gardens functions not only through communication, negotiation, workshare, and task-distribution but also, quite importantly, through aesthetic contemplation and creativity. Sound plays quite an important role here.

My artistic research with communities of eco-organizers and urban gardeners seeks to provide evidence for the efficacy of a range of community listening and sound practices that have successfully emerged from their own group dynamics. This artistic difference is at the crux of the group process I call social composition.

SONIC PERMACULTURE

In my previous artworks permaculture principles were key in thinking how to connect my sound art practice to ecology. Permaculture deals with examining our environment in order to evaluate how to design self-maintaining and self-regulating systems for energy descent: a future in which local systems reach near, or total self-sustainable energy efficiency by taking advantage of natural ecology. I asked myself, how could music and sound art align itself to permaculture's principles in order to help enable such a societal transition? In order to derive these "sonic permaculture principles" for sound studies and music theory I have, in a previous article, interrogated the permaculture founder's own idealized concept of nature and the arts in indigenous societies with reference to recent ethnomusicology scholarship (2014a). With this preparation I proceed to further ask in following sound art works as a preparation to interviews and recordings, how exactly in practice does sound and music connect to essential concepts in permaculture such as "energy," "yield" and "waste" (Mollison and Holmgren 1978, Holmgren 2002)? To answer these questions, I used three methodologies applied to field research conducted together with urban gardeners in my artworks: firstly, I investigated and (re)imagined sonic and musical symbioses between gardener's urban lives and the garden, and between cultural issues and that landscape's requirements for yield in particular cities. Secondly, I considered modes of sonic "performance" in the everyday that emerge from aspects of the garden's functioning in its urban environment. My theory of social tonality (2014b) provided a structure with which to relate the second methodology above to the first, using music theoretical concepts. Thirdly, given this theory, I considered what would be necessary to convert the gardens productively into better spaces for sonic performance in the specific constraints of their urban situation.

Permaculture was developed in the late 1970s, and its founding concepts tend to mirror certain prevalent essentialisms of the time. Like many ethnomusicologists then, such as John Blacking and Mantle Hood, Mollison (1978) projected his perceptions of the utopian nature of societies of indigenous cultures onto qualities of their music and arts. Also, like R. Murray Schafer, the innovator of acoustic ecology and the term "soundscape" (1977), Mollison had an almost messianic fixation on an idyll of the natural, in contrast to the urban, environment. More recent writing on sound art and sound studies has taken a critical distance to Schafer's approach, in for example, LaBelle (2010), Schulze (2013) and others. Musicologists have likewise distanced themselves from creating over-simplified dichotomies between the West and "the Other," tending rather to adopt a rhizomatic hearing of musical influence, as in Steingo (2016) and Sakakeeny (2013). Although conceptual frameworks have become more sophisticated since the inception of these fields, it's impossible to deny that the arts are indeed deeply connected to patterns of the natural environment and that in many cases indigenous arts are closer to it; in recording a garden soundscape perhaps, this connection to the indigenous arts is particularly imminent.

Invited guests giving instruction or workshops were never amplified in the garden, electronic sounds are generally unwelcome despite the presence of a bar or kitchen, musical guests come more from folk, traditional or "shamanistic" musical genres – one can hear the sound of how permaculture communities identify with the "other"
in the aesthetic sounds they make; the idyll of nature still has a powerful and tenacious influence in an urban garden, so although on an intellectual level as academics or activists we may not fail to recognize the fallacy of the human/nature dichotomy, the belief of the myth of the "purity" of nature and of the "non-Western" still exerts influence in sounds we can't ignore. Instead of negating or denying the continued active influence of these essentialisms, we can use inherent contradictions in them as a source of productive and provocative artistic tensions that also deconstruct and challenge them.

The core ethics of permaculture: "care for the earth, care for people, and respecting the limits of nature on production and fair distribution of surplus" (Mollison 1988: 2, Holmgren 2002: 1) imply a connectedness between natural and human agency to which musicology and sound studies have increasingly awakened. The patriarchal implication that only humans have agency, a founding bias of ethnomusicology and acoustic ecology, is of late receding from writing on music and sound generally. The prioritization of considering earth as a system first, before engaging human priorities, like in the plant philosophy of Marder (2013), for example, is also at the heart of recent new materialist perspectives on sound like from Douglas Kahn (2013) and Steven Goodman (2009). It is also evidenced in writers on music, like in the field of eco-musicology.[1]

Permaculture's main ethics statement similarly suggests we become attentive first to climate, living matter, soil content, etc., before human needs, since our continued existence depends on these factors; and if we heed this message, our listening potentials change accordingly. The sonic is a material force acting not only through the agency of humans in food production but also through the agency of elements: atmospheres, water bodies, soil nutrients, etc. New materialist perspectives suggest that the very meaning of ecological sustainability is variable, not only from one culture to the other at the base level of economic, social, and ethical assumptions, but also at different levels of non-human priorities, i.e., even listening itself need not be from only an anthropocentric perspective. For example, recent research shows that many flowers pollenate much faster upon sensing the vibrations of a bee's wings: flowers then have then been recognized as one kind of hearing mechanism of plants.[2]

Holmgren (2013: 6) states, "permaculture principles are brief statements or slogans which can be remembered as a checklist when considering the inevitably complex stations of an artistic process .. All elements in a system have 'needs,' 'products' and 'behaviors.'" As such it should partly only be a matter of logical deduction and partly a matter of creative synthesis to work out how music and sound art help Holmgren and Mollison's permaculture principals function better in a garden. Appadurai (2013) points out that the same cultural flows can both hamper and help their own freedom of movement across boundaries. How music and sound production influences nurture for the earth, production of food, shelter, wellness, and responsibility in relation to a surplus, is in fact not a straightforward question. Even Holmgren realizes that the attempt to develop "more appropriate governance, economy and culture, including art and myth" with permaculture principles "may be too big a leap" but that "it is possible to at least use them for evaluating the diverse cultural phenomena we find ourselves in" (Holmgren 2002: 47). In the same spirit, I did not wish to recreate sound studies or musicology from the bottom up using permaculture principles, but instead to use permaculture as leverage for the sonic imagination based on new ethical perspectives. Rather than creating inflexible epistemic categories with which to coordinate agricultural and sonic/musical vocabulary therefore, I started by fishing with a large net for broad intersections of sound, music and ecology, and then to refine the results through an analysis of the field research.

As far as "energy decent" is concerned in any case, one intersection is obvious: following the primary permaculture ethics would mean that we should calibrate our artistic work less towards "productivity" (however that might be defined in terms of artistic output, finances, science or social status) and more towards care; it would mean to transcend exerting "control" and focus more on facilitation, to be concerned not only with virtuosity, but virtuosic cooperation. The framework of composing sociality, wherein a sound work becomes part of the larger authorless collective work, follows directly from this recognition. As Uri Gordon writes of permaculture in the context of capitalism,

> "care for the land and the people," transposed into broader cultural terms, would involve facilitating that self-development of the plant or the person, the garden or the community, each according to its own context — working with, rather than against, the organic momentum of the entity cared for. Whereas in monoculture (or industry, or existing social relations) what is sought after is the opposite — maximal control and harnessing of natural processes and labour power (Gordon 2008: 137).

One intense appeal of the permaculture courses which have helped it proliferate around the world is that the foundational writings of permaculture farming (Mollison and Slay, Holmes), as well as the foundational texts of sustainable agriculture itself (e.g. Fukuoka, Russell and Albrecht), require exegesis with the sensual experience of a specific garden, as Holmes says, "the landscape is the textbook" (Holmgren 2002: 16). Only by being in one garden, by seeing, smelling, and hearing a particular place, its people, its natural materials and its plants, while the local gardener "performs" the telling of her experience, can other gardeners learn what to do and how to tend the land there. This sensorial difference is the same as any experience of learning through hearing and aurality vs. reading the written word: experiencing the sonic territory oneself rather than only speculating about it is how we learn through sound. In this way not only does the landscape "become the textbook," but also becomes a teacher, a map and a way of existing in the world.

Gardens were a very fruitful place to investigate the interplay of the three categories of sonic perception whose interaction are key to the theory of social tonality: ambient, musical and linguistic sound, while also experimenting with co-creation, gift economies and other concepts. Although I made some progress ethnographically, artistically and theoretically, I consider my series of sound artworks, compositions focused on urban gardens and transition design (Irwin et al 2015) in one way or another, just tests; lacking the time and funding required for extensive social composition to take place, they generally lasted, at most, only a couple days. As such I accepted certain limitations, but these pieces helped me formulate a way of working which has potentials to be taken further in longer-term projects.

GARDEN WORKS: 2012 – 2017

In my piece, *Sonic Permaculture: Resonances of the Urban Garden* which premiered at the Errant Sound Project Space in Berlin in winter 2017, as part of the series "In the Sound Field: Perspectives on Field Recording – Installations and Performances," composer Andrew Noble played outside on the sidewalk in the sun as "Performance for Action" for friends from social activist groups, including members of "Break the Silence" Initiative in Gedenken Oury Jalloh e.V.[3] Meanwhile, inside the project space, Noble's voice and ukulele was mixed with field recordings of the urban garden Himmelbeet e.V. and processed with electronics by composer Keith O'Brien and dispersed through the room in four channels. The social composition is multiple kinds of event simultaneously: solidarity concert, garden work and sound artwork. If extended over a longer period (the installation was up for only one day) other interesting formations between

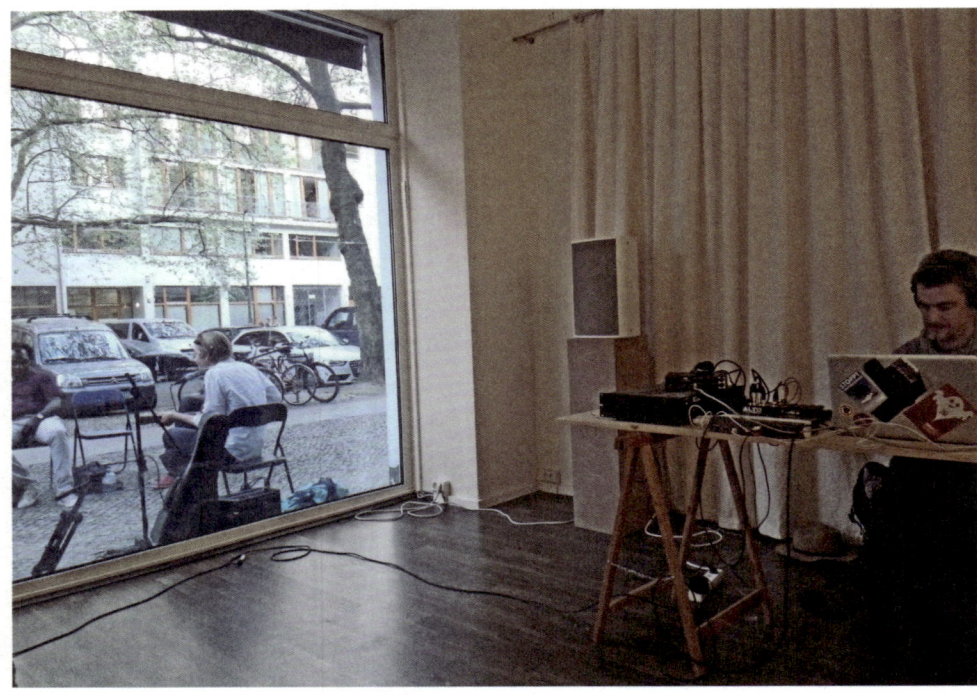

↙ : Sonic Permaculture: Resonances of the Urban Garden, Errant Sound, Berlin, 2017

CALLING ALL PEFORMERS!

who we are:
We are all those who wish to use our skills as artistic performers to constructively engage with and participate in struggles for social justice. We could be you.

what we do:
Performance for Action is a decentralized campaign, where performing artists (musicians, actors, performance artists, authors, poets, dancers, artists, etc.) conduct street-performances in order to raise money for legal fees and repression costs for political, human rights, and social-justice activists.

where we do what we do:
We recognize that many of us depend on street-performance as their sole or primary means of subsistence. As such, we do not wish to in any way infringe on anyone's ability to do so. Further, as members of a cultural industry, we believe in taking social struggles to the institutions where we might often be given a voice. For these reasons, we have chosen to perform in front of institutions where cultural performances usually take place "officially" (theatres, concert houses, gallery openings, academic institutions, etc.). Thereby aiming our performances as calls for solidarity directly at cultural consumers as well as at the cultural institutions themselves.

when we do what we do:
Any one of us performs whatever we have to perform any time where and when a high profile institutional cultural event is happening, typically directly before or after as an audience is arriving or leaving the event.

why we are doing what we are doing:
We believe strongly in the role that activists and organizers play in fighting for a better world for all of us, and believe that we can show our solidarity on the one hand, while also actively participating in social struggles by using our skills and perspectives as performers on the other.

how does it work:
Do you perform, professionally or as an amateur? [Use this form, or go to [website] to print out a copy of this short statement and a copy of the logo (or get creative and make your own),] go and perform what you have to perform in front of (for example) a theatre an hour before the performance begins as the audience is arriving (or after as the audience leaves). Transfer the money people donate to [account]. We are in contact with a broad network of activists and their lawyers and ensure that the money goes where it is needed. For our launch event in the Club Transmediale Vorspiel, the money will go to the Initiative in Gedenken an Oury Jalloh e.V. It doesn't matter what you perform, or how much you receive. What matters is that we work together.
(Performance for Action 2017)

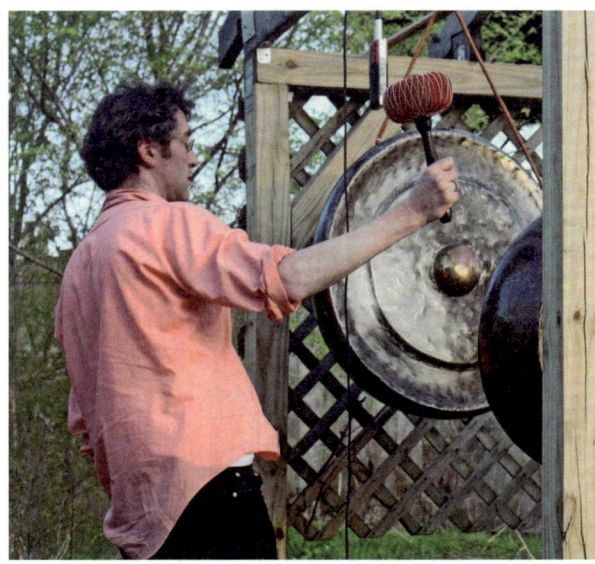

←: Gongburgh: Steeltown Forests, Hazelwood Food Forest, Pittsburgh, 2012

these social systems (sound arts space, activist groups and community garden) could be developed.

Similarly, in my piece *Gongburgh: Steeltown Forests* (2012) I experienced that my simple act of bringing two *gongs*, a *saron* and a *suling* from the University of Pittsburgh gamelan to the site of the Hazelwood Food Forest (a Pittsburgh Permaculture urban gardening project) one day, it gave the organizer a way of activating volunteer work from more members of the garden for a longer time than usually was possible. By being present, playing music on the instruments, and recording it in combination with the garden and the social life of the gardeners, new possibilities and energy were initiated in the space. A different mood than was usually present was created and a larger amount of energy and inspiration was created in comparison to the amount of energy needed to simply bring the instruments there. Often traditional design, not only of systems, but of structures make a big impact on social composition. My act of similarly transforming the Forest sign into a stand for the gongs had a similar effect.

By interacting with and recording the University of Pittsburgh gamelan in the Hazelwood Food Forest and combining it with sounds of interviews, a gamelan blacksmith, a current steel plant in Warren, PA, and a recording of steel factories of the old "iron city" of Pittsburgh, various imaginary economies were speculatively projected through sound (as the steel production, urban gardening, social life, gamelan production and music making transmuted and permuted in various combinations). A full version of the composition is offered on the internet in return for donations to the Hazelwood Food Forest. The principles of permaculture horticultural practices were used as a metaphoric template for the process of composition in this piece to explore social composition. The availability of the piece through social networks created a site for additional community contributions which earned the garden some hundreds of dollars towards materials for a gate and planting materials.[4] To expand the imagination of the musical/social possibilities around a garden, in my piece *Phonosynthesis* (2014) I played five children a recorded soundscape of

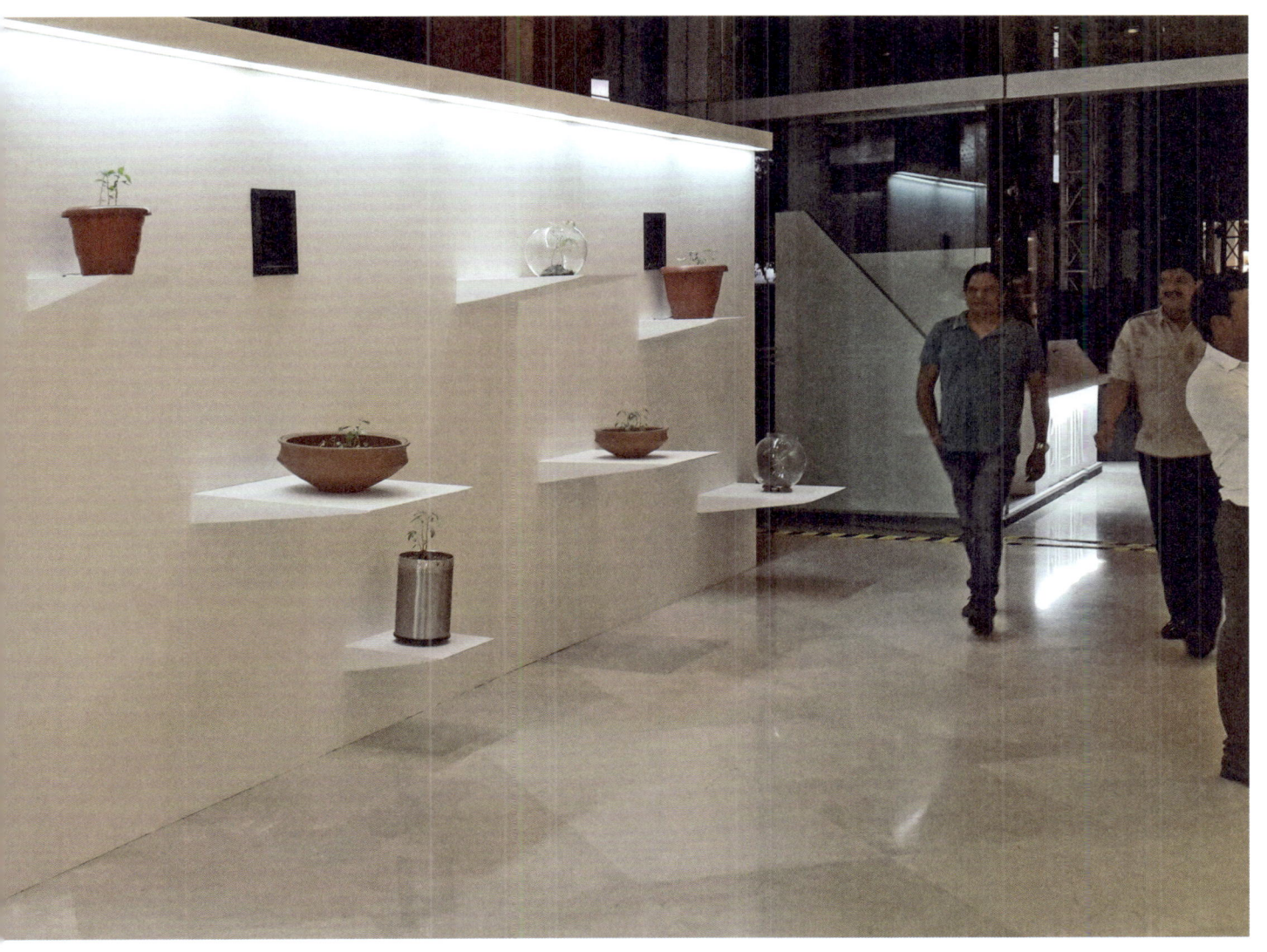

↑: Playing in the New Organic Terrace Garden of the UB City Mall, Bangalore, India 2015

an area in Dahlem, Berlin, where Permakultur & Terra Preta were planning a project garden during their piano lessons. The children were then asked to improvise fitting music for the soundscape that they just heard, and their improvisations were recorded. I encouraged the gallery visitor to play the transcriptions of the children's pieces on a toy piano for the five plants to hear. These five herb plants were then planted in the new permaculture garden planned on the site where the original soundscape was recorded. The sale of the recordings went to help the new garden project buy seeds and supplies. Inspired by the permaculture gardening principle of "observation and interaction" with the natural environment, this piece explores the circulation from the soundscape of urban gardens in Berlin, through the imagination of local piano students, to the participant in the gallery and back.

Phonosynthesis features a "do nothing" approach to music composition. Different from John Cage's non-intentionality, "do nothing" composition is inspired by

Masanobu Fukuoka's (1978) "do nothing" farming. Fukuoka's lifelong agricultural accomplishments and writings were a major influence on the development of permaculture in the 70s by Bill Mollison and David Holmgren. By a farmer "doing nothing," plants were allowed to live, and thrive organically. I hoped through plant life's ability to absorb vibrations of sound that are behind, beyond or underneath hearing, or in which hearing may merely be a sort of residue, the process of permaculture urban gardening and the children's musical experience would both be enhanced and enriched in the "energy cycling" (another permaculture principle) of music's sociality. By simply setting up a scenario in the gallery for others to play music based on transcriptions which were originally recorded by children, I didn't have to actively compose anything for the music to come about (hence a "do nothing" composition). The music arose organically out of the pedagogical / exhibition scenario.

While I was living in India in 2014–15 I had an opportunity to further my work focused on heightening ecological awareness through social connections conjectured with music. In my installation in the Art Bangaluru, contemporary art festival in Bangalore, India, *Playing in the New Organic Terrace Garden of UB City Mall* (2015), I brought Joshua Samuel, a student and talented cellist to meet Dr. B N Viswanath, who founded an Organic Terrace Garden initiative in Bangalore.[5] The sound material for the artwork is a compilation of discussions and music that were recorded on this date at Dr. B N Viswanath's roof garden in a neighborhood of Bangalore. The sound of the installation was channeled not only through speakers but also via transducers placed on flowerpots of different materials to use them as sound conducing objects. The plants that were seen in the installation were subsequently donated to businesses in UB City Mall roof terrace (the mall was the site of Art Bangaluru) for them to take care of and hopefully start their own roof terrace food garden. Hopefully the irony was not completely lost on everyone. On certain evenings Joshua came and accompanied the installation live on cello.

To explore the possibilities for a community to come together more through a sound art documentary process and installation, I initiated *Green Interactive Biofeedback Environments – GIBE* (2015) which took place at "UrbanplanTen," an urban garden project at Copenhagen's Urbanplanen social housing area. Members of the urban garden project were encouraged to donate music collections from worn out media they had. In this way a "sound compost" was created for the

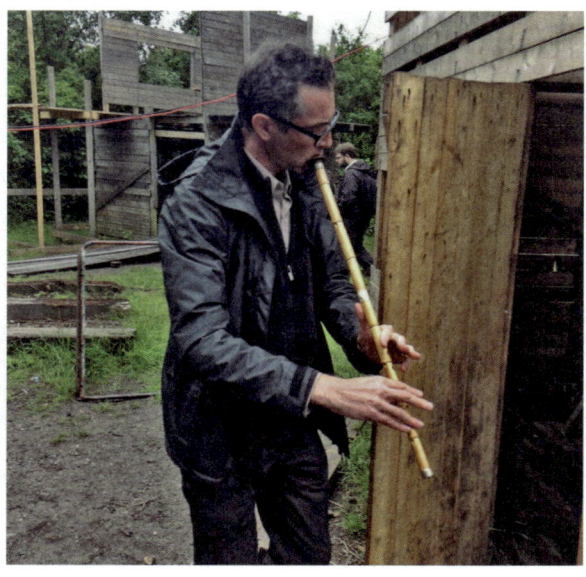

↗: Green Interactive Biofeedback Environments – GIBE, UrbanplanTen, Copenhagen, 2015

→: Sonnenbeet Gemeinschaftsgarten at Haus der Statistik, Berlin, 2020 project while I also interviewed them about the personal meaning of these recordings and their experiences regarding the garden's effects on community life. Added to the sound compost were field recordings that we collaboratively carried out. While the members cope with socioeconomic disadvantage and cultural differences, the group imagination of urban sound as a communal project suggested that listening could be made into a highly effective tool for the social survival of the garden. During the work, Danish and Turkish resident gardeners talked about how they had bonded over different musical, as well as culinary, aesthetics enjoyed in their homes during a chilli tasting session. The artwork provided a useful and welcome framing to reflect on this positive experience with their neighbors. The sound compost became a rich source of shared material that, if the project had continued, could have perhaps become a means of finance and investment on various levels of interaction with the garden, through crowdfunding and activities that took place on site. An open-air sound installation at the garden completed the artwork and allowed the participants in the work to come together, also with their children, and hear the community in a different way, including the remixed sound compost, garden soundscape and interviews. A resulting album of audio tracks is also available online.[6]

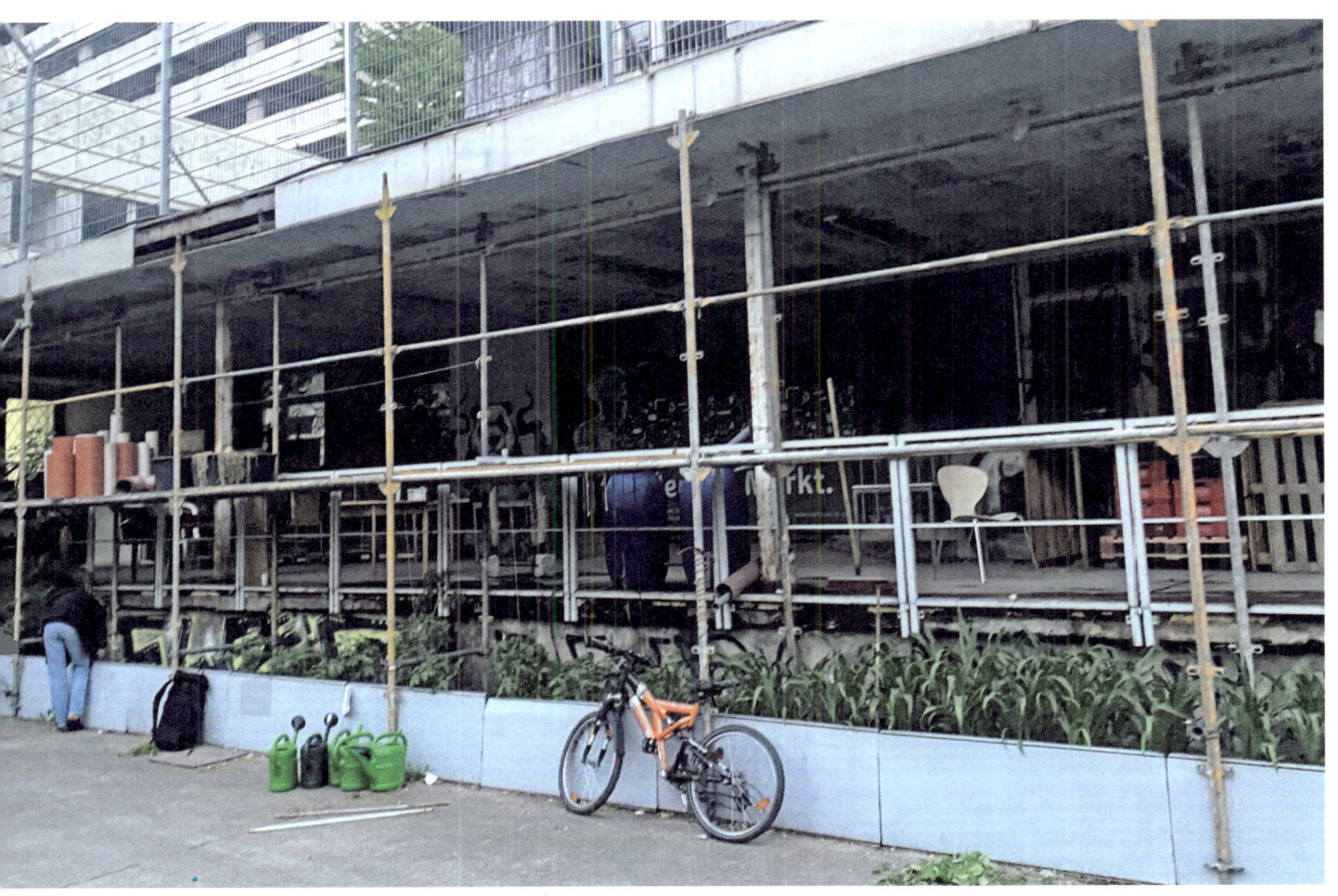

KLANGKOMPOST ON CELLPHONES: FURTHER GARDEN WORKS 2020-2022

After a hiatus of a couple years, I returned to the topic of urban gardens in 2020 by visiting several gardens in Berlin and recording or performing music in them myself, sometimes with other musicians and/or with the addition of the "Klangkompost" cellphone choir. During the pandemic, outdoor performances took on a new meaning and dynamic. From 2020–21 I visited and did research at the Berlin urban gardens Peace of Land,[7] Himmelbeet,[8] Sonnenbeet at Haus der Statistik[9] and a roof terrace garden at Kunsthaus Acud. By 2021 because of urban development of different kinds, all these garden collectives had to leave their original plots. At the time of this writing, both Sonnenbeet and Peace of Land still have not yet obtained a new permanent home.

My instrumental improvisations (on baritone saxophone, kaval and South Indian flute) at the sites of the gardens were an attempt at "accompanying" the soundscape of the gardens: wind, talking, traffic, birds, distant sounds were all echoed or enhanced in some way by our playing. At Peace of Land I recorded myself and cellist Guilherme Rodrigues as we listened, playing "as the garden" in this way. In one initial visit to Himmelbeet violinist Elo Masing and I made a recording of ourselves in the urban garden soundscape. On our next visit there we brought more musicians: we were joined by Ingólfur Vilhjálmsson on bass clarinet and Caroline Tallone on electro-acoustic hurdy-gurdy. On this occasion we were also accompanied by a small choir of people playing back quiet sounds on their cell phones to add a "layer of myth" to the soundscape. The cloud of sound generated by a choir of cellphones interestingly has a soft and supple sound in contrast to the potentially annoying sound of a single micro-speaker. I call this a layer of myth, because this cloud of cellphone sound is sometimes indistinguishable from the other sounds of the acoustic aural environment at the gardens and creates an uncertainty between fact and fiction on the site. The tiny digital sounds are also hard to locate. I supplied a playlist of both atmospheric and musical sounds for the cellphone choir to play, and all were encouraged to add to the playlist from their own collections or home recordings of gardens to form a "sound compost." Lastly, cellist Ulrike Brand and I also recorded at a since temporarily defunct roof terrace garden atop the entrance of Kunsthaus Acud in Berlin-Mitte.

At a show in October 2021 at Errant Sound (entitled "Sounds of Endangered Urban Gardens and Sound Compost Preludes"[10]) artifacts documenting the events were exhibited as two main pieces. In the first, cellphones playing both the soundscape with our live music and files from the sound compost were installed, positioned in a ring around the perimeter of the room as a 12-channel surround installation. The cellphones were slightly amplified through the resonant acoustic effect accomplished by placing them in small flowerpots as stands. This simulation created a demonstration of the effect, or partial reenactment of the work of the audience on site at the garden soundscape in those events. Secondly, in the separate but attached entry section of the Errant Sound space, a documentary video of the event with the larger group of musicians playing at Himmelbeet was shown with the sound on headphones. In this way the video of the Himmelbeet event purposefully collided with the cellphone choir sound in the room.

December 2022, the works were presented again at Errant Sound in the framework of "Anima Mundi 2."[11] The collaboration started between Miejski Ośrodek Sztuki (MOS) in Gorzów Wielkopolski and Errant Sound in Berlin, including Liebig 12 as cooperation partner. Curators Janine Eisenächer and Bartosz Nowak decided to include the work as it related to environmental questions and ecologies of listening in urban situations which were central to the exhibition. Invariably

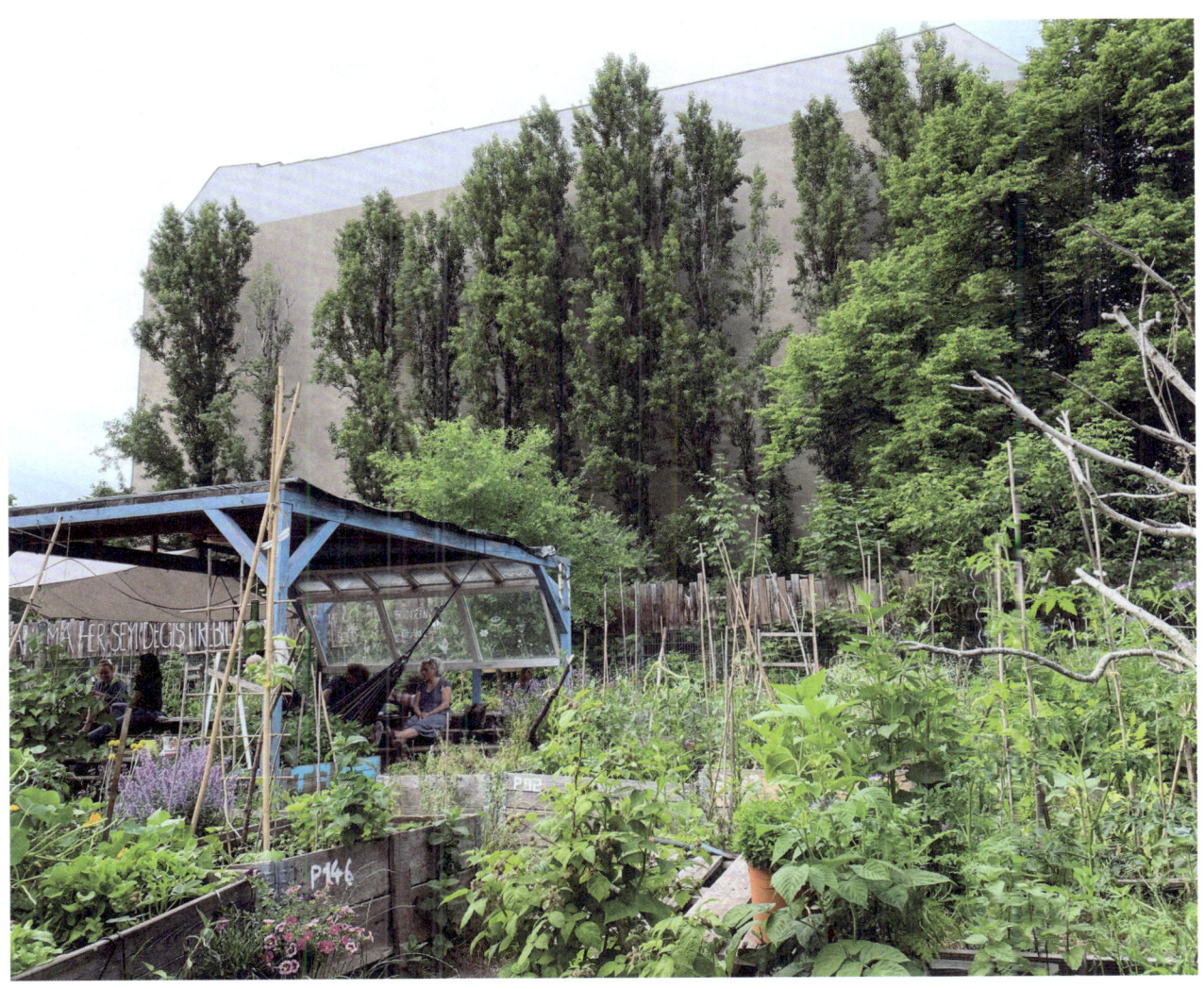

↗: Himmelbeet e.V. Gemeinschaftsgarten, 2021

the Berlin garden collectives were welcoming and curious. The door is open to further collaboration. It became clear that the potential for sound work in urban gardens in Berlin is very great, and openness for the effort is universal. These short, experimental events in at-risk gardening communities may have planted a seed of more communal sound work to come. Or perhaps at least leant a higher awareness for some of their members of how their oases of plant life in the middle of the busy city harbor not only the potential for food, but also sonic nourishment.

SOCIAL COMPOSITION

The soil of a specific geological area is often given a heightened significance by the people who identify with it as "their nation." The land's soil in some instances is even considered sacrosanct in this respect. A community can bond with a garden in a similar way, one which even contends with their loyalty to other identities, making a garden a special, autonomous kind of territory where barriers of cultural difference can be overcome. Different individuals, groups, peoples and nations tend the land differently, and plant different crops. The way that they plant and harvest have differing rituals associated with them. Their poetry and music assign the land, gardens and food different metaphors for differing affects. All of this can come into play during the planting of a garden and the attention given to the experience of it.

Music and an artistic awareness of urban sound may have the power to transform spaces into sites of communal ritual, but can a site for used for communal gardening be transformed into a venue for the public appreciation of art? I asked the gardeners how feasible they think it would be to have invited music performances and sound interventions at their sites, and if so, who they would ask. I also asked them how they think the recordings that they themselves might have been making of the garden and of the city might feature in these possible concerts as well. These inquiries gave the works a self-reflective aspect informed by the communities who were central to them. Answers varied, and many gardeners were skeptical of the idea. Creating a space for sound art or music entails other (often unpaid) labor and not everyone was sure that it could indeed enhance the atmosphere for the necessary (and most important) work of the garden enough to make it worthwhile. In some urban gardens in Berlin however, the idea of outdoor concerts in the garden had already long since caught on, like in the "Allmende-Kontor" garden project at Tempelhofer Feld.[12]

By creating these sound art works, during which I was following my intuition about how to develop new relationships between composition and communities through sound, I realized I could call what I was aiming for "composing sociality." In this process I sought to give up authorship of the artistic product, while simultaneously staying in a more traditional role as artist/composer. Composing sociality is a move away from the concept of the composition of a work, and towards the design of different tools, processes and relationships in which a group of people participate, in which an artist/composer is just one member. A kind of community "worlding" including a heightened awareness of sound.[13] A designer may rearrange inputs and outputs, and their presentation, to allow new forms of sociality to emerge, while an artist dealing in the realm of "the social," usually imposes a scenario where sociality is constructed. Primarily in the process of composing sociality therefore, the full evacuation of "authorial" control over others foregrounds the collective, and non-human agency (vs. the idea of individual "genius" and human agency.) The results of the emergent collectivity can in this process re-integrate the artist/composer's work via its being embedded (and embodied) in the collective social interactions. I don't presume to be able to do more than make an aesthetic object by myself, but, in the case of composing sociality I make artwork within this larger collective artwork of how a community is in the world which takes precedence and is the focus of the work. Although I don't control the group artwork, as an artist, I am interested in the quality and strength of the social relationships that form, just as the curator, the politician, the organizer and some social workers may do, for example, when they experimentally try out new models for relations between people in society for some social or political purpose. Furthermore, more than imposing a top-down aesthetic structure as a particular authorial work which I can use to accrue status or capital, I am more interested in focusing on how the community creates everyday aesthetics of work and social interaction into artform(s) which help them cohere and develop around ideas and activities that they hold dear.

The conventional idea of the artist is that they have the freedom to tend to all the wildest (re-)inventions of the human imagination, which is a wonderful task, but over the long stretch of history, it has also become a heavier and heavier burden as the work concept has gradually expanded so far as to practically have finally collapsed. In this contemporary view informed by the 20th century avant-garde and social practice art, the sound artist traditionally has the responsibility of teaching the listener / participant an entirely new way of (hearing/) being in the world. The process of composing sociality admits the possibility of a backseat role for the artist in this process, where, rather, the worlding is driven by the communities themselves. A collectivity is more appropriate for this task in any case, both cognitively and ethically.

If social tonality is the way tonal vocal inflections might be heard and impact within the context of the aural environment to confirm or negate social structures which arouse, heighten or ameliorate cognitive dissonance, so composing sociality takes on board the development and change within these structures as a potential "material." Although relinquishing control of the artwork means that the artist is no longer author, they still participate in its creation. And letting go control of an emergent artistic work offers the artist the potential to adapt their individual artwork to the collective's work systems to enhance or strengthen its aesthetics and understand their own output better as they see how their own preferences resonate within it.

My experiences of social composition in urban gardens have led me to the following conclusions about work that I would like to pursue in upcoming projects: transcribing the recordings of performances of garden space, the talk and negotiations around planning land treatment, as well as described experiences of making urban agriculture more self-sustainable through art and music. This would be to analyze the social tonality in and about urban gardens as inspiration to come up with more experiments with the collective perception and creation of sound. Gardeners and I could record not only an oral history of the gardens and work there, but also register musical effects of the gardens' acoustics by recording work going on there at different times. We can also record the sound of other work taking place elsewhere related to the garden, promotional, commercial and intellectual. Gardener's and visitor's various aesthetic preferences in sound and music in other contexts can be investigated further in order to theorize relationships between ways of listening, local culture and group garden work, i.e., to record other sounds of the city and music, in order to contextualize the sound of the garden within them. These recordings, observations and diagrammatic representations of sound could be made not only by me but also by the gardeners themselves. In this way, by exchanging opinions and visions of how creating a project around listening in/about the gardens might improve its overall chances for success, a larger picture of cultural differences can emerge: various concepts of time, of friendship, of the natural environment generally, of the conceptualization of space(s) of music in relation to these networks, etc. Could an ensemble made up of composers could work with the gardeners if desired, simultaneously asking themselves the same questions to see how they best integrate music into the garden work and see if it is possible to meaningfully and purposefully assist both the work of the garden and their own creative endeavors? Music and gardens may not always complement each other or benefit from coming into a new relation, but it's worth trying, to discover in which contexts they can, and why, or why not.

REFERENCES:

Appadurai, Arjun (2013). The Future as Cultural Fact. New York: Verso Books.

Becker, Judith (1979). "Time and tune in Java." In A. L. Becker and Aram A. Yengoyan (eds.), The Imagination of reality: Essays in Southeast Asian coherence systems. Norwood, NJ: ABLEX

Buchanan, R. (1992), "Wicked Problems in Design Thinking", Design Issues, 8:2, 5-21, Cambridge MA: MIT Press.

Christian, Diana Leaf (2003). Creating Life Together: Practical Tools to Grow Ecovillages and Intentional Communities. Gabriola Island, BC: New Society.

Copeman, Dick (2007). "Permaculture: Design Principles for Urban Sustainability." In Anitra Nelson (ed.), Steering Sustainability in an Urbanizing World: Policy, Practice and Performance. Burlington VT: Ashgate.

DeNora, Tia (2015). Music Asylums: Wellbeing Through Music in Everyday Life. Burlington VT: Ashgate.

Devine, Kyle (2015). "Decomposed: A political ecology of music." Popular Music 34/3: 367-389.

Dyson, Frances (2014). Tone of our Times: Sound, Sense, Economy and Ecology. Cambridge MA: MIT Press.

Eshun, Kodwo (1998). More Brilliant Than The Sun. Adventures in Sonic Fiction. London: Quartet Books.

Feld, Steven (1990). Sound and Sentiment: Birds, Weeping, Poetics, and Song in Kaluli Expression (Conduct and Communication). Philadelphia: University of Pennsylvania Press.

Bianchi, Frederick (2016). Environmental Sound Artists: In Their Own Words. Oxford University Press.

Fukuoka, Masanobu (1978). The One-Straw Revolution: An Introduction to Natural Farming. Emmaus, Pennsylvania: Rodale.

Gilmurray, J. (2017). "Ecological Sound Art: Steps towards a new field". Organised Sound, 22(1), 32-41. doi:10.1017/S1355771816000315

Gordon, Uri (2008). Anarchy Alive! Anti-authoritarian Politics from Practice to Theory. Ann Arbor: Pluto.

Haraway, Donna (2016). Staying with the Trouble: Making Kin in the Chthulucene, Durham and London: Duke University Press.

Holmgren, David (2002). Permaculture: Principles and Pathways Beyond Sustainability, Hepburn, Victoria: Holmgren Design Services.

Holmgren, David (2013) "Essence of Permaculture", downloaded from https://holmgren.com.au/essence-of-permaculture-free/ May 2023

Irwin, T. (2015), "Transition Design: A Proposal for a New Area of Design Practice, Study and Research." Design and Culture, 7(2), 229-246.

Irwin, T. Kossoff, G. Tonkinwise, C. & Scupelli, P. (2015), Transition Design 2015, Pittsburgh, PA: Carnegie Mellon University.

Kahn, Douglas (2013). Earth Sound Earth Signal: Energies and Earth Magnitude in the Arts. Berkeley: University of California Press.

Kunst, Jaap (1973). Music in Java: It's History, it's Theory, and it's Technique. The Hague: Martinus Nijhoff.

LaBelle, Brandon (2010). Acoustic Territories: Sound Culture and Everyday Life. New York: Continuum.

Lippard, Lucy R. (2014) Undermining: A Wild Ride Through Land Use, Politics, and Art in the Changing West. New York: The New Press.

Marder, Michael (2013). Plant-Thinking: A Philosophy of Vegetal Life. New York: Columbia University Press.

Mollison, Bill (1988). Permaculture: A designers manual. Tyalgum: Tagari.

Mollison, Bill and Reny Slay (1991). Introduction to Permaculture. Tyalgum: Tagari.

Oddies, Richard (2012). "Other Voices: Acoustic Ecology and Urban Soundscapes." In Ingrid Leman Stefanovic and Stephen Bede Scharper (eds.), The Natural City: Re-Envisioning the Built Environment. Toronto: University of Toronto Press.

Odum, H.T. (1996) Environmental Accounting: EMERGY and Environmental Decision Making. New York: Wiley.

Pijanowski, B.C. (2023) Principles of Soundscape Ecology: Discovering Our Sonic World.

Quigley, Sam (Producer). (1989). Copper, tin & fire: gongsmithing in Java [VHS]. Boston Community Access and Programming Foundation.

Sakakeeny, Matt (2011) "New Orleans as a Circulatory System" Black Music Research Journal 31/2.

Schulze, Holger (2013). "Das Genre der Soundscape: Eine Kritik und Verteidigung der Soundscape im 21. Jahrhundert." Infrastrukturen des Urbanen: Soundscapes, Landscapes, Netscapes (pp.109-128). Bielefeld: Transcript Verlag.

Schulze, Holger (2012). "Adventures in Sonic Fiction: A Heuristic for Sound Studies." Journal of Sonic Studies 4/1.

Schulze, Holger (2020). Sonic Fiction. New York: Bloomsbury.

Schieffelin, Edward (1979). "Mediators as Metaphors: Moving a Man to Tears in Papua, New Guinea." In A.L. Becker and Aram A. Yengoyan (eds.), The Imagination of Reality: Essays in Southeast Asian Coherence Systems. Norwood, NJ: ABLEX.

Solomos, Makis (2023). Exploring the Ecologies of Music and Sound: Environmental, Mental and Social Ecologies in Music, Sound Art and Artivisms. New York: Routledge.

Spaid, Sue (2012). Green Acres: Artists Farming Fields, Greenhouses and Abandoned Lots. Cincinnati, Ohio: Contemporary Arts Center.

Spiller, Henry (2004). The Traditional Sounds of Indonesia. Santa Barbara, CA: ABC-CLIO.

Stewart, Kathleen (2010). 'Worlding Refrains' in M. Gregg & G. Seigworth (eds) in The Affect Theory Reader. London: Duke University Press, pp. 339 - 53.

Gavin Steingo (2016). Kwaito's Promise: Music and the Aesthetics of Freedom in South Africa. Chicago: University of Chicago Press.

The Sounds of Steelmaking. (1965). One Billion Dollars in Progress [LP]. US Steel. (courtesy of Rivers of Steel National Heritage Area).

Voegelin, Salomé (2014) Sonic Possible Worlds: Hearing the Continuum of Sound. New York: Bloomsbury.

Weiss, Allen S. (2008). Varieties of Audio Mimesis: Musical Evocations of Landscape. Berlin: Errant Bodies.

Wishart, Trevor (1996). On Sonic Art. UK: Harwood.

Woodruff, Jeremy (2014a). "Remaking Pittsburgh: Permaculture Soundscapes" Journal of Sonic Studies 7/1

Woodruff, Jeremy (2014b). "A Musical Analysis of the Peoples Microphone: Voices and Echoes in Protest and Sound Art" (Doctoral dissertation). Pittsburgh: University of Pittsburgh.

Woodruff, J. (2020) "Composing Sociality: Towards an Aesthetics of Transition Design". Groth, S.K. & Schulze, H. (ed.) The Bloomsbury Handbook of Sound Art. Bloombury Academic.

JANINE EISENÄCHER

Ready

ON THE ACTION-BASED SONIC KNOW-HOW AND AUDITORY KNOWLEDGE IN SOUND PERFORMANCES WITH THINGS

Making

[...] *to begin to experience the relationship between persons and other materialities more horizontally, is to take a step toward a more ecological sensibility.*[2]
Jane Bennett

The material culture of sound, hence, is as much a technological culture as it is part of body practices, of popular culture, of fashion fads of artistic practices, and of intimately obsessive idiosyncrasies, of nauseous percepts and voluptuous affects [...].[1]
Holger Schulze

INTRODUCTION

With the exhibition and performance series READY MAKING, as well as with the research method of memory dialogues called *Mind the Sound*[3] embedded therein, Steffi Weismann and I have realized an artistic-curatorial research project in the context of Errant Sound from 2019 to 2022, which has examined in more detail "sound-practical actions"[4] with things in the genres of sound performance and performative sound art.

READY MAKING – On the object-based know-how and auditory knowledge in sound performance with things [5] consisted of six sound art exhibitions including sound performances, concerts, lectures and discussions, each of them focusing on a different aspect related to the main research subject. *#1 The agency of things*, March 29th-April 12th 2019, Errant Sound, Berlin; *#2 Materiality of space and spatial listening*,

July 10th-12th 2020, Errant Sound, Berlin; #3 *Sonic Affordances*, May 23rd – 24th 2021, Errant Sound and Flutgraben e.V., Berlin; #4 *Microphoning/Microscoping*, July 2nd-11th 2021, Errant Sound and Hošek Contemporary, Berlin; #5 *Resonating bodies and media apparatuses*, March 25th – April 3rd 2022, Errant Sound and Flutgraben e.V.; *#6 Sounds and bodies in movement*, July 1st – 10th 2022, Errant Sound and Dock 11, Berlin. *Mind the Sound*[6] is part of *READY MAKING* and was developed by the author to research on how to gain access to the embodied action-based know-how and auditory knowledge through sonic memories, i.e. through remembering and describing sound-practical actions with things. Performance and sound artists as well as composer-performers and curators related to the fields took part in this memory dialogue, which was carried out by Janine Eisenächer and Steffi Weismann, and recorded on video. Edited excerpts of this video archive were exhibited as a video work in the context of the exhibitions *Readymade Grüüschschsch-------* (TART gallery, Zurich/ Switzerland, 2019), *READY MAKING #1*, and *sonomemo – sound and memory* (Errant Sound, Berlin, 2019).

The German term "klangpraktisches Handeln"[7] was coined by the musicologist Elena Ungeheuer, with whom we were in further conversations on this topic following the *Sounding out the Space* conference in Dublin, Ireland, in November 2017.[8] This "certain tautology,"[9] as she put it, serves to highlight the actual doing or modulating with one's own hands or other parts of the body in the process of sound production, of a sonic action with a thing. A "sonic action" ("Klanghandlung"), on the other hand, can also be the mere amplification of a sound by a microphone positioned in the room, the playing of a sound file, or the simple (not explicitly sound-shaping) moving up and down of a knob on a mixing console. In this context, it does not only mean intentional, purposeful actions with a clear beginning and end, but also, following the phenomenological understanding of Maurice Merleau-Ponty,[10] both intentional and non-intentional actions, activities or processes that arise suddenly and unexpectedly from the live situations and moments, or actions in which the goal and course of the doing itself change in the very process of doing, from improvising to interrupting or ending an action. Another term that is connected to this subject is "handling," in which the dimension of a certain know-how is already announced. Here, to be able to handle something means to have an implicit or somehow acquired "know-how"[11] or "knowing,"[12] which is, as Michael Polanyi highlighted in the 1960s, an experiential knowledge of how something can be or is to be done, which comes into being through doing or anticipating, sensing it. Consequently, and in the words of Michel de Certeau's action theory,[13] *READY MAKING* is about exploring the specific use ("Gebrauch") and the conversion ("Umfunktionierung") of things as well as the scope ("Spielraum") related thereto in the context of artistic practices or creative practices, strategies and tactics in everyday life.

We invited artists, musicians, composers, composer-performers and performers from the fields of performance art, sound art, visual and media arts, contemporary and experimental music, real-time-music (Echtzeitmusik), dance and theater to share with us their relationships and practices of their artistic-sonic work with things. In a wide variety of sound installations, kinetic sculptures, (interactive) performances and concerts (sound and concert performances as well as dance and lecture performances) as well as in interventions in public space, we were able to practically explore and reflect together on how we (can) practice, embody, learn, remember, actualize, (re)apply and experience the manifold human-thing-relationships through sound-practical actions with things. Throughout the six exhibitions with their individual performance and discourse programs, we also discussed the epistemological functions of sound-practical actions with things with scholars from musicology and sound studies, communication and media studies, dance and theater studies. We asked ourselves: What knowledge, what forms of know-how and knowing are produced, acquired, applied and performed through them? According to current epistemological approaches, we took an expanded concept of knowledge as a basis and understood it as processual, situated, embodied, experience-based, context-bound, implicit or tacit, and changeable, and not as something fixed or stable that can only be cognitively conveyed and acquired through language. The English term "knowing," as mentioned above, is more suitable because it includes the active procedure and the processuality of knowledge – in its production, application and experience. Nevertheless, for the English subtitle we chose the term "sonic know-how" to emphasize the implicit knowledge of how to do something, i.e. the knowledge of, about and in an action, and the term "auditory knowledge" to differentiate it from know-how or knowing and to underline the individual physiological conditions of the hearing apparatus as well as the individual listening archive or knowledge in one's mind.

SOUND-PRACTICAL ACTIONS WITH THINGS AS PART OF AN AESTHETIC ACTION WORLD ("HANDLUNGSWELT") AND KNOWLEDGE PRODUCTION: THE SOUND PERFORMANCE AS A MODEL OF HEARING COEXISTENCE, ENTANGLEMENT AND STORYTELLING

Central to the project was the genre of the sound performance because, in general, it is here where sound-practical actions with things take place most clearly. Regarding the interplay of body, space and time as well as of the factors live situation, audience, materials, and things in the space, the sound performance has a certain model character for practicing ecological, phenomenological and political actions and relationships. In the course of the series and research, we extended the field to performative sound art to also include sonic performances or performativities in which the explicit human (inter-) action or doing was no longer necessary in the situation of presenting the work. Here, the things were activated, for example, by motors, sensors, mechanically or electronically produced vibrations, particle or wave movements, temperature changes or electricity.

At the same time, the things themselves as well as the relations we develop with them were just as important to us: they are knowledge carriers and cultural memory at once. They are not only produced differently and change their consistency or materiality, e.g. with changes in temperature. They change in different cultural contexts, according to other aesthetic relations and meanings of actions and sounds, their effects and their affordances, their (potential) spectrums of action and their agency, not least their concrete and associated sound worlds. In this way, not only different practices, customs and narratives are interwoven with the supposedly same things worldwide, but also manifold individual and collective know-hows of doing and listening as Jean-François Augoyard and Henry Torgue argue: "[...], sound is also shaped subjectively, depending on the auditory capacity, the attitude, and the psychology and culture of the listener. There is no universal approach to listening. Every individual, every group, every culture listens in its own way."[14] I would like to paraphrase and add: There is no universal approach to doing. Doing, listening, and things are all connected to sonic and body practices, to multi-sensory and corporeal practices, and consequently, they change in different contexts. This is why we favor the term "sonic" here instead of "acoustic" or "auditory" to include all aspects of the very materiality at play in a situation. In doing sound-practical actions with things, an action-based and a sonic know-how emerge at the same time, and – as sounding and listening –

they are profoundly material in themselves. Therefore Christopher Cox speaks of a "sonic materialism"[15]: "Sound is not a world apart, a unique domain of non-signification and non-representation. Rather, sound and the sonic arts are firmly rooted in the material world and the powers, forces, intensities, and becomings of which it is composed."[16] So far we have differentiated the following concepts and terms of knowledge: "sonic know-how" or "sonic knowing" ("Klang- und Hörwissen"), "auditory knowledge" ("Hörwissen") and "sonic memories" ("Klangerinnerungen"). In both self-experimentation and in realization with other artists, Steffi Weismann and I have experienced in *Mind the Sound* that there is an immensely diverse and broad spectrum of (remembered and described) sound-practical actions with things, of sonic know-hows, auditory knowledge, and sonic memories, as well as of ways and means of their recreated perception, their physical, verbalized or vocalized description or expression.

READY MAKING intended and still intends to gain findings about the extent to which action theory, which has often neglected the sonic dimension, needs to be further developed toward an aesthetic theory of action that includes the sonic and multi-sensual. Against the backdrop of ecological and ecofeminist theories, that are becoming more relevant (again), and an increasing attention to a new materialism,[17] through which the perception of the living or animate matter in our (surrounding) world has begun to change (again), the questions of how we act or do things at all and with whom also arise in a new and different way. In the project we therefore do not speak of everyday objects and materials as of objects, but of "things."[18] In doing so, we follow the school of thought of the object-oriented ontology[19] and, in particular, the political theories that deal with the interaction of human and non-human actors, actants or energies, such as those by Bruno Latour, Jane Bennett or Timothy Morton, among others.

These authors criticize the object-subject-dualism of Western philosophy and attribute to objects their own "thing-power,"[20] to things their own form of agency and resistance or resilience, as a result of which the diverse human-thing- and human-environment-relationships are understood, for example, as a "network" (Latour),[21] as an "assemblage" (Bennett),[22] as an "environment" (Morton),[23] as a "string figure" (Haraway)[24] or as a "relationscape" (Manning),[25] which all are characterized by a particular performativity related to their interconnectedness or entanglement. In relation to our research subject we consciously recognize the things as co-actors, co-performers, and co-players. We understand this diverse juxtaposition as a togetherness in which various relations of co-production and co-existence are articulated. Donna Haraway, in *Staying with the Trouble* (2015), memorably has described the extent to which we are in an ongoing state or process of "being-with,"[26] engaging in "sym-poiesis"[27] rather than in the long proclaimed and celebrated "auto-poiesis."[28] In this sense, the explorative, sensitive, and delicate collaboration with the things that surround us practiced by the (sound and performance) artists and composer-performers presented here also stand against the idea of a pure individuality of performers or artists. Both stand for an opening and an openness towards things and their material coexistence with us humans, towards the multiple "modes of existence"[29] ("Existenzweisen") or ways of relating that each one of them has with a specific thing.

For this reason too, the title *READY MAKING* sets the art historical concept of the readymade – the found object (*objet trouvé*) that is merely placed in another or the art context – in motion, in performance, or also: into the categorical performative. It means a doing and a processuality, a material activity and a mode of being at the same time: an al-ready making. It is the interplay of sounding and listening with the tactile and visual dimension of our actions that opens up a sensual-aesthetic and ecological-political space for perception and action. This text is the first brief summary of only some of our findings and research results so far, which cannot be presented here in full detail or meet the demand to completeness. This is a task to which we will devote ourselves more intensively after this publication. On the basis of selected works and excerpts from lectures, the following section will discuss a few aspects of sound-practical actions with things in sound performances focusing on agency, acoustic toying[30] and affordance.

AGENCY, ACOUSTIC TOYING AND AFFORDANCE: THINGS AS ACTANTS/ACTORS, CO-PERFORMERS AND CO-PLAYERS, KNOWLEDGE CARRIERS AND CULTURAL MEMORY

The concept of agency expresses the power or capacity to act or do (something), which initially referred to human beings, for example, marginalized groups or persons with lack of access to certain activities, institutions and decision-making structures. It can be extended and applied to animal or plant creatures as well as to all things in general, not without certain limitations as to what can be meant by agency or action in each case. Clearly, things do not act and behave like humans. But if we follow the object-oriented ontology and thus no longer the strict binary opposition and vertical hierarchy of subject = active and object = passive, we allow ourselves to look at our interactions and network of relationships with the world in a horizontal way and can open ourselves to the things' own qualities, characteristics and capacities. This relative dehierarchization is accompanied by a new sort of attention and sensitivity towards the things, in Jane Bennett's words an "attentiveness."[31] How can we practice or perform this attentiveness?

In the listening room for *READY MAKING #1*, which Steffi Weismann and I had developed for the beginning of the project, we presented a selection of things from everyday life like art objects on pedestals at eye, ear and hand height, and we provided them with various instructions for actions and listening, so-called recipes. While the term "instruction" ("Handlungsanweisung") is rather contextualized in the field of performance art, the playfully named recipes can also be called a score ("Partitur"), which is their adequate equivalent in the context of sound art. The audience was invited to try out our collection of *Grüüschschsch-Readymades*[32] quite individually, to explore them sonically and playfully, and, in doing so, to appropriate the action and listening instructions physically and sensually. These were two recipes we had tried out before at the TART gallery in Zurich:

GRÜÜSCHSCHSCH – READY MADE #7
2 sponges, made of different pressed foam materials, ca. 11x8x4cm
Stroke the wall with a sponge in a slow wave motion. Change the pressure so that the wall moans softly.[33]

GRÜÜSCHSCHSCH – READY MADE #9
10 nails à 25mm, galvanised, and 10 nails à 50mm, galvanized
Throw one nail at a time at or onto a surface in the room. Vary the time interval and throwing speed while listening.[34]

Selected for different haptic and sonic materialities, the listening room corresponded to a colorful sonic playground. Accordingly, tinsel was waved back and forth, blackboard chalk was rubbed close to the ears, steel and aluminium sheets were made to vibrate, and sponges were pulled, pushed, pressed or rubbed along the wall. The most diverse things, materialities, and actions on and with them could be heard and listened to. A wonderful space emerged with noises and sounds between cracking, crackling, rustling, squeaking, screeching clink-

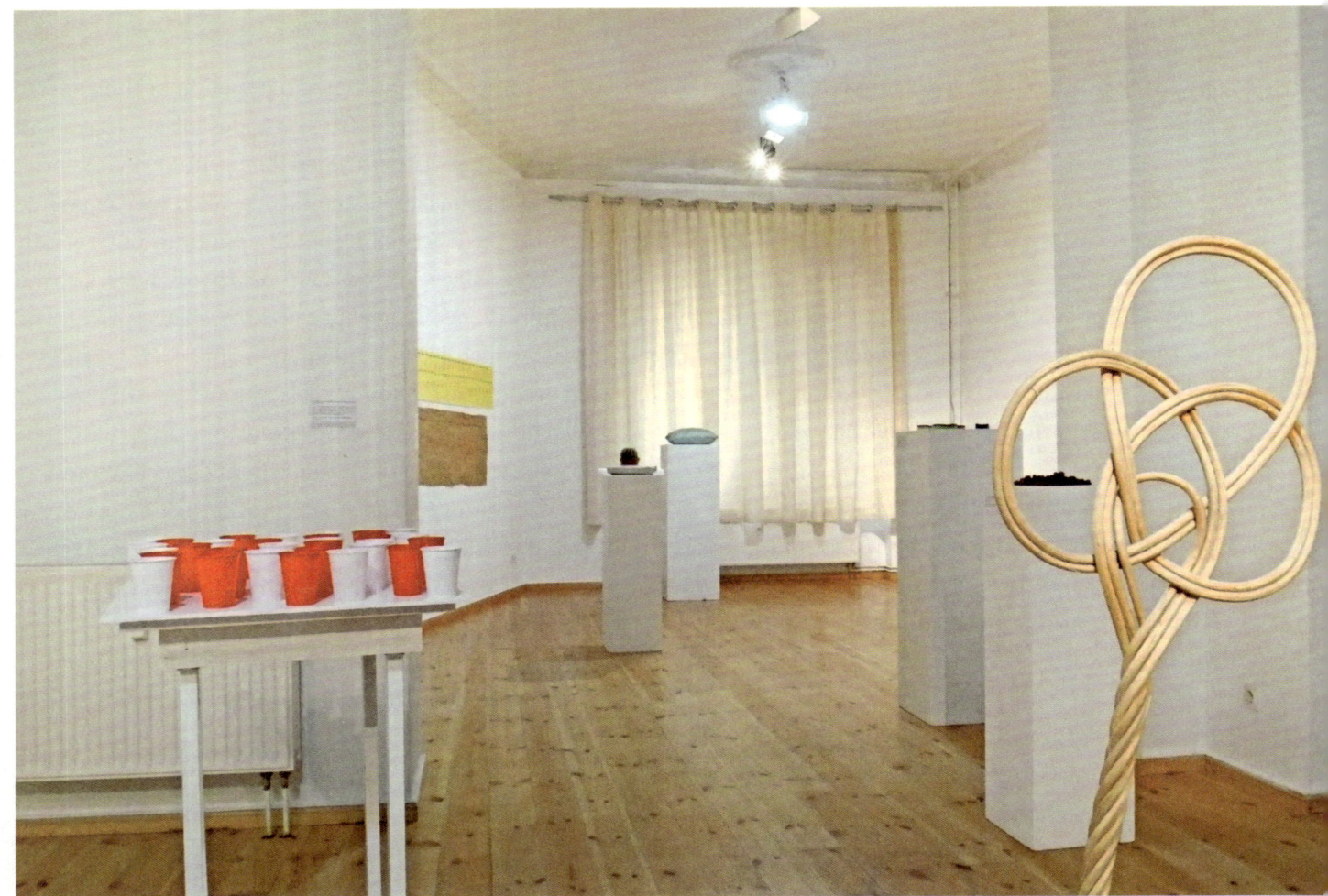

ing, popping, hissing, whirring, grinding, snapping, humming, and of listening to each other. However, there is no exactly fitting word for many of these very unique and peculiar friction and vibration noises and sounds. If one resorts to anthropomorphizing them like we did in the recipes, the things start talking, singing, moaning or whispering – but these are not adequate descriptions of the noise or sound, nor of the particular action. *READY MAKING* and *Mind the Sound* were thus used as opportunities to develop an extended language through playful descriptions that either attempted to verbalize the noise and sound or that, in this attempt, included the sound-practical action with the thing, for example, the "snapping away-sound" or the "sound when jumping away from the scissors," the "gentle unrolling-and-tearing-sound of an adhesive tape," the wagging-sound, the sound of nails falling or rolling back and forth.

Particularly, in our duo performance of *READY MAKING #1*, we were interested in the individual execution and discovery of the materials, in the encounter with their sonic affordances and their agency: How does this thing sound when I perform this movement or this action with it? In what way does it sound different when I hold or move it differently? What happens when I don't (any longer) try to control it to produce a certain sound? How do I listen to the thing? What does it do to me as it sounds? And how do my sound-practical actions change in the course of what I hear or listen to? Between the respective handling, manipulation and modulation on the one hand and the sonic properties and resistances on the

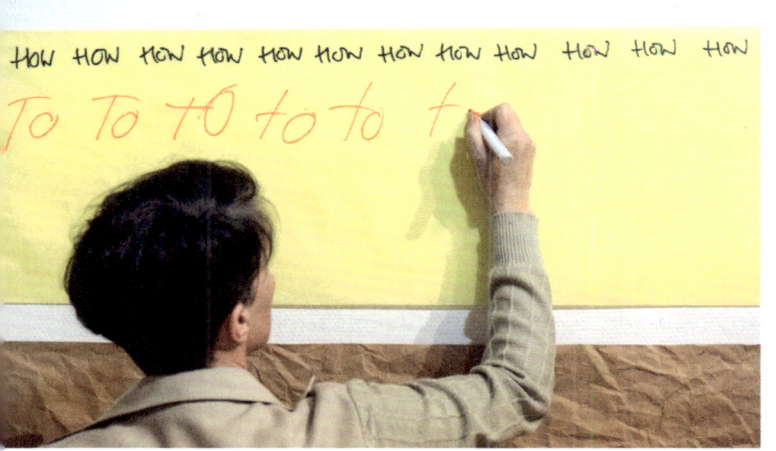

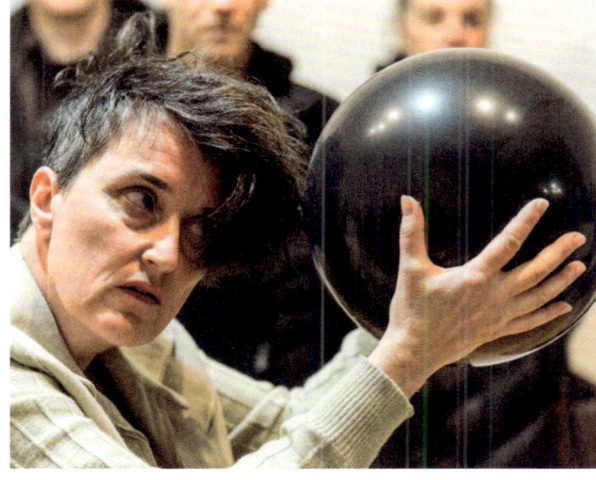

←/↑:
Exhibition view.

←/↑: Steffi Weismann / Janine Eisenächer performing.
All photos: Golo Föllmer

other, the visitors, we as performers and the things could encounter each other in a sound-practical togetherness.

The first decisive finding on sound-practical actions with things is that we never only listen to and haptically feel *one* thing, i.e., the thing itself in its material quality. We always listen to and feel at least two things, i.e. the surface, spatiality, and materiality also of the other thing or material on and with which the process or activity takes place. When cutting the straws with scissors (see *Grüüschschsch-Readymade #6*), we simultaneously listen to the cutting sound of the scissors – through which we learn something about the material, the heaviness and size of the scissors (metal) – and to the shorter cut plastic straw in the form of a sharp-sounding plastic noise that is created by cutting and bouncing the piece of plastic away from the edge of the scissors. This sound becomes higher the shorter the straw is cut. Consequently, we always listen to at least two things, materialities, and sounds. Another example from this performance is writing with two Edding markers on a long strip of yellow sketch paper from a roll attached to the wall: While Steffi Weismann and I each wrote a different word repeatedly in a line, staggered in time, we ourselves as well as the audience could listen to both the materiality of a full Edding 3000 with a round tip as well as to the properties and resistances of the sketching paper, which was smooth but still crackled and rippled slightly through the writing. This paper reaction in return had an impact on our writing ability and our respective writing rhythms, so that here and there there were small audible and perceptible

100 / 101

deviations in the sonic writing process. The second relevant finding is that we, as listeners of sound-practical actions with things, can also either precisely hear or audibly guess which action, activity or body movement leads to this noise or sound. Parts of the audience, who were standing in one room during our opening performance and could not see that I was throwing small metal nails at the ceiling in the other room, were at least able to understand that a soft, bright metallic sound appeared in the upper part of the room followed by a somewhat louder dull metallic sound on the wooden floor. They could hear or through listening envision the quite silent action of throwing and movement of falling. That we always hear this interplay of several materialities and the process of a movement or action make these findings very important because they make clear that sound-practical actions with things are always a doing-*with*, a sounding-*with* and a listening-*with*. The agency of things, which become equal co-performers here, lies in the fact that they cannot be controlled and handled perfectly or flawlessly by us humans, and that they can change their (known) properties in each and every situation in relation to our movements, daily form, nervousness or the like, as well as in relation to the humidity, temperature, air circulation and so on in the actual space or environment. Thus, they can also act, react and sound unexpectedly differently. Their agency or maybe even our co-agency also lies in the process that I call, with Jens Roselt, a "*phenomenological dramaturgy*" ("phänomenologische Dramaturgie").[35] By this I mean the process of creating a development or suspense with an action or activity guided by perception, in this case auditory perception. In a performance or performative process, when the action or action-based sound of a thing or material takes the leading role for a shorter or longer period of time in the further course of the performance or process, the performer follows the sound and thing-material through listening and explores in the very process how they both develop. At this moment, the performer holds back his*her*their control over the situation and opens up to the experimental, the unknown, the unexpected. A situation of a heightened sound presence and co-presence, of an experienced co-existence and co-agency emerges. For us, such a situation in the performance of *READY MAKING #1* was our interaction with the rinsing sponges (as they can now be heard on the Errant Sound-LP in the piece *Material Touch: Sonic Readymades for 4 Hands*).[36] The sponges came to a halt, slowed down or went along with our arm and hand movements. Here and there, they resisted our rubbing or pulling on the various surfaces and textures. The dryness of the sponges as well as the two different foam sides required a certain handling, which we only explored and experienced in more detail in this moment. We didn't rehearse beforehand, and we didn't repeat the actions in this way after the performance. These situations or moments can only happen, they are an "event,"[37] and they end either through an action or reaction of the thing, through an impulse and the following decision of the person performing, or through other, external influences or interruptions. It therefore follows that we have to give things space to encounter them again and again in order to perceive their agency or our co-agency. How does this relate to the action-based sonic know-how we gained in advance?

The fact that we chose the rinsing sponges has to do precisely with their affordances and our approach of a playful, experimental misuse ("Zweckentfremdung"). With their special materiality, they had an appealing character for us and interesting sound potentials beyond their function as rinsing sponges, which we know as such in their materiality from the everyday practice of washing the dishes. Soft, rough and smooth, dry and wet, with different options of handling and combining them with different surfaces or other things: we started from potentials based on an everyday action-based sonic know-how without ever having assumed or being able to know how these sponges could sound together with us on a plinth or a wall. An embodied, situational and experiential knowing was supplemented and actualised through the (performed) sound-practical actions with things by another embodied, situational and experiential knowing, which then is a newly acquired and implicit action-based sonic know-how. We have received the sonic affordances and integrated them into our way of a playful, experimental and research-focused handling. For this sort of encountering things Michael A. Conrad and I developed the term "acoustic toying," based on Conrad's concept and term "toying," which today – to emphasize the materiality – I would rather call "sonic toying":

[...] Acoustic toying is a perceptive attitude and practice. It is not only about perceiving things in the environment as toys, but also about playing with objects in order to make them sound. The attitude is to keep the acoustic anticipation as low as possible in order to explore objects more intuitively and intersensually – a "purposeless play,"[38] as Cage once said, or, to use Haraway's terminology: acoustic toying is all about to stay in trouble with sounding objects. This presupposes a process of decolonization. UN-LEARN. UN-KNOW. RE-THINK. RE-FEEL. RE-LATE. The attitude of re-encountering objects makes them sym-poietic partners in our world-making, with "string figures of sound" emerging. Sound Fiction. We resonate with objects and objects resonate with us.[39]

Things communicate and resonate with us, they "speak" to us, "talk" to us, they arouse desire, the lust to play with them or the desire to own them. They "tell" us stories, remind us of places, of people or other living beings, of experiences. They offer us one or more ways of using, of playing with them. This "offering character" of things is described by the aforementioned term "affordance," first formulated by James J. Gibson in his book *The Ecological Approach to Visual Perception*. According to Gibson, affordance corresponds to what the environment or an object offers us visually: "what [the environment] offers [to the actors], what it provides or furnishes, either for good or ill."[40] The term was later coined by Donald A. Norman in his theory of perception from the perspective of the design of everyday objects and architecture, such as cups, teapots or door handles. Affordance was understood by him as the relationship between object and subject, more precisely as "a relationship between the properties of an object and the capabilities of the agent that determine the object and the capabilities of the agent that determine just how the object could possibly be used."[41] The affordances don't exist only one-sided, but the relationship is still characterized by a use- or function-bound hierarchy between subject and object. Michael A. Conrad emphasises the collaborative aspect, meaning that these affordances – here, the object qualities designed by humans for the ideal use of the object by humans (in the case of produced objects) – unfold in the relationship between a person and the respective object – with its qualities as a thing: "[…], it seems more appropriate to say that affordances *unfold* in the relationship between me and the object, between my knowledge and desire and its resistance, the part of it that refuses, that objects […]. Objects become the vanishing points of our imaginations."[42] For sound-practical actions with things, these unfolding affordances, i.e. both the respective form, materiality, surface texture and their correspondingly designed – or also evolutionarily formed – offering character as well as the respective relationship between the person (here: the performer or artist) and the thing play an essential role. In focusing on the acoustic-auditory dimension relevant to *READY MAKING*, we asked whether there are sonic affordances in particular? If so, what would these comprise?

In his lecture *What Do Sounds Need, What Do We Grant Them – Or Not? A Few Considerations on the Affordances of the Sonic*, held at READY MAKING #3, cultural and media scientist Holger Schulze opened up a broad field in which sonic affordances unfold and asked what "affordances of sounds – of sound events, sound effects, or sound practices"[43] could be (see in this book, pp. 69 – 78). In the definition of the term "sonic affordance," co-authored with cultural scientist Carla J. Maier, they state: "Every instrument incorporates its own discursive and material attributes which become sonic affordances for instrumentalists or sound artists who play, interpret or manipulate the instrument."[44] The discursive and material attributes of every thing and situation are part of its sonic affordance. For the research subject dealt with in READY MAKING, we can equate "instrument" with "thing" – both are co-players, co-performers. Schulze identifies "four constituents that might be shaping the affordances of sound in a given intervention or artwork"[45] – which are: "[…] (a) the situation, (b) the instrument, tool or apparatus, (c) the actor, be it human or non-human, a singular or a collective group of actors, and (d) the particular activity in its time-based and relational structure."[46] All four aspects of sonic affordances are characterized by their specific materiality, and they are all determined and limited by their materialities: "The options are not limitless. They are given. They can be played with. But they only rarely can be expanded beyond these limits."[47] Their affordances for sound production and sound perception are likewise: they offer a limited scope and influence whether something is done and the way something is done, for example, the attitude, posture and playing style, the duration and dynamics.

In Christian Kesten's sound performance *ding ding*,[48] the focus is on his own kitchen table with its specific history and character. From its drawer, Kesten gradually pulls out various things from everyday life

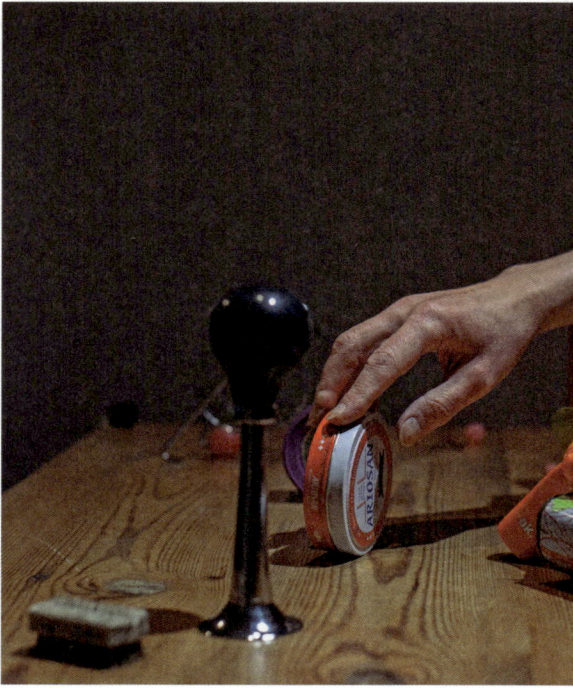

↑ / ↗: Christian Kesten performing. Photos: Julia Cremers

that are so special that not every person can immediately relate to them. Ball-shaped sweets, various aluminium cans, a music box, a small plastic hand fan, an old horn, a small metal running wheel, a small wooden brush: it is a selection from the performer's personal world of things and sounds, who is also a composer, director, sound and intermedia artist as well as a vocalist (in the ensemble Maulwerker): things from his everyday consumer life, souvenirs from his travels, perhaps also things found here and there. What seems familiar to us as an audience, however, are the materialities. Consequently, we have an association with them, i.e. an idea or inkling of how the things might sound. A small microphone is attached to each of the two corners of the table facing the audience; they amplify the noises and

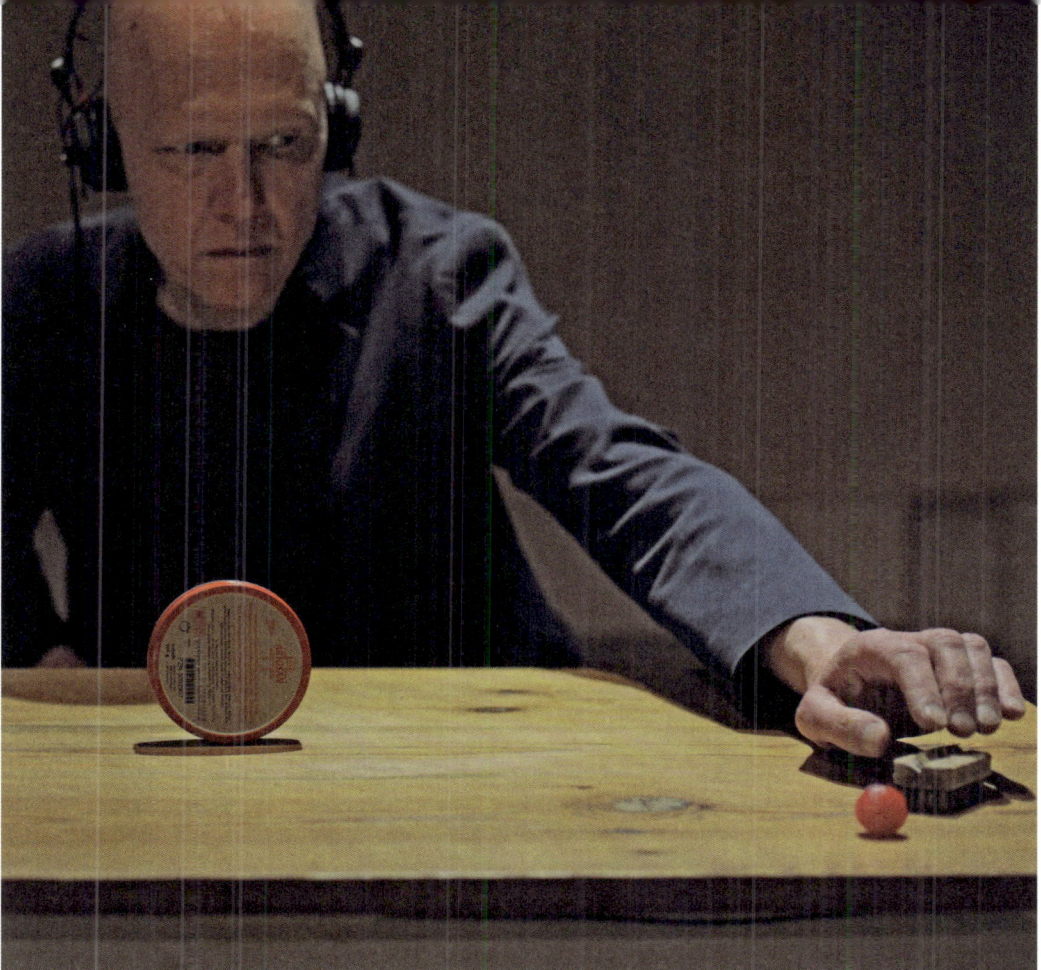

sounds of the things that the audience listens to through four loudspeakers – 2 in front of them, 2 behind them – while Kesten follows the subtlety of his sound-practical actions under his headphones.

At the beginning of the performance, the table is empty. Kesten opens the drawer of the table and first takes out a round tin can, which he carefully rolls back and forth on a spot of the table, and which comes to a stop there thanks to a slight dent in the tabletop. What we listen to here are the rolling movements of the round tin can on the wooden table. We hear both metallic and wooden sounds, their interplay. We hear and see through the slowing down and then the ending of the rolling that there is a resistance – the mentioned dent – which finally brings the movement of the can to a stop. In the course of the performance, Kesten takes other things out of the drawer, places them or puts them on the table, performs various actions with them – sometimes two or more things are combined – and simultaneously, he tells a true story of an observation and experience made in a supermarket. The rolling, vibrating, and rubbing noises, together with the quietly told story result in a precisely tuned composition that is nevertheless flexible and lively in itself. Particularly interesting are the moments when the audience's expectation of an object or material sound is not fulfilled, for example, when Kesten presses very carefully on the rubber case of the horn with his index finger: we do not hear a horn sound, but a gentle, quiet "breathing out and in" – an outflow and inflow of air – of the horn, sometimes we hear nothing – then

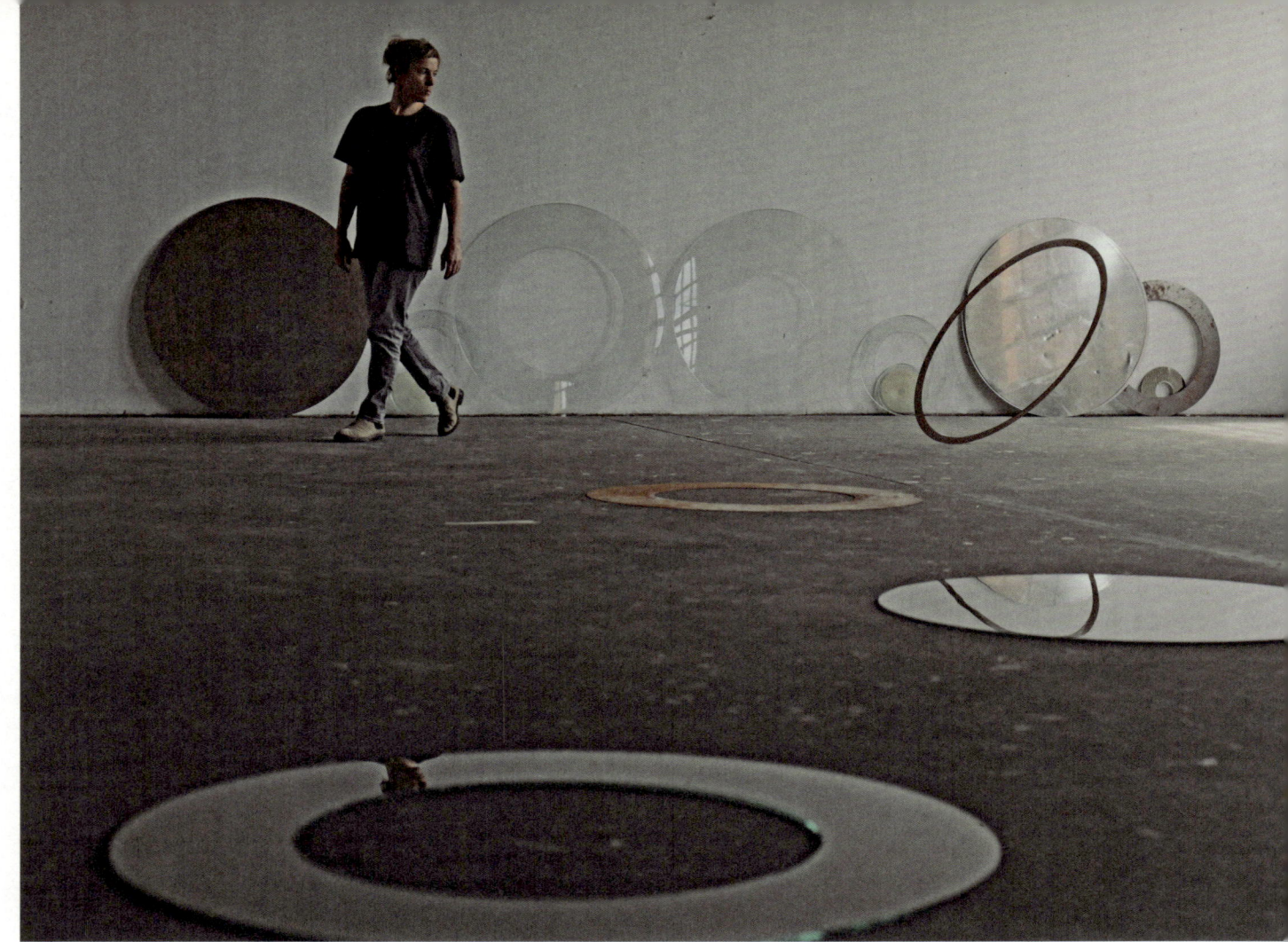

the pressure was too low and the material resistance too big. Here, too, we hear both Kesten's finger movement and pressure on the rubber material and the air-filled interior of the rubber case. Each of Kesten's hand movements and handling of things is precisely practiced – also equally rehearsed – and focused on listening. The rooms at Errant Sound are lit so that only performers and things are in focus. Other visual features of the exhibition and performance space disappear into darkness. Kesten follows the audible and perceptible qualities of things, their affordances, and gives their uncontrollable agency the necessary space: here and there, unexpected things happen, which sometimes make you laugh and are also allowed to happen. The subtle modulations in posture and movement of hand and fingers, in interplay with Kesten's overall upper body movement, illustrate the co-production and the doing-with of performer and things, whereby a connection between the things as well as between them and the performer is transported through the narrated story. Kesten has chosen a playful and onomatopoetic title for his sound performance *ding ding* (in English: thing thing or cling cling),[49] – which also reminds of the ding-dong-sound of a bell – newly produced for *READY MAKING #3*. It is both about the agency and respective affordances of things and about how these things stand next to and in relation to each other; how they (per-)form a composition, a narrative or a context, how they tell a story.

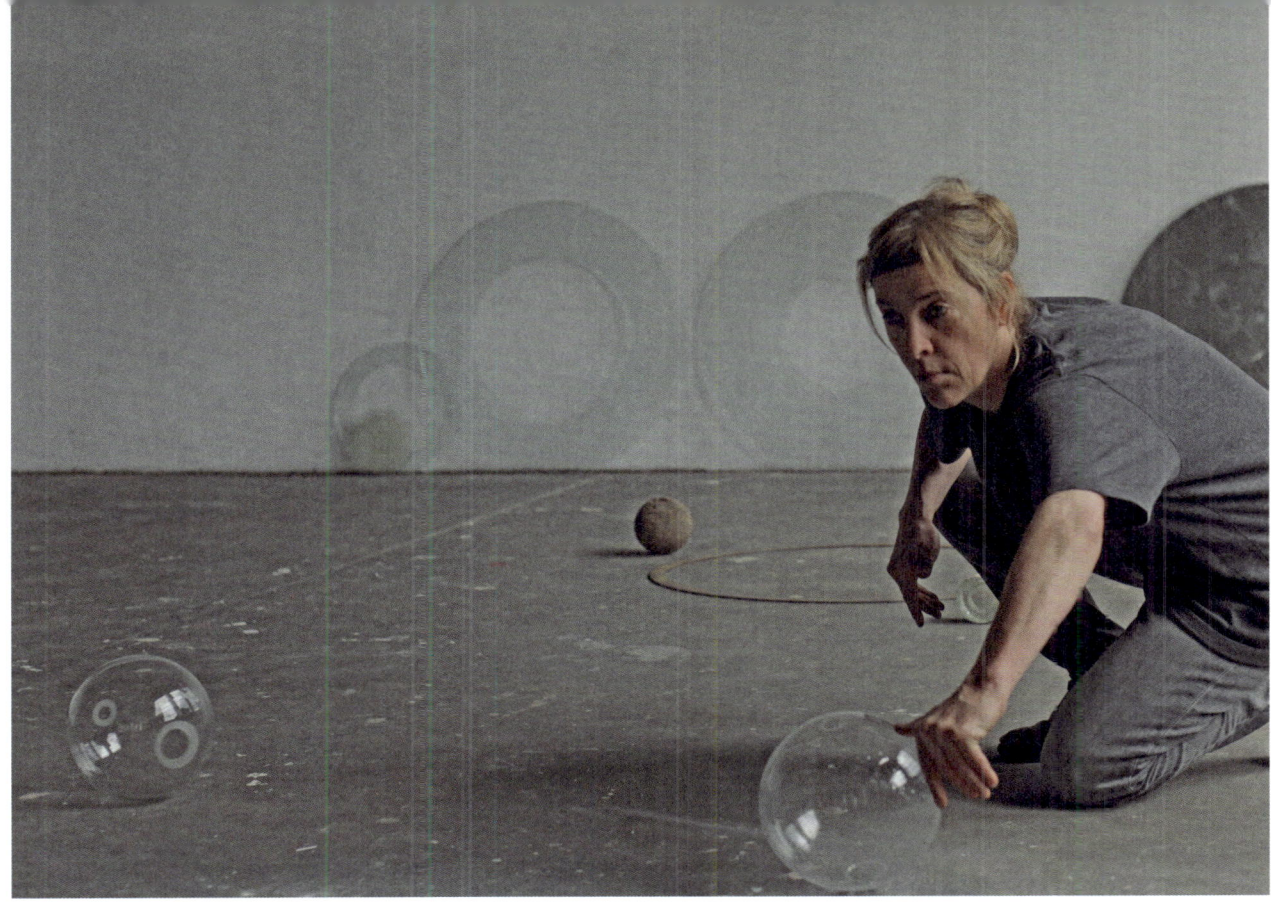

↖/↑: Gwendoline Robin performing. Photos: Julia Cremers

For her sound performance *Sous les lunes de Jupiter*, Gwendoline Robin has chosen a different kind of thing-world, a universe whose objects are sometimes much larger and heavier, but also more fragile and dangerous. Her glass and metal discs, specially produced by factory workers, which differ from each other in the way they are made, as well as the various glass and metal spheres, bring with them very specific aesthetics and sonic-material affordances that fit perfectly into the multi-purpose hall of Flutgraben e.V. – an old factory hall in an industrial architecture from the 1920s. We deliberately chose this hall for Robin's work because it needs a space of a certain size and a stone floor in which Robin can move around and on which things can move well. Robin, who is a visual artist and works in the fields of sculpture and performance, acts very physically with her things in this performance and does so in smaller and larger action radii, adapted to the concrete space.

The large glass and metal discs are set into various rolling or circling movements by her, mainly by her hands, in a well-balanced relationship between strength and gracefulness, which Robin follows with her whole body, placing herself in different positions, almost as if choreographed. She moves with the things and listens with the sound development of them: she keeps the discs moving, walks next to them or runs after them. She observes the course of the discs' own movement in relation to the gravitational and centrifugal forces and catches them – suddenly lying on the floor – with her hands just before they completely touch the ground. She also lets the discs circle to the end and vibrate, clattering loudly on the floor. She carefully balances the discs back and forth along her back on the floor. The various balls are rolled or spun on the floor with special hand movements – sometimes with, sometimes without spin – through the hall, sometimes slowed down or stopped by other discs lying on the floor, other obstacles or the audience. This creates both subtle and quiet as well as loud and brute vibration sounds of glass, metal and stone floor. There is a recognizable effort and tension in this physical collaboration with the things, in this play with the "planets" and their orbits as well as rotations, their gravitational and centrifugal forces, their potential im- and explosions. The more difficult to control and thus more risky handling of the things, which could also injure the performer if handled inaccurately or incorrectly, adds to the overall tension of the performance. The handling of the weight and dimensions of both things and the performer's own body, of the physical properties of human and non-human actors in space, effectively meets the sometimes delicate and spherical, sometimes brute and clanging sounds of glass and metal. Between continuous circular noises, long crescendo developments and a sudden, one second-long bang, we actually get acoustically-auditively into a universe – of sounds of glass on glass, glass on stone, glass on metal, of metal on metal, metal on glass, metal on stone, of glass and metal on human, and human on stone. Robin, who has been working with glass objects for many years, can hear the states and dynamics of her material very precisely from the different glass vibration sounds and their (frequency) development. Her performatively acquired, embodied action-based and sonic know-how indicates that and when the pane or ball will break before the familiar "cry of the glass." She is in an explicit corporeal, physical and sonic-material "interbeing,"[50] as Salomé Voegelin calls these processes of being-with and listening-with, with things. Depending on the course of an action or movement, depending on the development of the sound, she decides when it is necessary to intervene, to step in and to take action. She follows the affordances and the agency of things in the sense of a phenomenological dramaturgy.

In both performances it becomes clear to what extent the things chosen by both of them carry and communicate a material-bound action-based and sonic know-how and likewise a cultural history. They evoke memories of past times when certain materials were used more often than today (e.g. metal and glass instead of plastic), perhaps of days of one's own childhood. Some other things can be found in any supermarket or have the special quality of souvenirs from various journeys – interwoven with them are various discoveries, experiences and relationships of the respective persons. In this way, things are always knowledge carriers and culture memory that can unfold differently for each person – depending on their relationship to them. These examples show how intuitively, playfully and consciously artists deal with the affordances of things, and sometimes also act against them. In their inter-being and collaboration with things, they develop their own use as well as precise forms of handling, manipulation or action. They act and participate, improvise, carry out actions and processes, depending on their own skills (*manières de faire*[51]) and the knowing or know-how they have acquired (*savoir faire*[52]). The (composer-)performers have intensively studied the affordances of the situations, the things, of themselves and the others present as well as their activities – they know and deal with them. It is part of their artistic practices to bring these into a complex togetherness, thereby playfully exploring, artistically researching, giving space to or explicitly exhibiting the agency of things, and demonstrating new (relations and power) relationships. This action-based sonic know-how emerges between everyday life and art, pop culture and consumption; it flows in from numerous areas of aesthetic experience in life. The conversion of a use, the "redesigning"[53] ("Umfrisieren"[54]) in de Certeau's words, becomes the artistic and political strategy of a creative way of working or doing things in everyday life. These strategies also follow certain tactics and procedures, logics and mechanisms that have their place in the art world and in art history. The cultural field, like others, is permeated by economies, policies, and power relations, by conventions, regimes, and rules that are interrupted or become new traditions.

SUMMARY AND OUTLOOK —
FROM "AND" TO "WITH"

Sound-practical actions with things are part of and do explicitly create and apply reference systems, networks of relationships, and entanglements. The affective and emotional ties to a thing have their significant share in what kind of actions, in what quality and what sounds or noises are produced on and with it by a person. The aesthetic experiences and affects enter into the respective "world-making"[55] and "making-with"[56] of performer, things, and audience. They are done, experienced, embodied, and remembered. We can observe a further development from Gilles Deleuze's and Felix Guattari's thinking on multiplicity coined in the spatial structures of the "rhizome"[57] and "assemblage"[58] ("Gefüge"[59]), which was represented by the conjunction "and," to an even more relational, materialist and ambient concept of space and spatiality coined in the terms "entanglement" (e.g. Karen Barad), "string figure" (Haraway), "environment" (e.g. Bennett, Morton), and "relationscape" (Manning), which are represented by the preposition "with." This leads to another understanding of body and self in relation to other beings and things, to space, and to time, and this is where a new idea of storytelling sets in: it is about perceiving and listening-with the many different beings, things and stories that exist in different places

at the same time. It is about becoming aware (again) of our being entangled-with the world(s) we co-create and live-with – our co-relations and co-dependencies with other humans, non-human beings, and things, but also "the complicated web of dissonant connections between bodies."[60] Moving between these epistemological and ontological processes, it can be said that we're moving towards practicing and performing a "speculative onto-story,"[61] as Jane Bennett puts it. Consequently, within *READY MAKING*, the following two thematic strands were also relevant to us: the relations between mediality, mediatization and matter, and, as mentioned above, the manifold concepts and qualities of space and spatiality – both ranging from macro to micro and vice versa. The shifts towards a "sonic-as-spatial-practice turn"[62] or towards an environmental or ecological turn have many potential consequences for the conception, understanding and making of space and spatiality, in particular, in the field of sound art. What would sonic string figures or sonic relationscapes look, sound, smell, feel and taste like? How do we practice and perceive a "shared perceptual space,"[63] and how will new 3D- and 4D-audio environments and spatial audio-designs with loudspeakers and headphones influence our doing and perceiving the world (see text by Gerriet Krishna Sharma in this book, pp. 40 – 46)? Can we live and perform a "shared vital materialism,"[64] as Bennett claims, in which different sounding and listening perspectives do meet and can interact? Herein, the chance is to open up through the sonic to the manifold ways of doing, knowing and its relations, to the multi-sensory (inter-)actions of humans and non-humans, of matter and energies. An aesthetic action theory has to follow these actions and movements into and out of aesthetic experiences – not to culturalize societal, political or economic processes or problems, but to understand the complexity, diversity and multiplicity of local and global relations, know-hows or knowings, motivations, actions, and their perceptions.

NOTES:

1. See Holger Schulze, The Sonic Persona. An Anthropology of Sound. New York and London, 2018, p. 82.

2. See Jane Bennett, Vibrant Matter. A Political Ecology of Things. Durham and London, 2010, p. 10.

3. See: https://readymaking.com/ and https://errant-sound.net/projects/series/ Last visit: 07.10.2023

4. Translation of the German term "klangpraktisches Handeln" (Elena Ungeheuer) by the author.

5. The artistic research-project READY MAKING - On the object-based know-how and auditory knowledge in sound performance with things consisted of 6 Sound Art-exhibitions including sound performances, concerts, lectures and discussions, each of them focusing on a different aspect related to the main research subject. #1 The agency of things, March 29th-April 12th 2019, Errant Sound, Berlin; #2 Materiality of space and spatial listening, July 10th–12th 2020, Errant Sound, Berlin; #3 Sonic Affordances, May 23rd-24th 2021, Errant Sound and Flutgraben e.V., Berlin; #4 Microphoning/ Microscoping, July 2nd-11th 2021, Errant Sound and Hošek Contemporary, Berlin; #5 Resonating bodies and media apparatuses, March 25th–April 3rd 2022, Errant Sound and Flutgraben e.V.; #6 Sounds and bodies in movement, July 1st-10th 2022, Errant Sound and Dock 11, Berlin.

6. The artistic research-method Mind the Sound is part of READY MAKING and was developed by the author to research on how to gain access to the embodied action-based know-how and auditory knowledge through sonic memories, i.e. through remembering and describing sound-practical actions with things. Performance and sound artists as well as composer-performers and curators related to the fields took part in this memory dialogue, which was carried out by Janine Eisenächer and Steffi Weismann, and recorded on video. Edited excerpts of this video archive were exhibited as a video work in the context of the exhibitions Readymade Grüüschschsch------- (TART gallery, Zurich/ Switzerland, 2019), READY MAKING #1, and sonomemo - sound and memory (Errant Sound, Berlin, 2019). See: https://readymaking.com/ Last visit: 07.10.2023

7. Elena Ungeheuer in conversation with the author, recorded at the author's studio at Flutgraben e.V., September 30th 2019, Berlin.

8. Sounding Out the Space - An International Conference on the Spatiality of Sound, November 2nd-4th 2017, DIT Conservatory of Music and Drama, Dublin School of Creative Arts and GradCAM Dublin/ Ireland.

9. Elena Ungeheuer in conversation with the author.

10. See Maurice Merleau-Ponty, Phenomenology of Perception. New York, 1981. Orig.: Phénoménologie de la perception. Paris, 1945.

11. See Michael Polanyi, The Tacit Dimension. Chicago, 2009 (1966) and Knowing and Being. Chicago, 1994 (1969), pp. 123–207.

12. See Annegret Huber, Doris Ingrisch et al., Knowing in Performing. Artistic Research in Music and the Performing Arts. Bielefeld, 2021. Also Salomé Voegelin, Sonic Possible Worlds. Hearing the Continuum of Sound. London, 2021.

13. See Michel de Certeau, Kunst des Handelns. Berlin, 1988. Translated into English as The Practice of Everyday Life [1]. Berkeley, 1984. Orig.: L'invention du Quotidien. 1. Arts de faire. Paris, 1980.

14. See Jean-François Augoyard and Henry Torgue, Sonic Experience. A Guide to Everyday Sounds. Montreal and Kingston, 2005, p.4.

15. See Christopher Cox, "Beyond Representation and Signification: Toward a Sonic Materialism." In: Journal of Visual Culture 10 (2), 2011, p.145–61, here p.157.

16. Ibid.

17. The term "new materialism" was coined in the 1990s and describes an interdisciplinary and heterogenous way of thinking within academia, that investigates the interrelations between humans/ mankind, nature/ environment and technology/ science. Having partly been developed against the backdrop of climate crisis and environmental destruction, it is based on the critique of an anthropocentric thinking as well as on the understanding of our coexistence with other beings and things as entangled and interdependent through the vivid exchange of energies, matter and things. Prominent authors are, e.g. Donna J. Haraway, Karen Barad, Rosi Braidotti, and Jane Bennett. As mentioned in footnote 16, Christopher Cox speaks of a "sonic materialism," Holger Schulze also speaks of a "[n]ew sensory materialism" (Schulze, 2018, p.79).

18. The term "things" used here is rooted in the so-called object oriented ontology, which acknowledges that objects are not passive but instead have their own agency, power and matter-energy, that is and does, and in Bruno Latour's "actor-network-theory," in which things are considered as interactive actors/actants within networks of action (see footnote 20).

19. The "object-oriented ontology" (OOO) is a philosophical school of thought, which has further developed ontological, metaphyscial, and phenomenological thinking after Martin Heidegger, criticizing central parts of Immanuel Kant's thinking. To be oriented toward the object, here, means to reject the binary opposition of subject (active) and object (passive) and thereby the privilege of human existence over all nonhuman objects or forms of existence. Instead, objects are considered as active, living, animate matter with their own being and doing. The term "object-oriented philosophy" was coined by Graham Harman in "Tool-Being: Elements in a Theory of Objects" (1999) and rephrased by Levi Bryant as "object-oriented ontology" in 2009.

20. See Jane Bennett, Vibrant Matter, pp.1–21.

21. See Bruno Latour, "On Actor-Network Theory: A Few Clarifications:" In: Soziale Welt 47, no.4 (1996), pp. 369–381.

22. See Jane Bennett, Vibrant Matter, pp. 20–38.

23. See Timothy Morton: Ecology without Nature. Rethinking Environmental Aesthetics. Cambridge/ US and London, 2007, pp. 1–78.

24. See Donna J. Haraway, Staying with the Trouble, pp. 9–29.

25. See Erin Manning: Relationscapes: Movement, Art, Philosophy. Cambridge/ US, 2009.

26. See Donna J. Haraway, Staying with the Trouble, pp. 58–98.

27. Ibid.

28. Ibid., pp. 30–57.

29. See Bruno Latour, An Inquiry into Modes of Existence: An Anthropology of the Moderns. Cambridge/ US, 2013.

30 The term "toying" I relate to here was coined by cultural theorist Michael A. Conrad in several lectures related to his PhD research. See: Michael A. Conrad. Ludische Praxis und Kontingenzbewältigung im Spielebuch Alfons' X. und anderen Quellen des 13. Jahrhunderts. Spiel als Modell guten Entscheidens. Berlin/ Boston, 2022. We developed the term "acoustic toying" in our collaboration for the lecture performance at the conference Sounding Out the Space – An International Conference on the Spatiality of Sound, November 2nd–4th 2017, DIT Conservatory of Music and Drama, Dublin School of Creative Arts and GradCAM Dublin/ Ireland.

31 See Jane Bennett, Vibrant Matter, p. ix.

32 Readymade Grüüschschsch------ was the title of the exhibition that built the basis for READY MAKING #1 and the whole project. We called our sonic readymade-sculptures "Grüüschschsch-Readymades," using the Swiss-German word 'Grüsch' for the special thing sounds and noises in a playful way of writing and speaking.

33 See Janine Eisenächer and Steffi Weismann, Readymade Grüüschschsch-------, exhibition in the context of the LEFTOVER-series, curated by Livio Beyeler, TART gallery, Zurich/ Switzerland, February 16th 2019.

34 Ibid.

35 See: Jens Roselt, Phänomenologie des Theaters. München, 2008.

36 https://errantbodies.org/project/errant-sounds

37 With the term "event," which was also used by the Fluxus-movement for their happenings and performances, I refer to the "Ereignisform," as Jens Roselt names it, of both sound and performance. See Jens Roselt, Phänomenologie des Theaters. München, 2008. For further explanation on the philosophical and aesthetic dimension of the "event" see: Dieter Mersch, Ereignis und Aura. Untersuchungen zu einer Ästhetik des Performativen. Frankfurt am Main, 2002.

38 See John Cage, "Experimental Music." In: John Cage: SILENCE. Lectures and Writings. Middletown, 1961, pp. 7–12, here: p.12.

39 See Michael A. Conrad and Janine Eisenächer, "Hearing Coexistence: On the Spatiality of Sound and Acoustic Desires in Objective Encounters," Performance Lecture, presented on November 3rd 2017 in the context of Sounding Out the Space – An International Conference on the Spatiality of Sound, November 2nd–4th 2017, DIT Conservatory of Music and Drama, Dublin School of Creative Arts and GradCAM Dublin/ Ireland.

40 See: James J. Gibson, The Ecological Approach to Visual Perception, London, 1979, p.127.

41 See: Donald A. Norman, The Design of Everyday Things. New York, 2002 (1988), p.9.

42 See: Michael A. Conrad and Janine Eisenächer: "Hearing Coexistence: On the Spatiality of Sound and Acoustic Desires in Objective Encounters", Performance Lecture, presented on November 3rd 2017 in the context of Sounding Out the Space – An International Conference on the Spatiality of Sound, November 2nd–4th 2017, DIT Conservatory of Music and Drama, Dublin School of Creative Arts and GradCAM Dublin/ Ireland.

43 See: Holger Schulze: "What Do Sounds Need, What Do We Grant Them – Or Not? A Few Considerations on the Affordances of the Sonic.", Lecture, presented at READY MAKING #3, May 24th 2021, Flutgraben e.V., Berlin.

44 Ibid., also see: Carla J. Maier and Holger Schulze: "The Tacit Grooves of Sound Art. Aesthetic Artefacts as Analogue Archives." In: SoundEffects – An Interdisciplinary Journal of Sound and Sound Experience, Vol. 7 (2017), No. 3, pp. 20–35.

45 Ibid.

46 Ibid.

47 Ibid.

48 Produced for READY MAKING #3 Sonic Affordances, May 23rd–24th 2021, performed on May 23rd 2021, Errant Sound, Berlin.

49 Kesten also refers to the meanings in Mandarin: 钉钉 (ding4 ding1) to bring a nail into the wall, 叮叮 (ding1 ding1), onomatopoetic for the sound of a small object, 丁 (ding1) population, 丁丁 (ding1 ding1), a popular nickname, 定定 (ding4 ding4) to stabilize sth, to calm down. See: http://www.christiankesten.de/compositions_dingding.htm – last visit: 27. 09. 2023

50 See Salomé Voegelin The Political Possibility of Sound. London, New York, 2019, p.173.

51 See Michel de Certeau, L'invention du Quotidien. 1. Arts de faire. Paris, 1980.

52 Ibid.

53 See Michel de Certeau, The Practice of Everyday Life [1]. Berkeley, 1984.

54 See Michel de Certeau, Kunst des Handelns. Berlin, 1988, p.15.

55 See Donna J. Haraway, Staying with the Trouble, pp. 58–98.

56 Ibid.

57 See Gilles Deleuze and Félix Guattari, A Thousand Plateaus: Capitalism and Schizophrenia. London, 2021. Orig.: Capitalisme et schizophénie: Mille Plateaux. Paris, 1980.

58 Ibid.

59 See Gilles Deleuze and Félix Guattari, Tausend Plateaus. Berlin, 2007.

60 Jane Bennett, Vibrant Matter, p. 4.

61 Ibid.

62 See Ungeheuer, Elena: 'Toward a 'Space-As-Shared-Sonic-Practices Turn'.' In: Positionen 114 – Heroines of Sound, Mühlenbeck, 2018, pp. 49–51.

63 See Gerriet K. Sharma: Composing with Sculptural Sound Phenomena in Computer Music. Graz, 2016. Also: "Artistic Strategies in Shared Perceptual Spaces – Researching Sound as Space." Lecture, Kinetics in Sound and Space (KISS)-Colloquium, 17.06.2020, Hamburg.

64 See Jane Bennett, Vibrant Matter, p.13.

NICO DALEMAN AND JUTTA RAVENNA

Kinetic Sound Art

The use of movement as a means for exploring sound's spatial properties is a key component of the aesthetics of both kinetic sound art and contemporary electroacoustic music. Perspectives on the physical characteristics of sound brought about by psychoacoustic research at the turn of the 20th century allowed composers to reconsider the role of time and space as constituent materials of music. Within the current practices of electroacoustic music, this is evident in the insistence on virtual movement of sound sources through multichannel speaker systems, which is considered a central compositional and aesthetic aspect of the genre. Conversely, early 20th century kinetic sound art is associated with the traditions of musical automata and self-reliant musical systems, and with the emergence of "kineticism" in sculpture as seen in the works of Alexander Calder.

Linnea Semmerling and colleagues characterize kinetic sound art as "automated movement that produces sound" in order to create a thread between "the early music automata by de Vaucanson, self-playing musical instruments such as the pianola, the industrial machine sculptures of Jean Tinguely and the so-called 'audio-kinetic sculpture' by Stephan von Huene" (Semmerlin et al 2018, 235). We would also like to include happenings and certain compositions by György Ligeti and Steve Reich as manifestations of kinetic sound art.

A resurgence of interest in kinetic sound art in the last years can be attributed to different factors: The democratization and miniaturization of computer technologies (Rudi et al. 2018), a resistance to the predominance of the speaker as sculptural material manifested in the form of DIY instrument development and self-reliant sculptures (Bradley 2021), and the renewed interest in the exploration of sound materiality's aesthetics (Flø 2018). Likewise, the resurgence of spatial audio can be attributed to the advancements on headtracking technologies for VR and XR, as well as the developments of multichannel systems for film and music (e.g. Dolby Atmos).

We would like to examine the resurgence of kinetic sound art from an historical perspective, emphasizing the philosophical implications of the relationship between sound materiality and the concepts of time and space. The perception of movement accentuates the relationship between sound and space, making it a crucial element in the embodied perceptual dynamics between the listener and the (sonic) space. Concretely, we use Jutta Ravenna's kinetic sound sculpture *Zeiten-Pendel* (2021) as a case study where the relations of space and time are evidenced in the movement of speakers in space. First, we present a brief insight of the history of musical time, focusing on Henry Cowell and Erich Moritz von Hornbostel's theories of rhythmic and spatial perception of sound. Then, we contextualize *Zeiten-Pendel*'s sonic materials and aesthetic approaches to time, space and movement in relation to compositions by György Ligeti and Steve Reich. Ultimately, we discuss embodied perceptual and cognitive processes in *Zeiten-Pendel* within the context of kinetic sound art installation. We present *Zeiten-Pendel* as a coalesce of both trends of thinking space in music, where the musical material is a crucial result of the composition, but also employs the fluidity of kinetic art in order to explore perception of space and time through embodied listening.

TIME-SPACE IN KINETIC ART

Movement has an intrinsic relationship with time. Early timekeeping devices relied on the physical movement of sand or water. Later mechanical clocks operated through moving gears, levers, and pendulums. In both cases repetitive movement serves as a reference to measure and codify the passing of time.

In western musical practices, the invention of the metronome allowed musicians to synchronize to an objective reference of time, instead of relying on subjective descriptors based on affective characteristics (e.g. Allegro, Adagio, etc.). After Johann Maelzel patented the metronome in England in 1815, it became an indispensable device for musical practice thanks to industrial mass production. The use of the metronome and its consequences within musical interpretation has sparked discussions and disagreements that prevail until these days. The metronome highlights the tension between mechanical time and flexible time as a means of musical expression which is often used as an expressive device in western classical music (e.g., accelerando, ritardando, rubato, etc.).

The standardization of musical time also facilitated an empirical investigation of music, in the form of psychoacoustical research that explored relations of time in terms of frequency ratios as a function of time. In his 1930 book *New Musical Resources*, American composer Henry Cowell explains the relationship between the harmonic series, the construction of pitch scales and its relationship to rhythmic ratios (Cowell 1930). For Cowell, pulse and pitch are the consequence of different speed perceptions of a single phenomenon: periodic oscillations, which is evidenced in the mathematical relationships between the subdivision of pulses and the harmonic frequencies of sound. To exemplify this, Cowell commissioned Leon Theremin to create the *Rhythmicon*, an instrument that would create both rhythmical units and pitches following the harmonic series' relations.

During this period, Cowell undertook research of the polyrhythmic structures of Indonesian Gamelan Ensembles from Bali together with the director of the Berlin Phonograph Archiv, Erich Moritz von Hornbostel. As an experienced musicologist, Hornbostel had already conducted research on the relationship between

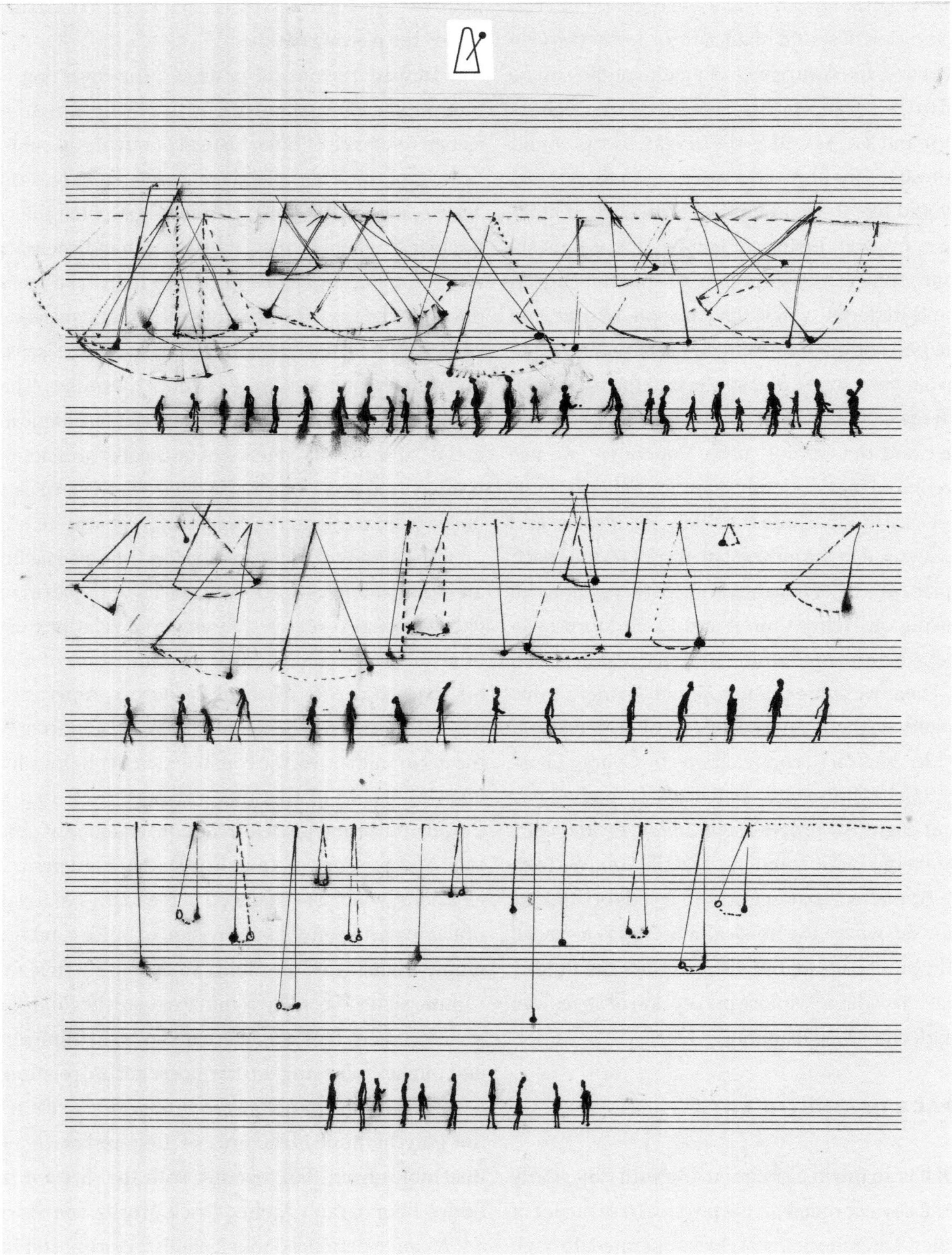

↑: Jutta Ravenna, Zeiten-Pendel, sketch, 2021

pulse and pitch, including also the spatial dimension of musical hearing. He claims that: "Pure time differences trigger clear and definite directional impressions, which even asserted themselves against opposing intensity gradients" (Hornbostel 1923, 88 – 9). Hornbostel identifies time differences in the offsets of acoustic events as a prerequisite of spatial hearing, which is independent of their intensity. That is, time differences become a crucial element in our acoustic perception of space.

Musical time perception is altered by the repetition of short musical gestures such as rhythmic pat-terns or the persistence of long-held pitches that create drone textures. Looping over short pat-terns removes the linear temporal and teleological character of western classical music based on harmonic progressions and melodic narrative development. By doing so, both drones and repeti-tion become an essential element for the creation an alternative perception of time, one that in-vites the listener to experience sound as a spatial phenomenon. Pierre Boulez coined the con-cepts of pulsed time and non-pulsed time in order to articulate the different forms of musical time perception: one in the form of measured time, the other in the form of floating time (cf. Deleuze-Guatari 1987, 262).

Likewise, practices of sound art installation entail a shift from pulsed time as form of narrative time – a progression of scenes in succession that retains a teleological nature – to non-pulsed time, where time becomes a sensuous and immersive experience. In this non-pulsed time, it is possible to expand the perception of discrete time towards the perception of a spacetime continuum. Through the potentiality of both spatial immersion and the freedom of movement of the sound perceiver and emitter, sound art installation highlights the sensuous experience of time as embodied experience of space. The use of physical or mechanical movement in sound installations enables the artist to summarize these two possibilities of time, creating an experience that is both spatial and sensuous, while also exploring space through differences of time and intensity between sonic events. Sound art installations have made explicit use of sculptural and architectural material to bound the perception of time to spatial experience: while the kinetic dimension of sculpture or art installation adds a concrete reference to time through the acts of (rhythmical) repetition and pulsed time, their sonic characteristic offers the opportunity to broaden the experience of time towards non-pulsed time, by transforming time into a sensual experience through embodied perception of space.

Kinetic Sound sculptures such as Nicolas Schöffer's *Chronodynamism* (1959) and Jean Tinguely's *Meta-Harmonie* (1978) manipulate spatio-temporal perception using mechanical repetition, while Stephan von Huene's *Totem Tones* (1969 – 70) and Marnix de Nijs and Edwin van der Heide's *Spatial Sounds (100dB at 100km/h)* (2000–1) manipulate temporal perception using constant tones and the interaction with the spectator. Beyond the immersive perception of time achieved by drone music (e.g. La Monte Young's *Second Dream of the High-tension Line Stepdown Transformer* (1962)), the presence of sculptural and architectural material creates a multisensorial and bodily relationship with the object, where its exploration and perception are contingent upon the possibility of movement both of the spectator and the sound source.

PENDULUM AS A MATERIAL IN MUSIC

Steve Reich's piece *Pendulum Music* (1968) uses pendular movement as the basis to create a musical composition. A set of hanging microphones is paired with a set of speakers laying underneath so that a feedback tone is generated when they are set in motion under the influence of gravity. This oscillatory movement is used in a musical process that is finite and goal oriented, determined by the mechanic characteristics of the system. Such systems are susceptible to states of chaos and self-regulation, analogous to cybernetic systems that fluctuate between entropy and homeostasis. Furthermore, the *Pendulum Music* refers to concepts of cybernetics on two distinct levels: as a homeostatic system, and as a feedback system. As the microphones are let loose and the feedback sound emerges as a single, discrete resonant tone, the oscillator system is in its most entropic part (the most chaotic one). As the piece develops, the tones become more continuous and create a steady feedback tone. The oscillator system is in its most quiet state, but the feedback system is the most active. The whole process could be thought as a transduction from kinetic energy to acoustic energy. Through a feedback experiment the oscillating microphones create a marking of time that eventually compresses into a continuous sound event that populates the space.

György Ligeti's composition *Poème symphonique pour 100 metronomes* (1962) makes explicit use of the metronome as a musical instrument. As the last piece from a series of Fluxus experiments, *Poème symphonique* seeks to associate and critique the state of contemporary music in Western Europe. On the one hand, the piece critiques the nihilism of the Fluxus experiments through its over-the-top description of the processes presented in the written score. On the other hand,

TEMPO	SLOW	
Grave	40 – 44	serious, heavy
Largo	44 – 48	wide, very quiet
Lento	48 – 54	slow
Adagio	54 – 58	calm
Larghetto	58 – 63	somewhat more fluid than Adagio
Adagietto	63 – 69	
	MEDIUM	
Andante	69 – 76	going
Andantino	76 – 84	speeding up
Maestoso	84 – 92	
Moderato	92 – 104	moderately fast
Allegretto	104 – 116	
Animato	116 – 126	slightly slower than Allegro
	FAST	
Allegro	126 – 138	fast
Assai	138 – 152	somewhat faster
Vivace	152 – 176	vividly
Presto	176 – 200	very fast
Prestissimo	≥ 208	as fast as possible

even as a "Happening" the piece shifts the focus from its performance or concept towards its musical character. Ligeti presents an experience of musical relevance, rather than a happening where sound becomes the byproduct (Drott 2004).

The metronome as a quotidian object for performers and musicians reinforces the dadaist essence of this Fluxus experiment (Drott 2004, 233). By adding multiple instances of the metronome, the piece undermines its main use as a regulator of musical time, while presenting an af-

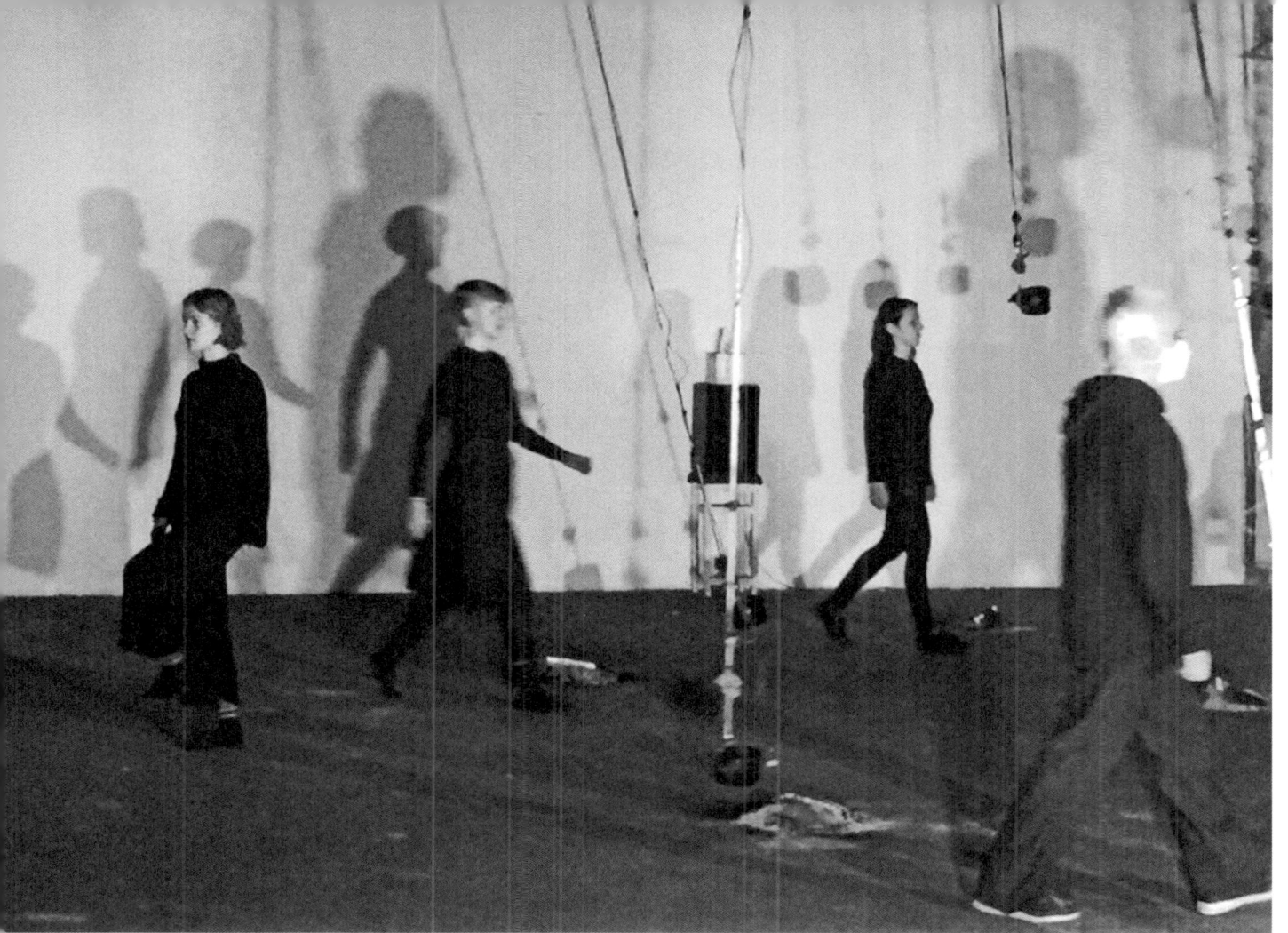

↑: Zeiten-Pendel Performance, 2021, (photo Dorothea Enzmann)
https://soundcloud.com/jutta-ravenna/zeiten-pendel-pulsating

front to the regulatory practices of concerts halls within everyday routines. Following Henri Lefebvre's concept of rhythmanalysis, *Poème symphonique* undermines the repetitive organization that "establishes itself, creating hourly demands, systems of transport, in short, [...] repetitive organisation" (Lefebvre 1992, 7)

Poème symphonique consists of one hundred metronomes are separated in ten groups on ten, which are to be set off by ten performers. The performers have the possibility of winding the metronomes to various degrees, which determines the duration of the piece: the longer the metronomes are wound, the longer they sound. Even though the tempo markings are to be chosen randomly, the standardization of the metronome marks according to perceptions of tempo create not only mathematical relations between them (i.e., they can be grouped as harmonics and sub-harmonics) but also a somewhat homogenous soundscape, where the proportions could be regarded as a distinctive musical "scale."

According to Ligeti, there are three phases in the form, homogeneity — gradual structuration — homogeneity (Ligeti 1982): One of relative synchronicity once the metronomes start, one of uncertainty where some of the patterns start to emerge, and one of relative synchronicity at the end, as the metronomes wind down. The piece begins with the simultaneous beating of one hundred metronomes at maximum density, where the individual voices cannot be perceptually distinguished, and end up by transforming into a dense texture. Its spectral characteristics are defined by the different relations and densities of rhythmic pulses. In the last section of the piece, as the metronomes wind down, individual metric layers become audible. Clear polyrhythms become audible, with their moments of synchronicity and asynchronicity. Because of the relative homogeneity of timbre of the metronomes, single voices are not to be perceived as individual, but rather as a large polymetric clock. Nevertheless, time differences make the clear impression that polyrhythms are happening in a particular space, even if it is in the space of a stage, or a stereo image.

ZEITEN-PENDEL

Jutta Ravenna's kinetic sound sculpture *Zeiten-Pendel* (2021) further develops ideas and motifs from Reich's and Ligeti's works by expanding and emphasizing the sculptural, spatial, and visual dimensions. One can consider Jutta Ravenna's *Zeiten-Pendel* (2021) could be considered as a music for metronome inspired by the final section of Ligeti's Poeme Symphonique. It distinguishes its musical components by making individual meters sonically transparent and audible in layers of time through a particular disposition of sound sources in space. Several motor-driven pendulums hanging from the ceiling with a speaker attached to one end function as upside-down oversized metronomes that represent timers in the room. Unlike in Ligeti's piece, space becomes an essential prerequisite in this kinetic sound sculpture. To explore the spatial sound and physical effects, the size of each metronome is varied and enlarged in accordance with architectural proportions. The pulse of time becomes perceptible in the sound installation in the synchronous / asynchronous swinging, in the breaking out of a common tempo, in the acceleration or deceleration of individual pendulum ensembles. *Zeiten-Pendel* distinguishes itself from Steve Reich and György Ligeti's compositions as a sculptural installation dedicated to the experience of time.

PHYSICAL AND MECHANICAL CONSIDERATIONS

Unlike Steve Reich's *Pendulum Music*, where a freefall pendulum uses gravity as its main force to generate movement, Jutta Ravenna's *Zeiten-Pendel* uses motor-driven pendulums that must in-corporate and respond to the laws of gravitational and centrifugal forces with respect to the current phase of oscillation. When the pendulum sets the pulse, the motor provides energy to either maintain the tempo, accelerate, or stop. The pendulum phase determines the timing and direction of the movement. As a result, a frequency modulation of periodic oscillations is assumed rather than a constant pendulum beat.

The physical processes of the pendulum mechanics are coordinated with the reproduced sound through position sensors and a computer software, so that sound is heard at the turning point of the pendulum. The computer program, influenced by the self-resonance of the pendulum, controls the movements between order and chaos, varying both the speed and deflection based on length and mass. The eight pendulums of different lengths are installed in two interlocking rows in such way that their movements can be grasped with a single glance, creating a field of possibilities for the choreography of the sounds based on the spatial matrix. In total, there are five modes: with sound oscillating synchronously or asynchronously, without sound oscillating, with sound at stand-still or without sound at standstill. The pulse of time is felt in different ways: in the synchro-nous/asynchronous swinging, in the breaking out of a common tempo, and in the acceleration/deceleration or standstill of pendulum pairs or groups.

Similar to the metronome, the oscillation frequency of the pendulum objects is determined by two factors: the weight of the pendulum head and the length of the pendulum arm. The ceiling height manifests the scale on which musical times are possible: taller ceilings are necessary for particularly slow tempos, which require long pendulum arms, while lower ceilings require shorter pendulum arms, which results in faster tempos. Originally, the pendulums were designed for a tower-like room in which the objects would swing back and forth above the heads of the listeners, which facilitates the localization of the swinging movements of the flying sound sources on the horizontal plane of the room.

As a means of spatial hearing and in order to facilitate the audibility of polyrhythms, timbre of the sounds becomes important for the acoustic differentiation of several time layers. The human psychoacoustic ability to locate non-pitched (i.e., percussive) sounds was exploited by using audio samples of drops, anvils, woodblocks, typewriters, among many others. according to the frequency spectra of the timbres, various speaker models are attached on the lower part of the pendulum arm, such as laptop speakers, flower-shaped police speakers and piezoelectric buzzers.

The sound plane generates vectors in the room, which are transformed by individual sound im-pulses distributed to various pendulums, generating an impulse response. The change of their spatial dispositions affects the listener's perception of the meter, which allows variations of sound-ing spatial vectors and other kinesthetic experiences such as diagonal, back and forth, or left to right. At times, different tempos move through the space, jumping from point to point, running back and forth on two parallel spatial axes, creating also rotational or jagged movements through the space. These movements are reinforced and contrasted by the physical movement of the objects, which further models the sound movement within the room.

Instead of the typical clicking sound, variable percussive material is combined via sampling, accen-tuating the polymetric structures and tempo fluctuations programmed in controlling. The human psychoacoustic ability to locate non-pitched (i.e., percussive) sounds is explored using audio sam-ples of drops, anvils, woodblocks, typewriters, among many others. according to the frequency spectra of the timbres, various speaker models are attached on the lower part of the pendulum arm, such as laptop speakers, flower-shaped police speakers and piezoelectric buzzers.

Zeiten-Pendel also operates within cybernetic states of chaos and homeostasis: the eight pendu-lums and their position sensors create a self-regulating feedback system that is influenced both by the physical laws of gravity, and by the phase relations between the swinging pendulums and the energy provided by the motors. The feedback loop ensures that the system remains in equilibrium, although it exhibits unexpected irregularities following the law of periodic oscillations and the gravi-tational and centrifugal forces. The slowing down and speeding up of the swinging pendulums is used as a form of musical ritardando/accelerando in the superposition of several pendulum meters.

SPATIAL PERCEPTION OF TIME

The perception of moments of synchrony or asynchrony is contingent upon a distance temporal and spatial distance to the pendulum ensemble. Due to the pendulum's size, longer observation times are required in order to perceive synchronicity. The metric tempos, their degrees of density, metric pulse sequences, durations, starting and ending points, and the selection of their timbres remain in constant flux by programing aleatory and stochastic procedures with the computer program. In the variation of the number of impulses, the perception of time dissolves again. Within a time period, liquid tempo values could be modulated (e.g. between 560 and 930 bpm) so that the pulse-pitch relations could also be perceived. The pulsating layers of time are closely related to the physical quantization of time, as the perception of speed, acceleration, and deceleration of the pendulums forms the underlying quantum of time: it materializes via the specific tempo in the unique back-and-forth swing of a physical pendulum object.

The phenomenon of synchronicity is deeply rooted in reality, and occurs in both macrocosm and microcosm. Planets and atomic particles oscillate in circles on their orbit independently of each other, although temporarily synchronously, to drift apart again soon and become asynchronous. This principle is taken up in *Zeiten-Pendel* and varied over time scales in space. Like with Boulez's concept of smooth space-time, the

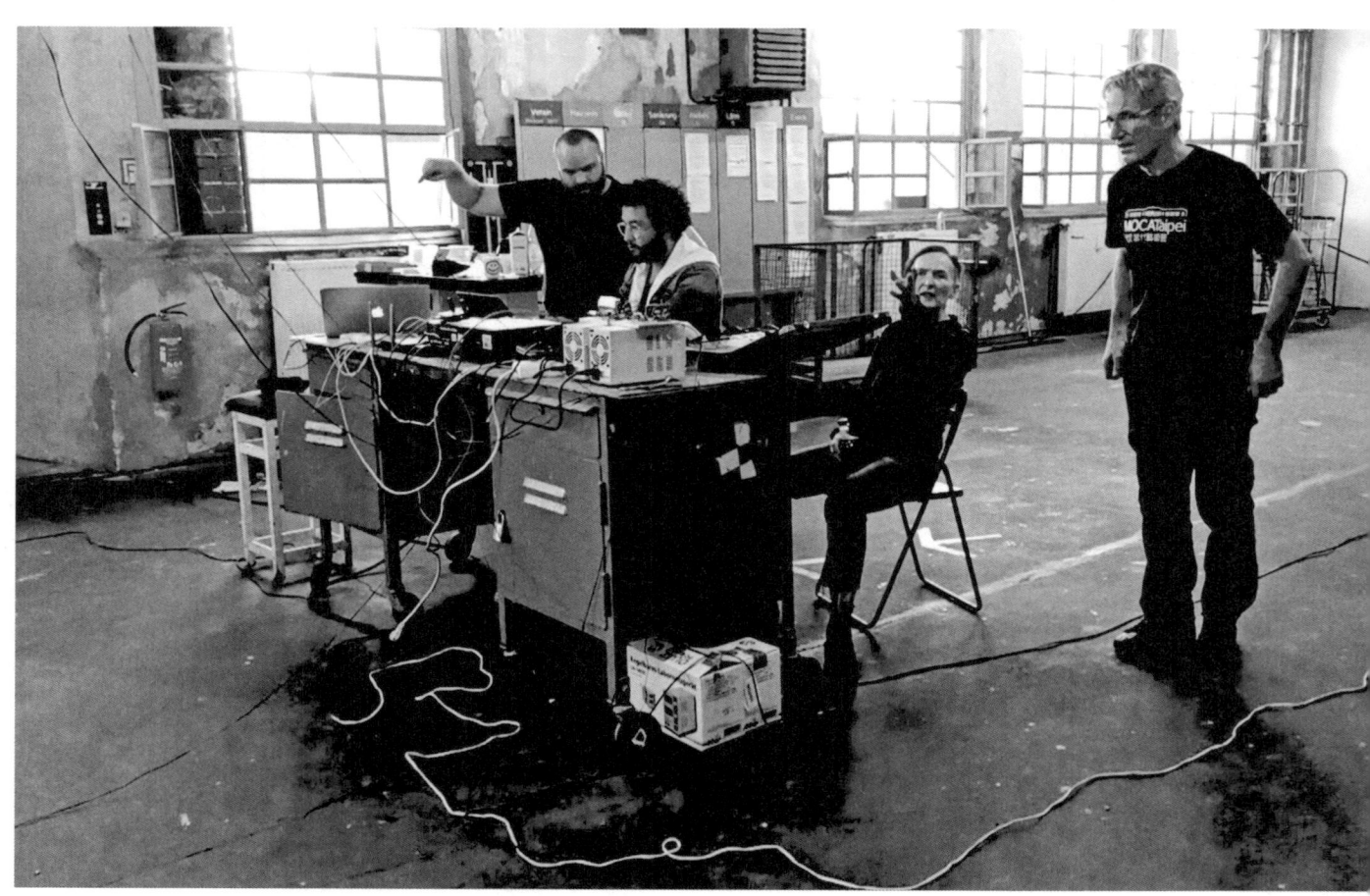

work bears the character of the passing of time not torn into time segments "counted to be occupied," but rather fluid, where "one occupies without counting" (Deleuze-Guattari, 1987, 477). The overlapping of several (metric layers and) tempi can result in episodes of phase resonance, while passages that occur in the border between synchronicity and asynchronicity provide an opportunity for engaging with the nuances of time perception. The shifts of heterogeneous tempi and the random formation of rhythmic figures is balanced between still-ness and movement by the insertion of silence or stasis, i.e. the standstill of the pendulum's engines.

LISTENERS AND BODIES

In *Zeiten-Pendel* the timing produced by the pendulums become indicators of musical time, making perceptible and comprehensible the density of different meters and of tempo fluctuations. By increasing the distance of the pendulum objects from each other the listeners are enabled to hear either meters individually, in pairs, or as an ensemble. Allowing listeners to walk freely around individual pendulums and linger in front of a moving object enabled kinesthetic experiences (especially with eyes closed) such as locating the sound source's hissing through the air from left to right and back again, or the perception of

←: Technical team: Paul Schuladen, Nico Daleman und Carlo Crovato with the artist (photo: René Henry)

↘: Jutta Ravenna, Zeiten-Pendel, Berlin Contemporary Music Month 2021
(photo: Emre Birismen)
https://soundcloud.com/jutta-ravenna/zeiten-pendel-pulsating
https://vimeo.com/632795070

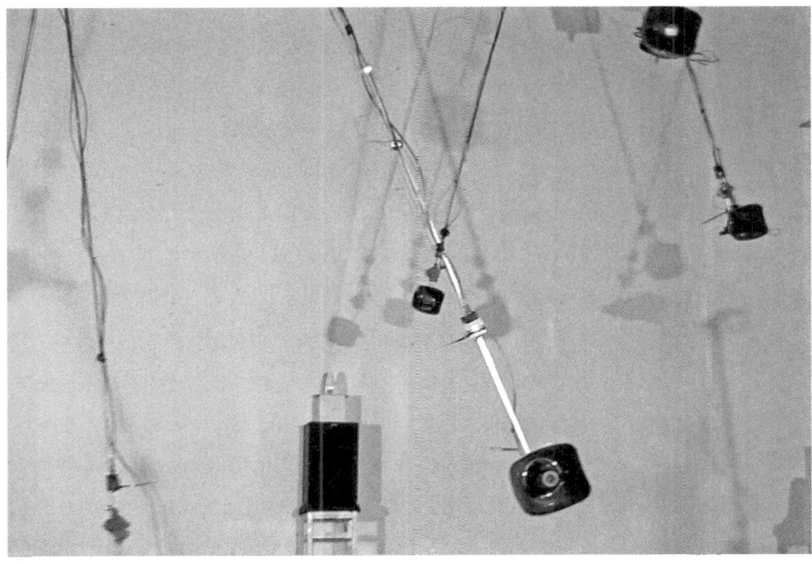

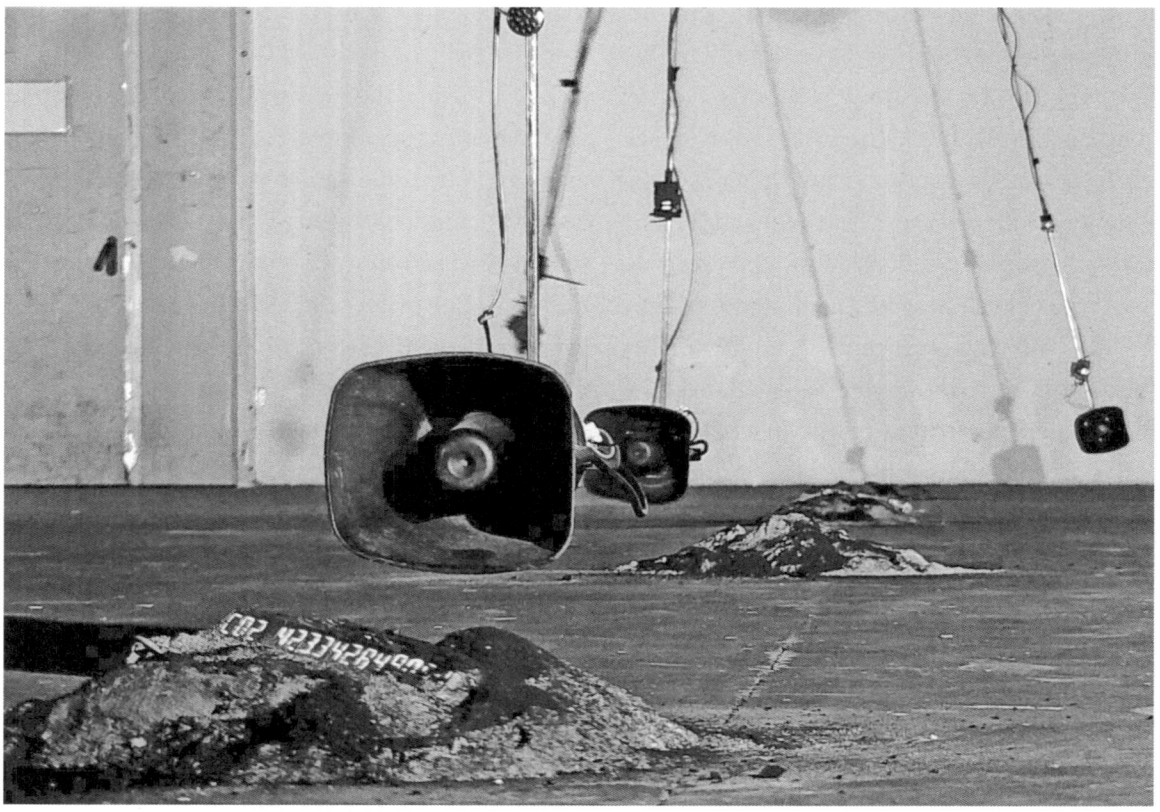

a very subtle doppler effect. According to the distance to the objects, the position of the listeners in the room determines the sound perception in terms of density. Via the sound movements of the pendulums in space, sound lines in different directions, spatial depth, and the right/left expansion of space becomes perceptible. Without the space and without a spatial situation in which the ear can move freely, it is not possible to conceive the different experiences of musical time that the work offers.

The experience of time is closely tied to the movement of objects. The subject's own movement is also affected by the the encounter with the physical objects, generating a sensory perception of bodies in space. Time is measured acoustically during the exploration of the kinetic sound sculp-ture with one's own body and with the help of the swinging objects in space. The smallest time intervals occurring in fractions of hundredths of a second can be perceived, not only through acoustic features but through embodied listening. However, it is not through and exact measurement, but through a subjective time perception, which is only possible by comparing several sound objects in space. In order to be able to perceive temporal differences, it is necessary to establish spatial proportions that refer to a single pendulum as a quantum. Phase synchronization, i.e. a controlled synchronous swinging of all pendulums, cannot be forced

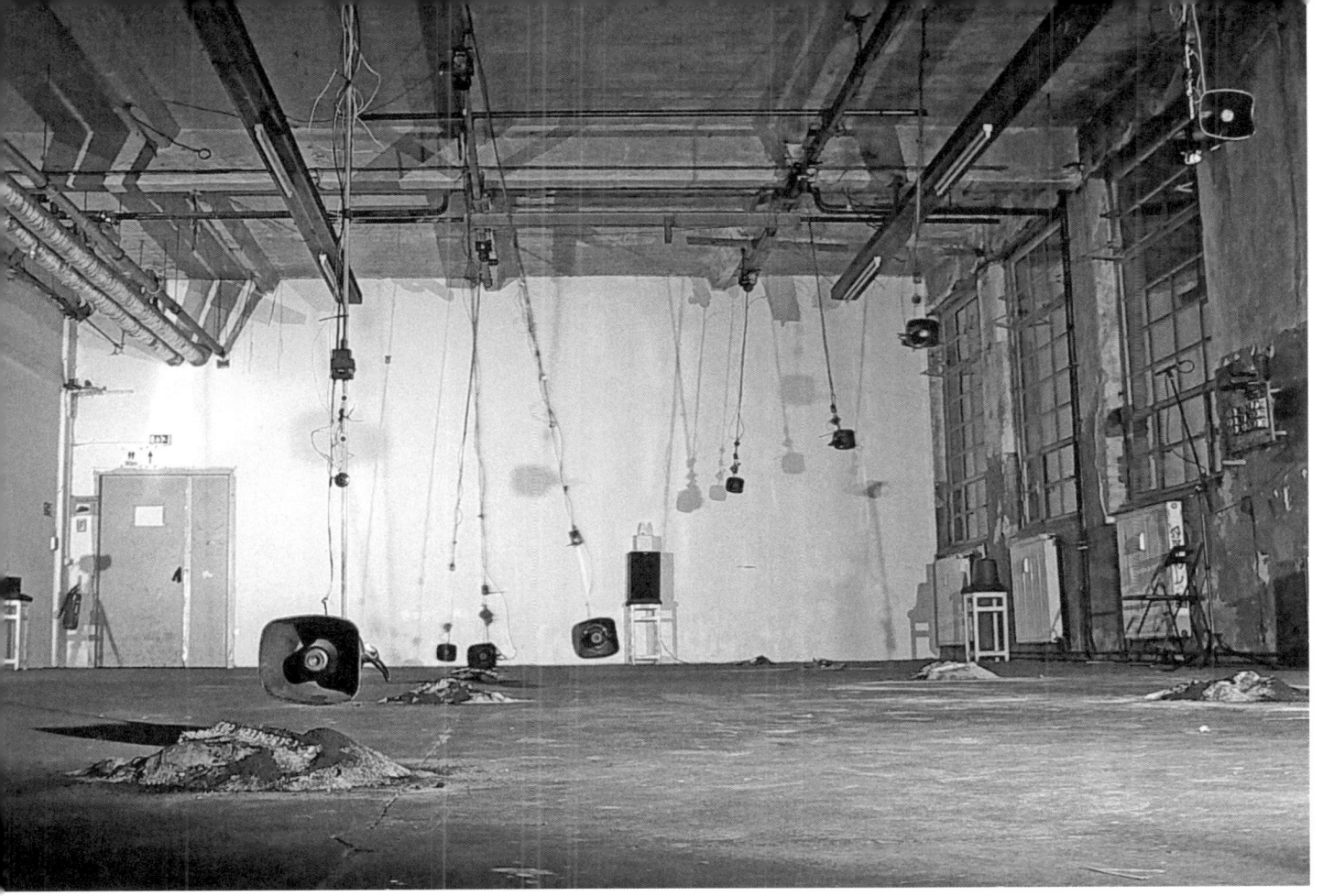

↖/↑: Jutta Ravenna, Zeiten-Pendel, Flutgraben Berlin, (photo: Emre Birismen)

and is instead left to chance. The listener can explore the time and space, and observe moments of random synchrony of the swinging pendulums, experiencing the fluidity of time.

CONCLUSION

Zeiten-Pendel presents a perceptual situation that establishes a relationship between time-space, body and movement. Instead of using metronomes as sound sources (as in Ligeti's work) or the pure movement of the pendulum through gravity (as in Reich's work), Zeiten-Pendel merges both approaches in a spatial sound installation that adds an embodied level to the experience of time. Movement is not only a crucial element of the recipient and the sculpture itself, but also a necessity for understanding the sonic and musical material. Polymeters are experienced not only in time but also in space, adding an ambiguous component through the synchronicity and asynchronicity of the correspondence of the oscillating samples. Unlike kinetic sound art, where materiality, post-speaker aesthetics or references to automaton practices are sought, Zeiten-Pendel thematizes time both as an experience and as aesthetic material. Indeed, beyond a search for sonic materiality, Zeiten-Pendel looks for an embodied perceptual experience that puts into perspective our relationship with the passage of time.

Through our resounding bodies, time is perceived through the perspective in which the present has an infinity and multiplicity of times (the past and the future), always resonating thought sound, and always creating singular possible worlds. The feeling of immersion as a form of exploration of acoustic spaces also reinforces the perception of non-pulsed time. Nevertheless, the use of space differs from an immersive perception of time and rather emphasizes, the perception of rhythmical structures in musical time.

BIBLIOGRAPHY:

Cowell, Henry. New musical resources. Cambridge: Cambridge University Press, 1996 [1930].

Deleuze, Gilles, and Félix Guattari. A thousand plateaus: Capitalism and schizophrenia. Translated by Brian Massumi. Minneapolis MN: University of Minnesota Press, 1987 [1980].

Drott, Eric. 2004. "Ligeti in Fluxus." In The Journal of Musicology 21, no. 2: 201-40. https://doi.org/10.1525/jm.2004.21.2.201.

Flø, Asbjørn Blokkum. 2018. "Materiality in sound art." Organised Sound 23, no. 3: 225-234.

Hornbostel, Erich Moritz von. 1923. "Beobachtungen über ein- und zweiohriges Hören. Psychologische Forschung". Zeitschrift für Psychologie und ihre Grenzwissenschaften 4: 64-114.

Lefebvre, Henri. Rhythmanalysis: Space, time and everyday life. Translated by Stuart Elden and Gerald Moore. London: Bloomsbury Publishing, 2013 [1992].

Gyorgy, Ligeti. 1982. Notes to the score of Poème Symphonique for 100 metronomes, U.E. 8150, (Mainz: Schott, 1982), n.p.

Rudi, Jøran, and Neal Spowage. 2018. "Sound and kinetics–performance, artistic aims and techniques in electroacoustic music and sound art." Organised Sound 23, no. 3: 219-224.

Semmerling, Linnea, Peter Peters, and Karin Bijsterveld. 2018. "Staging the Kinetic: How music automata sensitise audiences to sound art." In Organised Sound 23, no. 3: 235-245.

Stockhausen, Karlheinz. 1958. "Structure and experiential time." Die Reihe 2: 64-74.

LAURA MELLO / VANESSA DE MICHELIS

Beyond the Binaries: from Dystopia to *topia

*This text traces the articulations, challenges and decolonial insights that shaped the partnership between Errant Sound and a community of Brazilian artists during their two-year collaboration, curating and producing a series of sound art initiatives: Dystopia Sound Art Festival and the online Showcase of Brazilian Sound Art (2020); the symposium Listening as a Tool to Blow Up the Bubble (2020); and *TOPIA Sound Art Festival (2021).*

*Despite the scarcely documented histories of Brazilian sound art, it is possible to hear echoes of long-standing histories that reverberate through generations of Brazilian artists. The map accompanying the article highlights some connections that enabled the articulation of the *TOPIA Sound Art Festival.*

ERRANT SOUND AND THE INTERNATIONAL COLLABORATIONS OF THE DYSTOPIA FESTIVAL SERIES

Designed in 2018 by members of the Errant Sound group Georg Klein, Golo Föllmer and Jeremy Woodruff, the festival title shed light on the presence of the Greek word topos in sound art discourses. *Topoi* are spatial/place/geographic indicators that can either be used as prefix (e.g t*opo*graphy) or suffix (e.g u*topia*). In the case of the Dystopia Sound Art Festival (2018), the goal was hence to establish artistic collaborations between Germany and other "places with unusual past and open future,"[1] speculating on physical and abstract *topoi* in sound, approaching "dystopia" as a concept and tool to think outside the box.

In practice, every edition of the festival unfolds in two parts: one in Berlin and another in a collaborating country. The focus lies on practice, knowledge, and community exchange while having open calls and guests from other countries. So far, five editions of Dystopia Festival were organized: two in collaboration with Turkey (2018 and 2019), two with Brazil (2020 and 2021) and more recently, with India (2024).

The Dystopia Sound Art Festival in 2020, as a Berlin-Brazil collaboration, happened exactly between two lockdowns. Therefore, alongside the main exhibition at the basement of the old coin fabric Alte Münze, there was an online Brazilian sound art showcase (with 20 works) and a symposium to close the festival entitled "Listening as a Tool to Blow Up the Bubble." The following year's edition, supposed to take place in Brazil in 2021, took place almost entirely online.

In November 2021, the *TOPIA Sound Art Festival unfolded as a hybrid event showcasing 11 artworks created by both individual artists and collectives from Brazil, Turkey, and Germany. At this point in the text, one might inquire about the fate of the prefix *dys-* concerning the festival's initial concept of topos in its title. What prompted the transformation from Dystopia to *TOPIA Sound Art Festival?

*TOPIA: BEYOND THE DYSTOPIAN/UTOPIAN BINARY

In 2018, the year of the festival's inaugural edition, the world had not yet experienced the pandemic and wars in Ukraine and Gaza. As a result, "dystopia" remained largely a theoretical framework that offered an opportunity to think outside the box. Since the 2000s, themes and narratives centred on dystopia have experienced a surge in interest in various media, including books, movies, television shows, virtual environment narratives, and video/networked games.

However, during the organizational meetings of the *TOPIA festival edition, a significant shift in the curatorial understanding occurred. While studying the documentation of the previous year's partnership with Brazil (2020), specifically going back to the online symposium "Listening as a Tool to Blow Up the Bubble" it became evident that a broader perspective on the concept of *topos* was sought.[2]

In this delicate moment of isolation, a central discussion introduced by artist Pitter Rocha was recalled and resonated strongly with curatorial discussions in the early stages of what was to be the new Dystopia Brazil 2021. Rocha stressed that "while artists in the global north focused on dystopia as a festival theme, there were areas in Brazil, marked by poverty, where dystopia is actually a reality." Entire communities live on the margins of capitalist society, in abandoned buildings and debris, creating make-shift and hacked solutions for everyday life, and collecting social waste of clothing, food, and other materials to survive.

From this perspective, it is possible to start devising a decolonial critique of "dystopia," especially if seen exclusively as a conceptual tool for thinking outside the box by the white global minority – including white academic Brazilians and expatriate artists residing in Europe who have been steering these partnerships.

This understanding brought forth the challenge of curating artworks which articulate a broader spectrum of backgrounds, social contexts, experiences, and languages. Beginning with the festival's title, the aim was to emancipate *topos* from predetermined prefixes and to amplify visibility for less heard epistemologies. Hence, the decision was made to adopt the asterisk (*) as a symbol denoting all that remains unspoken and rebels against its non-existence in the current use of (artistic) languages. This deliberate choice meant departing from dys-topia or any prefixed term, embracing a simpler yet more expansive *TOPIA.

CURATING A MAP OF COLLABORATIVE HISTORIES

The 2021 edition required a more nuanced exploration of the collaboration between Brazil and Germany. It came to light that, despite the fact that decolonial discourses circulated somewhat widely, worldwide and virtually, global north countries still held all the infrastructure and financial capital to keep artistic expressions alive during the pandemic (and beyond). Curating the festival was a baby step in addressing the complex and asymmetric relationship between Brazil and Europe as nation-states and *topoi*, on an institutional, artistic and historical level.

The initial idea of collaborative curating a festival between Brazil and Europe slowly gave way to artists Laura Mello (in Berlin) and Vanessa De Michelis (in London) taking on the practical challenges. Since the official language was English, it was essential to secure funding to address the most important infrastructural asymmetry of the festival: language access. On a very basic level it became clear that the curatorial task extended, beyond the choice of commissions, towards ensuring artist care, international and intergenerational dialogue.

Ensuring that Brazilian artists benefited fairly from the festival's documentation and live events was the first step to enable a more horizontal circulation of discourses. Live translations, for instance, were available in both ways (English and Portuguese). In addition, commissioned artists were spread across 13 cities on Brazilian territory, extending far beyond the Rio de Janeiro São Paulo axis. Finally, for each commissioned work, documentation and social media image and video assets were provided, as well as a one-hour live talk between curators and each artist/artist groups.

*TOPIA promoted articulations between independent and academic discourses, expanding the notion of territories/topoi, exploring site-specific artworks, ecological territories, cultural and discursive spaces and the human body. The main thematic axes were "Artists, Audiences and the Visibility of Sound Art Festivals in Latin America and Europe" and "Migration and Diaspora in Sound Arts."

Through the festival's program, a myriad of Brazilian artists were represented intergenerationally such as Janete El Haouli, Isabel Nogueira and Lilian Campesato[3] whose more than 20 years long practices explore composition (electroacoustic, electronic and radio) and research focusing on migrant and feminist histories. Other participating artists, such as Paulo Dantas and Marina Mapurunga, who coordinate research centers in universities in Rio de Janeiro and Recôncavo Baiano (Electronic Sound Factory[4] and Sonatório[5]), have generously provided their space on the festival platform to showcase collaborative works with their students, a new generation of emerging sound artists.

Representing the northeast of Brazil there were two artists who are adamant in advocating for the inclusion of this often overlooked region in art histories: Tânia Mello Neiva and Rui Chaves. Lastly, a performance held in three countries by the Brazilian artists Mariana Carvalho (Berlin), Nirah Pomar (Florianópolis) and the Turkish artist Elif Soğuksu was the outcome of a residency partnership with SOMARUMOR – a long-run, pivotal sound art festival in Brazil.

CONCLUSION

As a contributor to Errant Sound's Dystopia Festival series, *TOPIA's main curatorial challenge was to understand decolonial practices as going beyond disseminating global south discourses and artworks to an European audience. Although this is not enough to tackle deeper is-

FESTIVALS AND PEOPLE NETWORK

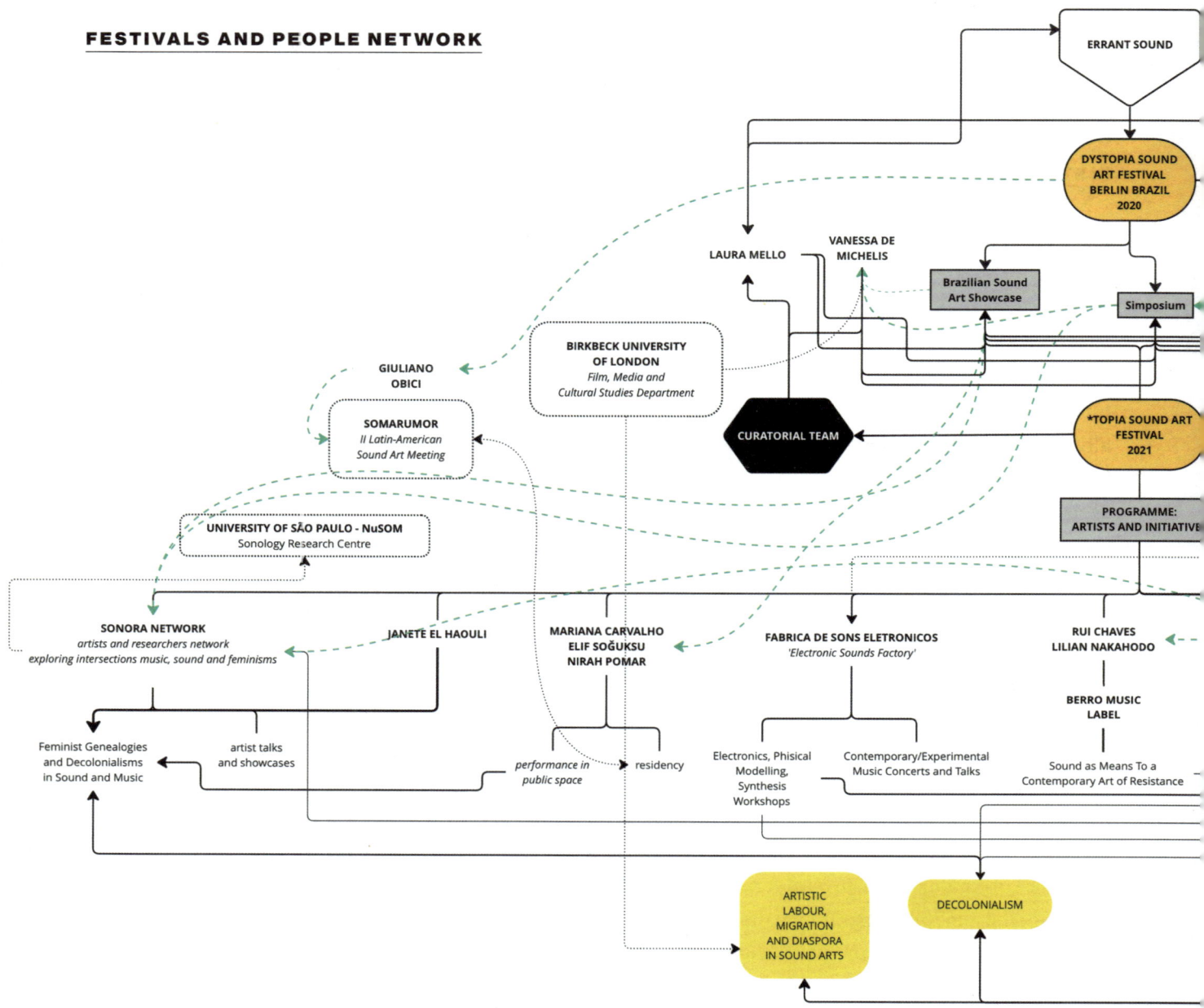

sues such as legacies of class and racial privilege in the arts, the festival has led to a unique initiative to make visible histories and genealogies of Brazilian artists in Europe.

Curating this festival has been an open-ended journey, and there are questions which are still resonating: is it possible to move beyond the binary dystopia/utopia by critically questioning the notion of topoi in sound art? And finally, to which extent the idea of equitableness is being practiced within arts funding initiatives between Europe and global south partners?

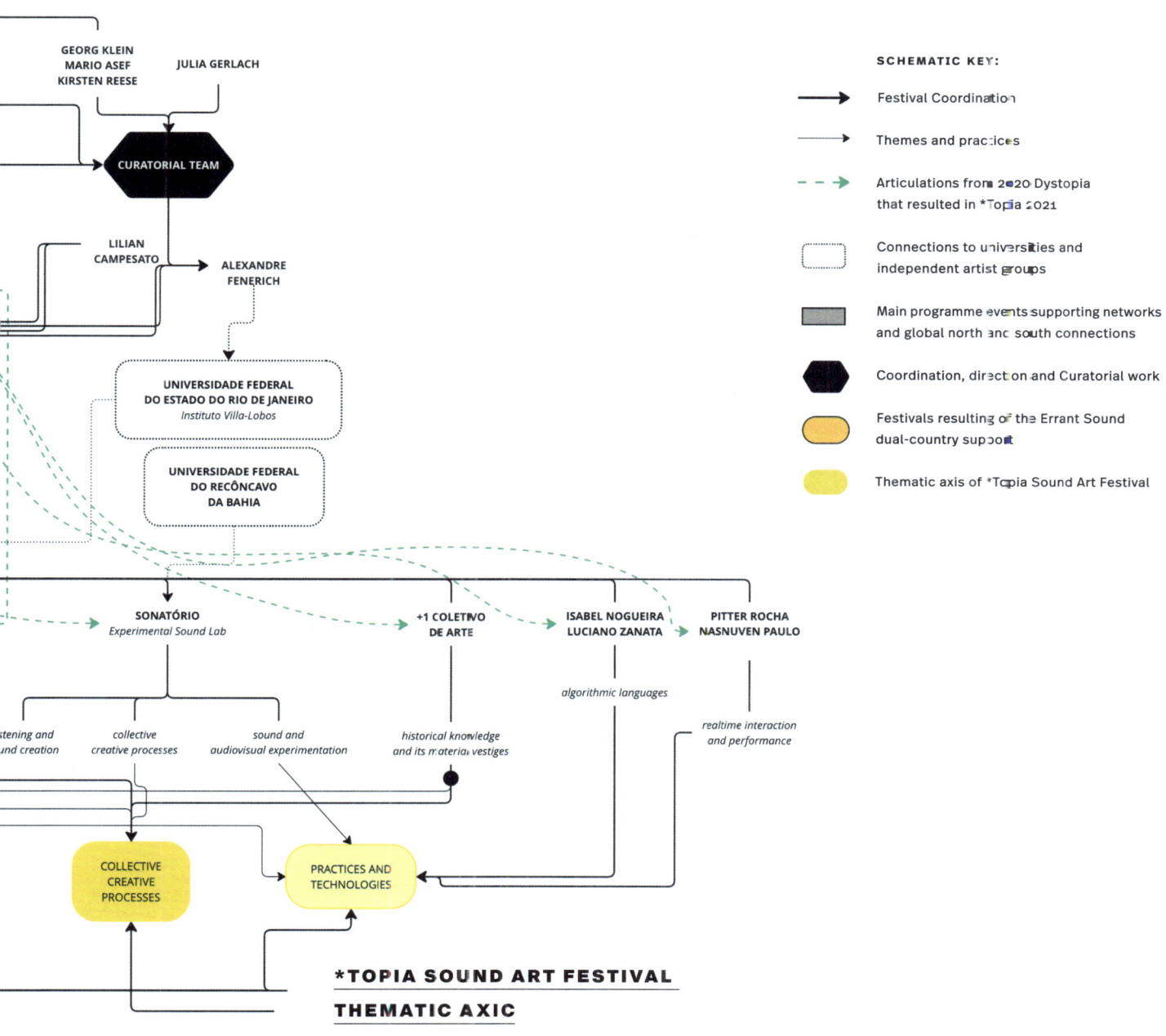

NOTES:

1. As formulated by Föllmer/Klein/Wooruff in www.dystopie-festival.net/2018/?lang=en

2. This encounter (held during the pandemic) brought head-on discussions between artists and scholars from across Brazil and Europe in an unprecedented joint platform: it served as a communication channel between the in person events in Berlin, Brazilian artists living in Europe and artists located in the Brazilian territory.

3. Who is a founder member of Sonora:Music and Feminisms – independent research group which also co-curated the Brazilian Sound Art Showcase in 2020

4. Fábrica de Sons Eletrônicos (University of Rio de Janeiro – UNIRIO)

5. http://sonatorio.org

BRANDON LABELLE

Listening between the Lines :

IN CONVERSATION WITH
LILIAN CAMPESATO

BRANDON LABELLE: It's a pleasure to be able to open this dialogue with you Lilian, and to continue our conversation from when we met in Rio de Janeiro, in May 2022, as part of The Listening Academy. To start, can you please introduce yourself, and say a few words about your practice – and what concerns you most in working with sound?

LILIAN CAMPESATO: First of all, thank you Brandon, for the opportunity to talk a little about sound practices, and especially about listening.

I would start by saying that my practice is a blend of reflective work and inventive actions involving sound, listening, art, and performance. I became increasingly involved in academic research while simultaneously discovering my artistic practice. Over the years, my artistic and academic work have intertwined. This connection between art and research appeared as early as 2005 when I explored the interactions between music and sound art in my master's thesis, and it was particularly significant during my doctoral studies when I developed an extensive discussion on the concept of noise in music. In more recent initiatives, I have had the opportunity to develop and test specific methods for applying a practical-theoretical approach that combines research and artistic creation. An example is the project "Microfonias: invention and sharing of listening,"[1] developed in partnership with the composer and researcher Valéria Bonafé. We base our actions on unconventional methodologies such as conducting recorded conversations, collecting audio testimonies, engaging in artistic correspondences, developing affective reports from listening and exploring alternative publication formats.

As an artist, I work mainly as a composer-performer. Most of the artistic works I've created depart from my own performance, from my experimentation with playing. Looking at my past productions, I realize that a creative path was built from a few axes: the collaborative work with other artists, the engagement with different means of expression and the exploration of voice and noise as crucial compositional elements. Both my solo and collaborative works span a wide range of resources and media involving interactive electronic processing and audiovisual resources that often rely on the creation of a performative poetics for invented instruments. In the last two decades, I have been deeply involved with experimental practices both as a sound artist and performer. One of my main interests relates to what I conceive as performative listening, which usually drives my compositional process. This active – often intimate and visceral – listening, reveals how I listen to myself and share my own listening with others.

BRANDON: Thank you Lilian, for sharing all these different aspects of your practice and ways of working. It's exciting to hear how your work is shaped by the interactions or crossovers between research and artistic practice, as well as your interest in collaboration, such as the *Microfonias* project with Valéria Bonafé. Could you share more about this project – what kinds of listening methodologies are you developing or inventing?

LILIAN: *Microfonias* is a project dedicated to listening. It is intrinsically collaborative and constantly evolving. Valéria Bonafé and I are both researchers and artists active in the fields of music, sound art, and sound studies. We had previously worked together in the feminist network we helped found, S*onora: Musics and Feminisms*.[2] The meetings that gave rise to *Microfonias* began in 2017, filled with the desire to create an alternative environment for research and artistic creation. It also contained a certain degree of guerrilla spirit against the conservative forces that had infiltrated both institutional and non-institutional musical and artistic settings. However, it's important to note that this alternative environment was gradually shaped during the meetings and guided by a particular ethics. This ethics is characterized by prolonged interaction, the regularity of meetings, and a relationship with work that transcends objectivity and productivity, blurring the boundaries between the personal sphere and research and work interests. The result is a place of trust that embraces vulnerabilities and a dynamic that respects the rhythms of creative imagination. Now, you asked me about methodologies ... Over the years, we have carried out various research-creation actions. I'll use the concept of "conversation" as an example of how these actions evolved into what we came to understand as a research method, which we refer to as the "conversation method."[3] Initially, we recorded conversations between the two of us, in which we shared and discussed the process of creating our own artistic works. These conversations were particularly important for initiating discussions about listening. These conversation sessions became materials for analysis and subsequent discussions, which we conducted through regular meetings over the course of a year. Gradually, beyond the topics discussed in the recorded sessions, the act of conversation itself emerged as an important subject to be investigated. As the meetings continued, our experience showed us that conversation in itself was a powerful means not only to present, reflect on, and analyze artistic works but also to convey ethical, aesthetic, and political values and to develop alternative biographical and poetic narratives. When we later reviewed the recorded conversations, we recognized the potential of creating textual transcripts to capture the dynamics of interactions, overlaps, and interferences inherent to the flow of the talks. These transcripts reflected our desire to share the nuances of what we were discussing, as a first attempt to escape the stabilizing effects of syntheses often found in verbal discourse, especially in academic texts. This enriching experience led us to embrace conversation as a method. Understood as a space particularly conducive to the expression of the subjectivities, the conversation allows for experimenting with both the other and oneself. Our extensive experience with the conversation method allowed us to expand our discussions about listening, moving beyond the initially selected artistic works and advancing toward broader aesthetic, ethical, and political debates.

Building on our experience with the conversation method, we developed three other actions aimed at encompassing different listening networks and conversation, including other women, other practices, and interactions. For example, our work with autobiographical audio testimonies of the Brazilian radio artist Janete El Haouli,[4] the production of affective reports from listening derived from the listening of other phonographic records,[5] and later, a non-verbal artistic correspondence action based on listening.[6] These actions enabled us to reflect on the creative process of other artists from their listening perspectives.

I believe that these actions are ways to explore creative forms of research and produce content that allows for the emergence of alternative methods for knowledge production. It's challenging to think about other epistemologies without considering methods that lead to innovative ways of observing the world. We intend to contribute to a broader understanding of the complex experience of listening through the experimental practice of inventing and sharing listening experiences.

BRANDON: I'm struck by the work you and Valéria are doing, and the explorative methods of shared listening as well as conversation. I've been reading again the work by Luce Irigaray, *The Way of Love*, where she develops an ethical model of speech, especially in order to support forms of radical sharing – what she terms *the sharing of speech*. For Irigaray, this is really about nurturing a new culture of voice, of speech, in attempts to overcome dominant forms of exclusion and silencing. Can we reflect more on the topic of conversation, of speaking and listening as a co-creative act? How does the conversation method relate to your experiences in Brazil – is there a situated politics, or a form of local engagement, that informs your work with conversation? How do the *vocal economies* of who speaks and where impact onto the conversation, the voicing you and Valéria are working at?

LILIAN: For Irigaray, love occurs when neither subject effaces the other, it is an ethic of exchange. She suggests that thinking about limits helps us build healthier connections among unique and limited individuals within a loving context, rather than dealing with relationships among bossy, self-sufficient, or all-powerful individuals in a system of mutual exchange.

When you start to reflect deeply on what is at stake during a genuine conversation, you realize that it implies interaction, it requires mutual action, and radical sharing that comes from a flux between the different bodies participating. Since the conversation implies an interaction between different bodies, we have to think about the quality of this interaction.

What truly constitutes the exchange between individuals during a conversation? From our experience, active listening plays a central role in addressing this question. In the course of a conversation, the willingness to genuinely hear and understand the other person ends up shaping what is communicated. This type of listening assumes the ability to be both influenced by and to influence the conversation, and it's an emotionally present form of listening. In a conversation, this presence can manifest through spoken expressions – such as asking questions, providing comments, or interjecting – as well as through physical gestures like maintaining eye contact or nodding. But also, it can be exercised silently by simply keeping an open channel for listening.

Regarding your second question, how does the conversation method relate to our experiences. I would say that first, this experimental method reinforces the identity and characteristics of those who engage in a conversation. Since this experience began with the two of us, two women artists, two Brazilians that engaged in a micropolitical cooperation, the results are deeply informed by that. How women listen to themselves, understand themselves, and express themselves. What happens is that we spend time together, we value random aspects apparently insignificant, yet intimate, singular. We avoid squashing the subtleties because they require time. This is why it's exceptionally challenging in straightforward speeches. It's difficult to carve out space for the nuances, but we believe that it is worth it. We call that a commitment to exercise a feminist politics of listening.

As for the aspect of local engagement, I haven't had the opportunity to reflect on that extensively, but I would say that our Brazilian culture greatly influences our approach in at least two paths. The first one relates to the prevalence of oral communication. We belong to an oral/aural culture. This is deeply rooted in our ways of thinking and acting, which directly impacts our cultural production. The second aspect is the emotional proximity and the heightened intimacy among individuals. This becomes evident, for instance, in affectionate exchanges through hugs, kisses, and displays of tenderness.

Concerning *vocal economies* of who speaks, I see speaking and listening, to some extent, as exclusive. Nobody listens while they are speaking, nor do they allow themselves to speak when they want to listen. However, the balance between speaking and listening is what helps define a communication policy: when someone takes on the role of listener or speaker, they are taking a political stance. This is why conviviality is so important. We realize that over the extended period of living together and conversing, we have the chance to truly learn from each other, to revisit our thoughts and, then, to modulate our ideas.

BRANDON: The question and practice of conviviality is something I also feel very connected to, and it's something we work on as part of The Listening Biennial, and also at Errant Sound, creating spaces and environments that not only support the creation of artistic, sonic work, but do so by also nurturing community. That balance between speaking and listening that you mention, does feel essential to maintain – how conviviality gives room for allowing for agreement and disagreement alike. I know you are also involved in the collaborative network Sonora, which supports the visibility of women's work in music and art. Can you share something about Sonora and your own work – have you developed or been part of realizing a work as part of the activities of Sonora?

LILIAN: Indeed, my work bears a profound imprint from my ongoing engagement with the Sonora network.

Since the first Sonora meetings back in 2015, the choice of actions and activities were always defined based on the participants' wishes. This characteristic was fundamental for the configuration of this network. Participants work through face-to-face meetings that are also transmitted via the internet. Over time, a vibrant weekly gathering environment has flourished. Being part of this community entails harmonizing individual aspirations with a collective spirit. Consequently, we have successfully fostered a political practice of attentive listening, speaking, and welcoming.

This was achieved through many hours of interaction in which conflicts are inevitable, making me wonder why I am dedicating myself so much to this. The answer is because I feel that I belong to a place where I can speak and listen to myself speaking to others. In this way, I am learning to build myself in relation to people different from me. Then I can also listen to other people, practice silence, pause, and listen to the various demands that arise. So, I believe that this builds a kind of community with its own ethics, with very diverse actions that are entirely based on people's desires, and through all of this, we realize that as feminists, as women, and as individuals, we are able to tell our own story, we are able to narrate ourselves in encounters with others.

Throughout all these years, I have been involved in organizing [collectively] various actions and activities for Sonora, including study groups, a series that features female artists and researchers discussing different topics, podcast production, symposiums, concerts, artistic occupations, and political demonstrations. However, I would like to specifically mention the artistic action called "Dispatches," a non-verbal artistic correspondence initiative that Valéria and I created at Microfonias, which later included the participation of several Sonora members.

"Dispatches" was launched during the early stages of the Covid-19 pandemic. In this practice, a "dispatch" refers to any form of artistic creation intended for a specific recipient. It could be a brief composition, a concise performance, a sound snippet, an image montage, a video, a poem, a photograph, or any other type of artistic work. Once created, it is sent to the recipient without any accompanying contextual message, aside from a title. Upon receiving it, the recipient embarks on a personal journey of listening while crafting their own dispatch in response, thus perpetuating the process.

In the correspondence exchanges between this group of thirteen women (nine Sonora members and four invited artists), sonic agency resonated in the artists' desiring posture of listening and being listened to. It was reflected in their auditory expectations and imaginations for what was to come. This immediately instigated them to create responses to each other's calls through artistic production in a movement that already implied the other in the creative process. In the course of this action, these women celebrated the bond, the encounter, opening their senses and letting their guards down. They formed a community founded on mutual care and collective solidarity, inspiring and nurturing each other.

The result of this artistic and research action along with a reflection on listening will be published in the *Unlikely Journal for Creative Arts* special issue on Resistance by the next year.[7]

BRANDON: It's inspiring to hear more about the Sonora project and community, and also to hear about the "Dispatches" project. It also seems to capture that sense in which listening can be practiced, as part of a greater movement of exchange and of building community, as well as finding or nurturing a particular ethics. The non-verbal aspect is also striking, opening up another space for relating, and also approaching our practices. You also mention the experience of conflict, and how important it is to also give room for disagreement as part of the communities or collectivities we are part of. To conclude our exchange here, let's reflect further on this. In what ways can we truly listen to those we disagree with, especially those who are farthest from our social circles? What kind of listening is this – or, what resources can we find to help us practice such listening? Is there anything that comes to mind for you – were there also conflicts, disagreements, critical responses emerging within the "Dispatches" that were productive?

LILIAN: Listening to the Other, listening to those who are different from me (or ourselves) is a vast subject, and I thank you for bringing up this discussion. In our hyper-individualized culture, it is common to perceive an inability to listen to others. Nobody listens to each other.

Listening is something you build, develop, in other words, it's a practice. Thinking about spaces of conflict, and misunderstandings, how can we truly listen to others? For transformative listening, it's necessary to promote a shift. It requires giving up the habit of listening to others from our perspective, our position, our values, and our interests. This kind of approach affirms our difficulty in listening, the refusal to hear and understand others, and it seems to give space to a desire for deafness, to close ourselves off. This approach, in a way, harks back to a colonizing form of listening, a form of listening that establishes a vertical power relationship: there is someone who speaks, who knows, who positions themselves as an authority, and someone who listens, accepts, obeys. It's necessary to give up the desire to defeat the other, to have our point of view triumph at the end of the conversation. But how can we be creative and coexist with diversity without giving up our attitudes and positions? It's just not possible. When you relinquish the desire to defeat the other, you realize that the participants in the conversation are not opponents but partners who can build and share ideas and can promote an openness to knowledge. However, this is a very challenging task, especially when the other is very different from you. I don't believe there's a formula to overcome this difficulty, but I believe that we can exercise our listening to understand differences not as barriers but as possibilities for understanding and growth.

I'll give an example that may seem somewhat radical but which illustrates the potential that open listening to embrace differences can offer. One of the recent actions I carry out with my colleague Valéria Bonafé within the *Microfonias* project takes place in the Luz neighborhood, a central region of the city of São Paulo. We have called this action "des-habitar escutas" (disinhabit listening). In recent decades, this region has become known for housing the so-called "Cracolândia" (crackland), one of the largest open drug scenes in the city, with a history marked by poverty and social exclusion. The Luz neighborhood also has a rich collection of cultural facilities, including museums, cultural centers, and an important concert hall in the city that are frequented by a socially affluent class and are inaccessible to those living in extreme vulnerability on the streets of the region. Therefore, it's a region of significant economic, social, political contrasts, and consequently, much conflict. Every time we go there, something special happens. These are chance encounters with people very different from me and Valéria. What stands out in these encounters is a sense of discomfort, a powerful noise that, for a moment, makes us lose the ability to communicate. It seems that all our conventions of communication and social interaction do not work there. They simply no longer make sense. So, it's necessary to (re)learn to communicate, and to interact. And that is the task of listening!

During one of our visits to Cracolândia, Valéria and I were talking to some artists who work in the area when we were interrupted by a man who, like hundreds of other people living in the region, was a crack user. He initiated contact by trying to sell a plastic ring and asking for a beer. It's important to note that initially everything about him was somewhat discomforting. He smelled of alcohol, and the abrupt way he approached us, interrupting our conversation, only reinforced our difficulty in interacting. He stood there, looking at us intently. I asked for his name, but he refused to respond, yet he stayed there smiling. Then, after a long period of silence, exchanged glances and nervous smiles, he began to produce sounds, as if imitating dog barks: "woof woof woof." He imitated a bark, smiled, and continued looking. I smiled, completely lost, not knowing what to say, so we remained silent. He barked several more times. At that moment, it was just me, Valéria, and him, and the discomfort of the situation led us to find a way to bridge the gap (or abyss) that existed between us and him. So, after a long period of silence on our part, and nervous giggles, I felt that I should bark back. And I imitated him: "woof woof woof." He smiled, and we communicated through barks for a while. In this moment of non-verbal communication, our conversation unfolded, and we, me, him, and Valéria, managed to create a genuine exchange. It was as if we had turned a key that unlocked our interpersonal relationship.

Practicing listening requires an effort to open up our own vulnerabilities, a movement that seeks a broad otherness. I'm very interested in a form of listening that is also produced between the lines, in the noise. This doesn't happen without effort! It's necessary to create conditions that allow us to liberate ourselves from an idea of listening inherited from modernity, which, like the mode of the subjectivity of the colonial-capitalistic regime, consists of anaesthetizing our vulnerability to the forces of the world, denying any alterity. Through listening, we can recognise the other, create narratives, share affections and feelings, and withstand uncertainty, anguish, and indeterminacy regarding the truth. Together, I and the other participate in a larger, open experience that is the desired exchange of languages (verbal and non-verbal too). Listening to others is relinquishing a position of power and allowing the experience, language, and presence to take center stage.

NOTES:

1 For more information, see: https://microfonias.net/

2 For more information see:www.sonora.me; https://www.youtube.com/watch?v=3NLPf7IgSuM

3 For an in-depth discussion of the conversation method, please refer to: Lílian Campesato and Valéria Bonafé (2019) *La conversación como método para la emergencia de la escucha de sí*. El Oído Pensante 7: 47 – 70. [Conversation as a Method for the Emergence of Self-Listening]. The article includes some examples of creative textual transcriptions we conducted based on recorded conversations.

4 This action resulted in the article: Valéria Bonafé and Lílian Campesato (2021) "'Many voices, resonating from different times and spaces': a script for an imaginary radiophonic piece on Janete El Haouli." Feminist Review, Sonic Cyberfeminisms, 127, 141 – 149.

5 This method was described in the article Valéria Bonafé and Lílian Campesato (2022) "Affective reports: from listening to writing, from writing to listening". OEI – Aural Poetics, edited by Michael Nardone.

6 Campesato, Lílian; Bonafé, Valéria. 2023. "Dispatches: Cartographing and sharing listenings". In *The Body in Sound, Music and Performance*, edited by Linda O Keeffe and Isabel Nogueira, 153–164. London and New York: Routledge.

7 Campesato, L.; Bonafé, V. "In between the lines: Listening to the inaudible, giving way to the unsayable." In Unlikely: journal for creative arts. Issue 9, Resistance. Ed. by Melody Ellis and Kim Munro. (Forthcoming)

MARIO ASEF

$$\frac{s<l>e}{\text{The Language}}$$
$$\frac{}{\text{of / in}}$$
$$\frac{}{\text{Things}}$$

The relationship between sound, language, and environment has been a subject of inquiry and exploration in many disciplines. For example in music theory, Brown (2017) highlights that the evolution of music and language in different societies is inextricably contextual, i.e. sounds are produced in some sort of accordance to our environments. One key concept that has emerged from these discussions is the idea of resonance. Resonance (from Latin "to echo") refers to the relationship between two vibrating systems. Co-oscillation or resonance of one body with another refers to the way in which sound waves interact with their environment, bouncing off surfaces, thereby creating reflections and reverberations that shape the way we perceive and experience sound. Another aspect in this regard is that language is not just a tool for conveying information, but also a medium through which we create and reinforce sociocultural structures and environmental interactions. As such, the sounds we produce and the words we use are deeply connected to our environment, reflecting and shaping the world around us (Maturana, 1998).

This text attempts an approximation on the relationship sound< language >environment [s< l >e]. By taking sound art works from an exhibition series I curated at Errant Sound called "Visual Approach to Sound,"[1] I will try to expose a way of understanding s< l >e not only as a structurer of our environment and of all the sound-ecosystems that inhabit it, but also as a pivot point to navigate environment through sound and language. Drawing from the exhibited works, together with my own artistic practice, this text showcases how artistic experimentation can contribute concretely to a contemporary understanding of the relationship s< l >e.

Even though the complexity interwoven between s< l >e remains inextricable, I will concentrate on distinct facets of sound, language, and environment to navigate my contemplations on the showcased artworks.

s<

In the realm of physics, sound is characterized as a vibration that travels in the form of an acoustic wave, traversing through a medium of transmission like gas, liquid, or solid matter. Within the domains of human physiology and psychology, sound refers to the process of detecting these waves and their subsequent interpretation by the brain. In terms of communication, sound is the result of organic or solid parts interacting through friction or undulations. Sound waves are empathic in the sense of being susceptible to their environment, transforming their own length or amplitude, tone and texture depending on the physical components of the surroundings. The same sound source sounds different depending on its surroundings. Imagine, for example, clapping your hands in a small room, a jungle or in an empty baseball stadium. In all these cases the source of the sound is your hands clapping, yet the resulting sound is very different in each case. Functioning as a perceptible signal received through one of our primary senses, sound serves a multitude of purposes across various species, encompassing the realms of danger detection, navigation, predation, and communication. The distinctive sounds emitted are inherent to and indicative of diverse elements, including earth's atmosphere, water bodies, and nearly all physical occurrences like fire, rain, wind, waves, and earthquakes. Furthermore, numerous creatures, including frogs, birds, and both marine and land-based mammals, have evolved specialized organs for sound production.

In contrast to sight, the complete obstruction of environmental sounds is beyond our capability, as our bodies perceive vibrations even when our ears are obstructed. We live pierced by sound and, through it, by our environment (socially, politically, naturally). At the same time, we are environment. From the most recondite corner of our guts populated by bacteria to the last mineral exploited to produce our cell phones – we are made of our social-political-natural environment (Bennett, 2010) and connected to it through sound. Inextricably situated within environment, we dialectically co-produce and perceive it. Sound can therein express the conditions of an environment to us. We are able to hear if an environment is in balance or in conflict. In times of war, for example, the most consistent sound (apart from screaming people, bombing airplanes and machine guns) is the silence of hiding people and animals.[2]

In an ongoing series by Berlin-based artist Clarissa Thieme, in which she engages with the Hamdija Kreševljaković Video Archive in Sarajevo, she documents war as a point of departure for the development of multimedia installations.

The installation *Can't you see them?*[3] investigates subjective testimony in the context of collective traumatic events, such as the Yugoslav wars, and their reconstruction through technical and juridical means. It examines how these events are reconstructed using technical and juridical methods, aiming at uncovering the gaps that emerge between the language of individual recollection and their transformation into mechanisms of historical representation. Central to Thieme's project is a 45-minute video footage sourced from the Hamdija Kreševljaković Video Archive, captured by Nedim Alikadic during the initial stages of the 1992 siege of Sarajevo.

Using motion tracking, the artist performed a metadata analysis of the video's shaky handheld camera that is facing an unforeseeable threat. Calculating its position and movement, she then fed this data into a light-projecting motion control system. The work focuses on what is visible and "replaces" the camera lens with a spotlight. The resulting light jerks, changes direction, and trembles. Due to these movements the whole object produces sounds – a body full of fear and anxiety behind the moving images.

The work was displayed at Errant Sound in two parts: the sounds of the original video was audible via a speaker placed in the middle of one room while the spotlight, with its mechanical movement, was placed in another. I find it important to highlight the sounds of the original video here. In a conversation[4] with Clarissa Thieme and Jan Verwoert, I addressed the immense role sound plays in analyzing specific historical trauma. In the original video one could hear the scared voices of people talking and the noises of the camera's microphone scratching the windowpane. These sounds, apart from being a form of reconsidering subjectivity in historical objectification and a representation of production processes of sound/video recordings, are witness to the terror of war through their technological disruption (mic scratching glass = shiver, distress) and the disruption of language (the conversation is distorted) through technologically-generated sound. Even if we are not able to understand the spoken language in the video, we do connect affectively with those voices – in a language beyond language. The screeching of the microphone on the window makes our skin crawl, makes us feel that nothing good is about to happen. We can see through Thieme's work how sound, apart from being an index that evokes the physical (technological/cultural) conditions of our environment, affects us on an emotional level which connects us intimately with our immediate socio-political environment. And it is precisely this intimacy, this involvement, that implies taking a position in front of the acoustic environment which we are part of. To that extent, listening also bears responsibility. To listen is to simultaneously be embedded in a myriad of categories – be it spatial, emotional, cultural, etc. In this context, attentive listening also implies a freedom of choice that our cities (and our political systems) often do not offer. Thus, there are situations of consensual listening / forced listening that we navigate in search of balance, or what we could call an "empowered listening."

Listening creates environment. Until it reaches our ears, sound first takes multiple paths, refracting on the surfaces that make up the surrounding space and transporting all these materialities plus the materiality of its source. A sound is always its environment; it transports and amalgamates it. Just as sound is the language of things, we unite with things through sound and they unite with us in a kind of uninterrupted dialogue.

"To listen is to enter that spatiality by which, at the same time, I am penetrated, for it opens up in me as well as around me, and from me as well as toward me: it opens inside me as well as outside, and it is through such a double, quadruple, or sextuple opening that a 'self' can take place" (Nancy, 2007: 14.).

According to Jean-Luc Nancy, inter-subjectivity in listening involves being attuned to the presence of the other and engaging in a mutual exchange of meaning. It emphasizes the shared responsibility between the listener and the speaker to actively participate in the process of communication. Furthermore, inter-subjectivity in listening challenges the notion of a single authoritative voice. It acknowledges the plurality of voices and perspectives in a dialogue and seeks to create a space for multiple voices to be heard and valued.

The concept of inter-subjectivity in listening finds a curious counterpart in physics describing how solid matter vibrates: Phonons, for example, are quasiparticles that represent collective vibrations of atoms or molecules in a solid material. They are the fundamental units of lattice vibrations, which contribute to the transmission of heat, as well as the propagation of sound and other mechanical waves in solids. In a solid matter, atoms or molecules are not static but rather vibrate around their equilibrium positions. These vibrations can be described as waves traveling through the solid's lattice. Phonons are the quantized versions of these vibrational waves, similar to how photons are the quantized particles associated with electromagnetic waves (Hunklinger, 1982).

This plurality of vibrations is what we could call "the voices of matter." The sound of rocks and glass, metals and concrete structures are also inter-subjective pluralities that express collectively the vibratory movements to which they are exposed.

A project by Erik Smith, *AABBCCDV*,[5] shows an installation and a vinyl piece, that capture the poignant instance of a building's demolition – a structure that once housed various Miami art organizations and artist-run spaces. Among these was the "Dimensions Variable" art space, which utilized the building for exhibitions and studio purposes over the years. However, in 2012, they were compelled to vacate the premises to pave the way for new development endeavors. The building's demolition was meticulously recorded and subsequently resonated within the Errant Sound exhibition space voicing so the materiality of an urban development, a narrative woven as much from speculative growth and renewal as it is one of negation and fragmentation.

The exposed sounds express not only their materiality – concrete, cement, stones, iron, etc. – but they also are the symbolical expression of their structural entanglement with late capitalism, post-industrial processes of production and consumption; in this case, within space organization, construction and transformation based on a violent intervention in the environment. The sounds of cracking and crushing walls, the aggressive "breathing" of the excavators and their pushing and crashing attempts are the voice of a system that administers space in order to control the habitat of humans within an urbanized natural environment.

!

In Heidegger's philosophy, language is not merely a tool for communication but a fundamental aspect of human existence. He argues that language is the medium through which our understanding of the world is shaped and expressed. Heidegger emphasizes that language is not a neutral or transparent vehicle for representing reality; instead, it actively shapes our perception and interpretation of the world (Oberst, 2011). For him, language is deeply intertwined with our being-in-the-world. He suggests that our existence is rooted in a pre-linguistic understanding or "primordial attunement" that underlies our engagement with the world. Language then emerges as a means of expressing and articulating this attunement.

Humberto Maturana, a Chilean biologist and philosopher, has a unique perspective on language. He emphasizes that language is not about describing an objective reality but rather about constructing a shared reality through coordination and agreement among individuals. He argues that language is not separate from our cognitive processes but is deeply integrated in our way of being and knowing. Like Heidegger, he sees language as a crucial aspect of human social systems and an integral part of our way of being in the world. This opens up a realm where language can be seen as different forms of communication between members of the same species or even between humans and non-humans.

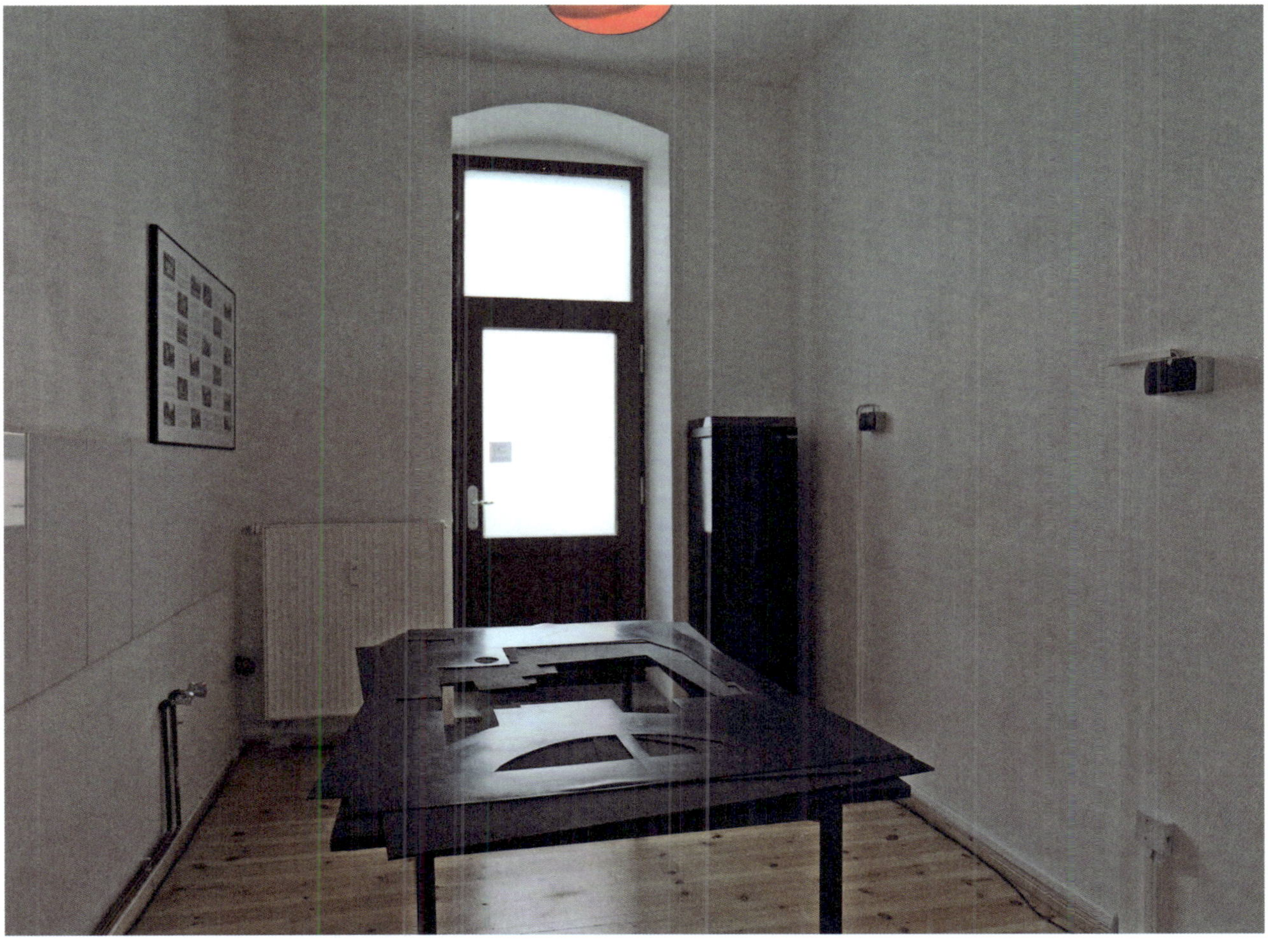

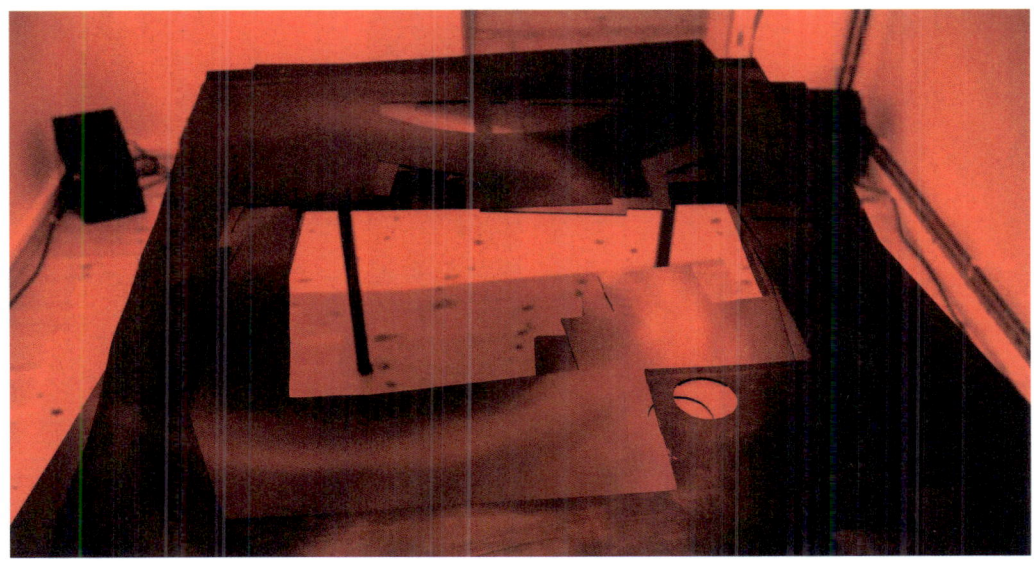

↑/↙: AABBCCDV.
Installation view Errant
Sound 2014/19.
Photo: Erik Smith

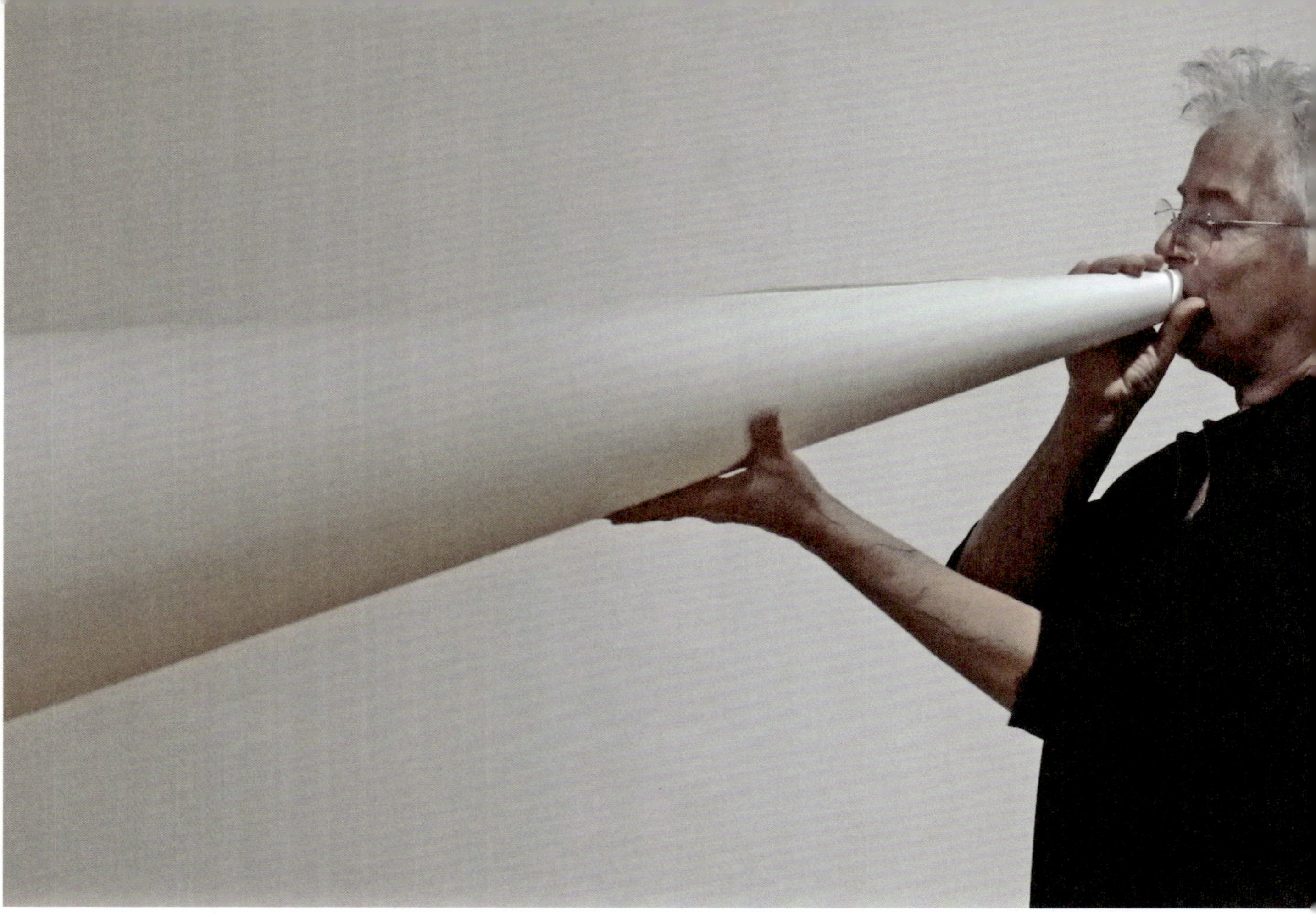

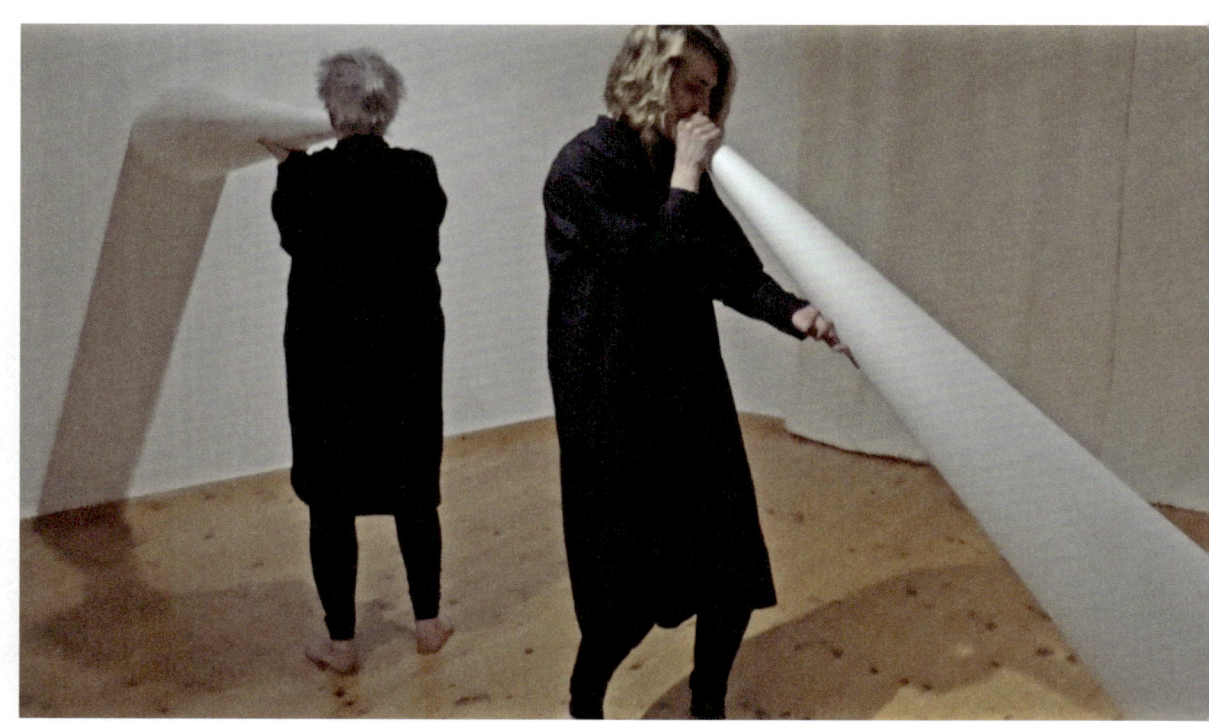

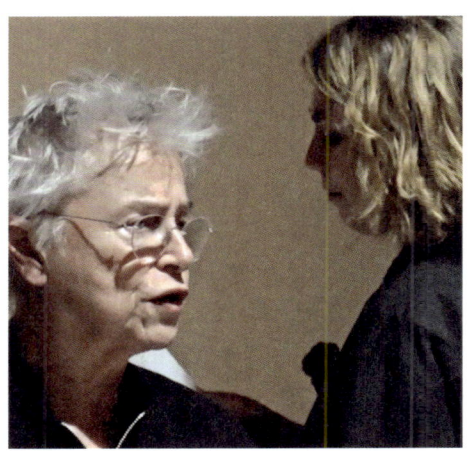

↖/↙/↑: May I ask you? Performance view Errant Sound 2023. Photo: Mario Asef

Language, according to Maturana, serves human beings to symbolically and conceptually shape the reality that surrounds them in order to adapt it physically to their needs and desires. In other words: words demand the world to be like the words.⁶ In a recurrent way, language is continuously installed in our perception of the world, updating the "effect" of the real, and establishing an interface of the interaction between us and our environment. Therefore, language shapes our emotions and influences our interactions with others and our environment (Maturana, 1998).

Reading emotions, for example, is the basis of a healthy friendship, in which the relationship is a field of interactions based on gestures, words, and silences. Kirstin Burckhardt and Lisa W Carlson are artists and friends working with performance and voice. They have developed a way of encountering each other which they call "brutal with love" – also the title of their collaborative book project.⁷ The performance *May I Ask You?*⁸ (2023) at Errant Sound was the first time they read excerpts from their transcribed conversations and publicly shared their practice of voicing, deep listening, opening up and thereby gently inviting attendants to a space of radical and caring honesty.

They use a practice that I would call "the practice of language kneading." They create intense intimate conversations, which they transcribe and re-enact in a centrifugal way to extract the most essential components of emotional talk. It is about voicing and listening, writing and reading and then going through these steps again. In the performance, the friends also embrace each other and listen to each other's breaths, they move away and grunt or click their tongues; they shape that organic inter-subjective space delineated by sound and consensual listening. Moving beyond words, emotional sharing and friendship is their practice. This, indeed, means to navigate an unmapped space where symbols are not clearly delineated. The voice, after a while, becomes an archaic tool for expressing the inexpressible. A cacophony of a text impossible to be written. Moving through affects they create an interlingual space.

Writing acts here, like in bioinformatics, as a way of capturing the trace – in this case the emotional trace of the voice and the voice itself – and bringing it into a storable format – in this case writing translated as data. "As data, the traces are secured and disambiguated. They are deprived of their precariousness, their tentative nature, their preliminary character, the measure of indeterminacy that is inherent in the trace" (Rheinberger, 2023: 22). For this reason, the process of reading the "data," as the artists do, has to recapture the "precariousness" of the emotional trace in order to re-establish or re-enact the emotions. This is where the great artistic exercise of Burckhardt and Carlson lies, precisely in being able to reanimate the emotional trace and tracking it in its transformation.

The dispute between spoken and written language (voice/trace and writing/data) is as old as the appearance of writing itself. Aristotle compared writing to painting, accusing it of a "false vivacity" (Lüdemann 2011). Derrida questions the very foundations of such distinctions and hierarchies. In his book *Of Grammatology* (1967) "The distinction between signifier and signified coincides with the distinction between the sensible (signifier: sound, letter) and the intelligible (signified: concept, imagination, meaning, mind, logos) and thus remains bound to the model of language as representation" (Lüdemann 2011: 75).[9] He points out that some differences between reading and writing are neglected when speaking and used the term "différance" for this: a made-up word that changes the "e" from the French word "différence" (difference) for an "a" causing no change in the pronunciation. Derrida's critique of logocentrism separates the material sign (the letter) from oral language and from what is meant.

The relation between phono/trace and logo/data has gotten an addition: the machine. Relocating "[…] the [process of] transition from trace to data into the machinery itself, has enabled its automation and thus made the whole procedure invisible […]" (Rheinberger, 2023: 22).

After the last industrial revolution (or should I call it an update?) that replaced human physical labor with robotic machines, we are witnessing today a renewed social fear that machines could be able to replace human intellectual labor.

Against the backdrop of artificial intelligence, Tao G. Vrhovec Sambolec's work *Reading Voice*[10] (2018 – 19) explores the zone between a read and a spoken word as an event in time. The process of cognitive engagement through reading is intentionally interrupted, creating a series of dynamic intersections between the reader's physical presence and the written text. At the heart of this installation lies an isolated booth designed for a sole observer. Within this space, a digital screen presents the text, accompanied by an eye-tracking mechanism and software that transforms the reader's visual focus into an auditory experience by immediately rendering the phonemes they fix their gaze upon. The reader is thus confronted with the cacophony of their own reading produced by the apparent chaotic movements of their eyes.

Like in a Zenon paradox, Sambolec's machine dissects the fluid dynamics of reading into fragments that defy seamless reassembly, giving rise to magnified micro-moments. The work shows us with evidence how incongruent the interpretations between trace and data can be when computer automation is added to the trace-data process. It is within these disjunctures that novel opportunities emerge, granting us the capacity to peer beyond the confines of mere words.

A written word is silent but writing itself is not. Writing produces sounds secondary to the syntactic and semantic aspects of the text; the sound of a computer keyboard, the sound of a pencil on paper in all its qualities and combinations, the sound of a printer, etc. Even though the sound of writing is not considered sound of language, as the Derridian "différance," the sound of writing cut off the "signified" from the duality "signifier-signified" and so can offer a way out of the self-talk circle of the "inner monolog" (Husserl, 1966).[11] Quite differently from the voice that reads what is written, the sound of writing makes evident the materials that are rubbed to draw the letters. That sound interests me in terms of cultural expression as it is the sound that amalgamates the surfaces, space and objects that surround the text. The sound of writing introduces us to the materiality of writing. In this way, the sound of writing can be considered a way out of phono- and logocentrism since the voice here is the materiality of writing itself.

Derrida recognizes phono- and logocentrism as Eurocentric:

> Insofar as phonocentrism and logocentrism are for Derrida simultaneously "eurocentrism" and thus bound to a specific geopolitical space, their reconstruction […] implies of a specific political critique (Lüdemann, 2011).[12]

If writing is understood as a symbol for phono- and logocentrism that is in turn a symbol of Eurocentric colonialist geopolitics then its sound can express, according to its materiality and context, the dynamics of capitalist production and the ecosystemic interconnections of those processes and our environment. Therefore, the sound of writing without the visual confirmation of what is written denotes a symbolic act of resistance against phono- and logocentrism that hides its semantic intention.

> e

The meaning of the term "environment" has evolved over time and can have different connotations depending on

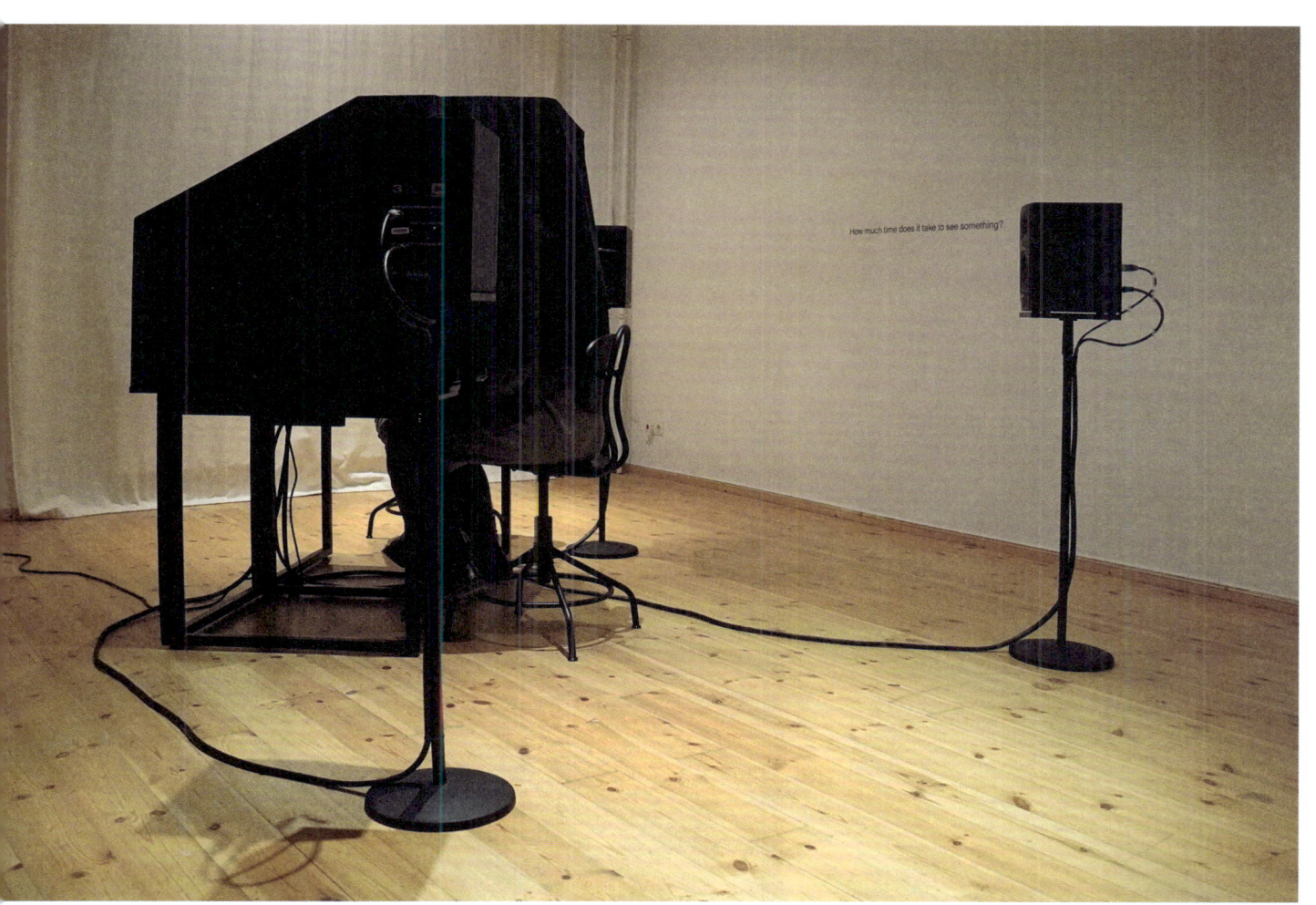

↑: Reading Voice. Installation view, Errant Sound 2020.
Photo: Mario Asef

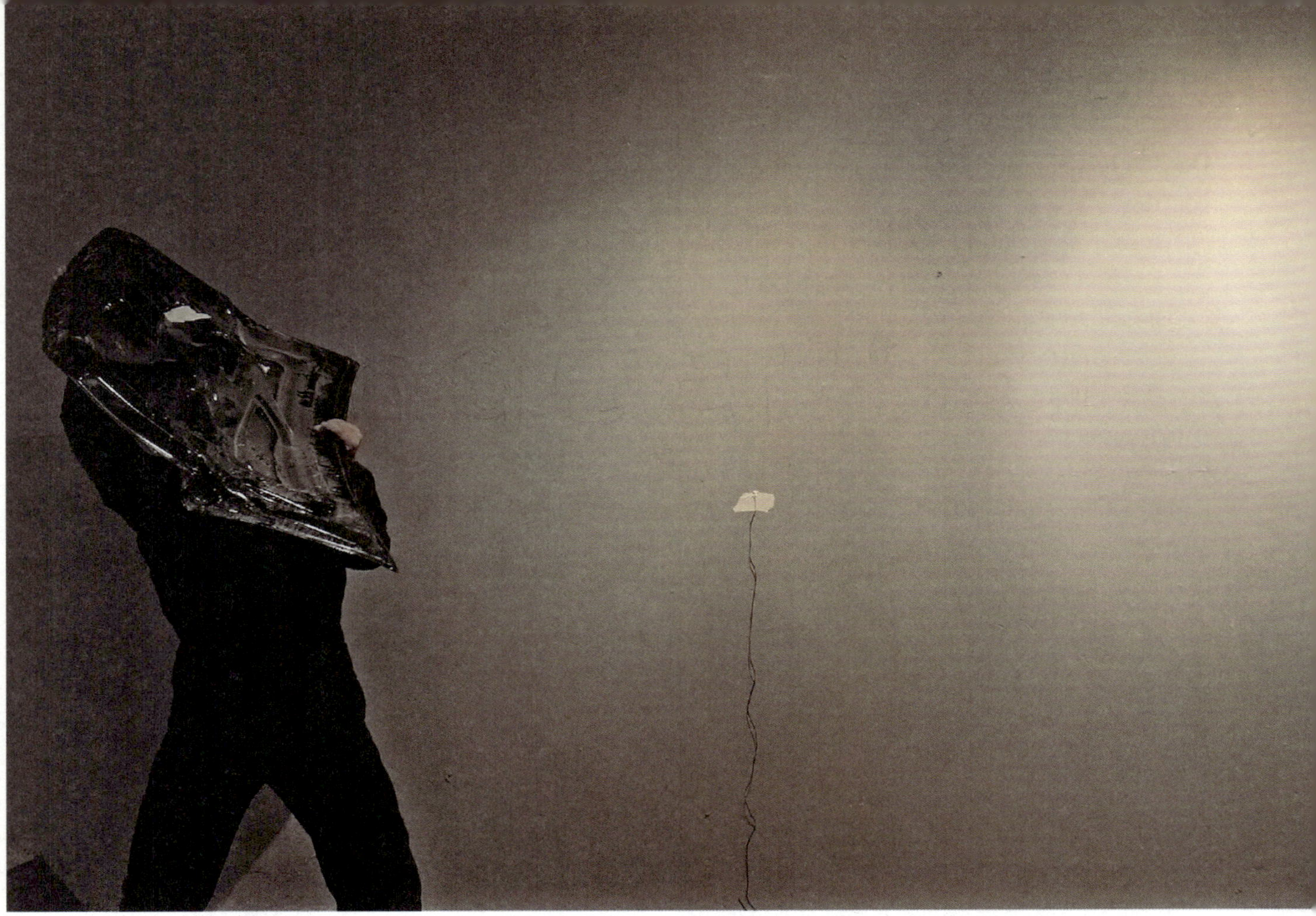

↑/↘: El Lenguage de las Cosas.
Installation view Espacio Odeón,
Bogotá, Colombia 2020.
Photo: Zoila Silena Arias

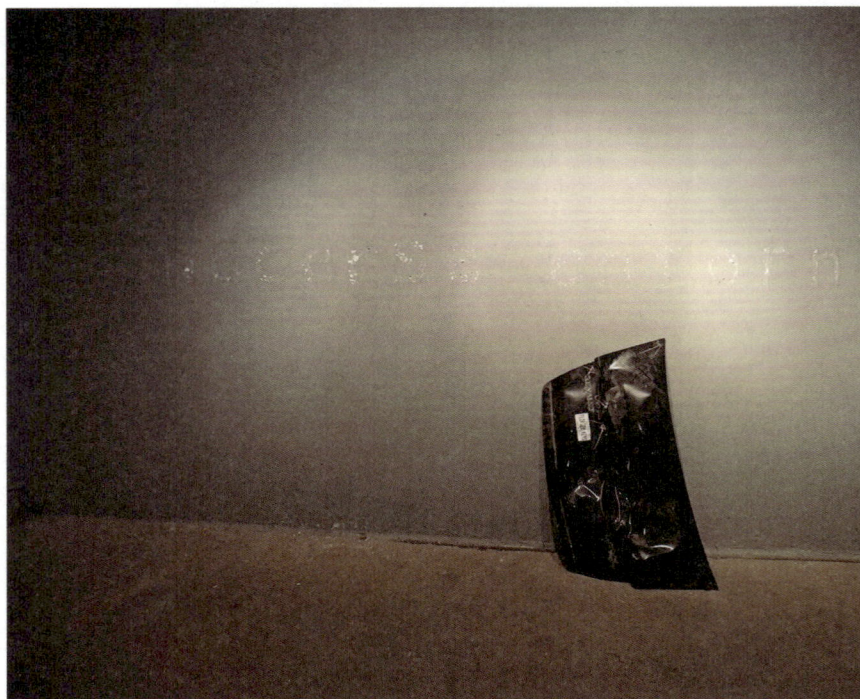

the context in which it is used. Today, the term "environment" generally refers to the physical, biological, and social systems that surround and interact with societies, sometimes human.

Modernity has established a model of relationships between humans and their natural environment as opposite terms. This is known as the nature-culture dualism, which is a mechanistic concept of nature of which Descartes – the so-called father of Rationalism – was its ideologue. This concept has become ingrained in the universal way of understanding the world over the last four centuries.

Rationalism relies on classical mathematics and mechanical concepts to describe the world and the organisms that populate it, ignoring much more complex, unexplained and still not well understood processes such as growth and reproduction systems like genesis: in science, a suffix referring to the beginning, development, or production of something (for example, gametogenesis is the development and production of the male and female germ cells [the gametes] required to form a new individual) (Nicholson, 2014). Our world economic system depends on and embraces this mechanistic understanding of nature today more than ever. To describe this development, Jason W. Moore coined the term "capitalocene." For him, "capitalism is not an economic system; it is not a social system; it is a way of organizing nature" (Moore, 2015).

In its broadest sense, the environment encompasses all of the "natural" and human-made elements of the world, including the atmosphere, water bodies, land surfaces, and ecosystems, as well as the built environment, such as cities, transportation systems, and infrastructure. Increasingly, the concept of the environment is also being expanded to include social and cultural factors, such as political systems, economic structures, social norms and values and technological ecosystems.

This recognition of the interconnectedness of social and ecological systems has led to the development of new approaches to environmental management and sustainability, such as the concept of "social-ecological systems"[13] and the "circular economy."[14]

Overall, the concept of environment today reflects a growing understanding of the complex and interdependent relationships between human societies and the so called "natural world," and the need for holistic and integrated approaches to addressing the environmental challenges of the 21st century.

For Bruno Latour, for example, humans are part of nature and not its opposite. In his work, particularly in his book "Politics of Nature: How to Bring the Sciences into Democracy" and the concept of "The Parliament of Things," Latour criticizes the traditional Western dualistic view that positions humans as distinct and separate from nature. He contends that humans and their cultural activities are an integral part of the natural world without a strict divide between the two. According to Latour, culture is not something outside or above nature but is deeply intertwined with it.

Latour suggests that all entities, whether human or non-human, have agency and should be given a voice in decision-making processes. He argues for a more inclusive and democratic approach that recognizes the agency and interconnectedness of all elements in our world, including both human and non-human actors. But how would these "voice" sound like? Do things have a voice?

In this context, sound can be understood as being capable of showing the intertwinement of nature and culture. And here is where the idea of "agency" (Deleuze, Guattari 1980) becomes crucial in relation to sound since it is related with a "becoming" and it is not tied to a stable and predefined subject or self. Rather, it emerges from the interactions, flows, and connections that take place within complex systems. Perhaps the agency of sounds

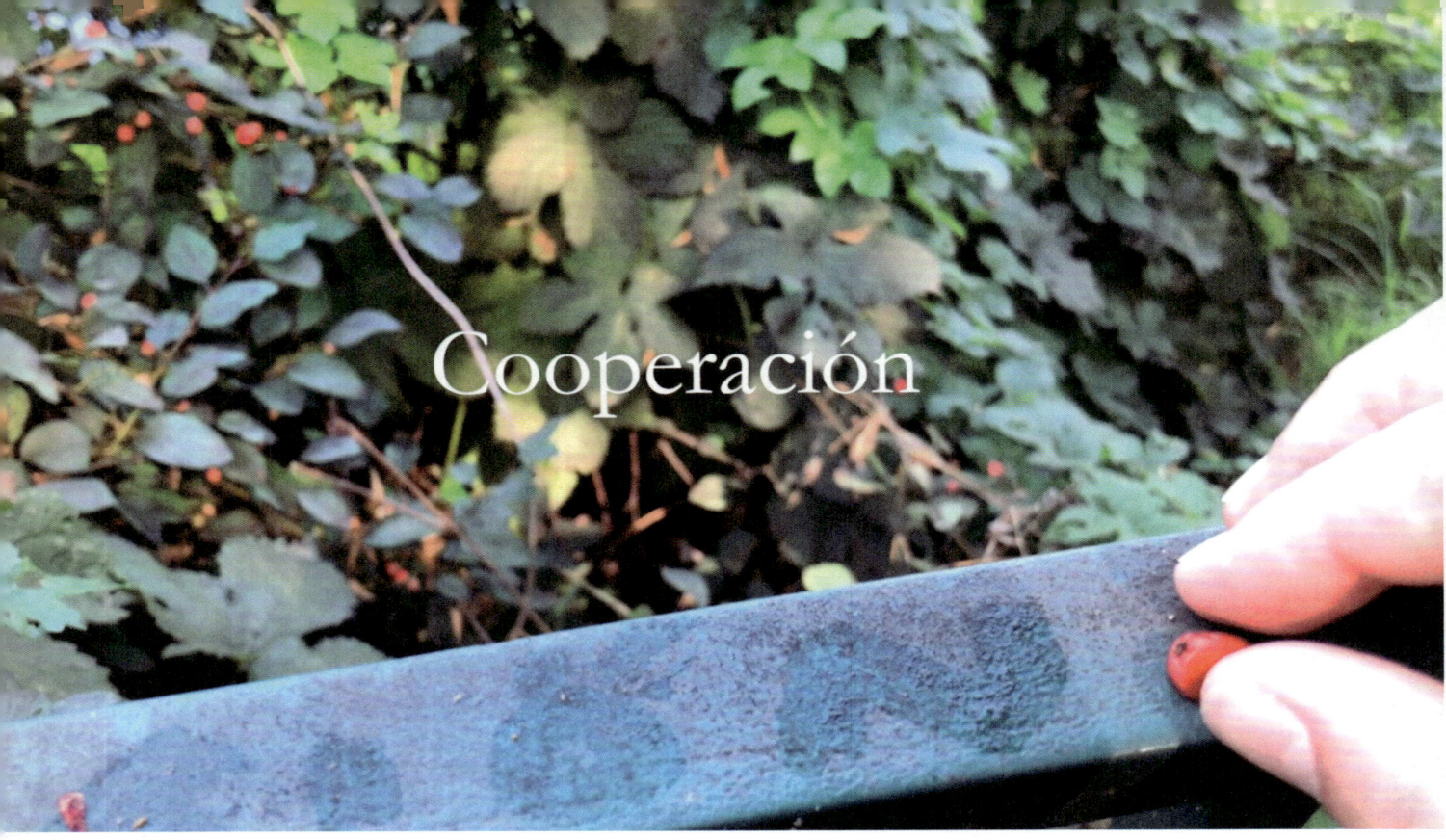

Cooperación

produced by human beings is the acoustic expression of a language with which we express ourselves and interact with our environment. Industry with its machines, the banging of construction sites, the gardener's shears, music and even the silence of computers can all be considered a language through which the semantic design of our socio-natural environment expresses itself.

The sentence "Sound is the language of things" from my Ecologica dictionary[15] is the point of departure for a project in Bogotá, Colombia.

El lenguaje de las Cosas[16] (2020) is an installation performance I produced for FESE (Festival Estación Sonora Experimental, Colombia). This project is inspired by the Wayuu culture and its language-environment relationship. The Wayuu community is located on the La Guajira peninsula, situated between Colombia and Venezuela. According to a Wayuu founding myth, the earth, or Mma in the native language, was fertilized by the father of rain, or Juyaa, thus giving rise to all living things. Rain is a metaphor for the power of language, called Pütchikalü (meaning: word or meaning). Both Pütchikalü (the word) and Juyaa (the rain) are dynamic and bring life. The word arises from the union between the earth and the rain, between the permanent and the transitory, between the arid and the fertile. For the Wayuu, the world, so to speak, is discovered and also fertilized through language.

For this project, the phrase "hacerse entorno" (to make yourself environment) was written on a wall of the Espacio Odeón (Bogotá, COL) by scraping its surface with a junk object from the streets of Bogotá. Both the wall and the junk object were connected to contact microphones that picked up the sounds produced by the friction. These sounds were recorded in separate channels. Once the action was finished, the junk object was left leaning against the wall and the recorded sounds

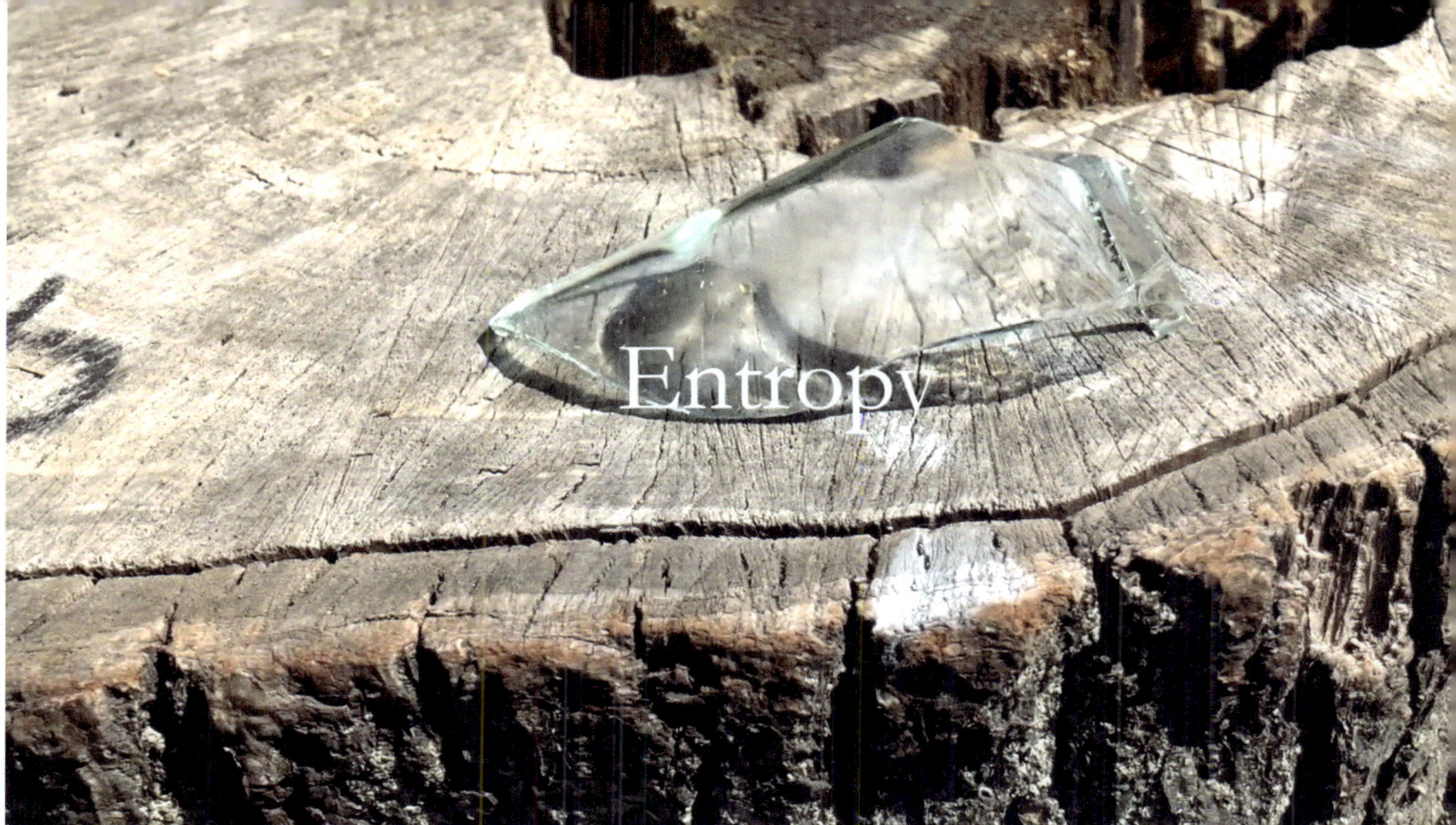

↖/↑: El Lenguage en las Cosas. Video still
2021. Photo: Mario Asef

were played back into the room. The sounds generated by the scraping/writing on the walls resonated in the exhibition space as a remnant of the vibrations and the physical encounter of object-wall-writing.

Taking the trace back to its "precariousness" and introducing it into the machine (the audio recorder) displaced the spoken word from Western phono- and logocentrism by creating, through the machine, an automated gap that is representing the means of language production and reproduction rather than the intended semantic meaning.

More and more we are able to recognize the "voice of things and creatures" that we have believed silent. Plants, for example, "emit ultrasonic airborne sounds when stressed. The emitted sounds reveal plant type and condition. Plant sounds can be detected and interpreted in a greenhouse setting. Many animals, including herbivores and their predators, respond to sound. Recently, plants were also demonstrated to respond to sounds, e.g., by changing the expression of specific genes, or by increasing sugar concentration in their nectar. Thus, if plants emit airborne sounds, these sounds can potentially trigger a rapid response in nearby organisms, including both animals and plants."[17] Thus, the voice of plants are also part of our acoustic environment, even if unheard from us humans, they can communicate in a cross-species interaction.

On walks along the Weigandufer and Kiehlufer canal in Berlin Neukölln I arbitrarily appropriated objects I found along the way (including glass, little berries and leaves) with which I wrote unintelligible words on different surfaces of the environment. The action was spontaneous and was recorded with the camera and microphone of my mobile phone. The intention was to capture, in a more direct and simple way, my experiences during the walks obviating the historical and symbolical load of the urban space by inscribing it with subjective meanings. In this way, I attempted an appropriation of the environment with conceptual relations to graffiti; but instead of capturing identity in a signature/logo, it is about the association of the written terms and their interrelation, in addition to the fact that the writing remains mostly invisible to those passing by.

El lenguaje en las Cosas [18] (2021) is a video work I produced for FESE 21 (Festival Estación Sonora Experimental, Colombia) and a further development of my earlier work *El lenguaje de las Cosas* from 2020. The video recordings show fourteen stations and two walk segments accompanied by a text in the exhibition space.

The words scratched on the surfaces were not intended to be legible by the rest of the people outside the process but to condition the subjective link of the artist with the given environment. It is an intimate approach where phonons and airborne sounds interact within the dynamics of writing. This subjectivity is of great importance for the "inscription" of an individual in a given social and urban environment, since it is not the space itself – its proportion, light, form and materiality – that defines our relationship with it, but the set of experiences and emotions in the environment that establishes a link and generates identity.

The sound of writing changes according to the material of the objects and the scratched surfaces. This accentuates the circumstantiality of the act of inscription (of engraved writing) itself and reveals the fragility of the terms and their relation to the so-called "real." Thus, the sound tells us rather about the physical circumstances – and perhaps the sociocultural conditions of these – than about the meaning of the written words. This, however, does not weaken the semantic force of the terms but reinforces it symbolically by means of unintelligibility itself. The impossibility of hearing and recording the phonons and airborne sounds produced by writing confronts us with the illegibility of traces.

s< l >e

In conclusion, human beings, as semiotic beings, are immersed in the intricate fluid dynamics of s< l >e. It is through sound and language that we interact with our environment (socially, naturally, technologically). Words not only serve as a way to name things, but they also carry our intentions toward those things and this shapes our interactions. Sound at the same time is an expression of the environment and can serve us as an instrument to communicate, assimilate, and understand our position within the environment. The trace-data-machine complex of bioinformatics is an approach that, also in the arts, helps us to understand and express phenomena, while also exposing the limitations of this complex. In this context, listening has a great epistemological potential. The agency of sound as "the language of things" enables us through listening to communicate within an ecosystem. Maybe precisely because humans are also emotional beings and are affectively connected to language, objects and sounds – in the face of the Western approach to the environment, and as a form of resistance in post-colonial times – the sound of writing, of colliding objects, of organisms, vocal machines and the affective cacophonies of individuals, accentuate the "différance" in the search for a way out of the Eurocentric phono-logocentrism that shapes the current globalist vision of the world. Within this constellation, listening is an essential tool not only for incorporation but also for the construction of a better relationship between sound< language >environment.

NOTES:

1. The exhibition series Visual Approach to Sound aims at reflecting on sound from the perspective of visual art. For this series, visual artists were invited to present works that are based on the forms and methods of visual art, but which also have a central acoustic aspect.

2. IFAW (International Fund for Animal Welfare) –. Animal, people and war: the impact of conflict. 2022.

3. Clarissa Thieme. Can't you see them? a solo show at Errant Sound November 2019 curated by Mario Asef.

4. Touching the Void. A Conversation Between Clarissa Thieme, Jan Verwoert and Mario Asef. ArtMargins.com

5. Erik Smith, AABBCCDV (a project created and first presented in Miami, FL (US) in 2012) in "Displacements" a solo show at Errant Sound April 2019 curated by Mario Asef.

6. Mario Asef. El Lenguaje en las Cosas. Video work and text. 2021.

7. Kirstin Burckhardt and Lisa W Carlson. Brutal with Love. Vexer Verlag, Berlin 2023.

8. Kirstin Burckhardt and Lisa W Carlson. May I ask you? a performance evening at Errant Sound March 2023 curated by Mario Asef.

9. Translation from German by M.A.: "Die Unterscheidung von Signifikant und Signifikant fällt mit der Unterscheidung von Sinnlichem (Signifikant: Laut, Buchstabe) und Intelligiblem (Signifikant: Begriff, Vorstellung, Bedeutung, Geist, Logos) zusammen und bleibt damit an das Modell der Sprache als Repräsentation gebunden."

10. Tao G. Vrhovec Sambolec. Reading Reading (2017–) a solo show at Errant Sound November 2019 curated by Mario Asef.

11. Husserl's understanding of inner monologue involves the examination of the flow of thoughts, ideas, and meanings that occur within individual consciousness. Inner monologue refers to the internal dialogue or self-talk that takes place within one's mind. It involves the articulation of thoughts and the internalized expression of ideas without external verbalization. According to Husserl, the act of speaking leads us into a circle of self-affection from which it is difficult to step out. "I speak and hear myself speaking at the same time. My voice comes out of me and at the same time, through the ear, enters me again. (Lüdemann 2011, p. 59). Translation M.A.

12. Translated from German by M.A.: "Insofern Phono- und Logozentrismus für Derrica gleichzeitig "Eurozentrismus" und damit an einen bestimmten geopolitischen Raum gebunden sind, impliziert die Rekonstruktion [...] eine bestimmte politische Kritik."

13. The term "social-ecological systems" was popularized by Elinor Ostrom, a political scientist and economist, who won the Nobel Prize in Economic Sciences in 2009. While Ostrom did not necessarily coin the term itself, she played a crucial role in developing and advancing the concept. Her work focused on the interactions between social and ecological systems, particularly in the context of managing common pool resources and addressing collective action problems.

14. The term "circular economy" gained prominence through the work of multiple scholars and organizations. The Ellen MacArthur Foundation, a British-based organization, has been instrumental in promoting and shaping the concept of the circular economy. They have conducted extensive research and advocacy, highlighting the importance of designing out from waste and creating a regenerative economic model that emphasizes resource efficiency, recycling, and reuse. While the term might have been used prior to their efforts, the Ellen MacArthur Foundation has been influential in popularizing and mainstreaming the concept.

15. Mario Asef. Ecologica. Dictionary of the artist. 2018.

16. Mario Asef. El lenguaje de las cosas (The Language of Things). FESE 2020, Espacio Odeón, Bogotá, Colombia.

17. Sounds emitted by plants under stress are airborne and informative. Cell. Articles. https://www.cell.com/cell/fulltext/S0092-8674(23)00262-3

18. Mario Asef. El lenguaje en las cosas. FESE 2021, Espacio Odeón, Bogotá, Colombia.

19. Link to video: https://vimeo.com/652199736

BIBLIOGRAPHY:

Bennett, Jane. Vibrant Matter – A Political Ecology of Things. Duke University Press: Durham, 2010.

Brown, Steve (2017) "A Joint Prosodic Origin of Language and Music." Front. Psychol. 8:1894.

Deleuze, G; Guattari, F. Mille Plateaux. Paris: Minuit, 1980.

Heidegger, Martin. Sein und Zeit. Max Niemeyer Verlag, 1993.

Hunklinger, S. "Phonons in Amorphous Materials." Journal de Physique. Colloque C9, supplément au n°12, Tome 43, décembre 1982. Page C9 – 416.

Husserl, Edmund. Zur Phänomenologie des inneren Zeitbewusstseins (1893 – 1917) Husserliana – Edmund Husserl Gesammelte Werke, Band X. Verlag: Martinus Nijhoff Verlag;, 1966.

Latour, Bruno. Das Parlament der Dinge. Suhrkamp Taschenbuch Wissenschaft, 2018.

Latour, Bruno. Das terrestrische Manifest. Edition Suhrkamp, 2019.

Lüdemann, Susanne. Jacques Derrida zur Einführung. Hamburg: Junius, 2011.

Maturana, Humberto. Biologie der Realität. Suhr-kamp. Frankfurt am Main, 1998.

Moore, Jason W. Capitalism in the Web of Life: Ecology and the Accumulation of Capital. New York, NY: Verso, 2015.

Nancy, Jean Luc. Listening. Fordham University Press: Fordham, 2007.

Nicholson, Daniel J. "The Machine conception of the organism in development and evolution: A critical analysis". Studies in History and Philosophy of Biological and Biomedical Sciences 48 (2014) 162e174.

Oberst, Joachim, L. Heidegger on Language and Death: The Intrinsic Connection in Human Existence. Bloomsbury, 2011.

Rheinberger, Hans-Jörg. Split & Splice: a phenomenology of experimentation. The University of Chicago Press, 2023.

Søren Brier. "Language as an ecological force". Tarasti, E. (ed.) (2005): From Nature to Psyche. Proceedings from the ISI Summer Congresses at Imatra in 2001 – 2002. Period, 30/06/10 ; Acta Semiotica Fennica.

ROBERTA BUSECHIAN

We are what we hear and how we remember it

On a cognitive level, we always filter sounds through our own socio-cultural background. A sound is perceived in respect to the context within which it is presented and is subjectively associated with semantic and cognitive patterns. Listening to a German song in Paris could be strikingly different from listening to the same song in Germany, as the thought patterns they trigger will probably vary, just as the underlying message they convey may vary, too. Evidently, groups of people may share similar cultural backgrounds and, thus, may have a similar understanding of a soundscape; notwithstanding, connotations vary widely with respect to individual idiosyncrasy and emotional state, unique mental representations, imagination, and personal memories. The interesting point about evoking memories through recorded sound, is that unclarity about when and where I heard that sound before, where it connects to my biography. More musical sounds are maybe more easily or more fully bringing us back to our past, which happens with a traditional song or melody we know from our childhood. There appears

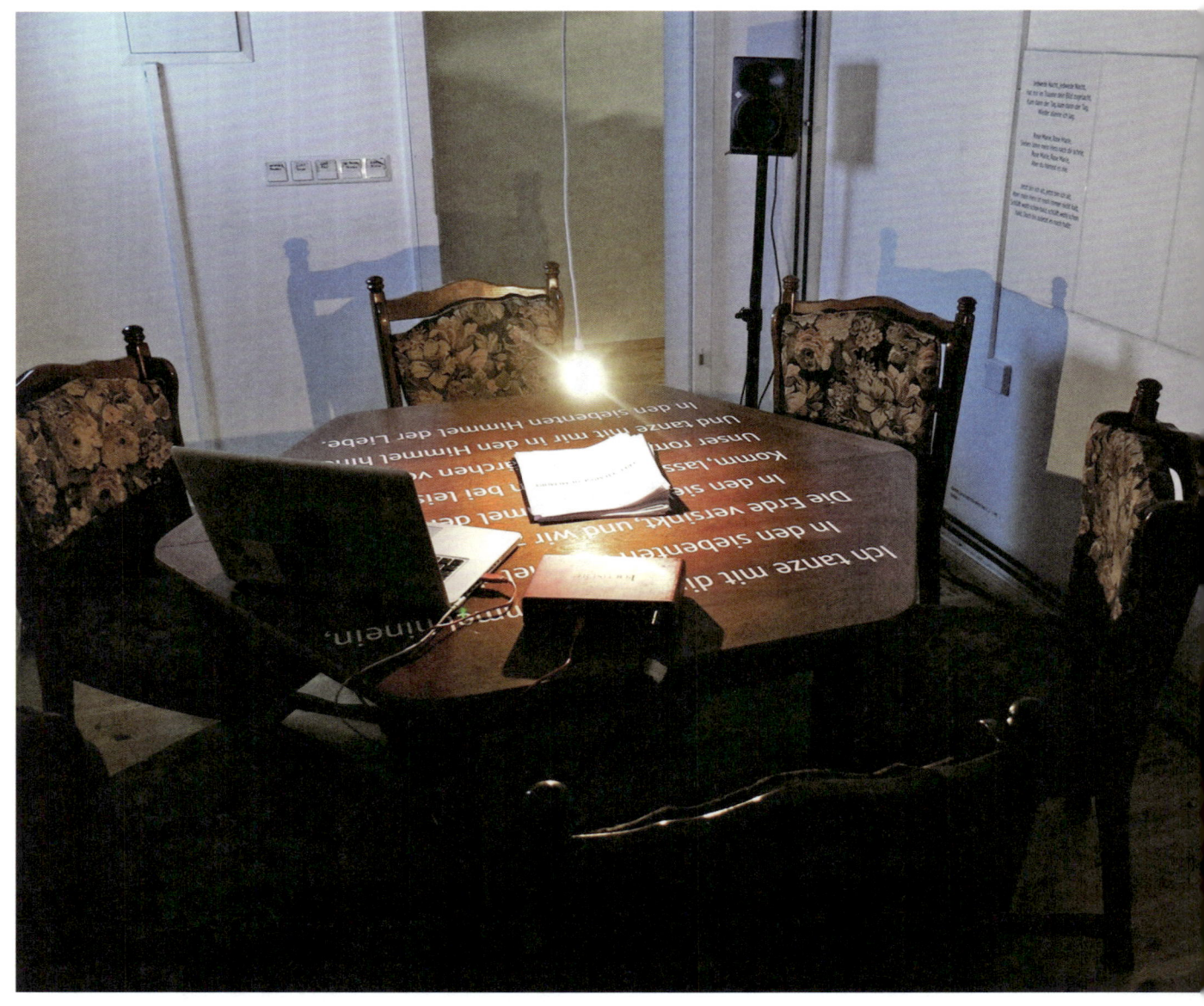

↑: "Freezed arise of Memory" (2019), sound installation by Roberta Busechian, Courtesy of Roberta Busechian.

to be evidence that the most memorable moments of listening to music derive from the feeling of surprise. In general people (and animals) prefer mostly familiar stimuli and stimuli that can be anticipated.[1] Conscious thinking tends to obscure the effect, which suggests that the exposure reaction originates unconsciously.

Regarding music, there is a way to go deeper in the understanding of what we call *arise of memory*[2] on a musical level when studying the work of music therapy with dementia patients (D. Muthesius, J. Sonntag, B. Warme, M. Falk, 2010). In music, if the rhythm – or the meter – is stable over the course of listening to a passage, it can help to predict elements of the music itself. On this regard, there are many hypotheses about why musicians use repetition (94% of musical passages lasting more than a couple of seconds are repeated in certain parts of the composition), while in spoken word a high number of repetitions is rare, except in the case of demonstrations, religious rituals and ceremonies. Music from this point of view is extraordinarily repetitive compared to other stimuli in our daily life. Musical repetitions create a transition from short-term memory to intermediate-term memory and implement involuntary conscious memorizations. In terms of duration and capacity for procedural analysis of information, musical units, such as motifs and themes, can be taken into account for short-term memory. Also, constant repetitions of a motif do not necessarily fixate the stimulus in short-term memory; the same repetition can fixate music in long-term memory, though,[3] and these long-term memories at times can re-emerge while listening to a piece of music on the radio, hearing the sound of a passing car, or while our steps remind us of a certain musical rhythm. Episodic memory – the long-term memory – creates real expectations that inform our future listening experiences by means of activated memories. For example, people suffering from dementia focus on the reality of their childhood and adolescence. Music here is based on their own resources: the formative musical experiences they made during their childhood and adolescence and prove to be "resistant" to oblivion. A person who has lost orientation and can no longer pronounce his/her name, could in some cases effortlessly sing a four-staged folk song.[4] The experience of being able to do so contributes to the preservation of identity, to the loss of anxiety and thus to a considerable quality of life. Emotionality, which in older people is much stronger than cognitive abilities, is deliberately stimulated with the help of familiar music and often leads to increased alertness and ability to verbalize: experiences from the old memory can be recounted. The external mobility also increases, and important vital functions are stimulated again through the movement lead by sound.[5]

Sound has apparently a number of therapeutically usable properties that can be applied in music therapy. In the project "Freezed arise of Memory" presented at Errant Sound for the exhibition "SONOMEMO" in 2019 I worked together with a music therapist, Prof. Dorothea Muthesius who is specialized in music therapy for Alzheimer and dementia patients. The aim of the project, which became a sound installation, was to record the moment of the arising memory during Muthesius' sessions of music therapy with seniors affected by Alzheimer and dementia. My intent was precisely the capturing of the moment when memory surfaced, the moment when out of nowhere, after singing/playing a folk song, in a silence, the person or persons participating in the session began to communicate. The communication itself was often not formulated in complete sentences, it happened rather with single words, speech fragments, verses, or laughter. Sometimes, however, something happened that clearly demonstrated how strong the connection between listening, memory, and the present is. What happened was that the person uttered a phrase clearly related to their present state, their inner state, their emotions in the here and now. One of these phrases was "Ich will nicht sterben" (I don't want to die) and "Ich sterbe bald" (I will die soon). This made me think about listening and the connection, if any, between music therapy and the process that exists in sound art, where a sound exists only in a given moment and can never be the same again.

This is because of the different situations that are created in the space where the sound is spread, and because of the different types of listeners, who, with their subjectivity interpret the sound work. To give an example, Susan Philipsz's sound installations, especially for those such as "Lowlands" (2008/10), using the sung voice (of the artist herself), as Alan Licht points out in *Sound Art*.

Revised: an emotional element is introduced that is often missing in traditional sound art works.[6] This could be reconduced to an electronic manipulation/deviation of sound which tends to be more abstract and where the emotional element is not perceptible at first glance. In Philipsz's installations, with the use of traditional music and in particular the voice, we move into a territory where the voice triggers emotional mechanisms and a different accessibility. This accessibility leverages the nonperformative factor of her work with the voice, stating that when she sings for her installations, she sings to herself, in an intimacy that creates a direct connection with the space and makes it perceived in a different way, making the listener feel more focused on her- or himself, heightening the subjectivity of the space in which one is.[7]

Feeling in space, feeling here and now, is something that has always been common to our relationship with sound. In both, sound healing practices of music therapy and sound art, listening is based on the connection between the environment and the individual. In music-therapeutic work, the individual accesses his or her memory through sound as a means of materializing the self in the present. In artistic work with sound, there are cases, such as that of artist Guadalupe Maravilla,[8] who speaks of "sound of healing" in which sound is used to purify the body in order to heal. During a battle with cancer, the artist undertakes a sound healing practice and realizes that sound is medicine. After that, he begins to practice sound healing for other cancer patients, for illegal immigrants, even taking his healing work inside a church. From a trained musical ear to the most untrained one, this approach assumes that there is a common ground of sound healing vibrations and frequencies which could be implemented in many fields, including the artistic one, having a deep and direct influence on listeners' psyche and body.

The upward interest and trend in sound healing practices brings listening and feeling sound vibrations to an interest and acceptance by a wide spectrum of audiences. Apart from traditional practices of sound healing as with singing bowls, crystal bowls and voice, the knowledge and technology we have today about the influence of determinate frequencies on the human body is opening a big area of experimentation also into electronic arts. Energy medicine or vibrational medicine was acknowledged already 20 years ago as faster and more effective to carry informations as chemistry.[9] Vibrational healing using sound, also subsumed under the term of sound healing, is nowadays used in both traditional techniques and in form of electronic vibration-frequencies.[10] Sound waves are, as we know, also vibrations and are charaterized by their frequency. Sound healing through electronic frequencies stimulates the body by a sequence of precisely tuned sounds influencing the functions of different body organs, but it also aims to restore the vibrational balance of the body.[11] Vibrational energy of sound is the main tool for Biosonology, a word derived from Bio [life] sono [sound] logia [dialogue]. This neologism created by Domenico Sciajno (www.sciajno.net) expresses the complex synergetic interaction that permeates sonic phenomena and the biophysical ones. We call it entrainment: when the physical energy influences us, our body cells will be affected by this energy. During a biosonology session, the person lies down on the floor listening to sound frequencies modulated by a Vortex based Synthesizer (created by Sciajno):

"[...] This sound synthesis is combined with techniques now established after more than 40 years of research in the areas of BWT (Brain Wave Training) and synchronized brain wave induction (BWE, Brain Wave Entrainment). The idea of integrating these two methodologies in biosonological listening sessions was developed by Sciajno precisely to extend its scope from the brain wave domain (BWE) to the domain of the whole organism (Vortex Based Synthesis). The Vortex Based sound wave production system devised by Sciajno is thus

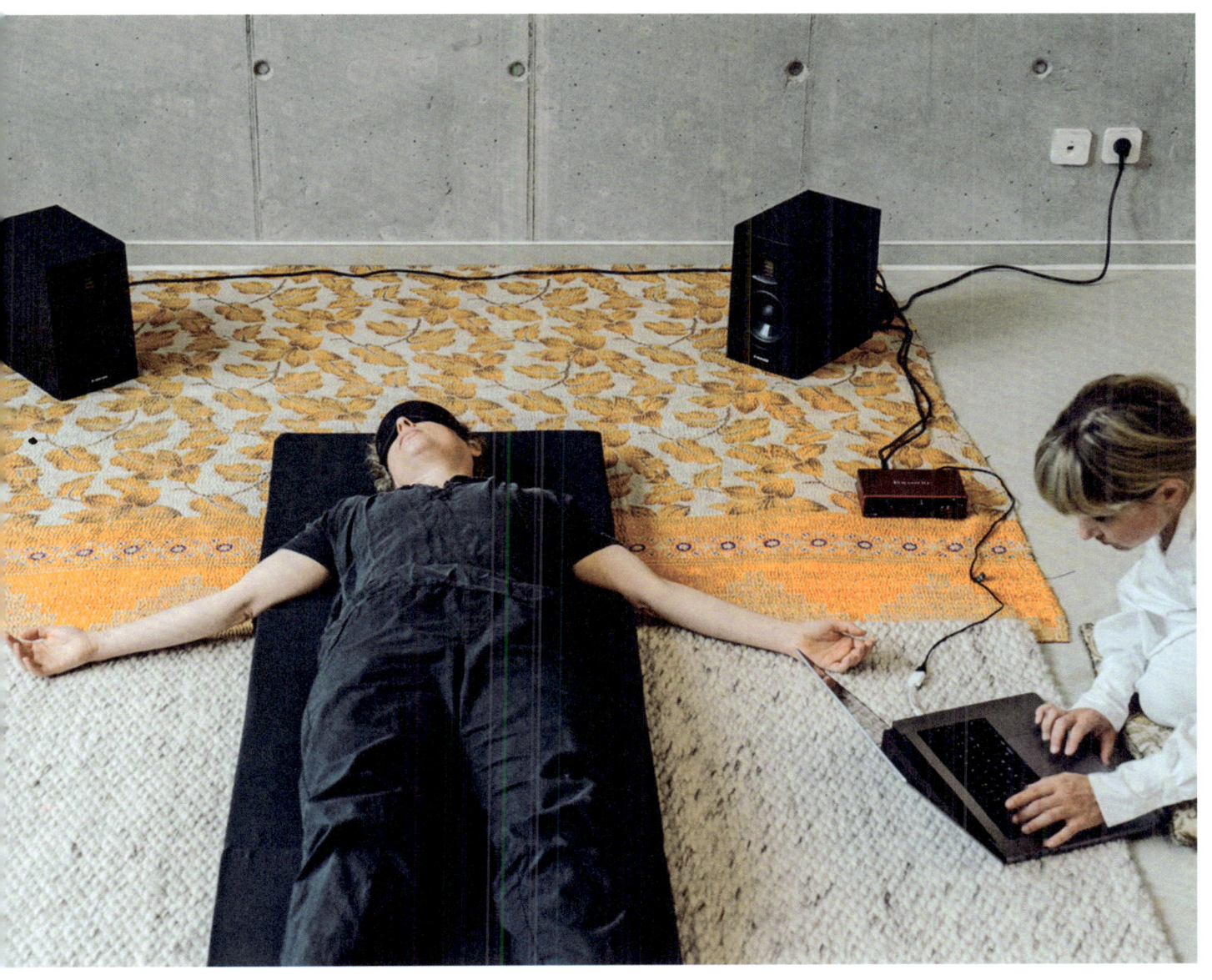

↑: Courtesy of Roberta Busechian. Photo: Ronja Falkenbach.

aimed at resonating not only brain waves but also the entire biophysical structure by exploiting the pervasiveness of one of our precious nerves: the vagus nerve. This represents a real fast track since it has a very special relationship with our auditory system. The vibratory nature of sound is a powerful tool to activate responses on organic consciousness to bring the body towards homeostasis through psycho-physical rebalancing […]."

Some sound artists and electronic musicians use this vibrational power of sound and its energy to work on both, activating the audience's awareness

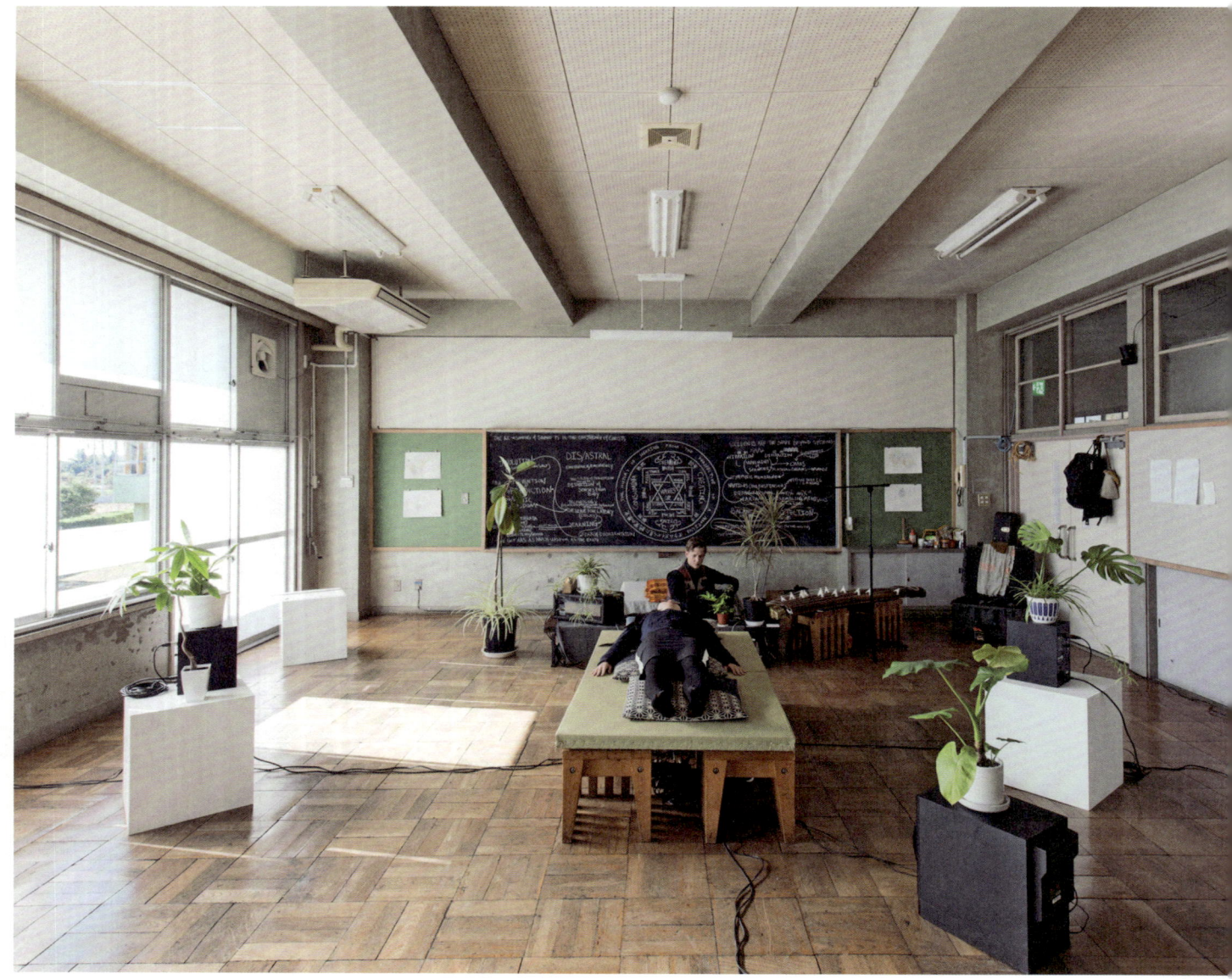

↑: Photo: Kato Hajime. Photo courtesy: ARCUS Project.

on their bodily presence and work on psychological aspects of sonic self-care. Aïsha Devi, producer, vocalist, and owner of the label Danse Noire, works on connections between altered states of consciousness, binaural frequencies, transcendence and the will to heal people with music. She also speaks about vibrational power of sound: "I connect the dots and I realize that the origin of what we see and what we don't see is vibration – its oscillation."[14] The aim to work on rituals through electronic music is nothing new, but there is a consciousness about the anthropological and political aim of electronic music which goes beyond the electronic music scene, clubs and its audience and embraces the primitive in electronic music, specifically the power of brutality, since changing your body only happens with strong turns-brutal actions. Letting frequencies invade our body, diffusing through our cells, as it happens in sound healing and in particular vibrational healing processes has also an intrinsic brutality, since it is mainly perceived via non-auditive tissues. Some sound artists dealing with sound healing are working within this overwhelming reality of vibration and how our body remembers it, like the beforementioned artist Guadalupe Maravilla who does healing practice that uses vibrations produced by gongs in exhibitions contexts. According to the artist, this practice "cleanse[s] the water in our bodies, which can carry stress, impurities, and, in some cases, diseases."[15]

Inside installative-performative sound art contexts arises the possibility to open sound practices involving also elements of sound healing, engaging with natural phenomena, geophysics, geology and animals as the artist Curtis Tamm does in his sound research (see below). That means presenting sound studies research practice in a setting which is both an artistic endeavor and a healing session. An interesting setting of such kind of installative-performative situations is the positioning of the audience-recipient in a Shavasana position (one of the most common body positions in Yoga), which is the posture of the body lying with the arms along the body and palms up. This setting, introducing a hybrid between sound healing session, performance, and installation, is available inside listening labs by Curtis Tamm[16] who spent time with seismologists to learn about the nature of waves, listened to the chants of blind shamans, and spent time with an engineer investigating the ability of other animal species to predict earthquakes. Approaching sound healing also as a trend and reflecting on this trend through listening sessions, where visitors lie down and are embraced by ultrasonic frequencies, brings sound installation practice on a border between analyzing contemporary auditive attention (evolved also in relation to sound healing settings and sound artistic research) and going deeply into creating new experiences of sonic-vibrational awareness.

Appropriating space through auditive awareness is a kind of resistance of contemporary listening. Going through our physical and mental knowledge of how sound and music can tell us about our past and our present seems to be a possible aural way to open less known dimensions of awareness. Both memory in sound therapy and vibrational power in sound healing could be tools for widening sound artistic practice into something we probably didn't define yet but which we may approach as an aurality of the inner human and non-human environment.

NOTES:

1. Huron, D., Sweet anticipation: Music and the psychology of expectation, (2006).

2. Roberta Busechian, artists website, accessed on 21st December 2023 https://www.robertabusechian.com/freezed-arise-of-memory

3. Huron, D. (2006).

4. Muthesius, D., Sonntag, J., Warme, B., Falk, M., Musiktherapie für Menschen mit Demenz, Frankfurt am Main, Mabuse, 2010.

5. Ibid.

6. Licht, A., Sound Art. Revised, Bloomsburry Academic, New York/London, 2019, p. 126.

7. Ibid.

8. Guadalupe Maravilla, artist website, accessed on 1st November 2023 https://www.guadalupe-maravilla.com/

9. Posted on Youtube by Avishai Barnatan (14 feb 2017): "Conversation with Dr. Bruce lipton about sound healing," https://youtu.be/O7MmSfo5b9U?si=wkkHuDfbqxjSw-cU (accessed 19.12.2023)

10. Biosonology: a practice of sound healing developed by Domenico Sciajno based on electronic frequencies.

11. Sciajno, D., "Vibrazioni Sonore per il Corpo e la Mente: La Biosonologia e l'arte in ascolto," Psiche 2, 2017.

12. Domenico Sciajno, Biosonology institute website, accessed 1st November 2023,< http://www.biosonology.org/www.biosonology.org/Home.html>

13. Domenico Sciajno, Biosonology institute ITA website, accessed 1st November 2023, <https://biosonologia-info.mailchimpsites.com/metodo-biosonologico>

14. Mariana Berezovska,"Rave Mantras With Aïsha Devi", BORSHCH, accessed 15th June 2023, <https://borshchmagazine.com/rave-mantras-with-aisha-devi/>.

15. Guadalupe Maravilla, MOMA website, accessed 16th June 2023, <https://www.moma.org/calendar/programs/206>

16. Curtis Tamm, website <https://curtistamm.net>, accessed 16th June 2023.

BIBLIOGRAPHY:

Albert, G., Sound sculptures e sound installations, essay from AAA – TAC (Acustical Arts and Artifacts – Technology, Aesthetics, Communication), 2010 – n.7.

Block, R., Dombois, L., Hertling, N., Volkmann, B., Für Augen und Ohren von der Spieluhr zum akustischen Environment, Akademie der Künste, Berlin, 1980.

Bosseur, J.Y., Sound and the Visual Arts, Dis Voir, Paris, 1993; Installation und Technologie, in Akademie der Künste, Berlin, 1996.

De la Motte-Haber, H., Zwischen Performance und Installation, Klangkunst. Tönende Objekte und klingende Räume; in "Handbuch der Musik im 20. Jahrhundert," Laaber, 1999.

Föllmer, G., Mitten im Leben. Klanginstallation, Klangkunst, Alltagsklänge, München, 1997.

Licht, A., Sound Art. Revised, Bloomsbury Academic, New York/London, 2019.

McLuhan, M., Understanding Media: the extension of man, McGraw-Hill, New York, 1964.

Minard, R., Sound Environments: music for public spaces, Akademie der Künste, Berlin, 1993.

Muthesius, D., Sonntag, J., Warme, B., Falk, M., Musiktherapie für Menschen mit Demenz, Frankfurt am Main, Mabuse, 2010.

Rebentisch, J., Die Ästhetik der Installation, Suhrkamp, Frankfurt am Main, 2003.

Sciajno, D., "Vibrazioni Sonore per il Corpo e la Mente: La Biosonologia e l'arte in ascolto," Psiche 2, 2017.

GOLO FÖLLMER

Hinges. Conversing about Do – Words

Artistic work with sound has become increasingly theorized over the decades. On the one hand, sound art has been reflected upon in greater depth using theoretical models. In the rapidly growing research field of Sound Studies as well as in Musicology and disciplines such as Media Studies, researchers are working on natural and urban sound phenomena, on popular music and mass media sound, and to a large extent on sound art practices. On the other hand, artists have increasingly underpinned their own activities theoretically and integrate their work into more complex reflections on epistemological, anthropological, decolonial, posthuman and many other questions. This volume shows that, maybe more than ever before, artistic work on sound is based on intensive theoretical reflection.

This essay focuses on the practical artistic approach to sound. It poses the question of the relationship between practice and theory. To this end, members of the project space group Errant Sound were asked about artistic forms of action and activities they use. In thirteen conversations with current and former members of Errant Sound, the specific practices that characterize their artistic attitudes were discussed.

The author suggested a "do-word" (one-on-one translation of the German educational term "Tuwort" which outrightly points to the performative character) to each person (e.g. experimenting, connecting, recording), on the assumption that the respective activity could be understood as an essential moving force of their way of working. Some terms were adopted ad hoc; others only turned out to be appropriate and productive during the discussion; for still others, alternatives were found.

In the conversations, it was discussed how the designated action occurs in the person's work, to what extent this constitutes the person's work and how it relates to theoretical considerations in connection with the respective work. This also implicitly raised the question of the extent to which talking about actions differs from talking about the experiences that these actions have deposited and, even more, from the products on which these actions and experiences are based.

During editing, the recorded conversations were textually transformed by leaving the interviewer out of the picture and condensing and concentrating the spoken text to a fraction of its original length, sometimes involving substantial rephrasing, into focused subjective reflections.

THEORY OF PRACTICE

Using a verb to emphasize action as an activity takes up ideas from the philosophical movement of practice theory or praxeology. Early approaches to this can be found in Edmund Husserl's transcendental philosophy. According to him, life-world activities must take place via the "body as the constitutive basis of thing, space, will and feeling" (Breyer 2019, 216, transl. by the author). For Husserl, a spiritual world of concepts and ideas cannot exist independently of practical experience, but arises directly from it.

Martin Heidegger follows on from these thoughts. According to him, conceptions and ideas do not arise through mere objectifying observation or abstract reflection, but in the course of "going along" with each individual experience in the course of human existence. The practical is thereby understood as executive or performative. (Breyer 2019, 222)

The performative is also addressed by Maurice Merleau-Ponty. He distinguishes the body as a carrier of physical and biological characteristics of the human being from the "Leib" as an instance of the psychological dimension of intentionality, which keeps us in constant interaction with the world. According to him, every situation is permeated by "lines of force" that evoke or require specific actions without the person acting having to be aware of them (Breyer 2019, 230). These attention-directing lines of force show a proximity to James Gibson's later concept of "affordance," precisely because Gibson locates them in an in-between of previously dichotomous concepts, in his case between living beings and the environment:

> There has been endless debate among philosophers and psychologists as to whether values are physical or phenomenal, in the world of matter or only in the world of mind. For affordances as distinguished from values, the debate does not apply. Affordances are neither in the one world or the other inasmuch as the theory of two worlds is rejected. There is only one environment, although it contains many observers with limitless opportunities for them to live in it. (Gibson 1986, 138)

Charles Peirce's pragmatism takes the praxeological concept a step further by understanding all beliefs as dispositions to act. For him, believing something, holding it to be true or judging it in this or that way always has a practical origin. This also dissolves the difference between thinking and acting, because according to him, both are mutually dependent, enable each other and are not operational without the other. Our experience of the world is therefore not shaped by what we encounter as observers, but by what we deal with practically and how we handle things (Kertscher 2019, 109).

> Thus we come to what is tangible and, conceivably, practical, as the root of every real distinction of thought, however subtle it may be; and there is no difference of meaning so subtle as to consist in anything but a possible difference in practice. (Peirce 1878, 337, translation by the author)

Finally, Pierre Bourdieu coined the term "theory of practice." With the concept of "habitus," he works out how patterns of perception, thought and action are socially appropriated and that they are simultaneously structured and have a structuring effect (Schäfer 2016, 10). Anthony Giddens then urges the dissolution of the dichotomy of "agency" and "structure" and thus also the dichotomy of "individual" and "society." According to Giddens, we always share practices such as doing and speaking, but also feeling and thinking, with others. For Giddens, commonality is a prerequisite for understanding the world and being able to act meaningfully in it (Kertscher 2019, 12). Both sociality and individuality therefore result from practices:

> By virtue of the understandings and intelligibilities they carry, practices are where the realms of sociality and individual mentality/activity are at once organized and linked. Both social order and individuality, in other words, result from practices. (Schatzki 1996, 13)

We are often not explicitly aware of how we do this. From a praxeological perspective, knowledge and the competent execution of situationally appropriate practices are understood as "tacit knowledge" (Polanyi 1985), i.e. as implicit knowledge that is "incorporated" in a very physical sense (Schäfer 2016, 13).

Philosophies of practice thus share the conviction that the long-dominant description of social interactions by means of dichotomous pairs of concepts such as subject and object, application and rule or individual and society is not tenable because none of these concepts can be considered complete as an independent entity (Bedorf 2019, 2). Philosophies of practice therefore start between the two respective concepts, and from their point of view, this in-between is precisely the practical action from which, for example, the individual and society mutually generate each other (Bedorf 2019, 3).

The concept of practice thus replaces the idea that a rule (e.g. counterpoint) can unilaterally determine an application (e.g. a piano piece) and that an application could therefore be derived from the consideration of a "given" rule. It replaces the idea that a subject (e.g. artist XY) can handle an object (e.g. sound) unilaterally and that the handling of the object could be explained by discussing the "given" subject. Practice theory rejects this separation, as neither rule nor application, neither subject nor object can be understood as "given" in themselves, because they only ever generate each other continuously. Practice theory thus conceives practical action and procedural practices as "hinges" that characterize the mutual conditionality and the interaction of affordances of the only seemingly dichotomous elements.

HINGES

In the following, thirteen do-words are discussed as just such hinges. Verbs are used that are not specifically significant in the context of music or art (such as "spatialize"), but which can be transferred to other areas of life (such as "move") and establish connections to everyday, social or political issues that the artistic approaches deal with directly or indirectly.

WORLDING

"Worlding [...] is an active, ontological process; it is not simply a result of our existence in or passive encounter with particular environments, circumstances events or places. Worlding is informed by our turning of attention to a certain experience, place or encounter and our active engagement with the materiality and context in which events and interactions occur. It is above all an embodied and enacted process – a way of being in the world – consisting of an individual's whole-person act of attending to the world."

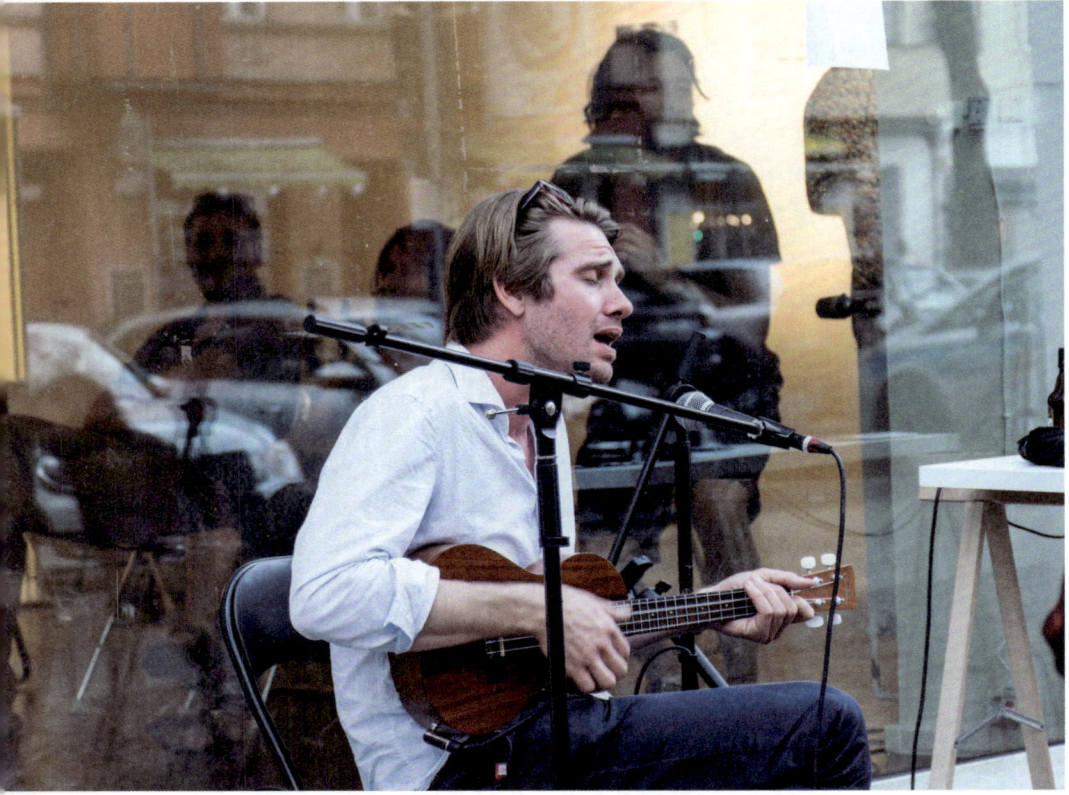

Source: Palmer, Helen; Hunter, Vicky: Worlding. https://newmaterialism.eu/almanac/w/worlding.html – accessed January 8th 2024

←: Performance for Action "Sonic Permaculture: Resonances of the Urban Garden" by Jeremy Woodruff; part of "In the Sound Field: Perspectives on Field Recording – Installations and Performances", series at Errant Sound @ Kollwitzstraße, 20. 05. 2017. With Andrew Noble, songs and Keith O'Brien, mixing and sonic performance.
Photos: Golo Föllmer

JEREMY WOODRUFF: Music is a very essential need for me, it's really like eating and breathing, it works its way into everything. So it's always like a big puzzle for me to understand the ways in which concepts that we are working on intersect with politics and technology, psychology, philosophy, and other disciplines in the humanities, exactly how they intersect with making music and in which ways there's a flow between the conceptual and the practical process of music making.

I like the verb "worlding" which is coming forward in certain academic literature recently, especially ethnomusicological writing. It speaks to the act of playing music in that worlding is like creating worlds, and I think it's actually comparable in a way with this concept of "musicking" from Christopher Small, which speaks about all sorts of aspects of making music on not only the level of performing on a stage and recording in a studio, but all of the other acts that go into forming music in the larger social consciousness.

Worlding has to do with this idea of how people personally affiliate with music because it gives them a different understanding and new access points to ways of being in the world. And that's also indicative of how music profoundly intersects with politics, therefore, that different types of music imply ideas of how people can be allowed to act and behave in different circumstances and what's permissible and what's not – in that various kinds of music are imbued with ideas of queering society or have more access to a collective view on forming the music.

This sort of transcultural aspect that pertains to worlding is very much in line with the way that I've been thinking about my work recently in terms of listening to sounds of protest and how they intersect with ways of expressing musicality as a powerful force, transcending normal means of speech and going into ritualized or heightened means of vocalization, which are highly musical, but not really a form of music.

I have involved myself in certain topics like protest, and ecology which have come back again and again. I had a crisis of sorts, which I think a lot of composers undergo, where there was a sort of disconnect between the abstract nature of music and the deep concerns about developments in the world and also the way that ideas can have an influence on culture, where very often experimental music can seem so detached from these concerns. I found that the only way forward would be to research things that I think have profound effect on the world, which included for me protests and politics and the ecology, the largest issues really on the world stage. It can be very frustrating for me, but also very, very productive because I have to find ways to bridge this sort of gap: in what ways does art actually affect politics? Is it the personal freedom of the artist which is creating a model in the world which then sets an example, you know, of freedom for everybody and is therefore politically effective? Or are there aspects in the work which actually can change hearts and minds, that can create what's called attitude change?

But then as a jumping off point for the creation of the art I'm stuck between this question as a basis and a lot of very abstract sonic ideas which I've developed over time having to do with how pitch behaves and how sound activates a space, just basic sonic effects which I find pleasing and beautiful and therefore poignant and important to me as an artist. I'm somehow stuck between these two positions and they go into the ring and battle it out. So as a result of this battle I arrived at this point of thinking about worlding and social composition as a modus to accommodate both things at once which is holistic rather than schizophrenic.

I come from a classically trained background as a composer of contemporary music. Also I've learned to play different instruments from my stay in India and Turkey, and also have a background in jazz. And if you look at the social emphasis of all these various sources, then where does that leave me? There's this craft-oriented music that I'm based in, that was my training, like orchestration and counterpoint and things like that. And then my exposure to conceptual action art and chance operations from John Cage were also very influential on me. One of my formative moments was playing *Imaginary Landscapes No. 4* in front of John Cage during his residency at Harvard in 1989, during the Norton Lectures that he gave there. His whole way of being and talking really was profoundly influential on me.

And I eventually had to come to the sensible conclusion that somehow in the way ideas come together, that it's not the composer who decides these things. Talking about worlding is instead rather like just being fascinated with the way things interact.

I think that one piece I did at Errant Sound in particular was actually very successful. There weren't very many people there. But for me it was a turning point just because all I did in a way was just put a few very different things together. The thing that makes it very special is that different people coming to this event would have perceived it totally differently, simultaneously as a solo concert on a kind of folk protest level, and an experimental electronic four-channel piece as a kind of installation, as a street happening, just: oh, they're playing outside. We don't even know if it's art.

And I thought of this "do nothing approach," which comes from Masanobu Fukuoka, organic gardening, where you let the garden just grow. You take a few weeds out, you do this and that, but basically the idea is that nature runs its course and in the end you get wonderful things. It's of course related to John Cage's ideas, but is not proprietorial. It's not claiming so much territory. It's not saying as much that this is my composition, my property which I own, in this box. It's leaving the borders open to say, I'm putting all of these things together and what am I actually doing? Well, not very much of anything – that's not my possession. As an artist you could say it's my work, but that aspect is less important than all the perspectives involved. What my presence, not my ownership there opens up is so much more interesting than "this is my work now". And I also like the idea that it happens without me, that all these connections are forming all the time. I simply contribute somehow and it all takes care of itself. But it doesn't have to be my own invention, or breakthrough, which I think is synonymous with the work of the academic and the pursuit of knowledge: that it's a collective activity. This is completely and automatically assumed in the academic arena and in the understanding that nothing in the field of human knowledge develops on its own, the idea of the Creative Commons. But still within the arts this idea doesn't have so much currency and that's a shame. And these collective processes are already natural too on their own like music, it's part of the natural environment, because it too is like eating and breathing, the way we react to each other, and come together in different social formations.

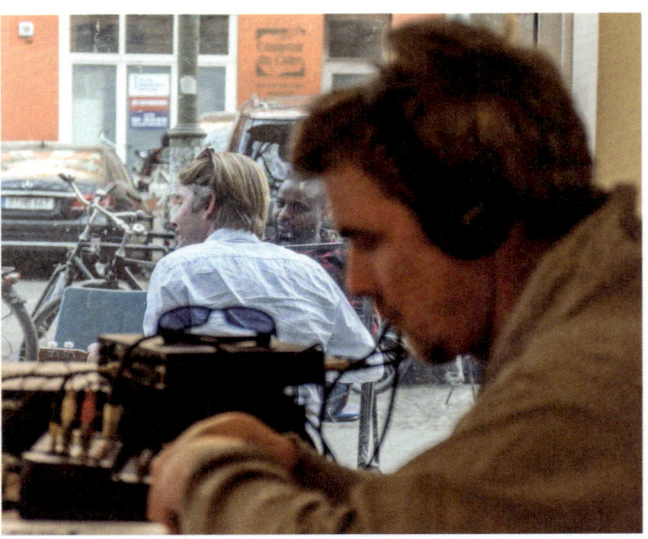

RECORDING

Recording sound linearly follows the course of time and writes a waveform that reflects the fluctuations in the air pressure of sound events. Recordings of sounds usually evoke ideas of the generation process when listening and refer to the associated objects. However, recording and editing recorded sounds can resolve this reference to sounding objects and virtually abstract sounds. Pierre Schaeffer described such sounds as 'objéts musicales'.

Source: Schaeffer, Pierre: Treatise on Musical Objects. An essay across Disciplines. Oakland 2017

→: A few of Hanna Hartman's "sound notebooks".
Photo: Hanna Hartman.

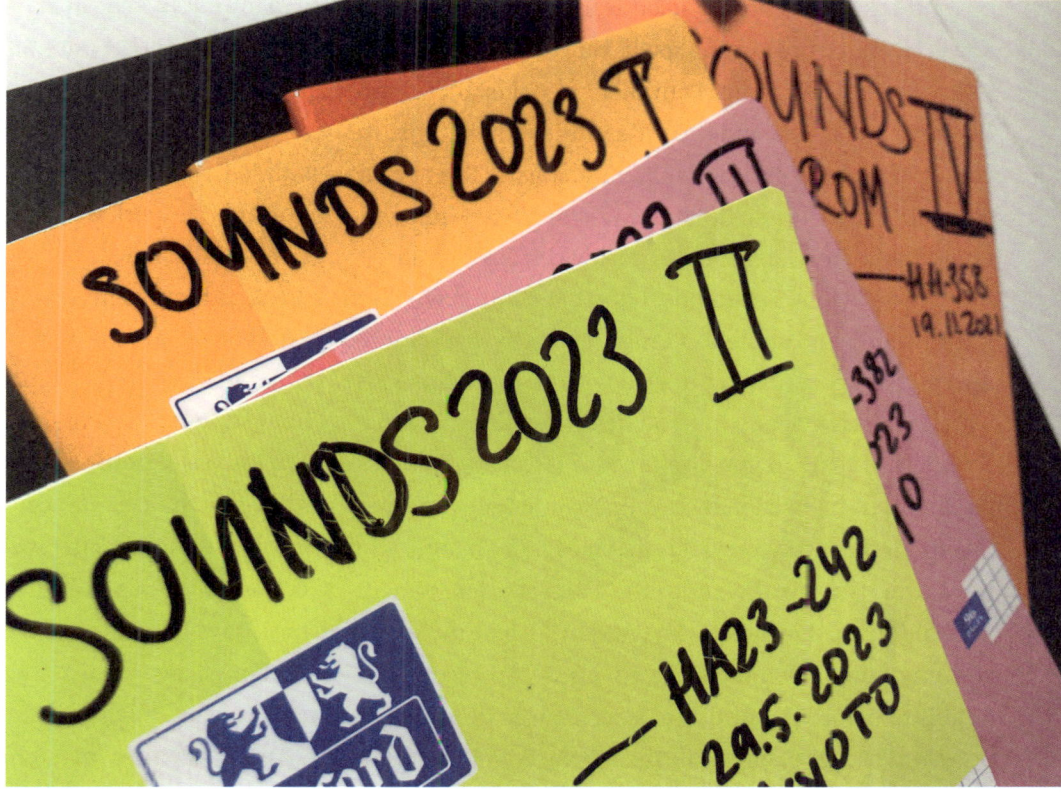

HANNA HARTMAN: I don't do field recordings. I just don't care about the atmosphere of a city or the surrounding area. I am interested in close-ups, but really so close that you no longer really hear what it is, but that you expose the sounds from the surrounding area, that they have a different meaning, that they become abstract. I record a lot in my apartment, especially in my hallway, I think it sounds best there. I want close-ups of things so they sound different.

Recording with OKMs [original head microphone] is totally boring because I don't hear what I do. With these recordings you get quite a good sound, and it's sometimes convenient to record anonymously with OKMs. But I think recording without headphones is like taking photos without seeing. It's just so blind. When I see people who record and don't use headphones, I think: "Okay. But you don't know what you do!" Therefore, of course I always use headphones. That is, so to speak, the meaning of the matter. Otherwise I would have no idea what I was doing.

When I wear the microphones open, with headphones and so on, and when I make it clear that I don't make a video, i.e. no pictures, only sound, then most people don't say no.

I think the recording itself is an abstraction, so to speak. Even the recording itself. But most importantly, I have several layers and I cut them free, I expose them. The multiple layers and the different layers that mix together create something else. This is music. To get rain, sound designers often don't use rain at all, but quite different tools. And I use tools to get away from the rain.

I usually look for sounds, I don't just find them. But sometimes I find some too. And that's why you should always have a recording device with you, because it's usually the case that what you hear then doesn't come back in five years. If you don't record it exactly then, it's gone. I went to Sweden by car, that was a long time ago. I went on this little ferry. It only takes half an hour and it was very stormy. I went to the Tax Free department and suddenly that noise, what's that? I had my zoom with me. I quickly took it out, up and I can record just a minute before the grids go down. It was the whiskey bottles that were shaken in the storm. Many different bottles, it sounded so great. A week later, I even called and asked if I could record, and I was allowed to. But it wasn't as windy as the previous time and there was no more sound.

It's mostly that I have an explicit idea, a topic for which I then make recordings, maybe in Japan or I want to record weaving machines, visit weaving mills and record old looms. That's always nice because I have a reason, so to speak, to get somewhere where there are interesting sounds that you wouldn't so easily get to otherwise. And then I make a lot of recordings, really as many as possible. I'm telling people: Okay, I'd like to record 20 minutes. But of course I would like to take six hours.

And when I've made a lot of recordings, I listen to everything and write down exactly what I have recorded in my notebooks, in my "Klang-Kladden." Later I can just go to my notebooks and look for it. "I heard something, ten or fifteen years ago, which had this pitch and sound." I take out the notebook and look up at how it sounded. And then I go to the hard drive and get the file out. And this work with listening and giving names and all this writing means that I get to know the recordings and store them in my head.

I have no idea what you hear and I will never know. What I'm listening to is simply music, but what I like has changed over the years. There was a long time when I didn't like electronic sounds. I even took ice recordings, and when you ride on ice, sometimes it sounds like an electronic singing. That's what I recorded and said: "Eh, no, that all sounds so electronic, I don't want to use that." These days I think it's super great.

For a new piece I always make new recordings. I have a vision of what I want to do and I am looking for it. And I also have my archive. And then I not only use the new recordings, but if there is a lack of sound, then I search for it elsewhere and often go to my archive. The recordings are like colors. And I use them to paint a new picture.

TRANSFORMING

Transforming: to convert, to reshape. Transforming is a component of many artistic actions. In music, for example, the aim of thematic transformation is to transfer a melodic theme to a new context and adapt it to this context, while retaining components and references to the material's origin. The technical component 'transformer' adapts electrical voltages to different uses of electrical energy. The term digital transformation describes changes in social structures in interaction with media developments. In many transmission, storage and presentation processes, media transform the aesthetic characteristics of the data presented.

Source: Ungeheuer, Elena: Ästhetische Pragmatiken analoger und digitaler Musikgestaltung. In: Lexikon Neue Musik, edited by Jörn Peter Hiekel and Christian Utz. Wiesbaden 2016, 77 – 87.

→: Site specific vocal performance "Per Diem" by the Psychedelic Choir. The members are Gosia Gajdemska, Irina Gheorghe, Ana Kavalis, Pauline Payen, Karoline Strys, Lyllie Rouvière and Leah Buckareff on bass. Errant Sound @ Rungestraße, 2. 9. 2023. Photo: Golo Föllmer.

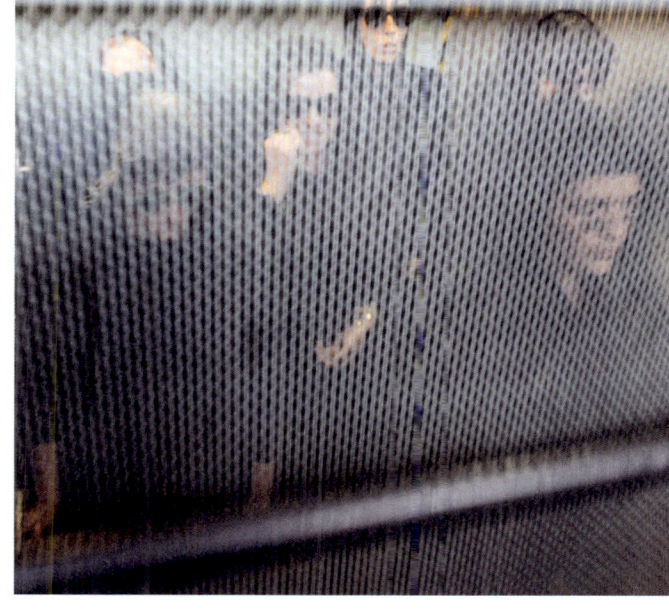

ZORKA WOLLNY: Sometimes we meet at the moment when people feel they are losing energy and they search for new ways to keep going. When we work together in a group we try to focus on transforming our doubts, fears and anger into something beautiful.

So the first point is the meeting and the second point is to create a place where people feel safe and welcome with all their opinions and questions. I think joining vocal workshops run by a noise artist is already defining a group that is quite open and has a will to connect, share and experiment together. While a regular choir is aiming for harmony and perfection, we create an atmosphere where every type of sound and every type of voice is welcome in the room. And before the public performance I remind the group that there is never a mistake, nobody knows what to expect from us. We're not singing a song, we are presenting a polyphony of voices, so as long as we listen to one another and give space the magical moments will happen.

Musically I'm taking it as far as I can. With some groups you can take it far, with some you have to accept a limit. If you work with amateurs and always with a different group you simply have to accept that. I'm not writing the composition and hiring someone to perform it. The people are the co-authors of the libretto, and I'm giving it the musical form, and this is where we meet. They are asked about their fears, wishes, opinions, favorite tunes. They represent themselves. It results with the piece that they fully identify with and this brings the strong emotional load into performance. One that one can never reach with the professional team of actors.

Sometimes I'm writing compositions for professional musicians or actors. It's hard to compare this to working with people who actually feel happy that they can express themselves. It's usually very moving and very touching to see all this polyphony and all these people who create this emotionally involving piece together.

It is working on what's there. Working in places that go through some transformation process, working with communities there, or transforming frustration and anger into music. It's not easy to talk about it because I'm not a trained psychologist. But after years of working with groups I know the group dynamic a bit, I know what to expect and what kinds of personalities are in every group. After seeing my retrospective exhibition in Dresden ("Voices/Stimmen," Kunsthaus Dresden 2023), one person said: It's like therapy on the society. That's funny because all this started for me actually having social difficulties, a long time ago. I'm working with people now for almost 20 years. But it started because I didn't understand the game. I had difficulties understanding social interactions. People were quickly offended and said: It's never fun with you. And you really don't know what's going on. So I had to propose my own game where I understand the rules and people are joining me to create a bit of a reality. I invite people to play my game and then I know what's going on. It's funny for someone who started from this nerdy and introverted position to become someone who is seen as giving other people a voice.

As we talk about transformation: I was always interested in architecture that is transformed from being something into becoming something else. What was, what can be, what is our imagination doing? You go inside the empty building with a bunch of musicians and you all have fun discovering.

These things start as an open process, improvising, listening to one another and listening to the space. And then slowly, bit by bit, we choose the best parts and we make a composition out of it. And even if there's fragments of text, the story has to be constructed in the audience. Working in empty spaces and buildings triggers the imagination of the audience. What was once there? What will it become?

I started from places, I started from architecture. "Concert for High Heels" (2004) was my first concert ever. An empty building of an official kind, late night, twelve women filling it with steps. Different characters, different schoes, walking, running, marching, 25 minutes long composition. Then I was working with objects for a couple of years. Telling stories of different places, different buildings.

And then slowly I discovered the voice itself can carry so much. And then it was a big step to go to public space where you don't have so much of the architecture and acoustics, and you have to rely just on text and vocal.

It's been a long way. The first seven years I was composing in collaboration with a girl who studied composition (Anna Szwajgier), and I learned a lot from her, not only about music but also how to address people. I always work in collaboration because it's easier to stay sensitive when you have four eyes, when you have two brains, two people monitoring the situation. Collaboration is extremely rewarding. You have a peek into somebody's mind, that's an amazing thing.

I'm not one of those artists who want to leave a heritage, like: When I die my work will continue. No, my work helps me functioning and making life more interesting. I explore other people's minds, I explore other people's emotions. I explore the relations between all these things, and then I understand better: people, relations, emotions, what they think, how they act. My work is my exploration lens.

INTERVENING

Intervention arises from the critical observation of actions. Interventionist concepts of action can be divided into five components: "(a) Actor who intervenes in (e) a defined situation on the basis of (b) specific intentions and (c) certain assumptions regarding the effects of his behavior with (d) certain measures in order to change it." The characteristics of the actor determine not only the choice of his measures, but also his criticism as such. Interventions usually relate to complex contexts, often involve many actors and are multi-stage in nature.

Source: Kaufmann, Franz-Xaver: Konzept und Formen sozialer Intervention. In: Handbuch sozialer Probleme, edited by Günter Albrecht und Axel Groenemeyer, Wiesbaden 2012, 1285 – 1305

→: Installation view of "TRASA" by Georg Klein, a video-based bimedial contact space connecting Berlin and Warsaw, September 25th – November 28th 2004. Photo: Georg Klein.

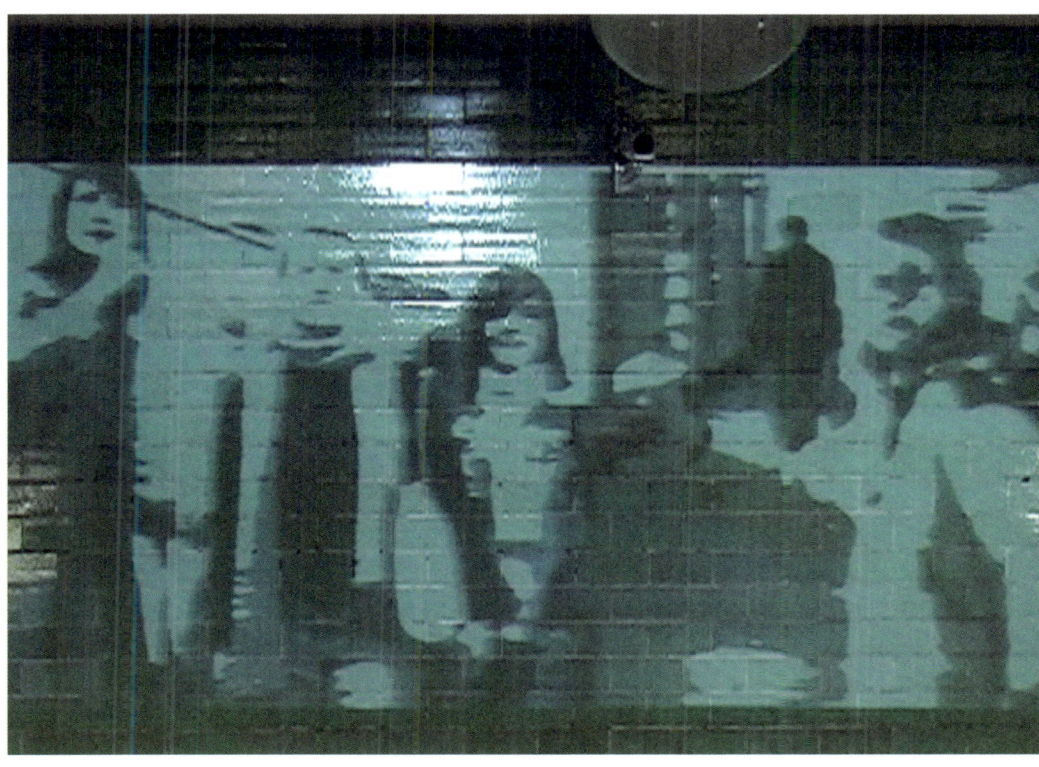

GEORG KLEIN: I have the impulse to intervene primarily in public spaces. Not in the gallery or the concert hall. What I find exciting about it is the unexpected reactions of passers-by, the randomness. This intervention in a place also means a very specific confrontation: first of all with the place itself. So what kind of architecture is it? What is the social situation like? What kind of atmosphere does a place have?

We are familiar with the topos of non-places that are used artistically. But it's not just that, although I do like to work in transit spaces where there is automatically a certain flow of people and vehicles. For me, the location often involves researching the place, finding out what conflicts there are in a place and conducting interviews with the people I meet there. And for me, that's almost the best phase of my work, to be involved in this research and to come across something that I can and want to work with.

I myself can be a kind of foreign body in this setting. For me, this is one of the functions of the artist: to get somewhere with a specific perception and try to absorb the atmosphere, everything that is there, and then transform it artistically. When I bring up conflicts in the process, this naturally involves a certain sensitivity. The reactions are very different. Some people can take it exactly as I want to show it, and others find it wrong. But at the end of the day, these are all confrontations that are part of it, right up to protests like the provocative project "turmlaute.2" (European Border Watch, 2007 – 2015).

I explained in an article that the term "intervention" comes from a military language, just like the term "avant-garde." I find it interesting that we have military terms for artistic things. At the same time, there is the difference that for me it is never about solving the conflict, but about the representation and reflection of this conflict. In other words, there is always a certain ambivalence. "Dark Matter" (2021), for example, is about seduction through right-wing extremist music and propaganda: getting involved in it for a moment and feeling what power it has, only to step out of it again critically.

For me, it is very important that there is something like an initial fascination, i.e. an attractiveness – here the sound in the space is decisive, possibly also visual elements – with the aim of first of all persuading the visitor to stay, especially in public spaces. It's not like at a concert: "I'm going to stay for an hour and a half and listen to everything, boring as it is," but in a public space the decision is made very quickly: "I'm moving on." That's the reason why this moment of attraction, or fascination, is a very good term for it, because it also shimmers a little ambivalently and suggests that you can discover further levels by staying. I often use language, which then appears not in the accompanying text but as spoken language in the work itself and can create various references, even if these are not unambiguous.

With sound in public space, the fact that you can't avoid it plays a major role. It's a dimension that comes with hearing and that the visual doesn't have. In my work in Marl ["Ortsklang Marl Mitte," 2002], graffiti slogans that were written or scribbled down were spoken and reappeared acoustically in the same place. This results in a completely different presence. The people walking across the pedestrian bridge couldn't avoid it, it was just there. I think this kind of presence is amazing. I often spread it out spatially, working with multiple channels and making the listening itself an attraction. This includes a basic atmosphere that sound can create particularly well, this immersion in sound when you enter a room. Finding the right basic sound for a situation is always a crucial task for me.

And with my interactive installations, the question arises: Who is playing this game? How do the bodies move in it? That's wonderful to observe. And it's nice that I can place myself in my installation to see the reactions incognito. I don't have to reveal myself and can simply talk to people. For example, in the installation "TRASA" (2004), which connected two public spaces in Berlin and Warsaw. There was an audiovisual connection that worked with a certain alienation. Seeing what people make of it, how they try to communicate and get caught up in a game, was incredibly instructive, almost like a sociological study.

When I transform spaces with my work, I create spaces of possibility, and there is something utopian in that. I change the everyday space and show that there is also another reality, so to speak. Regardless of whether this happens through light or sound, it takes you into another space. It's more of a transcendental space that is removed from everyday life and perhaps also carries you beyond this conflict. For me personally, this is perhaps also due to the fact that I have had a lot of therapy experience myself. In therapy, you go through the conflict to get to something else.

CONNECTING

In communication processes, people connect by creating reality with the help of culturally shared codes and assessing the extent to which their individual realities and assessments coincide or differ. Communication goes far beyond speech acts. It is often assumed that the perception of a connection is essentially created through non-verbal communication and is linked to transcendental, non-rationally accessible processes.

Source: Beck, Klaus: Cultural Studies. In: Lexikon Kommunikations- und Medienwissenschaft, edited by Günter Bentele, Hans-Bernd Brosius and Otfried Jarren, Wiesbaden 2013, 155 – 156.

→: Audio Walk/Intervention "Living Radio 2018" for 4 observers, 2 musicians and 100 radio listeners by Laura Mello and Wolfgang Musil; part of the "Dystopie Sound Art Festival Berlin". Kollwitzplatz Berlin 2018.
Photos: Golo Föllmer.

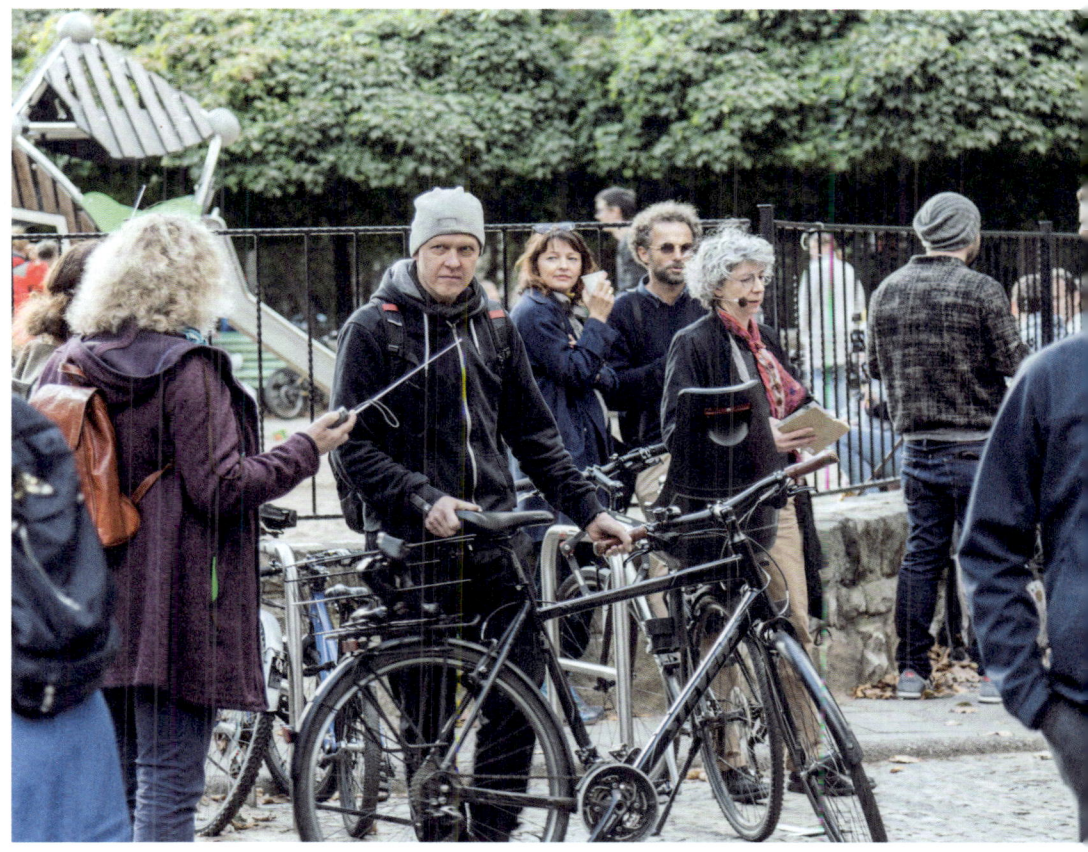

LAURA MELLO: I see music as a cultural phenomenon that is created through communication. I have studied music as a ritual: What happens in the theater, what happens in the concert hall, the listening experience, the sitting together, also the social history of music. I think people should know more about the connections between music and society and not go to a concert to represent. Sounds are essential for the connection between people. A fetus can hear as early as the fifth month of pregnancy.

My method is to communicate. But when I create my pieces, I always have the desire to make connections. I spent two years studying with journalists and PR people. That's when I realized that I don't want to be an advertising person. I believe everything can be connected to everything. And ultimately, everything is at least economically connected anyway. That's why there are always many connections in the background in my work, both musically and aesthetically and in terms of content. I have a very emotional relationship with radio. Exactly 40 years ago, there was the biggest flood in Blumenau, Brazil, and my parents had already had water at home twice. The third time, we were right at the top, where there was no water. We were hosting people and there was no running water for two weeks, no electricity. The only thing we had were battery radios. And the studios that weren't under water were broadcasting. That was very memorable: the radio was the only connection to the outside world. As a child, of course, it was great, we had an extra week of vacation, our parents were all drunk and we had to eat everything from the freezer. And afterwards I often took part in radio quizzes as a child.

With "Living Radio" [Kollwitzplatz 2018], the idea was that a microphone is a filter. I had gained experience with technology in Vienna. Then I realized that people are filters too, albeit in a completely different way. I invited performers from four different cultures with different mother tongues. And in the score, there is a requirement that they first describe everything that happens on the square as neutrally as possible. One level further on, they should use adjectives and then go more and more into emotions. The aim is to create feedback between the performers and the audience on the square. If someone feels like they are being watched on the square, their behavior will change.

My 7" record "Ringing Still Life" has a double groove on both sides. There's also a personal story about it. In Brazil, there were children's radio plays on small 7" records like that, I knew them by heart, lyrics, music, I knew everything by heart. They were well arranged and that had a big impact on me: That someone goes to so much trouble to do something with the medium itself, to exploit the medium to its full potential. I also think it's great that the record hasn't died. Records are re-released and then people listen to them reverently. It's a nice ritual that really connects. This thing runs under a needle on one arm, embracing us all with sound. It's very tactile, very subtle, creates a connection through touch.

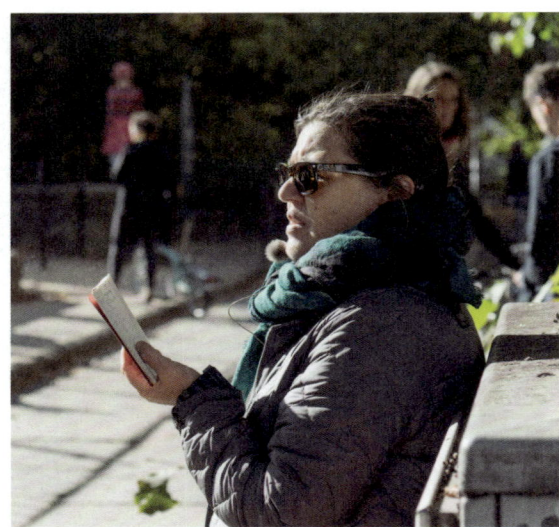

EXPERIMENTING

In the natural sciences, experimenting is often based on a set-up in which one parameter is varied while others are kept as stable as possible. In this way, it is possible to observe what changes occur in the structure when one parameter is changed. However, scientific breakthroughs are often achieved through errors in the experimental setup, i.e. through the intrusion of unforeseeable influences. In experimental music, openness to results is an important maxim, and this is often made possible by contingent processes. The audience's attention is often drawn to itself, thus essentially observing its own perception, which changes over time even if what it is listening to appears static or undifferentiated.

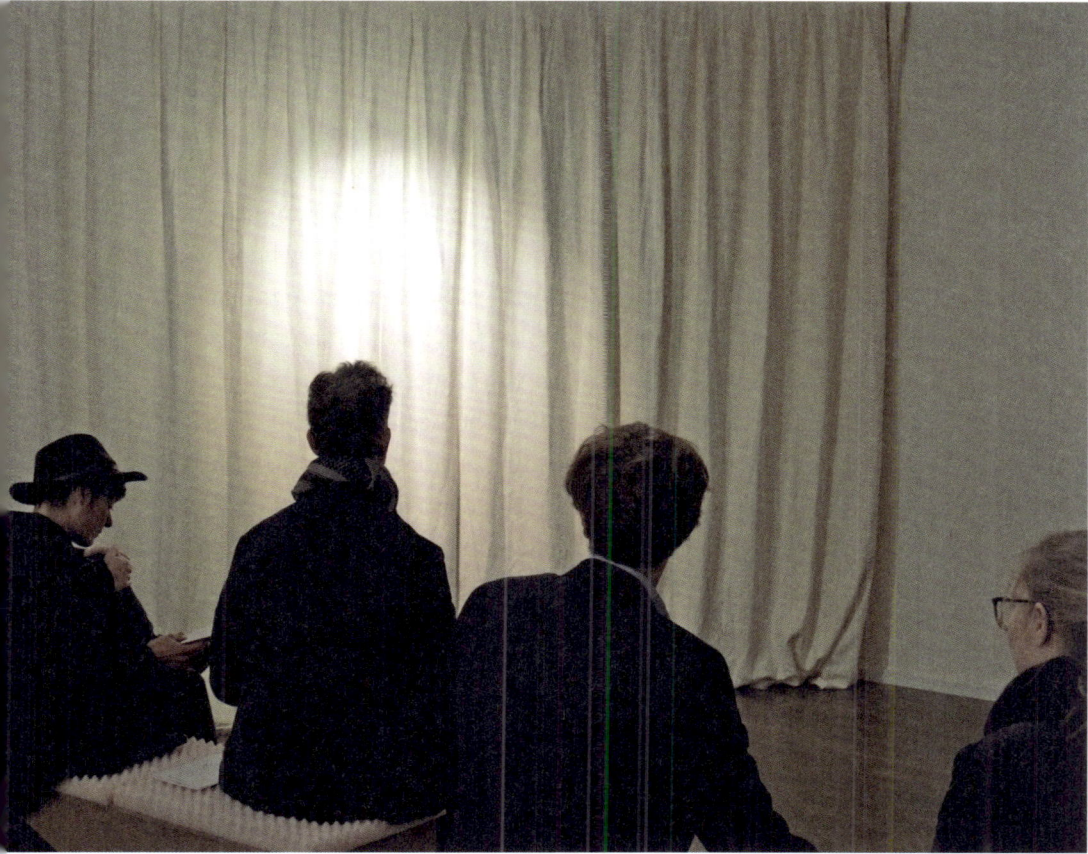

Source: Nyman, Michael. Experimental Music. Cage and Beyond, New York 1999.

←: Acousmatic Lecture by Hans-Jörg Rheinberger, 14. 09. 2017, Errant Sound @ Kollwitzstraße. Photo: Mario Asef.

MARIO ASEF: I see art as a medium for asking epistemological questions. I started out with observations of everyday things that didn't fit in, that I didn't understand. I constantly saw gaps where I thought: something like this contradicts the narrative of everyday life. I made a series of interventions in public space where I rearranged or moved elements. And the displacement creates a decontextualization, even though the context has not been changed at all.

In 2000, for example, I dug a hole on the grounds of the US military airport in Heidelberg. While digging the earth on the German side, a hill was created on the cycle path, which regulated the speed of cyclists.

I call these interventions *Empirics* (German: Empirien). Because all the considerations that take place in the studio – What would happen if I moved A to B? How would the space be read? How would this change the function of the public space? – I test these speculations empirically on site. What does the change mean semiotically, symbolically? What concept of architecture are we dealing with?

In another work, I donated things to museums undeclared. I added them to the collections at the exhibition venue. Visitors perceive this as part of the exhibition. I didn't install any works of art. For example, I placed a fox pelt next to a wild boar in a natural history museum. The question was: why is this dead animal on display here and not another one? I took photos as they carried the fox pelt away.

I always leave room for chaos in my experiments. Public space, however well organized, always has a certain amount of chaos. And my experiments have a place that is particularly open to chance and chaos. A scientist wouldn't do that, that would be death. It would be like a crack in the experimental model.

My processes are not contingent, they are very clear. But they have a leak. And that is by design. The leak is there to create chaos, to create chance. But I'm not aiming for aesthetic results. I have developed strategies to free myself from aesthetic constraints. I have a conceptual language, this structural methodology is my language. But it is not purely conceptual in the sense that you simply have to imagine it. You experience, you undergo a transformation that has an effect on you. I accept any results. Where other artists would say: that doesn't sound so good or that doesn't look so good, I focus on the process.

My last long-standing experimental format is the "Acousmatic Lectures." At first it was almost an excuse to invite interesting theorists to give lectures. But with the decision to use the acousmatic principle, I was confronted with how to let someone speak behind a curtain without it coming across as a cheap trick. So the experiment was: can Pythagoras' curtain still have an effect? If Pythagoras' curtain is a medium, what kind of transformative function does it fulfill?

I realized that I have to structure the format strictly in terms of space and time so that the lecture is choreographed from start to finish. The speaker and the audience must have separate entrances and must not see each other before or after the lecture. There is also no presentation of the speaker; the speaker simply starts speaking at some point. And he is not amplified, otherwise the speaker could have been somewhere else and we would have a kind of radio effect. When you hear the speakers' natural voice, you also feel their body in a different way than through a microphone. If it goes well, it makes you want to see the person after all. That's what it's all about for me: this desire has to arise. Otherwise it is not an acousmatic phenomenon.

Acousmatic phenomena also play an important role in psychoanalysis. The patient lies down and looks into the void. The therapist is just a voice. Silence plays a major role in Lacanian psychoanalysis in particular. The therapist tries to give as little input as possible. He only asks very short, concise questions and the silence is then the place where the patient reorganizes his thoughts. So we are talking about the absence of sound, and here again there is this desire to fill a void with visuals or whatever.

The experimental mode sets in as soon as you enter the room at the Acousmatic Lectures because you have to make a lot of decisions about how to deal with the situation, on both sides of the curtain. The lecturer also has to make a lot of decisions. Hans-Jörg Rheinberger said that he perceived this curtain as a kind of mirror, where his voice came back to him like an echo.

It turned out that speakers from different disciplines have different effects. Many people I have invited – e.g. Rheinberger as a philosopher and biologist, Sabeth Buchmann as an art historian – get in touch with me and say: Thank you for bringing this topic to my attention, because I find interesting connections in my field. I recently published a book where I describe the whole procedure. It's a kind of recipe so that other people can experiment with it.

The exact nature of the Pythagorean curtain and the role it played are controversial. Brian Kane believes that the curtain should be understood metaphorically and that there were two different lectures: one for the mathematikoi and one for the akousmatikoi. In any case, Pythagoras' curtain embodied a hierarchical structure. Anyone who wanted to enter the school first had to sit in front of this curtain for five years, just listening and not allowed to ask questions.

I have now reached a point where I would like to break this hierarchical structure of the Acousmatic Lecture. I'm thinking about creating an acousmatic dialog with several speakers on both sides of the curtain. Is it possible to give the acoustic voice a plurality? What is the best way to create an acousmatic dialog?

LEARNING

Learning is the acquisition of knowledge and skills. As it always takes place as 'additional learning' to already acquired capacities, it is to a large extent a restructuring of existing knowledge and skills. Biologically, learning occurs as the formation or reinforcement of neuronal connections in the brain. The 'intentional learning' of targeted learning processes differs from 'incidental' and 'implicit learning', such as that which occurs during disinterested observation or playful exploration of the world. What is essential about learning is that knowledge can be transferred to other contexts and enables self-learning processes.

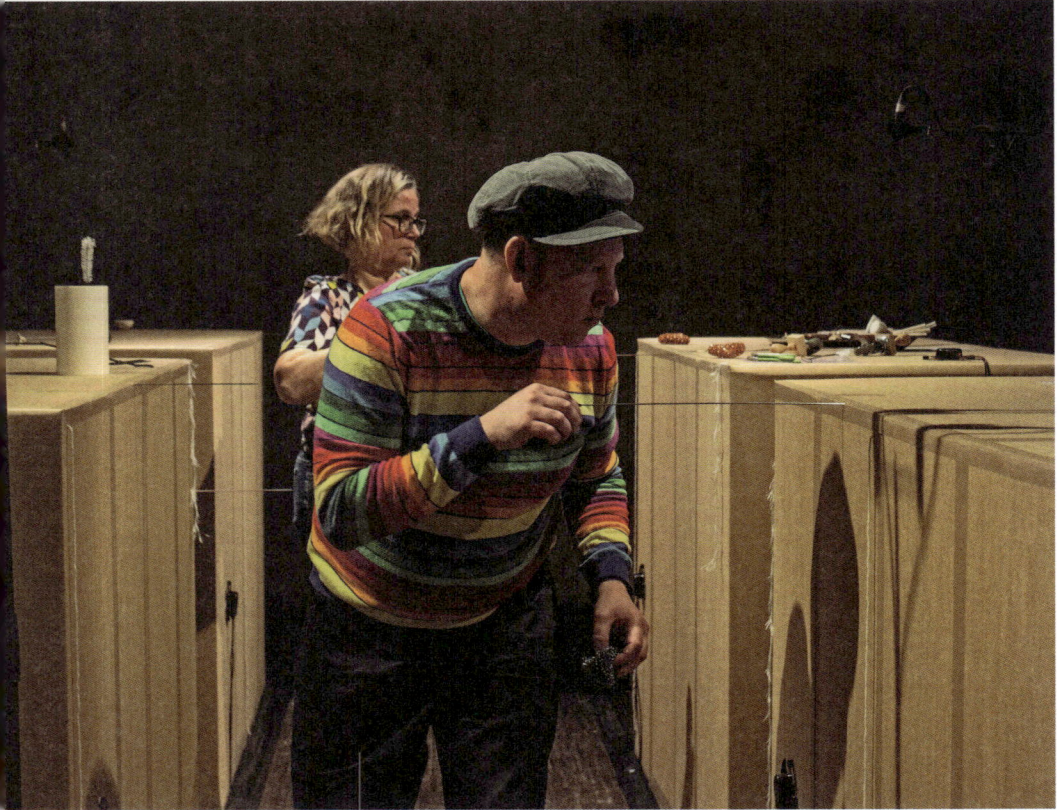

Source: Roelle, Julian; Lachner, Andreas; Heitmann, Svenja: Lernen. Theorien und Techniken. Paderborn 2023.

←: Performance as part of the exhibition "Jenseits der Wand" (Beyond the Wall) by Daniela Fromberg & Stefan Roigk, ausland Berlin, 7. 9. 2021. Photo: Heidrun Schramm.

DANIELA FROMBERG AND STEFAN ROIGK: Our work involves a constant search for materials. By using everyday materials, access to everyday life is central to our works. For me, almost everything starts from this room here, from my very private everyday life. We are always trying out new material and new sounds. I would say that we both like to explore material … and also find failure interesting. When you touch material, connect something, break something, dip it in water, then something happens that you didn't expect and then it becomes interesting.

The installation made of cardboard boxes ("Beyond the Wall") is the first artistic work that emerged from our cultural education projects, because we realized: Ah, that's not just interesting for children! We had to experiment to find out what sounds good INSIDE the box and what only sounds good OUTSIDE on the surface! There are lots of sounds that are really nice on the top that you can't hear at all inside or that can't be transmitted with the transducers.

We have been doing aesthetic research projects in daycare centers and schools for years. We started this as part of our artistic practice when our son was of nursery age. He wanted us to come over and do something with the children. This resulted in "geräusch[mu'si:k]" and we continue to do it because this work ultimately corresponds directly to our practice in the studio. In other words, we have a lot of interesting experiences. And it's great that we can bring people closer to the subject. But for us, it's not that different from working in the studio, because this exploration is so important to us artistically. I see myself entirely in the role of children when I make art: I explore my everyday life and try to develop rules and techniques from it.

In our workshops, we often give the simplest basic materials in large quantities to the group, i.e. a mountain of paper, lots of cardboard tubes, screw caps, pudding cups etc., which are then examined for their sonic possibilities.

So that it is clear: you can get a lot out of this insignificant, uniform material. Then we do small introductory rounds, and these introductory rounds develop into circle concerts or conducted concerts. And the children are empowered more and more each day to give more complex concerts.

We also encourage the children to bring their own things that make sounds, not musical instruments, but everyday objects: stuffed animals, toys, stones, matchboxes, garbage.

Exploring these sounds is also about motor skills. You learn them in the process because it's a lot about how you move objects together very delicately to achieve certain sound characteristics. We work a lot with dishwashing brushes that have a hard rubber suction cup at the back. You can use them to create a deep drone on many surfaces. It sounds like a monster, but you have to practice it because it only works at a very specific angle and only without pressure. I think this tactile skill is very important and you can learn it this way. Just like you have to spend a lot of time applying pressure to the violin bow to adjust your motor skills so that it works the way you want it to.

Sometimes, when we happened to be back in the same daycare center after nine months, there were children who were absolutely convinced that they didn't know us. But these children were still able to conduct. If you gave them things, they still knew how to make noises with them. They also knew that the last time we gave them a balloon with a dice in it, it made a great noise. We think that's good because we don't want the children to remember us, we want them to internalize techniques that they can transfer to other situations. In one daycare center, we built a sound cart. And the children have passed on the technique of making noises and playing little concerts with this sound cart to each other over several generations of daycare children. The trolley is in an area they call the research aisle, next to fish, guinea pigs and physics experiments. The children simply know how to use it and what it involves. The fact that they have passed on this knowledge shows that it is of value to them.

There were also children who took part more often and were able to reflect on the fact that their sound preferences had changed. There was once a boy who was maybe five and a half who said that he used to be incredibly loud and only liked loud noises. And now his favorite sound is the soft squeaking of a Playmobil figure's arms, which you can only hear very close to your ear.

It's always really interesting for us to see which things work with children. At the very beginning of our projects, for example, we were surprised when very young children started to playfully recombine our graphic notation signs and use them to make music together.

When working with the children, it is important to us not to impose a canon of values on them, but to be open. We say: listen to this, you can find it funny or stupid. Because you can't make a value judgment without experience. Everyone always says to us: Oh, and then you also squeak with polystyrene? Yes, we squeak with polystyrene! Because children don't find it horrible at all, because it's not painful for their ears. We've had lessons where someone has pressed polystyrene into a plastic cup and then squeaked with pleasure for 60 minutes!

There was once a childcare worker who thought that a boy wouldn't enjoy the project and would only throw things around unmotivatedly. But because we had conducted interviews beforehand, I was able to refute this: he only did it when he was instructed. In the interview, he also spent 20 minutes telling me why he thinks this tipping gemstones in plastic cups against the wall is so great: Because it sounded a lot like lava spurting out of an exploding volcano. So he had clear associations and a reason why he liked it. We don't want to restrict anyone, we want the children to find their own favorite sounds and they can only do that if they try things out and aren't presented with something by someone else.

Children can hear much better than they can see and are better able to process and remember what they hear. Unfortunately, everything in our everyday lives is always geared towards the visual. If children can be active with sound and noises themselves at a young age and are given this playful approach, then they can also relate more to experimental music. Adults are often much less able to do this because they don't recognize the playfulness of it and always think they have failed to understand something serious about it. That doesn't happen with children, this inhibition threshold is not there at all.

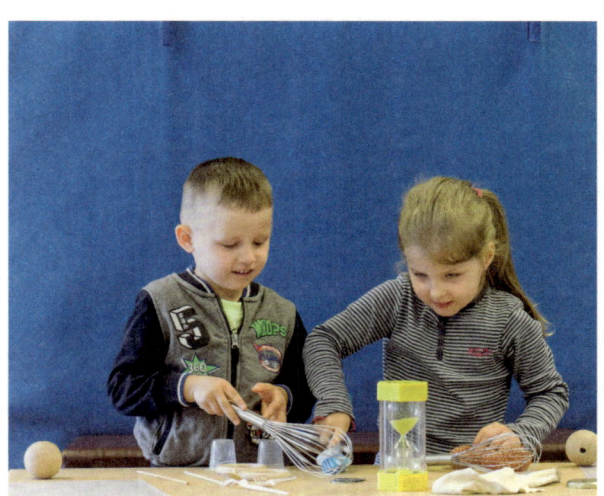

COMPOSING

Composing refers to the assembly of components into a larger whole and aims to create a work that is clearly recognizable in different performances. A composed work is also characterized by contingency; it could have been different and its characteristics cannot be fully grasped.

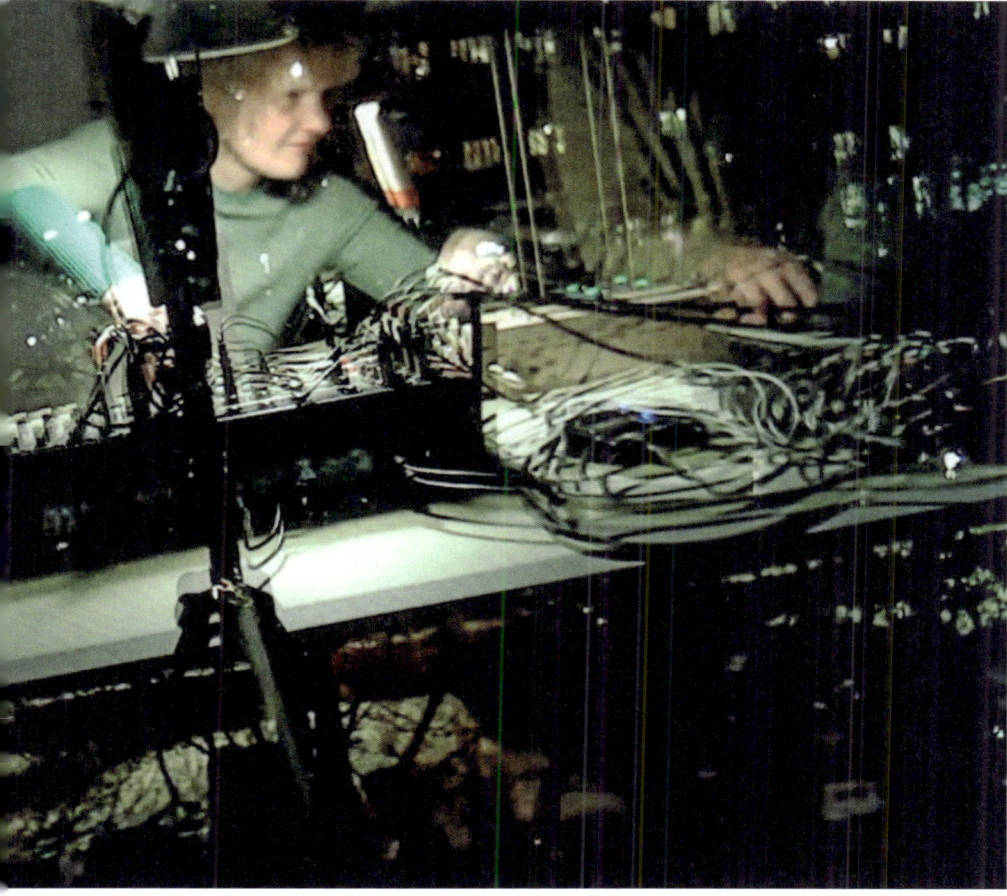

Sources: Composition, in The New Grove Dictionary of Music and Musicians, London 2002; Zembylas, Tasos et al: Praktiker des Komponierens. Soziologische, wissenstheoretische und musikwissenschaftliche Perspektiven, Wiesbaden 2016.

←: Live improvisation set by Kirsten Reese and Golo Föllmer from home location part of "Errant Sound Shutdown Night #5", 30. 1. 2021. Photo: screenshot youtube stream.

KIRSTEN REESE: Composing actually means putting things together, and I use this term because it is essentially what I do. To be more precise, I would perhaps say that today I research sounds or deal with the technical realization of a sound work. Or I negotiate with musicians, arrange rehearsals or send out technical riders. That would all be part of it. But in the true sense, composing for me means that I sit down and work on a sound work or composition.

I like the term composing. You can apply it to sound works just as much as to any other artistic work. One is the practical aspect: what do I do when I go to my desk?

The second is precisely this aspect, that I would like to call everything composing, to include everything that deals with bringing sound into a form, into a realization. And the third is how I really work with structures in concrete terms. By that I mean that even when I make sound works, sound installations for example, for me they are compositions, because I usually make works that are very strongly related to temporal structuring.

I am interested in content, in the sense of a certain richness or depth. That's why many works are research-based. That's why some works of fine art are not enough for me. I go to an exhibition and think, that's all well and good, but is it supposed to be a great work of art, such a small thing? For me, it's about what kind of theme a work has, what kind of vision do I actually have for a piece, and what kind of elaboration is appropriate?

It's not that I have rules beforehand and then I work through them. I would rather say that there is a guideline or a vision – although this is another typical case of there being no good audio terms. You'd have to say an aud-ion, haha. Or it's not an aud-ion, because I don't hear anything beforehand, but I think to myself, this piece is about this and that and it should achieve such and such. It often starts with the idea of a duration, this piece is 40 minutes long, for example, and the sound should be harsh and rugged – and so on.

I had this piece in a hot air balloon. I had the idea that I wanted to hear the sound as far as possible from the balloon. I wanted to hear the trumpet sound as far as possible, that was the guiding idea. That's not a rule for building a piece, but a lot comes out of it.

Sometimes the idea relates to a simple form. Something starts low, gets higher and higher and gets low again at the end. I have found that very simple basic ideas are often very sustainable. Often a form is created that is actually sequential, many small forms one after the other. First I look for material and then I put it together according to similarities or contrasts, dissimilarities.

Then I listen to it, or imagine it, and think about whether it should stay quiet a little longer or become louder. I condense the form, that's composing.

There are no fixed rules, rather principles. Take film music, for example, where the rule is always circulated that the music must not be too much in harmony with the film. I see it differently, because I think it's always about deviations that are interesting. Something runs parallel and then suddenly doesn't. Or there's a richness building out of proximity, but it's not a real proximity because two different media are interacting.

Composing is based on a will not to control, but to shape. Sometimes I don't know whether something has been solved correctly in terms of form, whether a part would perhaps have better been shorter or different parts more interlocking, for example. And then I think: yes, that might have been nice, but now that's the way it is.

My pieces often have a certain openness in terms of how they can be read. I have an idea of the composition, a form and an elaboration that I have notated for musicians in a score, or that meet a space and a situation in purely electronic, medially fixed sound works. But how something is realized is open. When you cook a recipe, you want a nice dish to come out of it, but you don't want to have control over the dish. I'm happy if the dish tastes different from the last time. It doesn't always have to taste exactly the same.

TINKERING

Claude Lévi-Strauss distinguishes the tinkerer from the engineer. According to him, the engineer tries to open up a passage for himself in the context of culture following a strict plan, for which he ignores the conditions of the environment as far as possible. The tinkerer, on the other hand, always voluntarily remains within the conditions; he is constantly in contact with what is happening outside. The tinkerer therefore not only speaks with things, but through them. He lets the objects speak. He starts something and then the thing speaks to him, says: I work best like this, or: This is where it gets interesting, etc. "To emphasize a movement that is not predetermined: that of the ball that bounces back, the dog that makes detours, the horse that deviates from a straight path to avoid an obstacle. Nowadays, the tinkerer is the person who works with his hands, using means that are absurd compared to those of the professional."

Source: Lévi-Strauss, Claude: Das wilde Denken, Frankfurt a. M. 1968 (1962), 29. Translation by the author.

→: Georg Werner in his tinkershop.
Next page: Performance by Georg Werner.
Photos: Golo Föllmer.

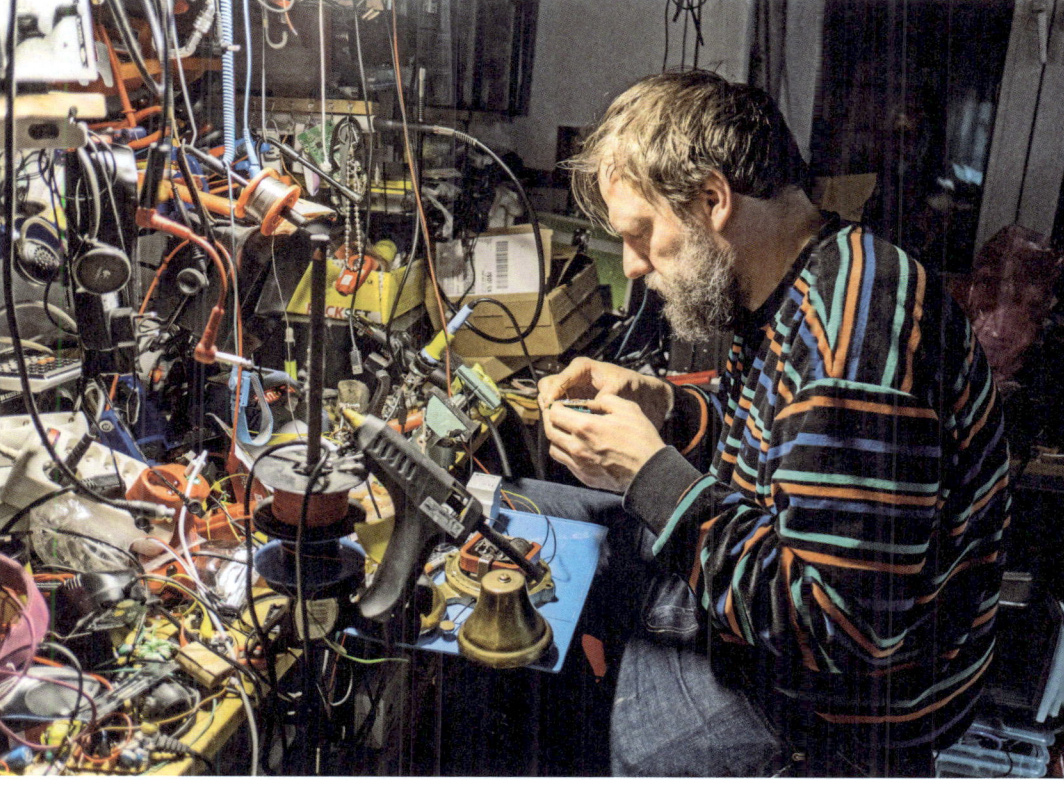

GEORG WERNER: I didn't really learn all this tinkering somehow. Tinkering is a lot of different things: exploring how things work, how materials work, how to repair things, how to create new things. And it's not a profession. I would rather call it a basic attitude.

The counterpart to the tinkerer, the engineer, basically needs a clear list of requirements in order to do his work. An engineer would always build things in such a way that they fit the application exactly, there's not too much to it, there's not too little to it, but it's exactly enough for the requirement. In some project phases, I clearly have to be an engineer and say okay, I have this-and-that budget, I have these-and-that requirements.

Trying things out takes place at different levels. The moment I understand a subject better, I can try out new things at a different level. And of course you need a basic understanding of how things work. Once I've achieved that, I can draw a circuit diagram, for example. And that's how I approach technological finds. Exploring in a way, but also with a kind of compass, where I can look for something.

Social responsibility plays a role here. First of all, I have the feeling that far too much is thrown away in our culture, far too much is simply consumed. You buy something and then something older is thrown away simply because it's older. I've already equipped various performances simply with electronic waste, and 3/4 of the stuff still worked straight from the dump. So that's the thing for me: breathing new life into things.

However, this tinkering type of repair is not just work, you also learn something in the process. If I take something somewhere and someone repairs it for me, it's probably more efficient because it takes less time and costs less money. But in the end, when I've figured out how it works myself and maybe I've also learned a technique or two to repair things: These are all things that nobody can take away from me. And that's actually a much bigger gain than the time or money I've now saved.

And then, of course, I hope that this somehow radiates or that it becomes much more normal on a social level to repair old things again and continue to use them. You develop a different relationship with the things that surround you, out of necessity: when you look at how we should deal with resources on our planet now.

I would tie my concept of art very closely to this image of the tinkerer. I think that the material must always have a voice. And you have to find that voice for yourself. Material speaks to everyone differently.

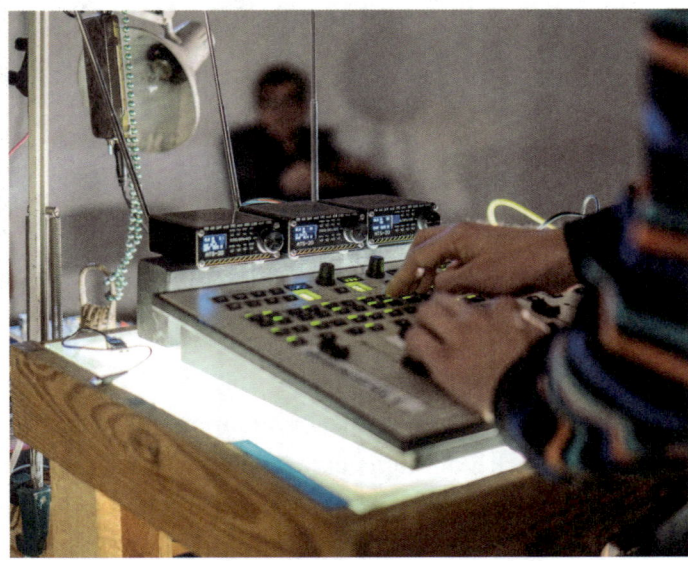

ACTING

Max Weber distinguishes between purpose-rational and value-rational action: the former is oriented towards material purposes and places conditions on the outside world, whereas the latter is motivated by ethical, aesthetic or religious values, for example, and is exercised independently of success. He contrasts these forms with affective action triggered by emotions and traditional action based on habits.

Pierre Bourdieu's theory of practice places practical action at the center of sociological considerations. Culture should not be understood by querying cognitive concepts, but is expressed in the actions themselves, as society and the individual mutually produce and define each other.

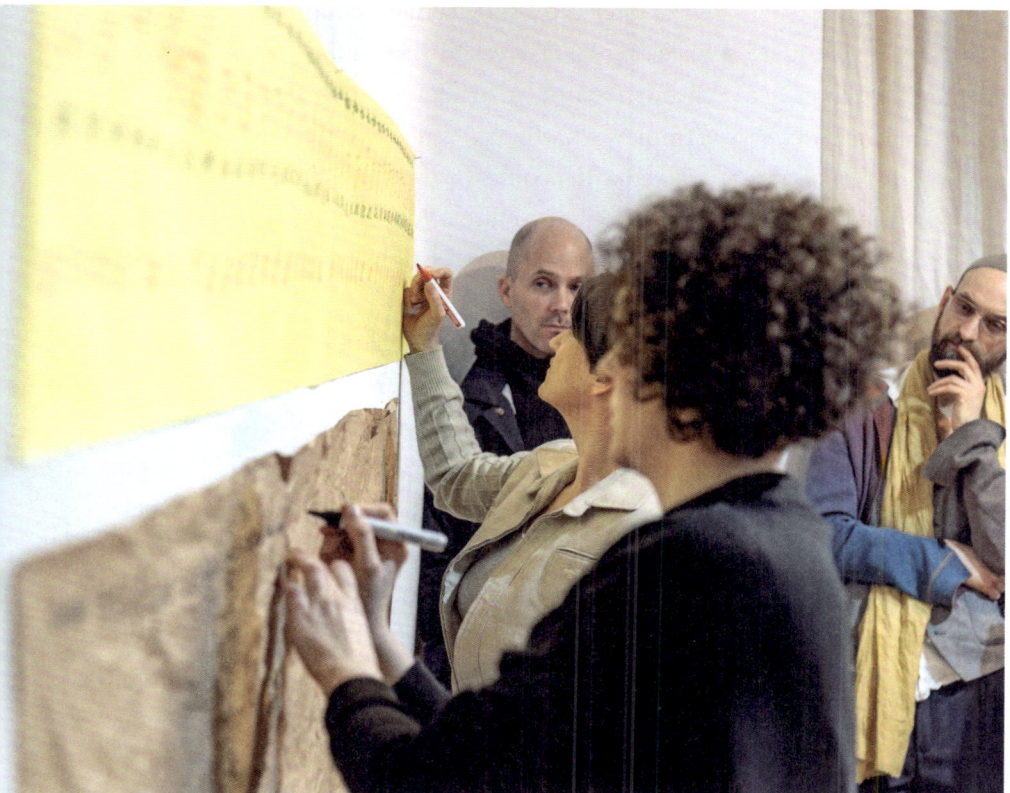

Sources: Weber, Max: Wirtschaft und Gesellschaft. Grundriß der verstehenden Soziologie. Studienausgabe. Tübingen 1980 (1922). – Bourdieu, Pierre: Die feinen Unterschiede. Kritik der gesellschaftlichen Urteilskraft, Frankfurt a M. 1982.

←: Performance at the opening of the new Errant Sound location at Rungestraße 20, as part of "Ready Making #1" – exhibition and interactive listening space by Janine Eisenächer and Steffi Weismann, 29. 3. 2019. Photos: Golo Föllmer.

JANINE EISENÄCHER / STEFFI WEISMANN:

JE: I am interested in noises and sounds, performance art and action-based material. I am specifically interested in action with things, with objects, materials, everyday objects. When I started researching action and action-based material sounds in performances in 2014, I looked up action theory, musicology and sound studies and found hardly any theory on the subject. There was a focus on listening, a lot has been written about listening habits, about listening in certain times, from social science, cultural studies and historiographical perspectives, linked to certain circumstances, to the place, to the person and to the voice. I have simply not found anything on the question of what relevance the action aspect has for working with sound. The discrepancy between my artistic work and the lack of scientific description was the starting point for me.

SW: When I think of action, what comes to mind is handling, the haptic dealing of things for which we already have certain experiences. But these everyday objects are then used in a different situation, which suddenly challenges our ability to improvise.

JE: For me, it's clearly about doing something with your hand, which is part of the concept of action. And then you have to differentiate what distinguishes this form of action from an action in a drama. There is a good reason why the concept of action is used here. So we've been using different terms all along. In fact: handling is one of them! It's about questions of modulation, manipulation, skills, use. And in all of these terms there is the moment of repurposing. We have often referred to this as playful misappropriation, because it's about taking things out of one context and into another and doing other things with them in order to break habits of perception, action and listening and open up new potential. We have a whole spectrum of such hand-words, do-words. And that's why there's always the question: is this acting, is it an action, is it an act, is it performing, is it operating? Who or what is actually acting with whom?

SW: We also talk about body knowledge, where there is a level of intuitive action, where you make decisions quickly and behave spontaneously. Also the question of how it compares to a musical instrument, where you also use your hands. We think about when it is an active intervention, when I shape something, and when I let the thing be itself. There is a French expression for this: laissez faire. When acting with things, we often seek a balance where control is not permanently with me as the performer, but where I allow myself to be guided by the resistance of this thing.

JE: In our "Ready Making" series, we work with the German formulation of "Hör- und Handlungswissen." By this we mean that there is a knowledge that arises in a simultaneous doing and listening, in the sound-practical action. We have translated this into English as "sonic know-how." It means an implicit, tacit knowledge.

SW: We soon came to the conclusion that we didn't just want to perform together, but that we wanted to offer the audience the opportunity to experience this themselves by providing an introduction through written instructions. In this way, we create a framework where a "multi-speaker experience" is created with people who just happen to come in and leave after ten minutes. Very complex sound experiences are created in incredibly simple, little planned interaction situations.

There are subtle differences in the best way to create such a situation so that people don't start chatting, so that the approach is easy to understand. The situation has to be pointed and clear and simple, but still have a multitude of possibilities so that it doesn't get boring after five seconds. For example, we had metal sheets and nails next to them. The instructions were: "You put the nail on the metal sheet, then pick up the metal sheet and bend and move it so that the nail turns and produces changing pitches." – a skill exercise where people have fun seeing how well they can balance and turn the nail. When several people do this, you have a buzzing in the room, completely electronic sounds that you can't identify.

JE: I have thought about why I do this work. What experiences do I want to give people? I wouldn't say: "What do I want to teach you?" but of course I want to share with people how easily they can do things differently, because for me that's an important attitude in life: that you don't have to do everything the way it's pre-designed for you. When it comes to listening and making sounds, after several years of working with contact microphones, I made a very conscious decision not to always amplify sounds. Also, I can no longer cope with this ubiquitous Ableton Live sound aesthetic. I want to train a different way of hearing, because I think it's a shame if we are no longer able to hear all of the things that actually surround us. At some point, it might all just disappear if everything only exists digitally. I don't want us to unlearn this hearing, I want us to live with more than just headphone experiences. You can learn so much about space and spatial sound just by listening to these simple sounds and actions. And that's why I, personally, don't have to go into this over-technoid or tech-savvy production of sound and space.

SW: I'm also interested in physical know-how. How do things react to certain chemical or physical influences, what role does moisture play? I like the contradictions when one level is very artificial and the other is perhaps more like a childhood experience. If I wet these green packaging chips with glass cleaner, I can make a crazy noise on a window pane. When I do something like that, I can be completely with myself. I can close my eyes and simply modulate the sound by applying pressure. That's also the educational work I do with children, this acoustic experience and creating it myself with the simplest things.

JE: In my work, I try to open myself up to everything I can perceive in the room, whether it's human or not. And that has something of a mindfulness process. Not that I perform it didactically for others, but I am simply like that in my attitude at that moment and I also love it when this is conveyed: the quality of dedicating myself to something with my entire presence and being in this existential space. That's why I'm interested in live processes with Ready Making, working in a room, with the acoustics, with the conditions. However, after four years of live processes, we have now reached the point where we are turning our attention to other things. How do we write about it? What does that mean on a record? What would it look like on a website? That requires a lot of transformation processes.

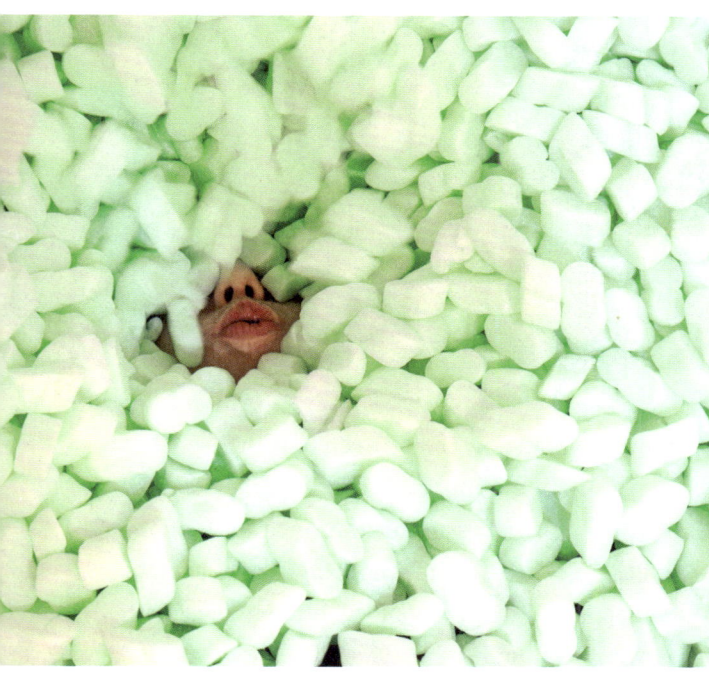

VOCALIZING / VOICING

In oral communication, vocalizing means expressing an idea or feeling with words, while voicing points especially to expressing anger or protest. In music, vocalizing means using the voice to make a specific sound, while in organology, voicing means fine-tuning timbre, attack, loudness etc. of each individual string or pipe of an instrument.

Roland Barthes distinguishes the formally-musically perfect, but in a certain sense lifeless pheno-song from geno-song, which allows the voice to grow "out of language and its materiality" from the "space in which the meanings germinate" (Barthes 1982, 272). For Norie Neumark, a central element of the voice is its ability to transcend the boundaries of the subject and connect subjects. '"Alterity" is the reason why we listen to other voices: because the voice conveys the fundamental and perceptible uniqueness of the person vocalizing.

Sources: Barthes, Roland: Die Rauheit der Stimme, in: id.: Der entgegenkommende und der stumpfe Sinn, Frankfurt a.M. 1982, 269 – 278. Neumark, Norie et al. (ed.): Vocal Aesthetics in Digital Arts and Media, London 2010. Translation by the author.

→: Performance "Nocturne Ritual" by Alessandra Eramo, Errant Sound @ Rungestraße, 11. 2. 2024.
Photo: Golo Föllmer.

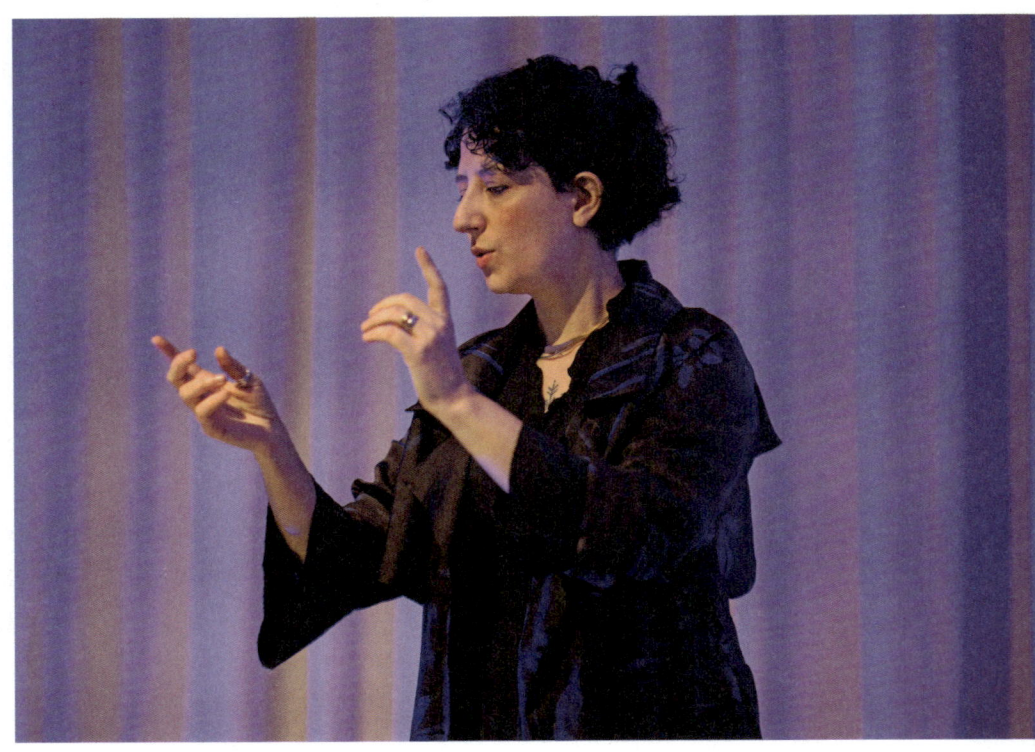

ALESSANDRA ERAMO: As a young woman, I dealt with my body on stage. I had also trained in bel canto, classical singing, but at a certain point I broke with this tradition. I didn't want to be the pretty singer with make-up applied on the stage. Sometimes I thought I would put on a hood and just disappear. My voice would remain. Later, I thought about how I could overcome these clichés of the singer. Singing in public is like a political act for me. That's why I'm interested in my voice in its many forms and as an expression of freedom. I try to explore the hidden acoustic territories of the human voice with extended vocal techniques.

I am fascinated by the fact that the voice contains very different emotions as well as physical tensions and always musicality. My performances are mostly composed pieces where trance states also play a role. I have often observed how trance arises in my body.

I am thinking of the conceptual proximity of evocation and invocation. Evocation refers to the fact that I can evoke states with my voice, in myself and in others. Invocation is the summoning of spiritual beings, a kind of magical activity in which performers "call into" their own bodies or thoughts.

My work has to do with suggestion and memory. I look for something that is present as a sound idea or memory and I bring it out. For me, this process is connected to the power of the repetition of prayers or chants, as I could hear them during my childhood in Basilicata and Apulia at funerals or other magical-religious rituals. Women would recite the rosary for hours until the words dissolved and became meaningless, and while invoking a saint or a Madonna, the women would create a kind of drone-music concert with an immersive experience of the sound of the voice.

In my solo live performances for voice and often also for electronic instruments, there is always a situation of exchange between the audience and me, something is taken, something is given. I speak, I sing during a concert or in public, and my voice suddenly acts like a body that moves from me to the ears and memory of other people. It is there, at this point, that the exchange takes place. The room also plays an important role in this. I am in dialog with it and always adapt to certain spatial situations. That's why my work tries to be site-specific. I really like it when the audience is close to me. It's like a ritual where the audience almost shares the smells with me.

A good two years ago, still during the pandemic, I realized the performance work "La Santa Monica." The title refers to an old Apulian divination ritual that combines elements of paganism and Christianity in an interesting way, a sound ritual that my great-grandmother performed. Women met on a terrace at midnight for this. After praying to St. Monica, they listened into the stillness of the night to the sounds sent by the saint: the cry of an owl, the whistle of a train, the barking of a dog, footsteps or the voice of a man. Each of these acoustic signs had a symbolic meaning for the women, which they then interpreted. I find it fascinating how these women worked creatively and imaginatively with sound, trying to understand their own reality and finding answers to their questions and problems through an oracle. For my performance "La Santa Monica," I created a new sound performance for which I combined field recordings from our current reality – which I recorded from my balcony in Berlin and also during my stay in Puglia – with text, drawings, a sound object made of salt and contact microphones, and composed a song to create a deep collective listening experience together with the audience.

I associate "voicing" with a voice that is conspicuous, that goes outwards and demands attention, here and now. I therefore perceive voicing as strongly political, as an expression of an acute need for visibility/audibility. At the same time, it stands for impulsive behavior. I identify more strongly with the term vocalizing. It contains the focus on structure, on a creative process that takes time and is not as impulsive as voicing. I understand vocalizing as more highly structured, a voice that refers to a solid base that already exists within us, like a sediment of materials, images, memories that are the foundation of our being.

I love the idea that the voice is alive. The voice can of course be trained to achieve a certain virtuosity, a certain sound and a certain color. But there is always a shadow behind it. And I am particularly interested in this shadow, precisely because we cannot create it through training and virtuosity. I can observe my hand, but only others can see my back. I need a mirror for that. It's similar with my voice. In this image, the mysteriousness of the voice becomes evident to me.

ASSEMBLING

The assembling of sounds can be understood as a compositional process in which heterogeneous building blocks are put together to a certain degree in a homogenizing way. This contrasts with collaging, in which the equally heterogeneous building blocks retain a recognizable reference to their origin. The principle of montage first appeared in film, where it was used to describe a meaningful arrangement whose rules had to be subordinate to the narrative. In music, montage can be combined with traditional form-building processes such as thematic-motivic work. However, montage procedures are particularly common in "avant-garde poetics", which emphasize media techniques or the connection between art and everyday life.

Source: Drees, Stefan: Collage/Montage. In: Lexikon Neue Musik, edited by Jörn Peter Hiekel and Christian Utz. Wiesbaden 2016, 209 – 212.

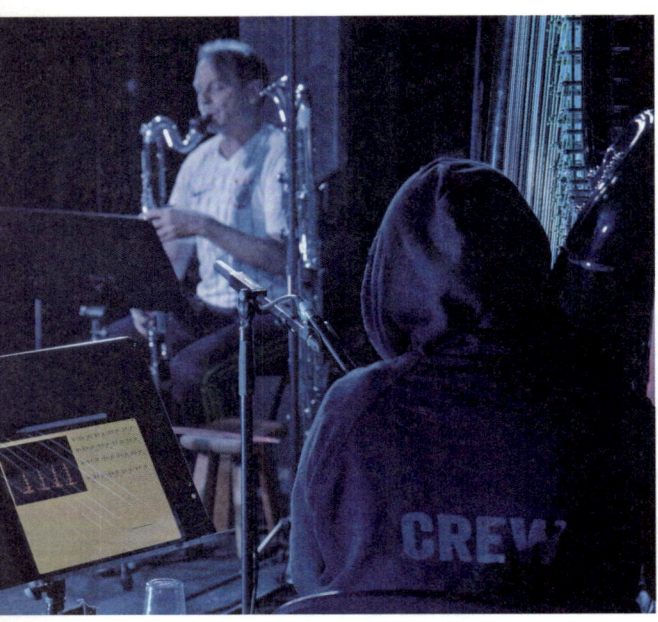

↙: Performance of "Brazil Now" by Thom Kubli with Ensemble Adapter at Alte Münze Berlin, 25. 10. 2020; part of Dystopie Sound Art Festival. Photo: Jonas Blume

THOM KUBLI: For me, assembling plays a role in two ways. One is to compose music through montage processes. The other is my work with installations, where I assemble technical and sculptural set pieces as material in order to achieve a certain functionality. Assembling always has something to do with functionality: For example, you install a sanitary facility so that water can flow through it.

I work with the demon of the machine. This means that I work on the machine until it does things that I no longer expect. You can get a machine to do things that you can no longer foresee. And then it starts to get interesting because you almost have a kind of organic counterpart. We humans have a habit of projecting animistic ideas into things. A machine means something to me if there seems to be a systemic structure behind it, but I can't see through it.

For the first two years of my studies, I just sat at home and read books, post-structuralists, sociologists, philosophers, Bourdieu, Foucault. And I studied systems theory, Heinz von Foerster, Humberto Maturana, biological principles. That was a great backup for building machines that could do more than just reproduce things that I told them to, but that had a life of their own. Systems theory gave me a vision for this.

I always put myself in the situation of working on projects with a high level of complexity, where systems collide that I have to bring together. This creates the emergency situation where I have to distil something from it that can produce information that is not messy. Because simply bringing messy and messy together makes no sense. And then I realize: Shit, this is insanely complex and technically overwhelming. At that moment, I have to learn to solve the whole thing. One consequence of this is to create forms of appearance that are aesthetically pleasing on the one hand, but also structured, transparent and clearly defined. I have the intuitive need to come out of a situation that is extremely overwhelming with something that actually depicts a structure.

We are all struggling with a certain degree of overload due to information overflow at every turn. The question is: how do we compensate for this? What do we do to somehow get out of the situation at the end of the day without feeling a loss?

If you think of assemblage as putting together or collaging set pieces, then it's basically a montage of different processes, where I'm not putting together results, but processes. For example, in my piece "Brazil Now." In the first part, there are the processes of capturing field recordings and the analysis by an artificial intelligence that allows categorization. And then there is a second part. This is the interpretation by an orchestra or ensemble of musicians.

I work with AI algorithms, but I don't let them decide on their own. There is human supervision, which means I have to like it. That's actually a bit contradictory, because the idea is that the algorithm produces things that are outside your aesthetic expectations. That's exactly what makes AI interesting, that you're forced to deal with things that you wouldn't do. It takes you out of your comfort zone. Of course, you can change parameters so that the results suit you better. But you need to know what you're looking for. You also need to know what criteria the intelligence uses. So you can roughly enter a target perspective and vary how strange the results should be.

For "Brazil Now," I met with the Ensemble Adapter with this archive of snippets that the AI picked out. I explained the principle: this is the aesthetic basis on which you try to create textures on your instruments, actually in a kind of mimicry, to create similar sounds or textures with the instruments and also to break away from the default. This resulted in a list of playing techniques that are available. The various playing techniques were then assembled in an improvisational, playful process with the ensemble, divided into phases and put together to form a composition that stands the time scheduled for the piece.

I made a lot of radio play music. We often produced with Dolby 5.1. One problem with this is the sweet spot. There is only one point in the room where the sound event is reproduced coherently. This led to an art-philosophical question: Is it okay to have only one ideal point and thus a hierarchization of space? Or do you have to produce in such a way that the sweet spot doesn't matter? That was an interesting discussion, to say: we have to get away from this sweet spot, we have to create equality. That means you have a completely different experience from every position you take. I worked on that for a long time: creating a narrative that gives rise to multiple narratives, depending on where you move in space, is very demanding.

When I make electronic music with software like Max/MSP, I often record it live on tape. This allows me to playfully create sounds and manipulate them over time. In the end, I have 50 or 100 set pieces that I assemble into a piece, e.g. in "Children of the Convclution" and in many of my radio play scores. This way of working differs from generative production, where I sit down at the piano and create a melody linearly. I have a much greater degree of surprise in the performances.

MOVING

A people-oriented theory of architecture sees space not as a mathematically defined container. Rather, space is created through movement. Only by walking through a space do its proportions, visual axes and auditory perspectives unfold. Architectural form and human movement combine to create a living space. Spaces receive and change their function through active and communicative use. This necessarily implies a dynamic relationship between space and time: the freedom to move. In sound installations, visitors can move freely through the space. This demands a multi-sensory perception of architecture and undermines the idea of a closed, completely definable artistic work.

The current standard for reproducing acoustic space, stereophony, reduces the listener to a specific location, the so-called sweet spot. This is located at one corner of an equilateral triangle with the loudspeakers at the other two corners of the triangle and prevents movement.

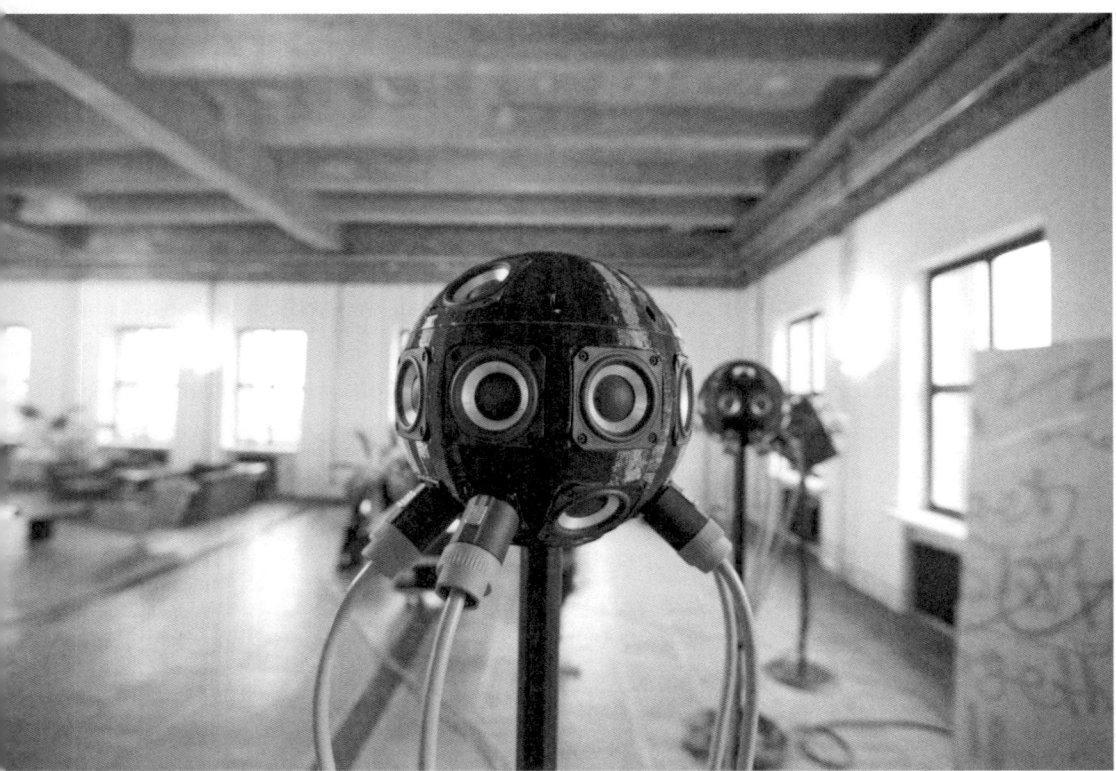

Source: Brüstle, Christa: Raumkomposition und Grenzüberschreitungen zu anderen Kunstbereichen. In: Lexikon Neue Musik, edited by Jörn Peter Hiekel and Christian Utz, Wiesbaden 2016, 88 – 102.

←: 393-Beamforming loudspeakers as mobile spatial audio projectors at spæs Lab Berlin.
Photo: spaes Lab Berlin.

GERRIET KRISHNA SHARMA: There are several reasons why space is suddenly so topical again, even though the spatial turn is older and we have long since dealt extensively with space and movement in sound art. On the one hand, the music industry is currently looking for the next kick. Stereophony is just a simulation of width with a bit of depth. At the end of the 1990s, a more comprehensive spatialization was attempted with Dolby 5.1, but it failed due to the German living room. In a German living room, there is a television at the front, a two-seater sofa at the side and a three-seater sofa at the back. You can't fit five speakers around it. But now there's something to feature again. In fact, there's hardly a studio that isn't considering jumping on this Dolby Atmos bandwagon because they desperately need something that's the new wow. And spatialization apparently provides that wow for some people, maybe because there's something flying over your head or playing guitar behind you.

I would never have expected the second reason: that headphones would come back so strongly in everyday life. I experienced this with the Walkman and it was fascinating – the city becomes a music video. The revival can also be explained by the fact that many people are encapsulating themselves more and more because it's getting louder and louder around us. And because the technology is close to the body, spatialization is now technically feasible through head tracking in the mind. This should be the precursor to the daily use of VR goggles. What you couldn't do before because the living room was in between is now on your body. I bought these Apple headphones for the Lab. I wanted to hate them. I put them on. Three minutes later I was consumed and never took them off. I forgot I had them on. Engineers, colleagues or artists who drop by the studio feel the same way.

That's media. There are algorithms at work that check out my perception. In the movies, we know that the cowboy isn't riding from left to right, but that there are lots of individual images that someone quickly pulls away in front of my eyes, and apart from that, the cowboy isn't there either. And yet we are immersed in the cinematic events as part of our everyday lives. In pop music, on the one hand, the spatial arrangements of the instruments are highly standardized. On the other hand, each instrument is often given a different reverb in the studio – these are downright utopian spatial constructions. And nobody goes up today and says: But that's not true! Because that is learned cultural practice.

3D audio is becoming increasingly popular in games and VR. In my opinion, the trend is towards an immersive design of everyday life and the world of work. In the workplace, for example, this becomes important where people assemble complex devices. Acoustics play an important role here: on the one hand as shielding against noise, and on the other as acoustic cues and work aids. That's also one reason why Apple is now featuring it in this way. At some point, you will move through virtual spaces with acoustic guidance as a matter of course. Some people can't imagine that yet, but 20 years ago I couldn't have imagined that everyone would be sitting on the streetcar and looking at their cell phones.

But 3D audio also takes us back to the caves, where so many things started. People are lighting fires, drumming, singing, using these huge reverb tails, immersion per se. The shadows flicker, maybe they take on substances, and the whole cave billows. And then, with painting and central perspective, there is suddenly a fixation on a single objectified view: You have to stand right here! The same in music with stereophony: stereophony has fixated us. I have never understood why we as artists resign ourselves to being reduced to the sweet spot in the stereo triangle.

The body is a body in motion. We are naturally given the ability to move towards or away from things through spaces. Now we have to ask: what does this mean if sounds exist in a technically staggered spatial arrangement and I can move through them? Who has the authority to interpret the arrangement of the elements here? What does my perception make of it?

Edgard Varèse formulated this idea of a 'journey into space' back in the 1930s, 'zones of intensity' and sounds that separate themselves from other sounds. He actually describes sculpture, i.e. objects, arrangements that stand in relation to one another. He uses a relative concept of space with polarities, in which space is created, not as a cage. Now, almost 100 years later, we have really achieved the Varèse utopia that has been a source of inspiration for science and technology for so long.

Many of the pieces I've made in recent years start by showing you around. As if you say: there's the kitchen in front, there's the bathroom, living room on the left. And then you live in there for a while. You first have to establish trust in the setting. That's still necessary at the moment, but maybe not in a few years' time. For me, the debate about space is about asking: What are the spatial sound forms that we can discuss? I am interested in technically provoked but divisible perceptions when I compose space.

All translations done by the author with machine support by www.deepl.com

SOURCES:

Bedorf, Thomas; Gerlek, Selin: Einleitung, in: Philosophien der Praxis, edited by id., Tübingen 2019, 1 – 6.

Breyer, Thiemo; Dzwiza, Erik Norman: Phänomenologie. Leibliche Fundierung und lebensweltliche Artikulation des praktischen Selbst- und Weltbezugs, in: Philosophien der Praxis, edited by Thomas Bedorf & Selin Gerlek, Tübingen 2019, 211 – 245.

Gibson, James J.: The Ecological Approach to Visual Perception. New York 1986.

Husserl, Edmund: Ding und Raum, Vorlesungen 1907, edited by Ulrich Claesges, Den Haag 1973.

Kertscher, Jens: Pragmatismus: Erfahrung als experimentelle Praxis, in: Philosophien der Praxis, edited by Thomas Bedorf & Selin Gerlek, Tübingen 2019, 105 – 139.

Peirce, Charles S.: Wie unsere Ideen zu klären sind (1878), in: id., Schriften I. Zur Entstehung des Pragmatismus, edited by Karl-Otto Apel, Frankfurt a.M. 1967, 326 – 358.

Polanyi, Michael: Implizites Wissen, Frankfurt a.M. 1985.

Schäfer, Hilmar: Einleitung. Grundlagen, Rezeption und Forschungsperspektiven der Praxistheorie, in: Praxistheorie: Ein soziologisches Forschungsprogramm, edited by id., Bielefeld 2016, 9 – 25.

Schatzki, Theodore R.: Social practices. A Wittgensteinian approach to human activity and the social, New York 1996.

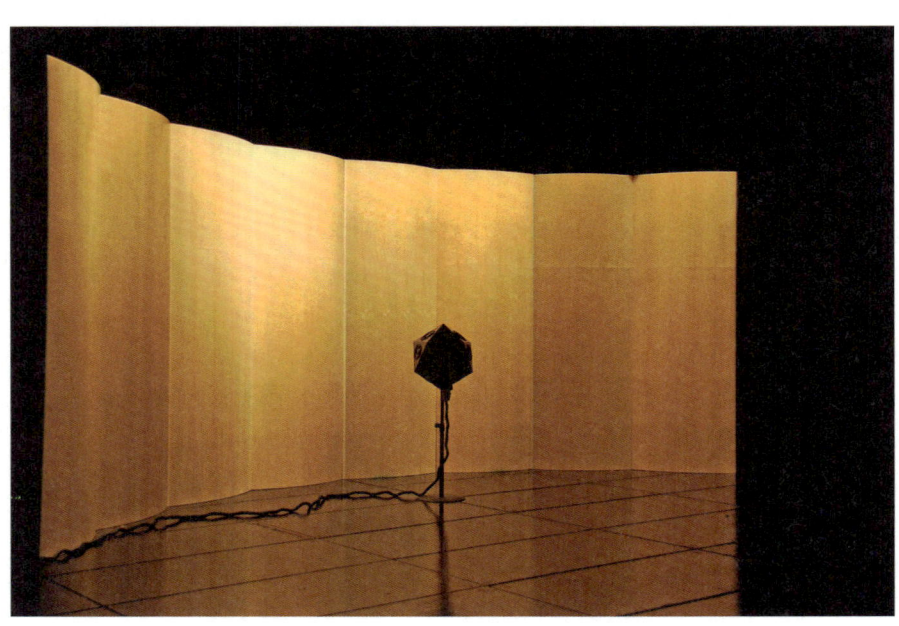

BIOGRAPHIES

MARIO ASEF is an architect and conceptual artist based in Berlin. His projects address both ecological and socio-political issues and confront questions related to their spatial and linguistic representability. His works are divided into three methodological categories: the field of language as a structurer of physical space, the field of history and writing about history as a construction of mediated reality from a post-colonial point of view, and the scientific field of transdisciplinary enquiry and exchange. He is co-editor of "Akusmatik als Labor: Kultur-Kunst-Medien." He is chairman of Errant Sound e.V. Berlin and is co-director of Dystopia Sound Art Biennial.

ROBERTA BUSECHIAN is a sound artist, researcher and biosonologist. She has lived in Berlin since 2012 and teaches theory, practice and activism in sound art. As a sound artist, she leads seminars and workshops in Berlin. She is interested in the effects of listening in the creation of shared aggregation points in physical space, especially the technological possibilities through live streaming and time shifting of virtually connected urban spaces. She is a member of Errant Sound. She conceives and realizes multimedia installations, conferences and workshops, sound installations and performances (e.g. London, Los Angeles, San Diego, Tijuana), conferences (e.g. IUAV University of Venice, Accademia di Belle Art di Brera, ICST – Institute for Computer Music and Sound Technology, Zurich, 2019 CENSE Annual Conference, Ústí nad Labem (CZE)).

LÍLIAN CAMPESATO is a Brazilian artist and researcher. Her practice combines reflective work and inventive actions involving sound, listening, art, and performance. Holding a PhD from the University of São Paulo, her scholarly work explores the politics of listening, with a particular focus on gender and its subjective dimensions. She critically examines hegemonic discourses in experimental music and sound art, reflected in her publications. Since 2017, she has developed the research project "Microfonias: intention and sharing of listening" in partnership with Brazilian composer and researcher Valéria Bonafé. Currently, she has been awarded a Marie-Sklodowska-Curie Post Doctoral Fellowship to be developed at the University of Copenhagen starting in 2025.

NICO DALEMAN is a Colombian-born sound artist and researcher based in Berlin. With a background in audio engineering and musicology, his research explores the influence of music technology on current practices of contemporary music and sound art, focusing on cybernetics, neuroscience, artificial intelligence, and non-western musical traditions. He is a member of the sound art collective Errant Sound and hosts the show "The Rest is Music" on Cashmere Radio.

DANIELA FROMBERG / STEFAN ROIGK are the founders of geräusch[mu'si:k], a multi-award-winning program for teaching sound art, which they run in particular in early childhood cultural education on behalf of the Berlin Senate. In addition, they each work as independent artists. Fromberg is a Berlin-based visual artist. Her intermedial approach focuses on sculpture, sound, photography and intervention in public space. She explores the potential of "poor" everyday materials from her personal environment, with a particular fondness for natural products, food, sounds, found objects and old building materials. She holds an M.A. Art in Context from the Berlin University of the Arts and was accepted into a national qualification program for the academic careers of female artists in Lower Saxony. Roigk is a sound artist based in Berlin. In his work, he pursues the intermedial interweaving of sound collage, installation, musical graphics and text-sound composition. The resulting works approach sound as a field for artistic and aesthetic research, taking it as both their departure point and central medium. As an artistic focus, he reflects on his own living and production conditions, examines the political potential of aurality and traces the subjective construction of reality.

JANINE EISENÄCHER is a performance and sound artist/ composer-performer, curator and researcher based in Berlin. The focus in both her artistic work and research lies on sonic epistemologies and hearing coexistence in performative sound art/ sound performances based on the manifold relationships between human and non-human actors/ agents, particularly, things. Together with Steffi Weismann, she carries out the curatorial and artistic research-projects "READY MAKING" and "Mind the Sound", and she pursues further collaborations with the composers and sound artists Andrei Cucu, Gerriet K. Sharma and Verena Lercher.

ALESSANDRA ERAMO is a Berlin-based sound artist and vocalist who works with performance and installation, sound poetry, video and drawing, exploring latent acoustic territories of the human voice and noise as socio-political matter. She develops interdisciplinary art projects that address questions of the body, memory, migration and identity. Her current research focuses on the invisible and the materiality of the voice, the tension between vocality and writing, performative rituals and trance-like states with singing.

GOLO FÖLLMER 2002 PhD on net music, 2007 – 2013 junior professor for audio culture research at the University of Halle. Texts on sound art, contemporary music, radio and acoustic media. 2010 – 16 Head of the Master's program 'Online Radio' and 2013 – 2016 of the EU project 'Transnational Radio Encounters'. Curatorial collaboration at sonambiente (Berlin 1996 & 2006), RadioREVOLTEN (Halle 2006), SoundExchange (Central Eastern Europe 2011 – 12) and Dystopie Sound Art Festival (Berlin 2018). Experiments with intermedia radio formats. Radio programs on music, sound and art; children's radio plays; features; sound installations and actions. Since 2020 Professor of Music and Media at the University of Halle.

HANNA HARTMAN is a composer, sound artist and performer based in Berlin. She has composed works for radio, electroacoustic music, ensembles, sound installations and given numerous performances all over the world. She often works with sounds taken out of their original context and thus perceived in their purity. Hanna Hartman seeks to reveal hidden correspondences between the most diverse auditive impressions.

GEORG KLEIN has a background in composition and works as a sound and media artist, often in public space and with a strong political background. His installations and interventions, sound walks and concert performances play with the audience's perception, question identities and position themselves in-between, on the border. He is chairman of Errant Sound e.V. and artistic director of the DYSTOPIA Sound Art Biennial and he works as a sound art professor and director of the master's program "Sound Studies and Sonic Arts" at the University of the Arts Berlin.

THOM KUBLI works as an artist and composer in Berlin. His practice is multidisciplinary, blending elements of composition, sculpture, and conceptual approaches. His installation pieces oscillate between spectacle and contemplation, exploring the social implications of physical space and virtual presence. Kubli often collaborates with scientific institutions like the MIT Media Lab or the Rensselaer Polytechnic Institute to devise new technologies and materials.

BRANDON LABELLE is an artist, writer and theorist focusing on questions of agency, community, pirate culture, and poetics, which results in a range of collaborative and extra-institutional initiatives, including directing The Listening Biennial and Academy. In 1995 he founded Errant Bodies Press, an independent publishing project supporting work in sound art and studies, performance, and contemporary political thought. His publications include *Dreamtime X* (2022), *Acoustic Justice* (2021), *The Other Citizen* (2020), *Sonic Agency* (2018), *Lexicon of the Mouth* (2014), *Acoustic Territories* (2010, 2019), and *Background Noise* (2006, 2015).

LAURA MELLO is a Brazilian/German sound artist and composer. Her work is the outcome of a practice of listening to the in-betweens, taking sound as the starting point to establish unheard connections. She explores the auditory dimensions of spoken language to deconstruct and reconstruct (de-)colonial perspectives, challenging established epistemologies. Laura's projects emerge in multiple formats and evolve from interdisciplinary and often site-specific investigations.

VANESSA DE MICHELIS is a London-based sound artist. Her compositions blend electroacoustic soundscapes, improvisation and live electronics. Her work explores minimalism, critical use of technologies and the politics of noise captivating audiences through immersive installations, soundtracks and live performances/dj sets. With a multidimensional practice spanning both arts management and education, she also freelances coordinating festivals and exhibitions (Co-Curator of *TOPIA Sound Art Festival – Berlin, 2021; Outreach Coordinator at the eavesdropping New Music Festival – London, 2021). Vanessa currently works as a Creative Technology Advisor at Central Saint Martins – University of the Arts London.

JUTTA RAVENNA studied fine arts and music in Düsseldorf and Berlin. She works as a sound artist with kinetic objects. In mobile loudspeaker scenarios of rotating, swinging or falling objects, she makes the significance of physical space for music tangible and comprehensible. The artist usually designs her installations in relation to a specific situation on site. Since 1994, she has worked in places such as lakes, disused shipyards, a gelatine factory, old churches and monasteries, radio buildings and universities. Ravenna was co-initiator of the series "Klangkunst im Dialog" (1996) and curator of the festival "Sonifications" 2017 of the Berliner Gesellschaft für Neue Musik).

KIRSTEN REESE is a composer and sound artist based in Berlin. Her works focus on the interrelation of immersive listening, body, social perception, loudspeaker constellations and electronic media. Research based projects work with site-specific aspects and 'found sound', field recordings as well as archival and documentary material. Ecology related works explore more-than-human, instrumental and algorithmic voices and their poetic transformation in compositions and installations, often in 'open spaces' such as urban and rural landscapes. Kirsten Reese teaches electroacoustic composition at the University of the Arts Berlin.

GERRIET KRISHNA SHARMA is a sound artist, composer, and artistic researcher. He studied Media Art at the Academy of Media Arts Cologne and composition, sound installation & computer music at the University of Music and Performing Arts Graz. In October 2016, he completed his doctorate "Composing with Sculptural Sound Phenomena In Computer Music" at the scientific-artistic doctoral school Graz "summa cum laude." Since 2004, he is specializing in sound spatialization, in media utilizing Ambisonics and Wave-Field Synthesis, and in transforming spatial sound into 3D sound sculptures. In 2020, he co-founded the spæs lab for spatial aesthetics in sound Berlin.

HOLGER SCHULZE is professor in musicology at the University of Copenhagen and principal investigator at the Sound Studies Lab. His research moves between a cultural history of the senses, sound in popular culture and the anthropology of media. He is the author of "The Sonic Persona" (Bloomsbury, 2018) and "Sonic Fiction" (Bloomsbury, 2020), he co-edited "The Bloomsbury Handbook of Sound Art" (2020), and works currently on "The Bloomsbury Encyclopedia of Sound Studies" together with Jennifer Stoever and Michael Bull.

ANTJE VOWINCKEL is a composer, sound performer and radio artist. Her main focus is on compositions with sound bites such as media speech or dialect melodies. She investigates direct connections between performance and digitality, exploring the human body and the environment as motor for a new oral, musical, collective and multiperspective poetry without script. She also creates performances in public space, using elements of everyday life to address new audiences. Her work has received international awards, most recently the Sound Cinema Award 2023. Member of the Academy of Science, Literature and Music (ADW) Mainz.

STEFFI WEISMANN is a freelance sound artist, composer and performer creating audio performances, mixed media compositions, interactive sound installations and interventions in public spaces. In recent years, the transfer of tactile experiences into sonic processes has played a central role. In addition to her solo work, she has long-standing collaborations with the group Maulwerker, Janine Eisenächer, Annette Krebs and others. She has been a member and co-curator of Errant Sound since 2019.

GEORG WERNER often works in collaboration with international artists und collectives in the field between art & technology. He is eager to learn and shares the knowledge he gathered along the way in workshops, lectures and seminars. His artistic approach is humble and multi layered – influenced by objects and situations, that he modifies, to be inviting to exploration and relation. Meanwhile they may raise the sensitivity of the viewers perception.

ZORKA WOLLNY is a composer, singer, performance and installation artist. Her works function at the boundary between music and visual arts and are strictly related to architecture. She collaborates – in a director-like mode – with musicians, actors and dancers and every time with members of local communities too. She works as an associate professor at Stettin Art Academy.

JEREMY WOODRUFF is Senior Scientist for Artistic Research at the University of Music and Performing Arts Graz (KUG). He is an artist, composer and researcher with many internationally presented works and numerous published writings. His work deals with diverse subjects including protest, urban gardens and transcultural music. He was a founding co-curator for the Dystopia Sound Art Biennial and most recently he is Artistic Director of the Sonic Borderlines project.

COLOPHON

Errant Sound Reader: Thoughts and Practices from the Berlin Artist-Run Space
Editor: Mario Asef, Golo Föllmer, Georg Klein, Brandon LaBelle
Translation: Patrick Lennon, Nuria Rodriguez
Design: fliegende Teilchen, Berlin
Back cover: Sven-Åke Johansson performing at Errant Sound, April 10, 2019. Photo: Golo Föllmer
Printed by druckhaus köthen
Pubished by Errant Bodies Press, Berlin / 2025
www.errantbodies.org
Distributed by DAP, New York & les presses du réel, Dijon
ISBN: 978-3-9825585-6-1

Senate Department for Culture and Social Cohesion | BERLIN